THE BRITISH MALTING INDUSTRY SINCE 1830

Cuthbert & Company's brewery and malting at Stonham, Suffolk, *c.* 1850. The old buildings were pulled down in 1882 and replaced by a 240 quarter malting which was worked by Pauls from 1890 until its closure in 1967. (*Jane Pratt*)

The British Malting Industry
Since 1830

Christine Clark

THE HAMBLEDON PRESS

LONDON AND RIO GRANDE

Published by The Hambledon Press 1998
102 Gloucester Avenue, London NW1 8HX (UK)
PO Box 162, Rio Grande, Ohio 45674 (USA)

ISBN 1 85285 170 8

A description of this book is available from
the British Library and from the Library of Congress

Typeset by Carnegie Publishing Ltd, Chatsworth Road, Lancaster
Printed on acid-free paper and bound in Great Britain by
Cambridge University Press

Contents

Illustrations

Between Pages 204 and 205

Figures

Tables

Appendixes

In Memory of

Lawrence Frederick William
Rowe

1922–1997

Foreword

When I started work for R. & W. Paul Limited in September 1962, I was allocated to the Malt Department under Jock Causton, my father's first cousin. Hugh Philbrick was in charge of production and he sent me to Stonham maltings, some ten miles north of Ipswich, to 'break me in' with a season's barley drying.

The day began at 6.30 in the morning with unloading the previous day's kiln of dry barley, which had to be shovelled into hods (tipping bins slung between two large wheels known as Boby carts) and pushed off the kiln floor and right across the malting floor to the barley elevator. Lorries loaded with coomb (2 cwt) sacks of barley had then to be unloaded up a chain hoist onto the kiln level. Each sack was barrowed onto the kiln and tipped. All the time that we were working on the wire floor of the kiln, the fumes from the damped down coal fires rasped the backs of our throats. By lunchtime we were all 'wholly dry' and so repaired to the adjacent pub to sink a few pints. I then took my lunch box and sat behind the hedge to eat my 'dinner'. Invariably a combination of physical exhaustion and the beer ensured that I then fell into a deep sleep, sometimes not waking until 4 p.m. Les Wicks, the foreman in charge, was very understanding and never reported me to Hugh Philbrick or I might not be where I am today!

Christine Clark has conducted a prodigious amount of research into the history of the British malting industry. She has discovered a great deal about my forebears that I did not know. She has detailed the histories of many malting companies which have long since ceased to trade or have been absorbed into one of the few malting companies which still survive today. Throughout her research Christine has sought to discover what it was that made some companies thrive whilst others went under. You will discover the 'secrets of success' as you read this book.

My friends and colleagues on the board of Pauls Malt Limited felt that such a wealth of malting history and information should be published for the greater edification and enjoyment of all who have an interest in this fascinating industry. Indeed anyone with no knowledge of malting will still find this book most absorbing.

The publication coincides with a period in which profits of the British maltsters are suffering from a combination of the strength of sterling and the fact that malting barley has been cheaper in continental Europe. True to the theory that one should invest during the bad times to reap the benefits when times are good again, Pauls Malt is just completing a £27 million investment in new capacity at Bury St Edmunds which will add 100,000 tonnes per annum to its output. Christine Clark's research indicates that a timely and bold investment policy is one of the ingredients of success in the long term.

I congratulate Christine on incorporating the results of her comprehensive and painstaking research into a book which is a pleasure to read and, for me, brings back many memories. I commend it to you.

George Paul

Preface

This book has been commissioned by Pauls Malt, Britain's leading sales-malting company. The decision to write a history of the British malting industry since 1830, rather than a conventional company history, was taken for two reasons. First, although for centuries malting has played a key role in the production of the national beverage and provided a principal bridge between agriculture and industry, it has been strangely neglected by historians. Peter Mathias, in his authoritative history of the brewing industry, has covered the years to 1830 in great detail.[1] Jonathan Brown provides an illustrated general introduction to the industry in a little over one hundred pages.[2] Yet there is no extended history of the modern (post-1830) period. Secondly, until quite recently malting was a sector comprising mainly small, private firms. Not surprisingly therefore extant records are sparse. The archive held by Pauls Malt represents by far the most substantial collection relating to the industry. Nevertheless its records, and those of the many companies it has absorbed, are patchy. In particular, few business records for these firms survive before the late nineteenth century. Information therefore has to be extracted largely from British Parliamentary Papers, the brewing trade press, obituaries and a few typescript company histories. To make the best use of the material which remains I have set the book in the broader context of the malting industry as a whole.

The history of Pauls occupies a central role in the story, for of the thousands of licensed maltsters in the 1830s the company is one of only a dozen to have survived into the 1990s. Indeed, it has evolved as one of the world's ten largest sales-maltsters (in terms of output). My focus has been to trace the changing structure of the industry over one and a half centuries. I have considered in some detail the competitive environment, both national and international, within which Pauls operated; the impact of taxation and state controls; the industry's close links with agriculture; and its relationship with, and until after the Second World War its dependence upon, the domestic brewing industry. Within this framework I have had to concentrate mainly upon the owners and their managers, an approach largely dictated by the sources. It is also, however, a view which reflects the business historian's

---

[1] P. Mathias, *The Brewing Industry In England, 1700–1830* (Cambridge, 1959), pp. 387–474.
[2] J. Brown, *Steeped in Tradition: The Malting Industry in England Since the Railway Age* (University of Reading, 1983).

interest in the debate about entrepreneurship and Britain's economic performance. Much has been written, in particular, about the strengths and weaknesses of the family firms which survived so long in Britain. Malting provides an excellent field for a discussion about them, since few industries have been more family-dominated.[3] This study, one of the few to chart a small-scale sector of the British economy, evaluates the success of founding families in preserving their firms across several generations; and their efforts to adapt to changing circumstances and, in recent years, to maintain international competitiveness.

In writing this book I have been very aware of the many advantages of being a *business* historian, for I have received so much encouragement and help from across the malting industry. I am especially grateful to George Paul and the directors of Pauls Malt, David Wilkes, Alan Pryke and George Hook, not only for their generous support but for patiently answering my many questions. I must, in particular, single out for especial thanks two people. First, Pauls' production director, Brian Seward: he has read my manuscript in its entirety and made many helpful suggestions; he has continually unearthed obscure sources; and not least through his enthusiasm for the project, he has made my task enjoyable throughout. Secondly, Dr Richard Wilson has read and commented upon my work and given freely of his time and expertise. His warm encouragement and wise counsel have been a great source of strength and instrumental in the completion of this manuscript. To both I remain deeply in their debt.

Many other members of Pauls, past and present, have aided me in a variety of ways: Hugh Philbrick, Peter Simmonds, Pat Hudson and David Ringrose, all past managing directors of the company; Ian Cantrell, Robin Pirie, Bruce Oliver, John Clayton, the late John Young, Bill Nelson, Derek Bemment and the late Les Wicks. James Craven Smith (Hugh Baird & Sons), Ian Ponton (Crisp Malting Group and IOB) and Guy Horlock (French & Jupp's) kindly gave me access to their companies' archives. Andrew Shelley (Muntons), Simon Simpson (J. P. Simpson & Company), Richard Wheeler (Edwin Tucker & Sons), George Abbott, Tony Chubb and Alan Macey (all formerly with ABM), Oliver Griffin (formerly with Moray Firth Maltings) and John Moody (formerly with E. S. Beaven, Guinness) all agreed to be interviewed about their experience in malting. Bruce Turner (Pure Malt Products) provided information about his company; John F. Alsip, president of Rahr Malting Company, Minnesota, kindly gave me access to his research on the international malting industry; Mrs Nancy Causton, Miss Betty Wharton, John Burke and Edward Sandars talked to me about their families.

---

[3] For two good reviews of the extensive literature see R. Church, 'The Family Firm in Industrial Capitalism: International Perspectives on Hypotheses and History', in G. Jones and M. B. Rose (eds), *Family Capitalism* (London, 1993), pp. 17–43; also P. L. Payne, 'Family Business in Britain: A Historical and Analytical Survey', in A. Okochi and S. Yasuoka (eds), *Family Business in the Era of Industrial Growth* (Toyko, 1984).

I am also grateful to the two secretaries of the Maltsters' Association of Great Britain, Clive Rattlidge and his successor, Ivor Murrell, who allowed me to see the Association's records, and to Judi Collins and Pam Bates who answered my many queries and made my visits to Newark so enjoyable.

Professor Roy Church, Professor Peter Mathias, Dr Terry Gourvish, Dr Roger Munting, Michael Miller, the late Dr Jim Holderness and Dr Mike Prior have all discussed my work with me and offered valuable advice. With great patience, John Barney guided me through the intricacies of reading company accounts. I should also like to express my thanks to Dr Fiona Wood, formerly of the Brewers and Licensed Retailers Association; to the staff of the Suffolk Record Offices, the Greater London Record Office, Lincoln Archives; and to Tim Warner of Newark Library. Alan Pool (Pollock and Pool) generously gave me permission to use his firm's invaluable statistics. Phillip Judge drew the maps and diagrams and Michael Brandon-Jones, of the School of World Art Studies and Museology, reproduced the illustrations. Dr Judith Middleton-Stewart and Robert Malster helped in the search for illustrations. I am grateful to Mavis Wesley for her many kindnesses, to Chizuko Wesley for assistance in preparing the final manuscript, and to Martin Sheppard of Hambledon Press for his help and guidance. Lastly, I should like to thank my husband, Robin, who has been a tower of strength and helped in many practical ways. I am grateful to them all.

Christine Clark   University of East Anglia

Conventions

Until the early 1970s, the British malting industry worked in imperial weights and measures, the basic unit being the quarter of malt or barley. It has subsequently adopted metric units of measurement. This format has been followed throughout the book. Rates of conversion are as follows:

> One quarter of malt = 336 lbs
> 3 cwts of malt = one quarter
> 6.67 quarters of malt = one ton
> 6.56 quarters of malt = one tonne
>
> One quarter of barley = 448 lbs
> (for some foreign varieties, one quarter = 440 lbs)
> 4 cwts of barley = one quarter
> 5 quarters of barley = one ton
> 4.92 quarters of barley = one tonne

Other traditional weights and measures:

> Two bushels = one strike
> Four bushels = one coomb, sack or barrel
> Eight bushels = one quarter
> Five quarters = one weigh or load
> Ten quarters = one last

Money is expressed in pre-decimalisation terms:

> One pound (£) = 20 shillings (s.) = 240 pence (d.)

Abbreviations

ABM	Associated British Maltsters
BIRF	Brewing Industry Research Foundation (now Brewing Research International)
BL	British Library
BLRA	Brewers and Licensed Retailers Association (formerly the Brewers' Society)
CAMRA	Campaign for Real Ale
GLRO	Greater London Record Office
HRO	Hertfordshire Record Office
LA	Lincoln Archives
MAFF	Ministry of Agriculture, Fisheries and Food
MAGB	Maltsters' Association of Great Britain
NIAB	National Institute of Agricultural Botany
NRO	Norfolk Record Office
PP	*Parliamentary Papers*
PRO	Public Record Office
SRO	Suffolk Record Office, Ipswich and Bury St Edmunds

1

Production, Location and Taxation, 1830–80

Malting is one of Britain's oldest rural industries. Usually made from best-quality barley, malt is the main ingredient of beer and also an important raw material in spirits. Thus malting stands half way between agriculture and industry: on the one hand, the purchaser of a major portion of the national barley crop and, on the other, the dependent of the drinks trade. In particular, the history of malting is fundamentally linked with that of its chief customer, the brewer. Writing in the 1840s, William Ford, emphasising the interdependency of the two processes, went so far as to urge that 'every Maltster ought to be a good Brewer, and every Brewer a good Maltster'.[1] Many brewers did make malt, but Ford reckoned as many as two-thirds of them were ignorant of this essential part of their business. The main reason for this was that, whereas brewing was universal throughout Britain, malting was focused increasingly upon the prime barley-growing regions in the sunnier, drier east. The light soils of East Anglia and the east midlands, for example, grew the finest malting barleys. Here the production of barley, the sale of malt to the urban brewing centres, and the return of capital to the countryside, were the linch-pins of the rural economy. By the early nineteenth century, no sector bridged the gap more effectively between the old, pre-industrial world, dependent upon the produce of the land, and the burgeoning industrial economy.

The origins of malting are cloaked in uncertainty. Most writers attribute the cultivation of barley, the discovery of malt and its role in the fermentation process to the ancient Egyptians.[2] From there these skills were transported to Greece and, before the first century AD, to northern Europe. Julius Caesar found that in Britain:

> they drink a high and mighty liquor, different from that of any other nation, made of barley and water. This drink is not so subtle in its effects as wine, but it is warming, even more nourishing, and leaves enough space for the performance of any actions before the spirits are quite vanquished.[3]

---

[1] William Ford, *An Historical Account of the Malt Trade and Laws* (London, 1949), p. 5.

[2] For details of the origins of malting see H. A. Monckton, *A History of English Ale and Beer* (London, 1966), H. Stopes, *Malt and Malting* (London, 1885) and W. R. Loftus, *The Maltster: A Treatise on the Art of Malting in all its Branches* (London, 1876).

[3] Quoted in T. R. Gourvish and R. G. Wilson, 'The Production and Consumption of Alcoholic Beverages in Western Europe' (typescript, 1993), p. 3.

Certainly, in Britain, where the temperate climate favoured the cultivation of cereals suitable for malting, ale quickly superseded other fermented liquors such as mead and cider. Details of its production during the so-called Dark Ages are lacking, but such was its popularity that in 970 villages were permitted only a single ale-house.[4] During the medieval and early modern periods much malt was made domestically, but some retail breweries, the larger monasteries and noble households malted and brewed on a bigger scale. At Fountains Abbey the 20 quarter malthouse made sufficient malt to brew 900 barrels of ale a year.[5]

Much of the story of malting, as Henry Stopes bemoaned, is portrayed most clearly through the legislation that surrounded it. The host of laws and licences to protect the consumer culminated in the hated malt tax which for almost two centuries occupied a central role in the public finances. The subject of the final section of this chapter, the malt tax prescribed production and influenced the structure of the industry and its relationship with the farming community; it brought together diverse interests to form the Malt-sters' Association of Great Britain; it spawned select committees and inquiries and occupied Parliament to a greater extent than many more important issues. Until its repeal in 1880, no single factor shaped the history of the industry so decisively.

Practically any grain can be malted, but most have characteristics which make them less suitable than barley. Wheat, for example, has a husk which is too fragile, while rice, with a high starch content, contains oils which can impart an undesired flavour to some brews. Nor is there any reason why other starch substitutes for malt cannot be used. The freeing of the mash tun in 1880 encouraged brewers to experiment with different materials, especially cheap imported maize, either in its raw state or as 'flakes', that is, subjected to heat partially to modify the starch. Yet despite the greater use of sugar and unmalted grain, malt has always been and remains the major raw material used in brewing.

In technical terms, malt is made by partially germinating barley under controlled conditions until enzymes modify the starch into soluble carbo-hydrates and proteins. When the conversion into malt has been achieved, growth is halted by drying and kilning; the kilning process also renders the original hard grain (which has had its cell walls broken down during germin-ation) into a friable, easily-milled corn. The crushed malt, or grist, is mixed with hot water, the resulting 'extract' providing the main source of energy for the fermentation by yeast into alcohol.

The traditional method of production, used almost exclusively before 1880, was that of floor malting. It was a process which had changed little over the centuries. *A New Treatise on Liquor*, published in 1759, provides as

4 Quoted in Stopes, *Malt and Malting*, p. 6.
5 H. A. Monckton, *English Ale and Beer*, p. 43.

apt a description of malting as any written up to 1880.[6] One factor especially inhibiting change was the all-important malt tax which prescribed in great detail each stage and much of the equipment used in malt production; another, as Stopes observed in 1885, was ignorance of the fundamentals of the malting process.[7] Apart from a brief foray into 'steam malting' in the 1840s, the forerunner of so-called 'mechanical malting' by the Suffolk malt-ster, Patrick Stead,[8] the main developments in the half century after 1830 were therefore in the scale of malting, rather than production itself.

At the start of the period, most maltings steeped between 25 and 35 quarters although many 'one-man' houses (so-called because one man did everything, from receiving barley to dispatching malt) steeped only 10–15 quarters.[9] In 1836, for example, the *Ipswich Journal* offered for sale a recently built malting featuring a 20 quarter steep, a working floor of 150 feet by 20 feet (a total of 3000 square feet) and a plate kiln.[10] William Ford, writing in 1849, still advocated a single floor; two were acceptable; but three, he argued, should be avoided because of the difficulty of hoisting grain to the upper floor without damage.[11] Thirty years later, two- or three-floor maltings were commonplace, like the 100 quarter malting built at Ipswich by Oliver Prentice in the 1870s with two kilns and two working floors of a total area in excess of 17,000 square feet.[12] But not until the end of the period were there real advances in the handling of malt and barley through the intro-duction of power-operated conveyers.

Any description of the production process must first be qualified by stressing the many differences in technique and practice across the industry. Regional tastes and market demands varied widely. Similarly, maltsters faced changes in the pattern of demand caused by the shift from porter and heavy-vatted beers to the lighter milds and bitter ales. Moreover, malting depended entirely upon empirical skills. Until late in the nineteenth century there were no analytical standards to guide the maltster, merely a few simple tests, such as the flavour and mealiness of the corns and the proportion which sank when immersed in a tumbler of water. Not least, the maltster was dependent upon the quality of the barley which, of course, varied from

[6] *A New Treatise on Liquor, Containing the Whole Art of Brewing All Sorts of Malt Liquor: By a Person Formerly Concerned in a Public Brewhouse in London* (1759).

[7] Stopes, *Malt and Malting*, p. 261.

[8] See p. 80.

[9] The conventional measurement of the size of a malthouse was its steeping capacity. In a normal season of seven and a half to eight months, most maltsters would average forty-two to forty-five steeps (i.e. three steeps a fortnight). Thus a 15 quarter malting had an annual capacity of 630–675 quarters, a 100 quarter malting, 4200–4500 quarters.

[10] *Ipswich Journal*, 19 March 1836.

[11] Ford, *Malt Trade*, p. 122.

[12] In 1859 John Crisp of Beccles advertised for sale a 130 quarter malting with six working floors; this meant the dimensions of the individual floors were unusually small. *Suffolk Chronicle*, 23 June 1877, 16 April 1859; Surveyor's Plan, 4 May 1877, MC6/18, SRO, Ipswich.

year to year. Most maltsters still bought local barley, often at markets like
the one at Warminster recalled by E. S. Beaven: the rows of sacks and samples,
the haggling, followed by the 'market ordinary' when maltsters and farmers
dined together in the local inns.[13] Already some looked further afield to the
fine-quality barleys of the eastern counties sent, via the coasting trade, to
London and the north. The coming of the railways from the 1840s broadened
most horizons, testing to the full the maltster's skill in handling barleys
grown on different soils, each batch needing different handling in the steep
and on the floor to exploit its full potential.

By far the greatest limitation on the malting process was its dependency
upon the prevailing climate. As barley germinates most effectively without
problems at air temperatures between 50° and 60° F, in normal years the
season was confined to the cooler months between October and May. On
rare occasions, as in 1831, when the demand for beer rose sharply after the
passing of the Beer Act, malting continued into the summer.[14] But 'cuckoo
malt', as summer-made malt was known, was generally of poor quality. The
weather also affected day-to-day working. Notably in cold spells, it was
difficult to maintain sufficient warmth to support germination. On the other
hand, one advantage of the malting season was that it neatly fitted the
pattern of the farming year. Thus labour could be hired after harvest and
return to the farm for haymaking the following spring or to other seasonal
occupations such as brick-making. In fact, the season began some time after
harvest, the barley then having dried in the sun and sweated in the stack.
Contemporaries attached great importance to using only mature, well-dried
grain, Stopes advising that a 'clear month' should elapse before malting,
although in wet seasons the grain was also gently sweated on the kiln to
overcome dormancy (thus ensuring even germination) and lengthen storage
life.[15] Finally, before malting began, the barley was graded and cleaned,
initially using hand riddles, then, from the 1850s, specially-designed screening machines.

The first stage of production was steeping: immersing the barley in the
cistern to absorb moisture and initiate germination. The water was changed at
intervals to prevent it becoming stagnant and the light grains, or 'swimmings',
skimmed off; together with the screenings these were sold for animal fodder.
With the malt tax in force (charged at a flat rate on each bushel of grain),[16]

[13] E. S. Beaven, 'Barley for Brewing since 1886', *Journal of the Institute of Brewing*, 42 (1936),
pp. 487–88.

[14] *PP* (1831), vii, p. 34.

[15] Arthur Young gives details of barley sweating by a maltster at Heacham, Norfolk, in 1804;
and Stopes refers to William Champion, who in 1832 recommended sweating before steeping,
but generally during this period sweating was limited to wet harvests. The construction of
separate barley-drying kilns became commonplace only during the wet phase of the late 1870s.
A. Young, *General View of the Agriculture of the County of Norfolk* (reprinted, Newton Abbot, 1969),
p. 256; Stopes, *Malt and Malting*, pp. 73–74, 321.

[16] See pp. 28–31.

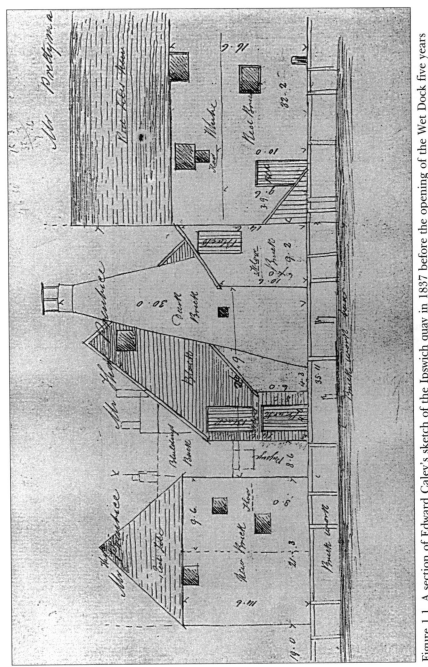

Figure 1.1 A section of Edward Caley's sketch of the Ipswich quay in 1837 before the opening of the Wet Dock five years later. This two-floored malting, steeping 15–20 quarters, was owned by Thomas Prentice. Its replacement, built by his nephew, Oliver, in 1877 was subsequently purchased by Robert and William Paul. (*Ipswich Port Authority*)

the volume of the barley was gauged by the excise officer at various stages of production, the first time after forty hours in the steep. This, however, was the legal minimum and most maltsters favoured a steeping of between fifty and sixty-five hours, depending on weather and quality, the plump, thin-skinned barleys requiring less time than hard, steely varieties.[17] The regulations also specified that cisterns (usually constructed of iron, slate or brick) be rectangular, shallow and with a flat floor to permit accurate gauging, which meant that at the end of steeping the wet grain had to be shovelled out by hand and then hoisted in baskets to the upper floors. To generate heat and encourage chitting, the barley was next piled to a depth of 30 inches into a square, wooden receptacle, known as the 'couch'. Again, this was a legal requirement. After a minimum of twenty-six hours the second gauges were taken with an allowance of 17.5 per cent made for the increase in volume. The grain was then spread evenly over the malting floor in a bed varying in depth from 3 to 12 inches. Here the final gauges were taken with different allowances applied: 33 per cent up to seventy-two hours and 50 per cent thereafter. Duty was then assessed on whichever volume was the greater.

The work on the floor demanded all the skill of the maltster. Ideally, to ensure a regular germination, an even temperature around 50–58° F was necessary.[18] This was achieved simply by varying the depth of the grain and manipulating the small shuttered windows along the side of the malthouse. A boost to growth could be given by sprinkling the grain with water, but this was thought to encourage fraud and was therefore strictly controlled until 1880. Subsequently, most commentators advised sprinkling. Ross Mac-Kenzie in 1921 advocated 2–3½ gallons per quarter, depending upon the season.[19] Throughout, the 'piece', as each batch of grain was known, was regularly turned by large, wooden shovels to maintain a fresh supply of oxygen and ploughed with rakes.[20] These operations prevented the growing roots from matting. Usually, there were two or three pieces, arranged in sequence of age, on the floor at the same time. As the first was loaded onto the kiln, the others were moved along the floor, leaving space for the next batch from the steep (see Fig. 1.2). The growing process took between ten and fifteen days, depending on weather, barley and the type of malt required.

[17] *Select Committee on the Malt Tax, PP* (1867–68), ix, p. 300.

[18] Most witnesses to the Select Committee on the Malt Tax considered the best average temperature for malting as 50° to 56–58° F. Ibid., p. 300.

[19] Frank Thatcher considered sprinkling should be carried out midway between turning, but 'under no circumstances' after five or six days on the floor; under the malt tax regulations, sprinkling was not permitted until *after* the sixth day. Frank Thatcher, *A Treatise of Practical Brewing and Malting* (London, 1905), p. 167; J. Ross MacKenzie, *Brewing and Malting* (London, 1921), p. 17.

[20] These were either made of wood or metal; 'stick ploughs', about four inches wide, were used to turn malt in areas inaccessible to rakes and shovels, particularly along the sides of floors and around columns.

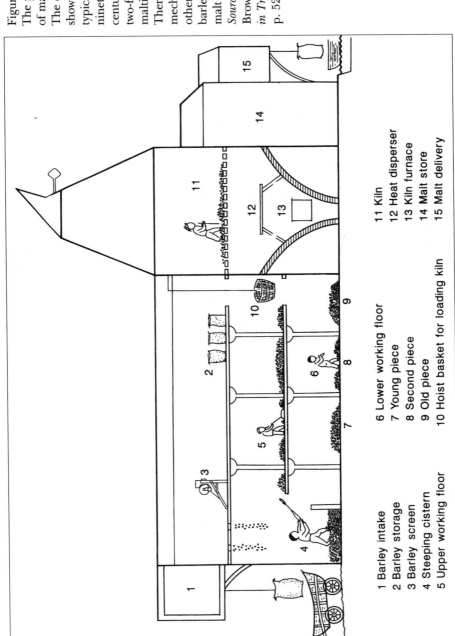

Figure 1.2 The process of malting. The diagram shows a typical early nineteenth-century two-floor malting. There is no mechanisation other than the barley and malt screens. *Source*: J. Brown, *Steeped in Tradition*, p. 52.

1 Barley intake
2 Barley storage
3 Barley screen
4 Steeping cistern
5 Upper working floor

6 Lower working floor
7 Young piece
8 Second piece
9 Old piece
10 Hoist basket for loading kiln

11 Kiln
12 Heat disperser
13 Kiln furnace
14 Malt store
15 Malt delivery

For the last few days, once the acrospire was between three quarters and the whole length of the grain, germination was checked by piling the grain high to raise the temperature and to reduce moisture, a process known as 'withering'.

The final stage of production was drying the germinated grain upon the kiln. This involved passing hot air through the green malt, which was laid in a bed 9–12 inches deep on the kiln floor. Early kilns merely comprised an open fire basket about 12 feet below the drying floor with a 'spark stone' (designed to disperse the heat evenly) above. A growing awareness of the role of kilning in determining malt quality led to a number of patents being taken out by 1880. More advanced kilns featured a bricked-in furnace with a separate heat chamber below the drying floor. Kiln floors also changed significantly, woven horse hair being superseded by iron and brass wire mesh, perforated tiles or iron plates, the latter used particularly for drying darker malts at high temperatures. Generally, it was the temperature of the kiln and fuel for the furnace which provided character. Stopes advocated oak to fire the later stages of kilning for porter malt and beech to give flavour for pales and ambers, but most contemporaries believed the smoke-less Welsh coke or anthracite was superior to either. Kilning lasted between three to five days, divided into two stages. First, the green malt was dried at about 90–100° F to halt germination. The temperature was then raised according to the desired end product, to 'cure' the malt. Ford, in the 1860s, suggested a range of between 130° F for pale malt and 180° F for dark malt, but by 1885 Stopes was arguing the benefits of temperatures in excess of these, even for pale malt.[21] Throughout, the grain was hand turned, in the green stage by iron forks, then wooden forks and finally wooden shovels. Not the most pleasant job, as one maltster recalled: 'on the last day no one complained of cold feet'.[22] Finally, the kiln was stripped, the malt screened to remove the 'culms', or dried rootlets (which were sold for animal fodder), the bins filled and the malt stored, usually for at least a month before dispatch to the brewer.

The production of pale and brown malts, with the emphasis shifting steadily towards pale, was the mainstay of the maltster's business. There was also, however, a range of coloured, or special, malts, which were valued for the colour and flavour they imparted to stouts, porter and dark ales. Patent, or black malt, in particular, had little saccharific value and was produced (usually from inferior grain) almost exclusively for its colouring properties. Properly made, it was malt first kilned and then roasted at a temperature of 420–50° F in a small, revolving roasting cylinder. Because it was difficult to distinguish between roasted malt and roasted barley, it provided a great opportunity for fraud. However, the Roasted Maltsters Act of 1842 laid down

[21] Stopes, *Malt and Malting*, p. 365.
[22] Mary Manning, 'Great Ryburgh Maltings', *Journal of the Norfolk Industrial Archaeology Society*, 2 (1976–80), p. 17.

such strict regulations and stringent penalties, limiting the length of the working day and requiring the maltster to site his roasting house at least a mile from his malthouse, that only a handful of licences were taken out.[23] The remaining coloured malts similarly involved variations to the basic process, either at the flooring or roasting stages. Chocolate resembled black malt, but was paler in colour. Crystal, which imparted a sweet, caramel flavour, was produced by roasting saturated green malt: grain was germinated for around five days, well-sprinkled to increase moisture content, then roasted for two to three hours rising to a temperature of 300° F. Amber, a paler, biscuit-flavoured malt, was made by drying the green malt more slowly and for longer than usual on a conventional kiln, the temperature reaching 140–60° F in the final stages. It was then cured at a temperature of 185° F. In later years the process was finished in the roasting cylinder with the temperature rising to 200–220° F. Lastly, harsh, biscuit-flavoured brown malt was finished on a wire mesh kiln floor and fired with wood. Faggots were used in the later stages to raise the final temperature to 300° F. The small batches of well-withered green malts were kilned in two to three hours and retained the wood-smoked flavour.[24]

Malt or, more precisely, the cultivation of barley, is the link between brewing and agriculture. Indeed, in his evidence to the 1808 Select Committee on Distilleries, Arthur Young reckoned that British brewers consumed no less than 26.4 million bushels of barley out of a total produce of 38.4 million.[25] Likewise, contemporary authors leave little doubt about the importance they attached to the malt trade. Writing in 1858, Bayne stressed its value to Norwich at a time when its textile trade had sadly declined: 'we have every reason to believe that the annual amount of it exceeds the annual value of all the manufactured goods in the city'.[26] In contrast, the modern historian has seldom acknowledged its contribution to the rural economy. The industry remains neglected and, all too often, the temptation has been to measure agricultural wealth simply by the price of wheat. Although it would clearly be wrong to deny the latter's central role in the arable economy, Peter Mathias has argued that 'wheat, the queen of cereals, has exercised a far wider dominion over the text-books of farming history than she ever enjoyed in the fields'.[27]

Any attempt to evaluate the relative importance of one sector of the arable economy is, of course, hindered by the lack of agricultural statistics until

---

[23] *Commission of Excise Inquiry, PP* (1835), xxxi, p. 390; G. Valentine, 'Roasting of Barley and Malt', *Journal of the Institute of Brewing*, 17 (1920), p. 574.

[24] I am grateful to Derek Bemment for information relating to the manufacture of coloured malts.

[25] *Select Committee on the Expediency of Confining Distilleries to the Use of Sugar and Molasses Only, PP* (1810), iv, p. 84.

[26] A. D. Bayne, *A History of the Industry and Trade of Norwich and Norfolk* (Norwich, 1858), p. 10.

[27] P. Mathias, *The Brewing Industry in England, 1700–1830* (Cambridge, 1959), p. 387.

the third quarter of the nineteenth century. Contemporary estimates such as those of Arthur Young, however suspect, nevertheless shed some light upon the general pattern of production. It is clear that by the eighteenth century a regional specialisation in the production of barley was firmly established. Barley was grown almost everywhere, providing animal fodder and meeting the local demands of small-scale brewing, but production of top-quality grain on a larger scale was determined by environment: by the drier climate, generally found in the eastern side of the country and, more specifically, by the light drift soils overlying chalk and oolitic formations. A broad belt, sweeping south from the Tees through Lincolnshire and Norfolk, south west through Cambridge and Bedford and on towards Hampshire and Dorset, encompassed most of this land and grew the best malting barley. In the words of one commentator:

> On our Clays, this grain generally comes off ... with a thick skin and tough Nature, somewhat like the Soil it grows in, and therefore not so valuable as that of contrary Qualities. But Loams and Gravels are better ... as all the Chalks are better than Gravels; on these two last Soils the Barley acquires a whitish Body, and thin Skin, and short, plump Kernel and a sweet Flour, which occasions those fine, pale and amber malts.[28]

By the 1720s Daniel Defoe observed great quantities on the banks of the Trent and in Cambridgeshire, where 'five parts in six of all [the corn] they sow is barley'.[29] The familiar advances in eighteenth-century agriculture saw yields and quality rise and the acreage under the plough extend, notably across north-west Norfolk and the heath and wolds of Lincolnshire. Here, on the great tracts of sandy soil, turnips flourished, cleaning the soil and providing winter feed for sheep. Barley followed: less demanding than wheat and, on these lightest of soils, able to replace it in the rotation, it enabled many acres of poor light land to sustain a profitable crop for the first time.

Unfortunately, the 1801 crop returns provide only a sketchy picture – with some of the key arable counties, in particular Norfolk and Suffolk, poorly covered.[30] Yet even from this limited evidence the geographical divide is clear: in Lancashire, only 8 per cent of the arable acreage was under barley; while in the Kesteven and Lindsey divisions of Lincolnshire, it was 25.9 per cent and 21.4 per cent respectively. Moreover, while nationally the production of wheat had far surpassed that of barley, in these two districts 54,848 acres of wheat were recorded to 54,063 acres of barley. The pilot study of Norfolk, undertaken in 1854, similarly puts the relationship between

[28] *The London and Country Brewer: By a Person Formerly Concerned in a Publick Brewhouse in London* (1759), p. 1.

[29] Daniel Defoe, *A Tour Through the Whole Island of Great Britain* (London, 1927), i, p. 78.

[30] Nearly 50 per cent of the total area of England and Wales was represented by the survey but in most counties coverage was such that any attempt to show the distribution of barley is severely limited. See M. Turner, 'Arable in England and Wales: Estimates from the 1801 Crop Returns', *Journal of Historical Geography*, 7 (1981), pp. 291–302.

the two cereals into perspective: in this, the greatest of arable counties, 189,881 acres of wheat were grown to 172,261 acres of barley.[31] From 1866 the national returns illustrate the full extent of this regional specialisation and its importance for the eastern counties (see Fig. 1.3). Between them, Norfolk, Lincolnshire and Suffolk accounted for more than one-fifth of the total barley acreage of Great Britain. Only Yorkshire, geographically the largest county, ever broke their domination, and only one other county, Essex, ever grew more then 100,000 acres.

Not all barley was made into malt nor, indeed, malt made from local barley. The substantial quantities of grain shipped to Scotland and the north east from East Anglia, for example, reflected the regional preference for locally made malt.[32] Generally, however, the reverse applied, not least because the quarter of malt, weighing only 336 lbs against the quarter of barley at 448 lbs, was cheaper to transport. The parallels between the distribution of barley across the country and the excise returns, which record the quantities of malt made in each collection district, are such that their relationship is beyond doubt (see Fig 1.4). The malt figures collected after 1830 have their shortcomings: the exact extents of individual collection districts are not always clear, and some were redefined over time.[33] Their real deficiency, however, is the unknown degree of evasion and the discrepancy between urban and rural collections. Yet while official figures clearly understate production, they do so most emphatically for the eastern counties, with their preponderance of country 'out-walks'. Yorkshire, with its six collection districts, dominated, but Lincolnshire (Lincoln and Grantham), Norfolk (Norwich and Lynn) and Suffolk followed, together accounting for almost one-seventh of total malt production in Great Britain.[34]

The demand for malt, as Mathias has demonstrated, did not initiate agricultural change.[35] By the 1740s a handful of counties already dominated malt production, emphasising their early pre-eminence as barley lands. There is little doubt, however, that it encouraged and sustained the improvement of light land farming from the late eighteenth century onwards. A comparison of the top ten excise collections in the mid 1700s with those

[31] *Report of Sir John Walsham on Norfolk Agriculture, PP* (1854), lxv, p. 291.

[32] Donnachie suggested that, despite a greater local emphasis upon specialised barley cultivation, by the beginning of the nineteenth century Scottish brewers and distillers secured around half their barley supplies from East Anglia. I. Donnachie, *A History of the Brewing Industry in Scotland* (Edinburgh, 1979), pp. 45–46.

[33] The Cambridge collection included Huntingdonshire and a very small part of Suffolk. There were sixty collections in 1832, but at times these were redefined; for example, during the year ending 30 September 1863, the Grantham collection became Stamford and Suffolk became Ipswich.

[34] In 1832 production in Lincolnshire was 2,073,441 bushels and in Norfolk, 1,616,155, together with 1,534,968 bushels in Suffolk, amounting to 5,224,564 bushels, 13.71 per cent of the total production of Great Britain (38,091,046 bushels); *Commission of Excise Inquiry: Fifteenth Report (Malt), PP* (1835), xxxi, p. 349.

[35] Mathias, *Brewing Industry*, pp. 393–97.

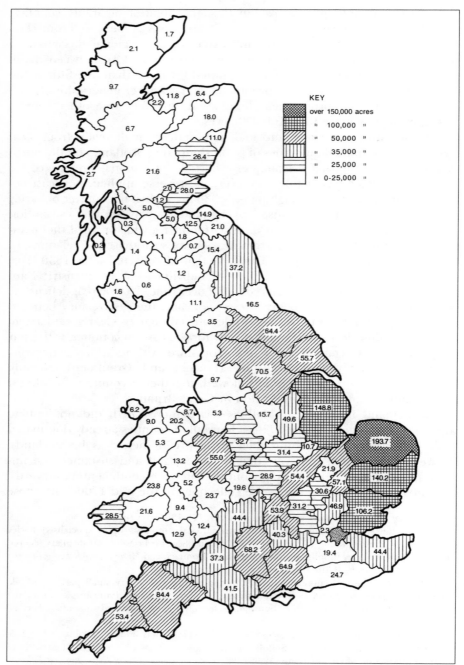

Figure 1.3 Distribution of barley cultivation, 1870. *Source*: *PP* (1870), lxviii, p. 363.

Figure 1.4 Distribution of malt production paying duty (by excise collection), 1832.
Source: *Commission of Excise Inquiry (Malt)*, *PP* (1835), xxxi, p. 349.

in the early nineteenth century clearly reveals the growing emphasis upon the eastern counties (Table 1.1).

Table 1.1
Top ten excise collections, 1741–1832

	1741	1760–62	1802	1832
1	Suffolk	Reading	Suffolk	Leeds
2	Bedford	Suffolk	Bedford	Suffolk
3	Reading	Bedford	Cambridge	Bedford
4	Surrey	Leeds	Surrey	Cambridge
5	Cambridge	Cambridge	Leeds	Hertford
6	Hertford	Lichfield	Lincoln	Surrey
7	Norwich	Surrey	Norwich	Grantham
8	Essex	Norwich	Reading	Norwich
9	Leeds	Hertford	Essex	Essex
10	Hampshire	Norwich	Grantham	Lincoln

Source: Mathias, *Brewing Industry*, p. 394; *PP* (1806), ii, p. 417; (1835), xxxi, p. 353.

Most notable was the rising position of Lincolnshire, with both its collections, Lincoln and Grantham, disclosing an ascendency based upon new rotations which in a few decades had transformed the county's barren heaths into intensively cultivated land.[36] The relative decline of Reading (fifteenth in 1832) and Hampshire (thirty-fifth) reflect the increasing dominance of East Anglia in the nation's malt trade. For centuries London had drawn its malt supplies from the surrounding arable counties, Hertfordshire, Bedford, Surrey (the last augmenting locally-grown barley with supplies from Berkshire and Oxford), and the more distant Reading and Hampshire collection districts. Hertfordshire, particularly, renowned for the quality of its brown malt, was the acknowledged capital of the malt trade. Ware and Hertford were two of several towns well placed on the River Lea and having a flourishing nexus of maltsters and merchants, factors and bankers, whose wealth was derived from the London brewing trade. Yet the increasing quality and quantity of Norfolk barley, coupled with rising prices and more accurate means of measuring extracts (which demonstrated the relative efficiency of pale over brown malts), saw the differential between the regions narrow. When, by the end of the eighteenth century, the great London brewers (Barclay Perkins, Whitbread, and Combe and Delafield) moved into malting,

[36] In 1801 Kesteven and Lindsey between them recorded 46,605 acres (19.8 per cent of the total arable acreage) of turnips and rape, an amount exceeded only by the three ridings of Yorkshire. M. Turner, 'Arable in England and Wales', p. 296; J. Brown, 'Farming Techniques', in J. Thirsk (ed.), *The Agrarian History of England and Wales*, iv, *1750–1850* (Cambridge, 1990), pp. 276–77.

it was to Norfolk, rather than Hertfordshire or the other old-established sources, that they turned.[37] Similarly, by 1840, Trumans were commissioning 27,000 quarters of malt in Norfolk, a further 21,000 in Suffolk, around 63 per cent of their total malt supplies; five years later, the two provided 69,853 quarters or more than 76 per cent of their total requirements.[38]

If there remains any doubt regarding the importance of these developments, we need look no further than the problems faced by the farming community after the repeal of the malt tax in 1880. Because the tax was levied at a flat rate per quarter, high quality barley, which yielded a higher extract than inferior grades, paid proportionately less duty and was therefore more cost effective for the brewer.[39] Contrary to farmers' expectations, however, the market for low quality grain failed to materialise. Instead imports continued to rise: the finest quality Chevalier being obtained from Chile and California in addition to vast amounts of six-rowed brewing barley from eastern Europe and America. The latter were not only cheap but well-ripened in sunny climates and therefore highly valued, especially in the wet years which marked the first phase of the Great Depression.[40] Nevertheless, the demand for the best British malting barley remained relatively firm. These are issues discussed more fully in Chapter 3. However, nothing underlines more clearly the continuing significance of the barley crop to the arable farmer than the vital role it played during these difficult years. Nationally, between 1874 and 1894 the acreage of wheat declined by 46.9 per cent. In Norfolk the figure was 40.8 per cent and in Lincolnshire 42 per cent. Likewise, there was some contraction of the national barley acreage, yet in these two great cereal-growing counties it increased by 13.8 per cent and 17.8 per cent respectively. These figures are important. First, they underline the demand side of the equation. When wheat prices collapsed, those of barley fell far more slowly and less steeply: during the decade 1874–83 the average price of wheat in Lincolnshire was 44s. 9d. a quarter, that of barley 35s. During 1884–94, wheat prices fell by almost 30 per cent to 31s. 5d. a quarter and those of barley by 17 per cent to 29s. In two of these years, barley recorded the higher price.[41] Similarly, in Norfolk barley

[37] Mathias, *Brewing Industry*, pp. 465–69.

[38] Truman Hanbury and Buxton, Barley Ledgers, B\THB\B\156–57, 1834–58. From the 1860s the trend reversed somewhat, the balance remaining around 50 per cent from East Anglia and 50 per cent from Hertfordshire until 1876 when the records cease.

[39] The yield from his malt was all important to the brewer's profits: 'The profits of brewing depend very greatly upon the extract given up by the malt: from this it follows that the probable yield is one of the chief considerations which we ought to keep before us when buying the material from which the extract is obtained. And this holds good whether we are purchasing barley or malt'. Graham Aldous, 'The Comparative Values of Malts from an Extract Point of View', *Transactions of the Laboratory Club*, 3 (1889–90), p. 140.

[40] After the wet harvest of 1879, Beaven recorded that 75 per cent of all the barley they had steeped that season was foreign grain. E. S. Beaven, *Barley* (London, 1947), p. 149.

[41] *Royal Commission on Agricultural Depression, PP* (1895), xvi, p. 253.

prices rose above those of wheat. These were averages. Where the crop was high-quality malting barley, it commanded a premium price. Even in the disastrous year of 1894, when the price of both cereals ranged between 16s. and 20s. a quarter, good quality malting barley fetched between 25s. and 30s.[42]

The figures also emphasise the crucial relationship between soil and barley cultivation. Barley flourished on light, well-drained soil, land that was often too poor to support wheat and had few alternative uses. It was less suited to the heavy clays. As one contemporary aptly suggested: 'poor land lying dry and warm must be allowed to bear better barley than rich land that lies wet and cold'.[43] Suffolk, for example, featured some of the most fertile land: the corn-growing belt running from Long Melford to Hadleigh and Needham Market, turning south to Ipswich then across High Suffolk to the Waveney Valley, where the light sands of the east grew some of the finest barley in the country. They had attracted one of the foremost maltsters of his era, Patrick Stead: 'I found the advantage of having a malting establishment at Halesworth beyond all other places ... on account of the quality of the barley ... in fact it is so good that I cannot find any so good anywhere else'.[44] But the greater part of Suffolk was heavy loam on clay and there was never the same opportunity as in Norfolk and Lincolnshire to extend barley production when relative prices shifted in its favour. It is no coincidence that Essex and Huntingdon, with their cold, heavy clays, bore the full brunt of the depression; and that Norfolk and Lincolnshire, at least on their poor light lands, suffered less. In these difficult years, it can be argued that barley was of even greater importance than wheat. Witnesses to the Royal Commission were surely justified when they explained how critical it was to their very survival: in Norfolk 'anything which affects the price of barley is a matter of greater moment ... than even the price of wheat'.[45]

Two further factors reinforced this growing regional specialisation: transport developments, which allowed the malt to be conveyed quickly and cheaply from the heart of the countryside, and the expanding markets of industrial Britain. Of course, given the universal nature of brewing, much

---

[42] In Norfolk during 1893 barley prices were not only higher than the national average, but above those obtained for wheat. This point is also stressed frequently in the diaries of the Gainsborough maltster John Sandars: 'Lincoln – barleys high, nothing under 35s. worth buying' and the exception: 'Bought barley in the market to sell at £1!'. *Royal Commission on Agricultural Depression, PP*, xvii, p. 385; Diaries of John Sandars, 2 Sandars 1/2/11, 15, Lincoln Archives.

[43] E. Lisle, *Observations on Husbandry* (1757).

[44] Quoted in R. Lawrence, 'An Early Nineteenth-Century Malting Business in East Suffolk', *Proceedings of the Suffolk Institute of Archaeology*, 36 (1986), p. 121.

[45] Similarly in Lincolnshire: 'The effect of these prices upon farmers in the wheat-growing districts, and in the great barley-growing districts of the Wolds, the Heath and the Cliff, will be very disastrous, because up to the present barley has been their sheet anchor and the nature of the soil does not lend itself to other systems of agriculture'. *Royal Commission on Agricultural Depression, PP* (1895), xvi, p. 235.

of the malt trade was of a purely local nature. Typically, the firm of Samuel Thompson & Sons, based in Oldbury, Worcestershire, supplied malt made from locally grown barley to small brewers within a narrow radius of their maltings.[46] Larger markets drew malt and barley from a more extensive hinterland: Bristol drew from north Wiltshire and, via the River Severn, from Gloucestershire; the leading brewers of Edinburgh and Alloa from the Lothians, the Carse of Forth, and Fife. Beyond this, however, and having a greater significance for the long-term structure of the malting industry, the flows were inter-regional, mainly from East Anglia into London; and from Lincolnshire and the east midlands to the rapidly-growing centres of large-scale commercial brewing in the north and west. Table 1.2, which contrasts the quantity of malt produced with that consumed by retail brewers in the eastern counties and in London, Liverpool and Manchester (the three lowest malt-producing collections in 1832), provides a unique statistical insight into this crucial relationship between urban and rural economies. In each of the rural collections there was a massive surplus of malt: in Norwich almost 75 per cent, in Suffolk, over 80 per cent. Its destination was the markets of London and the north.

Table 1.2

Malt produced and consumed, by collection, 1832 (thousand bushels)

Collection	Total production (i)	Total consumed by all brewers (ii)	Excess/deficit production (i–ii)
Norwich	1046.1	268.1	778.0
King's Lynn	570.1	320.3	249.8
Suffolk	1535.0	272.3	1261.7
Grantham	1049.8	495.7	554.1
Lincoln	1023.7	312.9	710.8
Manchester	9.3	1160.4	–1151.1
Liverpool	38.5	781.9	–743.4
London	46.3	4461.9	–4415.6

Source: (i) *Commission of Excise Inquiry, PP* (1835) xxxxi, p. 349; (ii) *Returns of Brewers' Licences, PP* (1833) xxxiii, p. 183.

By the eighteenth century, East Anglia was already well-established as the third major source of supply (after Hertfordshire and Surrey) for the London brewers; the Norfolk ports, in particular, dominating the coastal trade. The patchy survival of the port books denies any accurate insight into the quantities involved and the pattern of trade. Throughout most of the century Holland, and to a lesser extent Ireland, provided the main focus for malt exports, while barley was shipped coastwise. However, the loss of the Dutch

---

[46] E. F. Taylor, 'History of the Formation and Development of Associated British Maltsters, 1928–1978' (typescript, 1978), pp. 15–16.

market after 1780 and the growing attention of the London brewers indicate the increasing importance of the coastal malt trade. By the second quarter of the nineteenth century most of the malt and a large proportion of the barley landed at Bear Quay in London originated in East Anglia (Table 1.3).

Table 1.3

Coastal shipments of malt and barley from East Anglian ports and shipments into London, Hull and Liverpool, 1822–27 and 1836–38 (thousand quarters)

| | 1822–27 | | 1836–38 | |
	Malt	Barley	Malt	Barley
Yarmouth	85.3	150.3	101.2	165.3
Ipswich	96.4	25.0	89.0	36.3
Harwich	34.5	7.4	51.1	13.2
Colchester	23.2	9.0	34.2	10.4
King's Lynn	15.5	103.6	22.0	105.6
Wells	3.3	59.5	13.2	36.3
Woodbridge	7.2	26.4	10.2	34.9
Southwold	4.6	11.0	11.1	8.9
Aldeburgh	0.1	30.1	0.2	29.1
Cley	0.7	22.2	1.9	24.9
London	245.3	212.1	302.2	322.2
Hull	2.3	136.2	1.7	108.1 [1]
Liverpool	46.6	30.2	80.9	32.2

Note: [1] Includes imports into Goole

Source: *Return of British Corn, Flour and Malt, PP* (1824) xvii, p. 108; *PP* (1828) xviii, p. 332; *PP* (1839) xlvi, p. 81.

Yarmouth and Ipswich, in particular, dominated, exporting an annual average of 101,200 quarters and 89,000 quarters of malt respectively in 1836–38. Harwich in Essex, with 51,100 quarters, accounted for most of the remainder. In addition, Yarmouth exported 165,300 quarters of barley, followed by King's Lynn with 105,600 quarters. These ports were unrivalled by any other at this time; indeed Patrick Stead, in his evidence to the Select Committee on the Sale of Corn in 1834, claimed that Yarmouth was exporting more grain than any port in the world.[47] He may well have been right. He was one of the largest maltsters in the country, producing 15–16,000 quarters a year, of which on average 12,000 were sent to Trumans in London. He also shipped malt to Liverpool, Manchester and Brighton, and grain to London, Hull and Bristol.[48] Trumans also commissioned malt in Norwich,

---

[47] *Select Committee on the Sale of Corn, PP* (1834), vii, p. 50.
[48] Ibid., p. 57; Lawrence, 'Nineteenth-Century Malting Business', p. 117.

Narborough and Burnham Overy. Whitbread, after their amalgamation in 1812 with Martineau & Company, malted at Yarmouth, at nearby Southtown and at Whittington (near Stoke Ferry); Combe and Delafield malted at Yarmouth and Barclay Perkins at Norwich. Bayne reckoned that in the 1840s 20,000 quarters of malt and 100,000 quarters of barley were passing down-river from Norwich, Beccles, Bungay and North Walsham to Hull and Newcastle, with a further 80,000 quarters of barley shipped to Liverpool and Scotland.[49]

For King's Lynn it was the northern ports, Newcastle, Sunderland and, above all, Hull, which exerted the greatest pull. The huge quantities of barley imported by Hull (second only to those entering London) must have accounted for most of Lynn's trade, being a major source for the maltsters of the Leeds collection. The trade reflected the predominance of the small brewer in the West Riding and their demand for locally-made malt. Conversely, Liverpool, where the common (commercial) brewer dominated, imported more malt than barley. Perhaps it is Liverpool which shows most clearly the impact of a rapidly growing urban centre and its insatiable consumption of beer. In the twenty years after 1821 the town's population increased by a dramatic 107 per cent. Its demand for malt more than doubled; imports of barley, always less important, also rose by more than one-third.[50]

Completing the chain of supply, and almost as vital as the ports themselves, was the network of inland waterways which carried the produce of the prime arable land from the riverside market towns scattered throughout the region. Thetford in Norfolk must have been typical of many others. Brewing and malting were long-established trades, White's *Directory* for 1845 listing four large breweries and several malt kilns. Among them, Bidwells were both common brewers and sales maltsters, operating three maltings and, from 1841, supplying malt on commission to Trumans.[51] James Fison (founder of the twentieth-century company, Fisons) initially dealt in malt, seeds and artificial fertilisers.[52] By 1835 he had, in his own words, 'an extensive malting concern' and was representing the maltsters of the district at the Excise Inquiry.[53] The key to this trade was the Thetford Navigation which, from the seventeenth century, opened the Little Ouse from Thetford to Brandon, and on to the Great Ouse and King's Lynn. Thetford experienced the usual

---

[49] Bayne, *Industry and Trade*, p. 16.

[50] In 1834 there were twenty-two common brewers in Leeds, consuming 152,119 bushels of malt, and 1955 licensed victuallers and beerhouse keepers, 1481 of whom brewed their own beer. In Liverpool there were ninety common brewers, consuming 838,485 bushels of malt, and 2707 licensed victuallers and beerhouse keepers, only 249 of whom brewed their own beer. *PP* (1835), xlviii, p. 19. Between 1821–41 the population of Liverpool rose from 138,000 to 286,000. B. R. Mitchell and P. Deane, *Abstract of Historical Statistics* (Cambridge, 1962), p. 24.

[51] Bidwells, Valuation of Thetford brewery estate, 1889, BR 161/20, 161/28, NRO.

[52] A. Crosby, *A History of Thetford* (Chichester, 1986), p. 114.

[53] *Commission of Excise Inquiry, PP* (1835), xxxi, p. 370.

problems of neglect and mismanagement by its corporation, but the *Universal British Directory* of 1790 records that 'sometimes upwards of 200 lasts of corn were sent to Lynn each week'. Thereafter the trade must have expanded rapidly because between 1837 and 1841 the town's toll book shows an average of 25,844 lasts of grain transported annually.[54]

Throughout East Anglia, similar developments were taking place. The Bure from Aylsham, the Yare from Norwich and the Waveney from Bungay all naturally gave eight to ten feet of water, ample for the Norfolk wherries to transport corn and malt to Yarmouth and return laden with coal. Several maltsters, for example John Crisp, the Press Brothers and Mealing and Mills, owned their own wherries, while the Narborough maltsters J. & R. Marriott acquired the Nar Navigation which linked Westacre with King's Lynn.[55] In Suffolk, the Lark, Gipping and Alde were all navigable (at least by small craft) by the end of the eighteenth century, while at Halesworth the Blyth Navigation provided the vital link with the port of Southwold. It was a brewer who in the 1740s had first proposed the scheme. In 1847 another brewer, J. Cracknell, paid tolls on over 1000 barrels of porter, while Patrick Stead transported over 17,000 quarters of grain via the navigation.[56]

Turning north to Lincolnshire and the barley lands of the east midlands, the influence of transport was again decisive. Not surprisingly, as the main markets lay to the west and north, exports of malt and barley from the ports of Boston and Grimsby were negligible; at their peak, in 1822–24, less than 3000 quarters of barley left Boston annually.[57] Almost certainly, more malt and barley travelled the unrecorded overland routes than they did in East Anglia. At the end of the seventeenth century there were no fewer than seventy-six malthouses in Derby, from which it was estimated that 1800 bushels of malt a week travelled by road to markets in Cheshire and Lancashire.[58] The opening of the Trent Navigation in 1712 and the subsequent completion of the Trent and Mersey Canal opened the route to Staffordshire and the north. With the River Witham and the Fossdyke Navigation completing the link between Lincoln, Boston and Sleaford, brewers and maltsters gained access to a cheaper and more penetrating network and by the end of the century the leading Burton brewers were already buying their barley in Lincolnshire and East Anglia. The ledgers of Benjamin Wilson, for example, recorded regular purchases of 'water barley' in Grantham, Newark, King's Lynn and Ipswich.[59] Forty years later, William

54 *Universal British Directory* (1790), pp. 602–05; Navigation Ledger, T/NI/6, Borough of Thetford Records.

55 Roy Clark, *Black Sailed Traders* (London, 1961), appendix 1; J. Boyes and R. Russell, *The Canals of Eastern England* (Newton Abbot, 1977), p. 194.

56 River Blyth Navigation, Toll Book, EAW 9/25, NRO.

57 *Return of Corn, Flour and Malt, PP* (1824), xvii, p. 108.

58 Mathias, *Brewing Industry*, p. 423; Brown, *Steeped in Tradition*, p. 519.

59 Boyes and Russell, *Canals*, p. 258; Ben Ward, 'A Brief History of Bass, 1777–1977' (typescript); Benjamin Wilson's Malthouse Purchases Book, 1787–1803, Allied Breweries Archive.

White reckoned 24,000 quarters of malt were made annually in Grantham alone and dispatched inland via the Grantham Canal and the Trent.[60] Further to the north, the rivers and canals of Yorkshire similarly attracted a notable concentration of maltings; those at Wakefield, Mirfield and Elland gained the dual advantage of access to the barley lands of south Yorkshire and Lincolnshire and the markets of Manchester and Liverpool, as did those built beside the Chesterfield Canal at Retford and Worksop in Nottingham. As elsewhere, they reaped the benefits of the fierce competition between the rival canal companies to attract the malt trade.[61]

The half century after 1830 was to witness a further refocusing of the industry, prompted by the rapid extension of the railway network. The railways offered several advantages: they cut journey times and freight rates, opened up the national market and gave a year-round reliability unmatched by waterborne transport. From the beginning, they set out to capture the malt trade, offering a wide variety of incentives, including sites for new maltings. The Lion Brewery Company was given land close to Long Melford station by the Great Eastern Railway,[62] while Newson Garrett of Snape guaranteed to give regular freight to the railway in return for the construction of a private siding into his works.[63] Sacks and storage, both at local stations and in London, were free and, at least initially, freight rates were highly competitive. From Norwich to London by sea rates for corn were £1 6s. 10d. per last; by slow goods train, 10s. 10d., while malt at 1s. 4d. a quarter (1s. 1d. for 'large quantities'), represented a saving of 1s. 1d. a quarter over coastal rates.[64] Although generally companies quickly raised prices, they continued to offer 'special terms' in areas where they were in direct competition with coastal and river transport.[65] Some ports undoubtedly suffered. At King's Lynn and Yarmouth there was much concern at the loss of trade.[66] Conversely, at Ipswich the coming of the railway was complemented by the completion in 1842 of the new wet dock. Subsequently, the port occupied an increasingly dominant position in the coastal and foreign grain trades.

[60] William White, *Directory* of Lincolnshire (1842), p. 687.

[61] C. Hadfield, *The Canals of Yorkshire and North East England*, i (Newton Abbot, Devon, 1972), pp. 182, 193.

[62] Brown, *Steeped in Tradition*, p. 40. In the two weeks from 26 October 1878, 1075 quarters of malt were sent by rail to Blackwall at 1s. 5½d. Lion Brewery Company Barley Account, W 14/1, SRO, Ipswich.

[63] I. A. Peaty, *Brewery Railways* (Newton Abbot, 1985), p. 70.

[64] E. Doble, 'History of the Eastern Counties Railways in Relation to Economic Development' (unpublished Ph.D. thesis, University of London, 1939), p. 228. Doble shows that coastal rates were handicapped by extra dues charged at several eastern counties ports.

[65] Ibid., p. 236.

[66] 'The trade between Norwich via Yarmouth and Lowestoft has always caused the employment of steam packet and sailing vessels, but not now to the same extent as formerly. Five years ago there were sixteen regular traders, besides eight vessels running in the malt trade. Now there are only five malt vessels ... they make each week one voyage to London.' Bayne, *Industry and Trade* (1864). These were also years during which the total trade in malt was rising.

Likewise, the Manchester, Sheffield and Lincolnshire Railway Company constructed and owned docks which transformed Grimsby from a town of 8000 inhabitants in the 1840s to one in excess of 50,000 by 1890, changing the port itself from one which was insignificant in the grain trade into the largest importer of foreign barley in the United Kingdom.[67]

The real victims of the railways were the navigations. Despite cutting rates, few could maintain their trade. Within a decade of its completion, the Eastern Counties Railway from London to Colchester had undermined the viability of the Stour Navigation; tolls which in 1848 had reached £3400 had slumped to £1400 four years later.[68] Where previously many brewers and maltsters were involved in the administration of the navigations, they quickly recognised the potential benefits of the railways and were instrumental in their promotion. Their interests are evident among the shareholders of the Norwich and Yarmouth Railway Company, of which John Lacon, a banker and son of Sir Edmund Lacon, the brewer, was appointed treasurer. John Cobbold was the inspiration behind the Eastern Union Railway connecting Ipswich with the existing line at Colchester. Similarly, at the first general meeting of the Eastern Counties Railway Company in 1836, Thomas Prentice of Stowmarket argued forcefully that the line should pass through the town 'to secure the whole of the traffic of the west of Suffolk ... it would yield a sum of £20,000 more than as it at present stands'.[69] In 1867 Manning Prentice maintained not only that maltings had recently been built at almost every station, but that 'we malt all at home, which is at the railway station'.[70]

Many brewers and maltsters clearly gained from an extension of markets, lower freight costs and competition between ports and railways, and between the rail companies themselves. Many still purchased the bulk of their barley locally but widened their search in response to variations in price and quality. Besides his regular purchases at Lincoln and Brigg, the Gainsborough maltster John Sandars toured the main East Anglian markets, visiting Ipswich, Woodbridge, Fakenham, Lynn and Norwich.[71] The Scottish barley factors were likewise appraised, their specialities and customers noted and samples of grain sent to Gainsborough. Malt was dispatched mainly to the brewers of Liverpool, Stockport, Salford and, above all, Manchester, with days taken up in travelling to meet customers on a scale impossible before the advent of the railways. During the autumn of 1865 ten days were spent in Ireland visiting the main brewers, assessing their potential as customers. Typical was the entry made about Beamish & Crawford of Cork: 'saw their

[67] Alfred Barnard,

[68] Boyes and Russell, *Canals*, p. 87.

[69] Norfolk Railways, Scrapbook of Prospectuses, Timetables, Maps and Cuttings to 1889, pp. 21, 28, Colman Rye Collection.

[70] *Select Committee on the Malt Tax, PP* (1867–68), ix, p. 291.

[71] The evidence for this paragraph is taken from the diaries of John Edward Sandars, 1849–52, 1854, 1865, 1876, 1 Sandars 1; Letter Book, 2 Sandars 2/1, Lincoln Archives; Reference Book and Sales Ledger, PM.

main brewer and arranged to send samples – very fine brewery – all porter – wealthy'. Sandars' tour marked the beginning of a substantial and enduring trade with such major brewers as Guinness. Malt was sent, 'station to station', by rail from Gainsborough to Dublin, a new venture for the Great Northern Railway. Wherever he traded, Sandars kept a careful check on freight charges and maintained pressure on the rail companies to agree the keenest rates.

Few, however, exploited the network as thoroughly as the Burton brewers. Bass, for example, who were shareholders in the Midland Railway Company and provided over 90 per cent of their freight, saw their output more than double within a decade of the railway coming to Burton in 1839; twenty years later it had increased more than ninefold to stand at 290,155 barrels.[72] Similarly, in the single decade after 1850, consumption of malt in the Lichfield collection rose from under 900,000 bushels to almost 3.3 million. The Burton brewers all malted for themselves and by the late 1860s there were over one hundred maltings in the town. Such was demand, however, that the partners of Samuel Allsopps were still 'lamenting the want of malthouses' and commissioning malt at Grantham and Beccles.[73] Besides owning twenty-eight maltings locally, Bass leased another ten in Lincoln. They looked with increasing favour on the markets of East Anglia, establishing a network of carefully selected agents, such as H. Edwards of Woodbridge and James Everitt of Wells-Next-The-Sea, through whom they purchased a growing proportion of their barley. Indeed, by the 1860s, Owen noted that 'the traditional sources of supply to the east of Burton ... were of little importance'.[74]

These events marked a further stage in the continuing regional specialisation of the malt trade. For another century old-established malting centres, such as Ware, Newark and Wakefield retained an importance which reached far beyond local needs. But increasingly, the focus shifted to the eastern counties. Their ascendancy, with its roots in earlier centuries, was based upon a set of interdependent variables. On the supply side of the equation were the environmental factors: first soil and climate, when coupled with advances in agriculture, saw the region producing perhaps the finest barley in England. Secondly, developments in transport, which steadily opened up the national market, enabled malt to be dispatched quickly and cheaply to the centres of urban growth. On the demand side, it was rapidly expanding urban populations, with their own direct stimulus to the brewing industry, which were the key to this happy partnership between industrial and rural economy. That it was important to the farming community, to farmer, landowner and agricultural labourer, can scarcely be denied.

---

[72] C. C. Owen, *The Greatest Brewery in the World: A History of Bass, Ratcliff & Gretton* (Chesterfield, 1992), pp. 212, 222.

[73] Samuel Allsopp, Minute Book, 1a and 1b, 1865–87, Allied Breweries Archives.

[74] Owen, *Greatest Brewery*, p. 42.

'Since the reign of Queen Elizabeth ... no trade has laboured under so vast a complication of oppressions, from fiscal regulations, and other disadvantageous circumstances, as the malt trade.'[75] So wrote William Ford in 1849, reflecting that for more than five centuries the manufacture and sale of malt had been increasingly defined by government. From the early fourteenth century, a stream of legislation focused upon its quality and soundness, emphasising its importance as the brewer's main raw material in the national diet. A 'True Bill for the Making of Malt', for example, passed in 1548 and not repealed for 150 years, decreed that all malt for sale spend at least twenty-one days in 'floor, steeping and drying', for otherwise 'no wholesome drink for man's body can by any means be made thereof'.[76] A tax on malt was first imposed upon England and Wales in 1644 to meet the growing cost of the Civil War: malt made from wheat and barley paying a duty of 2s. per quarter; that from oats, 1s. 4d. a quarter. But it was in 1697 that the tax was first imposed in its well-remembered form, extended to Scotland sixteen years later and finally to Ireland in 1786. From then until its repeal in 1880 it occupied a central role in taxation policy.

From the 1690s, taxation was dominated by the need to meet the escalating costs of war, resulting in a growing dependence upon customs and excise duties. By the 1730s, excise duties provided, on average, no less than 50 per cent of the total income from taxation, of which the duties on beer (imposed in 1690) and malt accounted for half. Throughout the eighteenth century their contributions rose steadily and by 1789–92 had increased to £3.8 million out of a total revenue of almost £16 million, of which beer provided £1.97 million (12.3 per cent) and malt £1.84 million (11.5 per cent). In comparison, land taxes raised a total of £2 million, a figure which places the importance of the two industries in context.[77] The ability of the taxes to accommodate incremental increases meant they were again to play a vital role during the French Wars (1793–1815). Indeed, the inelastic demand for beer made these the simplest of all taxes to adjust: in 1802 beer duty rose from 8 shillings to 10 shillings a barrel, while malt duty was raised from 1s. 4¼d. a bushel to 2s. 5d., then in 1804 to 4s. 5¾d. a bushel. The following year, excise duties from the brewing industry (beer, malt and hops) accounted for 19 per cent of UK gross tax revenue, of which the malt duty alone provided two-thirds.[78] The end of war brought little respite; beer duty remained at 10 shillings a barrel, while malt duty was reduced to 2s. 5d.

---

[75] William Ford, *Malt Trade*, p. 6.

[76] If a quarter of malt yielded a peck of dust, the maltster also faced a fine of 20d.; quoted in Stopes, *Malt and Malting*, p. 9.

[77] P. K. O'Brien, 'The Political Economy of British Taxation, 1660–1815', *Economic History Review*, 2nd series, 41 (1988), p. 10; Mitchell and Deane, *Historical Statistics*, pp. 386–87; Mathias, *Brewing Industry*, pp. 356–57.

[78] Spirits contributed approximately another 10 per cent of tax revenue, hops only a minor proportion. Mathias, *Brewing Industry*, p. 357; *Accounts of Public Income of Great Britain*, PP (1805), v, p. 22.

a bushel, only to rise again to 3s. 7¼d. in 1819. After 1822 it stabilised, at 2s. 7d. a bushel until 1840 and thereafter – except during the Crimean War (1854–56) when it reached 4s. 3d. a bushel – at 2s. 8½d. (see Table 1.4). Throughout the half century after 1830, even when the duty on beer had been repealed, it continued to contribute approximately 10 per cent of the total income from taxation.[79]

Table 1.4
Main changes in the excise duties on malt, 1697–1880 (per bushel)

Year	England and Wales		Scotland		Ireland	
	s.	*d.*	*s.*	*d.*	*s*	*d.*
1697		6¾	—		—	
1713	—			6¾	—	
1725	—			3⅜	—	
1760		9		4½	—	
1780	1	4¼		8⅓	—	
1785	—		—			7
1791	1	7¼		9⅞	—	
1792	1	4¼		7⅞	—	
1795	—		—		1	3
1802	2	5	1	8¾	1	9½
1804	4	5¾	3	9½	2	3½
1816	2	5	1	8¾	2	4½
1819	3	7¼	3	7¼	3	6¾
1822	2	7	2	7	2	7
1840	2	8½	2	8½	2	8½
1855	4	0	4	0	4	0
1857–80	2	8½	2	8½	2	8½

Note: Between 1725–1822 the lower rates of duty in Scotland and Ireland reflected the poorer quality of the native barley.
Source: *PP* (1867–68), ix, p. 235; (1867), xi, p. 809.

To some extent the tax was mitigated by drawbacks and allowances, although these favoured some sections of the trade over others. Exporters of malt enjoyed a drawback of 2s. 6d. per quarter whenever the price of barley fell to 22s. or less (24s. before 1773), while indirectly the maltster gained from a ban on malt imports until 1860.[80] Exports, mainly to Ireland and Holland, fluctuated according to home demand but at their peak in the mid eighteenth century exceeded 300,000 quarters annually. The trade

[79] G. B. Wilson, *Alcohol and the Nation* (London, 1940), pp. 197, 308.
[80] Subsequently, malt imports attracted a customs duty of 25s. per quarter. Wilson, *Alcohol*, p. 62.

was dominated by the Norfolk ports, notably Great Yarmouth, in some years the county claiming the entire bounty. In particular, the export of 'long malt' (so-called because the acrospire, or shoot, protruded beyond the grain) to the Dutch distillers proved lucrative until the trade was destroyed by war with Holland in the early 1780s.[81] More difficult to evaluate was the impact of the tax itself and the allowances for its payment.

Duty was paid six weeks after manufacture, in normal practice, long before malt was sold.[82] The tax therefore increased demand for working capital substantially, especially in times of war when rates advanced sharply: at the start of the French Wars, every 100 quarters of malt entailed a duty payment of £54; by 1804, as much as £180. To ease the burden, maltsters could extend their credit to eighteen weeks (known as the 'five-month' credit) by giving bond and security of double their dues. Most availed themselves of this concession. Nevertheless, it was seen to favour the small man selling quickly in the open market (with the duty passed on in the selling price) and thereby deploying public revenue for his own ends. Witnesses to the 1835 Excise Inquiry, where fear of competition was uppermost, were loud in their condemnation of the 'speculators' undermining their trade. One reckoned three-quarters of all Irish maltsters 'could not be in *any* trade were it not for the capital given them by the law'.[83] As Patrick Stead, the most prestigious maltster of his generation, pointed out that it was precisely those who 'for their wealth and respectability were the most disposed to conform to the law' who were the hardest hit.[84] Yet while the excise concurred with these views, not until 1859, when Gladstone was determined to reduce the sixth successive budget deficit, was the extended credit first reduced to twelve weeks and then, the following year, removed.[85]

From the late seventeenth century there was also constant pressure to commute the separate duties on beer, ale and malt into a single malt tax, mainly because private brewing, largely the preserve of the well-to-do, escaped beer duty on payment of a minimal licence fee.[86] Thus the burden of tax fell disproportionately on the labouring classes. The greatest advocate for change was Adam Smith, who calculated that a single tax on malt of

[81] Mathias, *Brewing Industry*, pp. 425–32; J. D. Murphy, 'The Town and Trade of Great Yarmouth, 1740–1850' (unpublished Ph.D. thesis, University of East Anglia, 1979). Further drawbacks, benefiting brewers and distillers, were also paid on malt used in beer and spirits destined for export. By 1835 the rates were 8d. per gallon for spirits made entirely from malt and 5s. per barrel (36 gallons) of beer if brewed at the rate of at least two bushels of malt per barrel. *PP* (1835), xxxi, p. 361.

[82] Most common brewers drew their contracts slowly over several months; payment was three to four months after delivery.

[83] *Commission of Excise Inquiry*, *PP* (1835), xxxi, p. 387.

[84] Ibid., p. 386.

[85] During the first year, the reduced credit yielded an additional £780,000 revenue. *PP* (1862), lv, p. 771; S. A. Levy, 'The Brewing Industry, Politics and Taxation, 1852–1880' (unpublished Ph.D. thesis, University of Cambridge, 1992), pp. 77–78.

[86] Individuals malting for family brewing paid 5s. per head annually.

18s. a quarter would bring in substantially more revenue than all the existing duties combined.[87] Against this was set concern that opportunities for tax evasion were greater in the malt trade than in brewing. For, unlike brewing, which was mainly urban-centred, malting was a rural industry comprising thousands of small maltings scattered across the countryside. While maltsters in towns could be surveyed daily, in rural 'out-walks' which took the excise officer a day to ride, the rule was four times weekly; in more distant regions, only twice a week.[88] Moreover, the under-manning and lax standards in many remote regions meant that even these levels of surveillance were rarely achieved. Hence there was ample scope for evasion. The full extent remains unknown, but Peter Mathias, emphasising the many shortcomings of the excise statistics, estimated that by the end of the eighteenth century as much as a quarter of all the malt consumed in the British Isles may have escaped duty.[89] The case against commutation was further strengthened by the example of Ireland, where in 1795 the duties on ale and beer were repealed and that on malt doubled. So great was the incentive to avoid the tax that the quantity of malt charged with duty subsequently fell to an all-time low.[90] Doubtless, this delayed change in Britain. That it did take place in 1830 was due to a combination of factors: the high price of beer relative to other goods; the general depression in agriculture and rural unrest; concern at excessive spirit-drinking (which after 1830 remained double-taxed); and the need to compensate brewers for the imposition of free licensing.[91]

There is, of course, no definitive measure of evasion in the half century after 1830. Almost certainly, the passing of the Beer Act made little impact. In fact the produce of the malt tax rose sharply for a time after 1830, reflecting the growth in beer consumption stimulated by the Act.[92] Yet witnesses to the 1835 inquiry left little doubt that evasion was widespread. Several spoke of a long-established system of fraud in the woodlands of Suffolk and Essex and the west country, with malt sold at Bear Quay in London well below the price possible if duty had been paid. One of the leading Irish maltsters, John Alexander, thought as much as 20 per cent of all English malt escaped duty, although this may have been a response to the many complaints about the low price of Irish porter – supposedly underpinned by untaxed malt – which undermined the trade of English brewers and maltsters. But with two-fifths of all malthouses still located in

[87] Smith calculated that, on average, the combined duties on malt, beer and ale amounted to 24–25s. 'upon the produce of a quarter of malt'. Adam Smith, *Wealth of Nations*, v, chapter 2.

[88] *Commission of Excise Inquiry, PP* (1835), xxxi, p. 391, 397.

[89] Mathias, *Brewing Industry*, p. 343.

[90] P. Lynch and J. Vaizey, *Guinness's Brewery in the Irish Economy, 1759–1876* (Cambridge, 1960), pp. 81–83.

[91] T. R. Gourvish and R. G. Wilson, *The British Brewing Industry, 1830–1980* (Cambridge, 1994), pp. 3–11.

[92] Malt charged with duty in England and Wales rose from 26.9 million bushels in 1830 to 34.5 million bushels in 1834, *Commission of Excise Inquiry, PP* (1835), xxxi, p. 349.

the rural out-walks, there is little to suggest any real decline from the high levels of evasion of the late eighteenth century.[93] In contrast, by the 1860s the situation had clearly changed. Indeed when William Stephenson, chairman of the Board of Excise, claimed in his evidence to the Select Committee on the Malt Tax that the degree of fraud was 'trifling', he spoke not only for his officers but for the representatives of the trade. While unquestionably this reflected the growing efficiency of the excise, other factors played a role: the buoyant demand for malt; the refocusing of the industry around the railways; and, not least, the demise of the small maltster and growing number of large-scale producers, for whom an unblemished reputation was all important.[94]

One inevitable consequence of the great dependence of the public revenue on the malt tax was a complex web of legislation designed to prevent fraud and evasion on the scale described above. Certainly, in comparison with other trades similarly taxed at the point of production, the industry was closely scrutinised. This involved a system of licensing (the fee varying with the quantity to be produced) and inspection of premises to which the excise retained the right of access at all times. But the real bone of contention was the maze of rules and regulations which affected every aspect of production, from the construction of cisterns and number of working floors, to the keeping of barley books and malt stocks. Before starting production, for example, written notice was required (twenty-four hours for town malthouses, forty-eight hours for country) of the exact time and duration of steeping (within specified hours) and the quantity of grain to be wetted, this single operation attracting no fewer than fourteen separate regulations; ten with penalties of £100 and four with £200. The culmination was the 1827 Act, listing 101 penalties and fines totalling £13,500 should any maltster be unfortunate enough to break them all. By this time, few contemporaries could find their way through the legislation with any degree of confidence. According to Ford, the Act caused an almost 'total prostration of the trade'.[95] That it interfered with the maltster's daily business and his ability to satisfy his customers there can be little doubt.

Floor malting, as we have seen, depended upon the vagaries of climate and the quality of barley. Regional tastes and market demands also varied widely. Despite the regulations, in practice there could be no fixed rule about the timing of the production process or the exact procedure. In particular, the custom of sprinkling grain on the floor was rarely practised in Hertfordshire and East Anglia but commonplace elsewhere, reflecting on

[93] In 1834, 5052 of the 12,573 maltings in England and Wales fell into the category surveyed only twice a week or five times a fortnight, ibid., p. 119.

[94] The last two factors prompted the closure of many of the smallest maltings, in favour of new, larger units of production. In all, the number of maltings in the UK fell from 14,025 in 1835 to 9703 in 1867; *Select Committee on the Malt Tax*, PP (1867), xi, p. 10; (1867–68), ix, p. 282.

[95] Ford, *Malt Trade*, pp. 6, 10–11.

the one hand the needs of customers and, on the other, the characteristics of different barleys. The great London brewers, who bought their malt from the eastern counties, wished growth to be halted when the acrospire was three-quarters the length of the grain. In contrast, northern brewers and those in the west, many of whom were small-scale and whose production was less efficient, needed a greater degree of modification to obtain a good extract and, therefore, preferred the shoot to extend the full length of the grain. With distilling malt (made from inferior, steely barleys) the shoot needed to protrude. In both cases, barley usually had to be sprinkled with water on the floor to achieve this. Indeed, wherever it was grown in heavier, wetter conditions than the light soils of the eastern counties, barley required additional moisture to sustain germination.

The arguments about sprinkling – the fears of the excise versus the needs of part of the malt trade – rumbled on throughout the eighteenth century until in 1802 the practice was prohibited. Such was the outcry, however, that in 1806 it was permitted after eight days on the floor; although this was extended to twelve days the following year. This clearly favoured malt-sters in the eastern counties. Yet repeated protests by other sections of the trade made little impact, mainly because of the powerful lobby of the London brewers. Not until the 1827 Act, which, besides consolidating the existing penalties, brought in the 'certificate system', in effect a second method of gauging, whereby all malt sold required a signed certificate giving details of quantity, quality and destination, was the industry united in its struggle.

Barely six months after the passing of the Act, thirty delegates from the main malting regions met at the Bull Inn in Bishopgate Street, London, to form an Association of Maltsters of the United Kingdom. Some idea of the strength of feeling may be gauged from the 1800 members who quickly joined. Under the chairmanship of Sir Francis Doyle, a standing committee of three representatives of the Association, three of the Surveyors-General of Excise and Edward Portman, MP for Dorset, was formed to negotiate an effective and fair means of collecting the malt tax.[96] Almost immediately, the advantages of a united front were evident, with nearly two-thirds of the regulations and penalties repealed within three years. The 1835 Inquiry, acknowledging the past failure to consider adequately the interests of the industry, secured further reform. By the 1840s, of the original 101 penalties, only thirty-two remained several of which had been tailored to minimise their interference with daily work.[97] Unfortunately, little more is known about the Association, but its work clearly marked a turning point for the industry.[98]

By the time of the Select Committee on the Malt Tax (1867–68), attitudes

---

[96] *Morning Chronicle*, 4 December 1827; Ford, *Malt Trade*, pp. 7–16.

[97] Ford, *Malt Trade*, pp. 7–16; *PP* (1835), xxxi, p. 386.

[98] It is believed to have lapsed in 1880 when the malt tax was repealed, only to be refounded in 1917, when the industry was again threatened with government intervention.

had been transformed. There were, of course, a few complaints, notably about couching, several witnesses explaining that in warm weather the grain germinated in the couch increasing the swell and, therefore, the gauge. Others, like Manning Prentice, one of the leading Suffolk maltsters, thought the tax prevented 'a fertility of invention in the manufacture of malt, which there is not now'.[99] But most agreed that the more accommodating stance of the excise and the repeal of many irritating regulations ensured there was little interference with their trade. When, somewhat ironically after the long years of protest, the committee, believing the need for extra capital had 'created and tends to foster [a] large monopoly', recommended the replacement of the tax, the weight of the trade opposed its repeal. The benefits, in deterring new entrants, clearly outweighed both the financial cost and any constraints upon daily business.

In fact the only real objections came from farmers, who argued that the malt tax diminished demand for all but the best quality barley. Many farmers on heavy soils were therefore excluded from the malting barley market. When the end of the French Wars brought the collapse of cereal prices and deep depression to the countryside, the loss of the valuable premium was, in many cases, critical. In 1821, when average prices for Norfolk wheat and barley were quoted at 50–62s. and 18–21s. a quarter respectively – less than half their 1812 peak – the farmers of north-east Norfolk (whose rich loam was less than ideal for barley) presented the first of many petitions to Parliament.[100] The Beer Act of 1830 and the repeal of the Corn Laws sixteen years later exacerbated the situation; as a tax on raw materials, the malt tax was seen to contravene every principal of free trade. Moreover, British maltsters were slowly but surely supplementing their supplies with fine quality barley from France, Denmark and the Rhine.[101] The agitation steadily gained momentum: from 1860, the Anti-Malt Tax Association flourished in such far-flung centres as Northumberland and Norfolk, followed four years later by the Central Anti-Malt Tax Association, which extended the fight into the urban arena. The following year, the regular pre-budget deputation to the Chancellor comprised no fewer than thirty-three MPs (including Clare Sewell Read, the well-known agricultural writer) and representatives from twelve counties: 'filled all the passages and lobbies of No. 11'.[102] The result, two years later, was the Select Committee. But despite the chairman's casting

---

[99] *PP* (1867–68), ix, pp. 235, 282.

[100] *Norfolk Annals*, i, *1801–1850*, 13 March 1821; see also 3 January 1823, 16 January 1830.

[101] 'With the malt duty, only the selected foreign barleys of the finest description were used, and these always commanded high prices.' Robert Free, 'Barley from a Maltsters Point of View', *Brewers' Journal*, 1888, p. 603; Average annual imports of barley rose from 2,763,000 cwts between 1850–54, to 6,295,600 cwts in 1860–64 and 10,281,800 cwts in 1870–74. Mitchell and Deane, *Historical Statistics*, pp. 98–99.

[102] *The Times*, 10 February 1865. For a detailed discussion of the political debate surrounding the malt tax, see Scott A. Levy, 'The Brewing Industry, Politics and Taxation, 1852–1880' (unpublished Ph.D. thesis, University of Cambridge, 1992).

vote in favour of repeal, the inquiry achieved little; in fact, it highlighted the two main stumbling-blocks. First, that farmers were increasingly isolated in their opposition. While maltsters accepted some degree of constraint in return for the monopoly benefits, the brewers preferred the status quo. Secondly, there was the question of how to replace the lost revenue. The only real alternative was a tax on beer, a change resisted until 1880.

2

The Greatest Competitor: Malting and the Brewing Trade, 1830–1914

The identity of maltsters and brewers had never been entirely separate. In the prime barley districts, from Northumberland to Dorset, brewers had always made malt, some in excess of their needs. The great London brewers, who dominated the demand for malt, had also loosened their ties with the Hertfordshire factors and acquired maltings in Norfolk. Elsewhere, in the industrial north, where many brewers commissioned malt, and in the heart of the midlands, where sales-maltsters flourished upon the demands of licensed victuallers, the links were more tenuous. After 1830, as the scale of production increased and railways opened up the countryside, a growing number of brewers began to make malt, a trend which highlighted the vulnerability of independent maltsters. As E. F. Taylor noted almost a century later, 'the greatest competitor was the brewer who made his own malt'.[1] Many aspects of the relationship between the two sectors were mutually beneficial. Yet such was the balance of power, that developments in brewing were fundamental in shaping the organisation and structure of an independent sales-malting industry after 1830.

'A Cinderella industry – small scale, technologically unimpressive, enslaved to the distilling and, above all, the brewing industries', Richard Wilson's view of malting is in many ways apt.[2] First, as Fig. 2.1 demonstrates, the industry depended upon the derived demand for beer. In fact in some years after 1860 the malt consumed by retail brewers exceeded that charged with duty, a fact explained mainly by the carry-over of malt stocks from year to year. Of the remainder, a large proportion represented the malt used in private brewing, which in 1830 still accounted for one-fifth of beer consumption. After the removal of the beer duty, however, home brewing lost its obvious cost advantage (having been previously exempt from duty) and declined in favour of the more reliable product of the common brewer. In 1862 some 2 million bushels of malt (about 5 per cent of the total) were consumed by private brewers; twelve years later, only 200,000 bushels.[3]

---

[1] E. F. Taylor, 'History of the Formation and Development of Associated British Maltsters Limited, 1928–1978', p. 34.

[2] T. R. Gourvish and R. G. Wilson, *The British Brewing Industry, 1830–1980* (Cambridge, 1994), p. 186.

[3] G. B. Wilson, *Alcohol and the Nation* (London, 1940), pp. 56, 63.

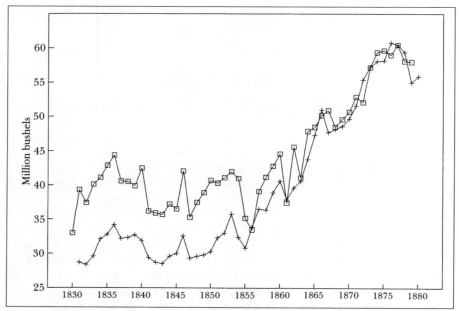

Figure 2.1. Malt charged with duty and malt consumed by retail brewers, UK, 1830–80 (million bushels).
Key: □ malt charged with duty; + malt consumed by brewers.
Note: Year end: 5 January following to 1854; 31 March thereafter.
Source: Mitchell and Deane, *Historical Statistics*, pp. 248–49; see Appendix 1.

After brewing, the most important use of malt was in distilling. In 1842–46, for example, an annual average of 3.96 million bushels of malt were consumed by distillers, mainly in Scotland.[4] From 1855, distilling malt was no longer charged with duty and was not included in the production statistics (thus explaining the rapid convergence of the variables in Fig. 2.1). But in the decade 1871–80, an annual average 6.5 million bushels of malt (mostly made by Scottish distillers) were used in distilling against 57.2 million in brewing, approximately 10 per cent of the total. Other uses of malt were relatively unimportant: a few thousand bushels for vinegar and yeast making and the production of malt-based foods; and exports, which throughout the 1860s averaged less than half a million bushels annually.[5] The repeal of the

[4] Over the period an annual average 3.21 million bushels were used in Scotland, *PP* (1847), lix, pp. 291–95.
[5] Around 200,000 bushels were used in the manufacture of vinegar and yeast in 1874. Malt imports were also negligible: until 1880 the malt duty acted as an effective deterrent; thereafter, brewers and maltsters preferred to import foreign barley rather than malt. The 1907 *Census of Production* recorded imports of 48,000 bushels, much of which was probably diastatic malt used in distilling. Wilson, *Alcohol*, p. 63; *Census of Production* (1907), Final Report, p. 477.

malt tax in 1880 brought to an end the annual returns of malt production. There is little to suggest any subsequent shift in the balance between production and consumption. Not until after the Second World War, and the growth of exports and the Scottish distilling trade, did the British brewing industry cease to define the malt market and, therefore, to determine the fortunes of independent sales-maltsters.

The second factor affecting the structure of the malting industry was the importance of malt to brewers. It was both their major raw material and the largest single element of total production costs. D. M. Knox, in her study of Whitbreads, concluded that for most of the nineteenth century malt accounted for more than two-thirds of production costs.[6] The sharp fall in barley prices after 1880 and increased extracts established a downward trend, but Richard Wilson has confirmed that as late as 1890–91 malt still represented 65 per cent of the brewing costs (excluding excise) of Lacons of Great Yarmouth.[7] Moreover, annual profits depended as much on the quality of malt as upon its cost. This was clearly underlined by Henry Buxton of Trumans in 1905. Reporting a fall in trade of over 112,000 barrels within six months, he had:

> no doubt that all our trouble this year, indifferent beer and inability to meet the public trade, is due to the quality of malt ... other materials are satisfactory, with the exception of the all important one – malt.[8]

There was also the problem, much discussed by the brewing trade press, of 'opportunism': the unscrupulous maltster who offered a fine quality sample at a keen price, only to deliver inferior malt.[9] Lastly, as the scale of many brewers' output rapidly increased, there was the need to ensure adequate supplies. On balance, it was the need to guarantee ample supplies of high quality malt which took precedence, even over cost.

---

6 D. M. Knox, 'The London Brewing Industry, 1830–1914, with Special Reference to Messrs Whitbread & Company' (unpublished B. Litt. thesis, University of Oxford, 1956), p. 123.

7 When excise is included, malt still represented 44 per cent of total brewing costs. Excise accounted for 33 per cent and hops 11 per cent, wages only 5 per cent and coals 2 per cent. Gourvish and Wilson, *British Brewing Industry*, p. 182. Even with the greater use of malt substitutes, Gourvish has illustrated that in 1896–1914 malt was always more than 50 per cent of the brewing costs of Steward & Patteson of Norwich. T. R. Gourvish, *Norfolk Beers from English Barley: A History of Steward & Patteson, 1793–1963* (1987), p. 77.

8 Truman Hanbury & Buxton, Monthly Reports, 28 September 1905, B/THB/A/121, GLRO. His opinion was shared by the *Brewing Trade Review*: 'We hold very strongly that of all the many factors influencing success or failure in the brewer's operations, the chiefest is the quality of malt'. 1 September 1893.

9 John Hanbury thought 'there are so many tricks in the trade ... it is difficult to rely upon bought malt. Some of the largest maltsters-for-sale have admitted to me themselves that they are only human'. Truman Hanbury & Buxton, Monthly Reports, 23 October 1905, B/THB/A/121, GLRO; see also, H. Lancaster, *Practical Floor Malting* (1906), p. 176. It must be remembered that there was no malting trade press to give the maltster's viewpoint.

For all of these reasons, brewers had every incentive to take control of their malt supplies by integrating backwards.[10] Many did so. Briefly, between 1855 and 1862, the annual returns of maltsters' licences distinguished between specialist maltsters and maltsters who were also brewers. While the number of licences in England and Wales fell from 6352 to 5458, the proportion issued to those who also brewed increased, from 34.8 per cent to 39.1 per cent.[11] Although there are no further excise statistics, the brewing trade journals, together with Alfred Barnard in his survey of the industry and company records, provide ample evidence of a growing involvement of brewers in malting.[12] Using Kelly's *Directory of the Wine and Spirit Trades*, Jonathan Brown calculated that by 1902, of the 1200 maltsters listed, 45 per cent were brewers.[13] Most conclusively, the Maltsters' Association of Great Britain estimated that by 1914 approximately 50 per cent of all commercial brewers made malt and that of the annual average of 7.66 million quarters of malt used for brewing and distilling (brewing, 6.58 million quarters; distilling, 1.08 million quarters), 52.4 per cent was made by brewers and distillers, only 47.6 per cent by sales-maltsters.[14]

The decision to integrate backwards rested of course upon several factors. The availability of capital and the expected returns from alternative investments were critical. The priorities also constantly changed: in many cases the acquisition of public houses, rather than malting capacity, became the focus for investment by the end of the nineteenth century. Equally important were the remaining factors of production: land and labour. As their scale of operation increased, many urban brewers lacked the space to malt at home. A growing number built maltings close to the source of supply. The Lion Brewery Company, for example, deliberated between extending their malt storage in London and building new maltings at Long Melford in Suffolk. Costs were similar; the deciding factors were a prime railway site and the services of an expert maltster, known to them for many years, to manage their enterprise.[15] Others solved this problem by merger and partnership, as in the case of Whitbread and John Martineau who amalgamated

[10] Hugh Lancaster suggested that substantial economies could be achieved by brewers if care and knowledge were exercised over the purchase of barley and the process of manufacture was carefully controlled, Lancaster, *Floor Malting* (1906), p. 177.

[11] *Returns of Maltsters' Licences*, PP (1862), xxx, pp. 499–500.

[12] For example, by 1890 the Lady's Well Brewery, Cork, had erected a five floor malting: 'Hitherto the firm have purchased all their malt, but in future, it is their intention to manufacture it themselves'. The Wardwick Brewery, Derby, was also in the process of building maltings which would enable it to meet its own requirements. A. Barnard, *The Noted Breweries of Great Britain and Ireland*, iii (London, 1890), pp. 409, 545.

[13] J. Brown, *Steeped in Tradition: The Malting Industry in England since the Railway Age* (University of Reading, 1983), pp. 29, 33.

[14] Statement from the Maltsters' Association of Great Britain, presented to the Prime Minister, Lloyd George, 16 April 1917.

[15] *Brewers' Journal*, 15 February 1878, 15 February 1879.

Figure 2.2 Hugh Baird & Sons were one of the first sales-maltsters to invest in a 'pneumatic' malting. Built at the end of the nineteenth century, their Glasgow malting supplied malt for the Scottish distilling trade. (*Hugh Baird & Sons*)

in 1812, the latter already owning maltings in Norfolk. For many urban brewers, especially those in the industrial north, malting was never a viable option: few had malting skills, few were experts in buying barley and few enjoyed the same close contact with farmers and merchants as their rural counterparts. Nevertheless, such was the balance of power between the two sectors that, even when brewers bought all their malt, they enjoyed considerable bargaining power over sales-maltsters.

Some malt was traded on the open market but generally this was of poor quality. Brewers and maltsters of any standing, wary of their reputations, were reluctant to buy and sell by this means.[16] The position of the malt factors, who acted as intermediaries, had also declined by 1830.[17] Increasingly, brewers preferred to obtain their malt either through commission or via forward contracts which were based on face-to-face negotiation.[18] With commission malting, the agent contracted to make malt on the brewer's behalf. The brewer provided the barley, or more usually the capital for the maltster to purchase his barley, and a fee to cover working expenses and the maltster's profit.[19] Contracts were made either annually, at the beginning of each season, or for longer periods – three and seven years being mentioned in Allsopp's minutes. Frequently, contracts were renewed year after year. Robert Lee made Allsopp's malt; John Crisp of Beccles made for Allsopps, Meux and Calverts; L. & G. Meakin of Burton and Patrick Stead of Halesworth for Bass and Trumans; while around half of John Sandars' production was commissioned by Greenall Whitley. Some, like Joseph Fairman of Bishops Stortford (one of the largest maltsters of his era), worked exclusively for one brewer, Trumans.[20] Unquestionably, their greatest asset was their reputation, for all were experts in the grain markets and recognised as

---

[16] According to witnesses to the 1835 Excise Inquiry, much of the ship-malt offered for sale at Bear Quay in London was fraudulently made. Low quality malt was also commonly mixed with better grades. *Commission of Excise Inquiry, PP* (1835), xxxi, pp. 389–92.

[17] For a detailed account of the role of the eighteenth-century malt factors and their decline, see P. Mathias, *Brewing Industry*, pp. 455–65; and C. G. Finch, 'The Hertfordshire Malt Factors, 1780–1835: A Study of Commercial Strength' (unpublished MA dissertation, 1976), HRO.

[18] By 1830 Trumans were commissioning malt from several commission agents, but every year purchased a proportion of their supplies through factors: John Taylor, previously their main supplier, who became one of their commission maltsters, and Samuel Swonnell, but mainly Randell, Howell & Randell of Mark Lane, probably the best known of the nineteenth-century factors. From the latter, they bought annual amounts which between 1860–70 ranged from 2827 quarters to 28,752 quarters. Individual transactions were mainly between 200 and 500 quarters. Malt was supplied by several well-known maltsters: Robert Paul, Oliver Prentice and Edward Fison (all of Ipswich), Robert Free (Mistley), T. W. Wilson (Hadleigh), John Crisp (Beccles), James Thorpe (Newark), William Rudyard (Lincoln) and Michael Sanderson (Wakefield). Truman Hanbury & Buxton, Barley Ledgers, B/THB/B/158, GLRO.

[19] For a discussion of the financial details of commission malting, see Chapter 5, p. 119.

[20] Richard Dewing of Fakenham, who owned only one 120 quarter malting, was also completely dependent upon Trumans; Mealing & Mills of Coltishall worked five of their seven maltings for Trumans, the other two for another brewer.

among the finest maltsters in the country. Indeed, Michael Bass considered that Patrick Stead was 'perhaps the best maltster in England'.[21]

The brewer who commissioned his malt penetrated the maltster's network of local contacts and obtained the expertise which guaranteed the quality of his malt.[22] Few exploited the system quite so effectively as Truman, Hanbury & Buxton. Unusually, among the major London brewers, they continued to commission rather than invest directly in malting. Their records provide a unique account of the relationship between the two sectors. They clearly dominated the arrangement, spreading their interests widely and never relying on fewer than eight maltsters scattered throughout the best barley lands of the Eastern Counties and, after 1873 (when their new brewery was opened at Burton), the east midlands and Staffordshire. They gained control over every detail of production and secured a vital communication network. Throughout the summer, their agents' reports flowed into London creating a comprehensive forecast of malting prospects. The first samples of barley followed. In return came detailed orders regarding the purchase of grain: price, quality and quantity, and not least timing, were all determined, with the agents always urged to move gently into the markets for fear of the impact of large-scale buying. Once the season had begun, every malting was inspected by Robert Pryor, the partner in charge of malt supplies, or the head brewer. Standards, moreover, were exacting. When in 1838 the partners compared the cost and quality of the malt made by each of their suppliers, they were informed 'that we shall cease to deal with those maltsters who stand worst and feel disposed to encourage those whose malt pays us best'.[23] Quotas were indeed adjusted: that of John Taylor, whose malt proved the most expensive and of low extract, was reduced from 8000 to 5000 quarters; that of Vickris Pryor from 14,000 to 10,000 quarters. Conversely, Henry Dowson of Geldeston, whose malt compared almost as favourably as Patrick Stead's, saw his 'make' rise steadily from his initial 1000 quarters to peak at 9000 quarters in 1845.[24] Again in later years, when there were many complaints about the malt made at Fakenham, Richard Dewing was informed that unless his standards rapidly improved his

21 Quoted in C. C. Owen, *The Greatest Brewery in the World: A History of Bass, Ratcliff & Gretton* (Chesterfield, 1992), p. 50.

22 John Sandars was in no doubt that 'owing to our connections with farmers and dealers we can make your malt far cheaper than you could expect to do it yourself'. Letter to Burton & Lincoln Breweries, 17 June 1890, 2 Sandars 2/2.

23 Truman Hanbury & Buxton, Thursday Private Memoranda, 12 April 1838, B/THB/A/129, GLRO.

24 The best results were achieved by Patrick Stead with average costs of 55s. 3d. a quarter and an extract ratio of 101.1, and Henry Dowson, 55s. 9d. a quarter and 101.9. At the bottom were Vickris Pryor, 57s. 3d. and 94.3, and John Taylor, 57s. 6d. and 95.3. The changes in quotas also to some degree reflect the growing ascendency of Norfolk and Suffolk over Hertfordshire barley for the increasingly popular lighter ales. Barley Ledgers, 9 March 1838, B/THB/B/156,157.

connection with the firm would cease.[25] Trumans similarly dominated any negotiations which determined the maltster's commission fee. In 1899, for example, the Burton maltster, Lewis Meakin, despite facing a sharp increase in wages for his seventy maltsters, was unable to obtain any increase in the fee of 5s. per quarter, a rate which had remained unchanged for many years.[26] Lastly, Trumans exploited any shift in the relative prices of malt and barley and malt substitutes. When in 1849 the partners of Trumans were 'all of the opinion that it will be advantageous to us in the future year to make *less* malt and buy *more* in the London market', their agents found their 'makes' reduced to 83,110 quarters from the exceptional 119,500 quarters of the previous year.[27] In 1884 the poor quality of English barley prompted the purchase of large quantities of old malt and a reduction in malt produced, while after the notorious harvest of 1888 stocks were run down and the proportion of sugar used was increased.[28] In every respect, the initiative lay with the brewer. Nominally, the commission-maltster retained his independence; in reality, there can be few clearer examples of quasi–integration.

The alternative was to buy malt on forward contract. In this case, the maltster purchased the barley on his own account, made malt and then offered samples to the brewer, whereupon contracts would be agreed for a fixed quantity and price. There is no means of determining the balance between this and commission malting; both were widespread, long-established practices and brewers and maltsters frequently relied upon a combination of the two. For many years, John Sandars made malt on commission for Greenall Whitley and the Cornbrook Brewery Company and sold malt on forward contract to Watneys, Guinness and a number of Manchester brewers, including Chesters, Wilsons, Beaumont & Heathcote, Yates and John Taylor. Nevertheless, by the close of the nineteenth century there were hints both in his correspondence and in Truman's records that

[25] Truman Hanbury & Buxton, Monthly Reports, 5 March 1885, B/THB/A/118, GLRO.

[26] The request followed a series of strikes in Burton during the autumn of 1898 and 1899 (see p. 124). Underpinning the refusal was the fear that 'it would be setting a bad precedent ... because once established, it is almost impossible to reduce, and there is a great danger of it becoming known and spreading to the Eastern Counties. It would be as well to keep in mind a shilling increase on our make all round would cost £6700 a year'. Truman Hanbury & Buxton, Monthly Reports, 9 May 1899, B/THB/A/118, GLRO.

[27] Truman Hanbury & Buxton, Thursday Private Memoranda, 1 February 1849, B/THB/A/129; Barley Ledgers 1844–55, B/THB/B/157, GLRO.

[28] When stored in airtight conditions, malt kept for at least twelve months. A good stock of malt could prove invaluable after a wet harvest. Trumans usually carried over six months' stock, but by December 1888 John Hanbury was buying 'only enough barley to steep at once, it is quite unsafe to go into stock being in worst condition this year than it has ever been'. In 1893, when barley prices and quality were favourable, Trumans bought heavily and carried over eight months' stock of malt. At the other extreme, in the difficult trading year of 1905, it was as little as two months. Truman Hanbury & Buxton, Monthly Reports, 10 October 1884, 6 December 1888, 4 June 1893, B/THB/A/118–119, GLRO.

commission malting was less suited to contemporary needs and evidence of a long-term shift towards contract buying.[29] Several reasons may be suggested. First, the vast range of malts, both English and foreign, each produced to detailed specifications, made separate contracts for a given quantity and price more appropriate.[30] Increasingly important were the changing circumstances facing brewers. The purchase of public houses, falling demand and hostility to the industry in general all focused thoughts on paring costs as never before. Even Trumans, the most committed to commissioning, discussed acquiring some of their Burton malt on forward contract. There was much to gain. Malt would be bought subject only to its being up to the sample offered. According to Arthur Prior, maltsters therefore would have:

1. An inducement to buy barley well.

2. Extra responsibility for careful production.

3. The exact amount contracted for would be supplied.

4. Stock can be kept much shorter.

5. Will tend to better quality – the maltster supplying the best malt will secure the best orders. Those who have gone to the expense of screening machines, good malt storage etc. will score.

6. There will be no question of malt being delivered having been made from a different barley to what has been passed.[31]

Not least important in this cost-conscious climate were the terms of contracts themselves. They enabled the brewer both to regulate the flow of working capital and to shift the burden of risk onto the maltster. By itself, the initial

[29] By 1924 the *Census of Production* indicated that only 366,677 quarters of malt, 14.2 per cent of the total UK production of sales-maltsters, was made on commission. In recent years an increasing amount of malt has again been made on commission.

[30] During the season of 1894–95, Henry Page & Company of Ware supplied thirteen brewers with a total of 83,010 quarters of malt. Over 60,000 quarters was bought by Combe & Company on forward contract. They received seven different types of malt: 'Foreign', Smyrna, Brown, No. 1 Ale, No. 2 Ale, No. 1 Amber and No. 2 Amber. The contract for No. 1 Amber, for a total of 11,500 quarters, alone involved twenty-seven batches delivered in 400 quarter lots and one of 700 quarters. Henry Page and Company, Malt Ledgers 1894–1905, D/EPa, B6, HRO.

[31] Somewhat irrationally, given the ultimate sanction of his initial point, his fellow directors still feared the opportunistic maltster. The debate was soon resumed. John Hanbury continued to support his commission maltsters, but by 1905 Henry Buxton added his voice in support of change: 'Our system of supplying ourselves with malt is altogether unsatisfactory, there seems every argument against continuing our present arrangements ... there are advantages in buying. We buy by analysis, and so get just what colour, moisture and diastatic power we need. Also we buy in large quantities, probably 1–5000 quarters, which would all be the same analysis – a great advantage to brewers who know just how the malt will work'. Truman Hanbury & Buxton, Monthly Reports, April 1903, 28 September 1905, B/THB/A/121, GLRO.

point was significant: instead of deploying capital for the steady purchase of barley, malt was paid for up to four months after the receipt of each delivery. But the real advantage hinged around the interaction between two further factors: that contracts, in terms of completion, were to all intents and purposes open-ended; and that they were struck on the basis of a small sample of malt, in effect, the maltsters' *expectations* of quality and costs for the coming year. Major contracts were made early in the malting season – before the maltster had completed his barley purchases; indeed, it was the projected contracts on which he based his estimates. His calculations therefore needed to allow for fluctuations in the price of barley.[32] Similarly, the malting 'increase' (the concept which related the quantity of barley purchased to malt produced) was a vital determinant of malting costs, but again one which could only be ascertained well into the season.[33] In normal seasons, and when trade was buoyant, the system worked smoothly. Brewers drew their malt regularly and the maltster's profit covered his uncertainties. But when trade was depressed, or the terms of trade turned sharply against him, the brewer offset his own loss, first by squeezing profit margins and secondly by delaying the completion of contracts. As John Sandars noted, 'though [maltsters] may get their orders, brewers do not take delivery for a year or two'.[34] Payment was also deferred. Thus in November 1897, when Combe & Company finally completed the contracts made the previous season with Henry Page & Company of Ware, £46,458 of a total of £119,458 was still outstanding.[35] Not until after Britain's entry into the Common Market in 1973, almost a century later, did forward contracts include an escape clause

[32] These problems were discussed in some detail in the *Brewers' Gazette*: '[The maltster] sells perhaps several thousand quarters from a sample of malt of which he may have only a few hundred already made. It is sufficiently easy to purchase 100 or 200 quarters of English or foreign barley of a certain quality at a moderate figure ... to obtain the total amount required of a quality precisely resembling the sample in every respect, he frequently has to pay a price exceeding that on which his calculations for his quotation to the brewer was based'. 11 April 1907, p. 263.

[33] Although traditionally trade was conducted by volume, the Sale of Grain Act of 1891 made it illegal to sell other than by weight. The standard units, already widely accepted, became the quarter of barley, weighing 448 lbs and the quarter of malt, at 336 lbs. The quantity of malt obtained per quarter of barley depended on the moisture content of the grain (which could be controlled by sweating) and the degree of modification. The latter varied not only from one season to another but, as barley matured in the stack, throughout the season. Thus John Sandars attached little importance to the results of individual steepings, but delayed his final calculations until his various maltings were cleaned at the end of the season. In most years he expected a small increase, of 1–2 per cent on English barley; but, during 1893–94, he calculated a decrease of 8 per cent. 17 June 1890, 1 December 1894, 2 Sandars 2/2.

[34] Letter to Frank Faulkner, 11 March 1893, 2 Sandars 2.

[35] This they offered to pay at the rate of £2000 weekly to the end of 1897, then £3000 weekly to mid February and finally £1000 weekly until completion on 16 April 1898. 7 January 1887, 1 December 1893, 2 Sandars 2/2; Letter from Combe & Company to Henry Page and Company, 10 November 1897, PM.

to protect the maltster.[36] This in part reflected the fragmented, competitive structure of the industry, but above all illustrates that the brewer again defined the parameters of what was in reality an intermediate stage in the process of backward integration.

Finally, many brewers took the relationship to its rational conclusion and combined all of these options: they made a proportion of their own malt and bought the remainder – either on commission' or forward contract – from sales-maltsters. In fact, this practice was widespread among the major brewers. In 1888–89, Bass made 186,834 quarters of malt at Burton and 47,552 quarters at Lincoln and Retford. In addition, 15,702 quarters were purchased and a small quantity made on commission.[37] That year their great rivals, Allsopps, produced 82,191 quarters in their maltings at Burton, 41,823 quarters were made on commission at Grantham and Beccles, and 12,399 quarters purchased.[38] Similar policies were adopted by other leading brewers: Guinness, Barclay Perkins, Whitbread, Combe & Company and William Younger of Edinburgh, all of whom had a long tradition of malting for themselves.[39] In part, this simply reflected inadequate capacity, especially during periods of rapid growth such as those enjoyed by Bass and Guinness.[40] But there remain marked seasonal differences in the proportion of malt produced and purchased, and these must be explained in terms of the brewer's strategy for stabilising production costs.[41] These, as we have seen, were dominated by malt costs, themselves a function of market demand and quality. With the latter closely linked to climate, both in terms of yield and storage potential, the impact of poor harvests was all too evident in brewing profits. Hawkins found that annual fluctuations in the price of malt and hops had a greater impact on profit margins than changes in any other factor cost, especially before 1880.[42] It was therefore essential for brewers to

36 Only after Britain's entry into the EEC, and the sudden doubling of barley prices which left maltsters selling contract malt at prices below the cost of barley, were the terms of contracts altered. Contracts are now negotiated on an annual basis and unfulfilled deliveries cancelled. I am grateful to Brian Seward of Pauls Malt for information about malt contracts.

37 Gourvish and Wilson, *British Brewing Industry*, p. 191.

38 Weekly Malt Returns, 1888–91, C/T/35, Allied Breweries' Archives.

39 Other partially integrated brewers listed in Barnard's prestigious volumes included Greenall Whitley, Ind Coope, Brains of Cardiff, Bentley & Shaw, Benskins, Marstons, Findlater & Company of Dublin and J. Calder & Company of Alloa.

40 Between 1840 and 1850, when Bass's output rose from 33,490 barrels to 78,330 barrels, malting facilities were far from adequate and in some years it was necessary to purchase almost half the malt used. Owen, *Greatest Brewery*, p. 49.

41 During the season of 1857–58, when the price of barley averaged 45s. 9d. a quarter, Bass malted only 57,000 quarters, 57.9 per cent of their requirements. The following season, when there were abundant supplies of barley at reasonable prices, they malted 89,000 quarters, 78.8 per cent of the malt brewed. Ibid., p. 62.

42 K. Hawkins, 'The Conduct and Development of the Brewing Industry in England and Wales, 1888–1938: A Study of the Role of Entrepreneurship in Determining Business Strategy with Particular Reference to Samuel Allsopp & Sons Limited' (unpublished Ph.D. thesis, University of Bradford, 1981), p. 707.

manipulate malt stocks skilfully and exploit every shift in the relative prices of malt and barley. In this respect, partial integration offered distinct advantages: production could be maintained at optimum levels and sales-maltsters used to bear the risk of fluctuations in demand. Thus in 1896–1901, when Bass saw their sales of beer advance steadily, purchases of malt also increased, to peak during the season of 1900–1 at 111,510 quarters (29.2 per cent of the total malt used). Thereafter, as trade fell, there was a steep decline to the all-time low of 2414 quarters (1 per cent of the total malt used) during 1910–11. In comparison, the malt produced throughout this period remained relatively constant.[43] That this strategy was by no means unusual was confirmed by the *Brewers' Gazette*:

> It is possible to mention cases of large brewers who have not during the period of depression made one bushel less of malt for their own use, but the falling off in their purchases has been almost incredible ... hence the bulk of the decrease in the manufacture of malt has fallen entirely on the maltster's shoulders.[44]

These were certainly some of the most difficult years that brewers had known but, as the same article concluded, 'their experience was incomparable to that of maltsters'. Many lost their entire livelihood. In 1918 membership of the newly refounded Maltsters' Association included all but a tiny minority of trading maltsters. Yet numbers, hovering around 240 against the 660 listed in Kelly's 1902 *Directory*, were a stern reminder of the hardships maltsters had endured since the turn of the century.[45]

Nevertheless, the relationship between the two sectors, conducted within the gentlemanly confines of the brewing world, was also in many ways supportive. Often bonds between brewers and maltsters, like those between the Lee family of Grantham and Allsopps, were forged over many years as commission contracts passed from one generation to another and were only severed because of the dire problems facing Allsopps after 1900. Similarly, some malting firms served Trumans for almost a century and, even if Trumans dominated the relationship, loyalty remained a strong bond. Thus during the difficult years after 1900 change was clearly resisted for longer than was desirable. Only in the autumn of 1905, when malt production was reduced to 53,000 quarters – in 1897 it had been 101,000 quarters – did John Hanbury finally admit:

> the crisis has come, it will be necessary to do something drastic ... The question is what to recommend for our benefit at the same time doing others the least possible harm. There are serious difficulties, getting rid of one or more means practically ruin to these individuals.[46]

---

[43] Gourvish and Wilson, *British Brewing Industry*, p. 191.

[44] *Brewers' Gazette*, 11 April 1907, p. 263.

[45] They estimated that only thirteen small maltsters had not joined the Association. Maltsters' Association of Great Britain, Minutes of Executive Committee, 23 September 1918.

[46] Truman Hanbury & Buxton, Monthly Reports, 23 October 1905, B/THB/A. 121, GLRO.

He had already prepared a detailed report of the circumstances of each maltster, the quality of local barley, carriage to London, and the standard of maltings. Next came the quality of barley. The real determinant, however, was hardship. Thus Richard Dewing, with a single malting in only a 'fair' barley district, survived because he pleaded it 'simply meant ruin'. In contrast, it was noted with great satisfaction that Mills of Norwich, a more substantial maltster who enjoyed private means, was 'not in the least disconcerted' when his long-standing contract was finally ended.[47] Indeed, the time devoted by such a major brewer to this single question is evidence in itself of a genuine concern for those whose livelihood they controlled.

In surveying the development of sales-malting after 1830, the historian faces several problems: the lack of extant records before the late nineteenth century; absence of family and business histories; and, not least, the thousands of small concerns involved. On the other hand, the statistics generated for excise purposes provide a rare and invaluable tool. Inevitably there are imperfections: the licence returns suffer from some degree of double-

Table 2.1

Maltsters' licences, England and Wales and Scotland, and malt charged with duty in Great Britain, annual averages, 1825–79

Year	Maltsters' licences			Malt charged with duty (million bushels)
	England and Wales	*Scotland*	*Great Britain*	
1825–29	10,161	3197	13,358	30.6
1830–34	10,170	2242	12,412	36.1
1835–39	9996	1969	11,965	39.5
1840–44	9017	1438	10,455	36.2
1845–49	7848	1022	8870	36.5
1850–54	7119	820	7939	39.4
1855–59	6302	676	6977	36.71 [1]
1860–64	5766	557	6323	41.1
1865–69	5226	478	5705	47.0
1870–74	4593	409	5002	51.5
1875–79	3944	345	4288	55.8

Note: [1] Excludes malt used in distilling from 1855; year end 5 January every year following, to 1853, 31 March thereafter.

Source: Wilson, *Alcohol*, pp. 385–87; Mitchell and Deane, *Historical Statistics*, pp. 248–49.

[47] 'He talked mainly about investments and stocks of various kinds and also about his motor-car for which he recently paid £500 ... and said that as he had worked at [malting] for some thirty years he considered he was entitled to a break.' Monthly Reports, 17 February 1906, B/THB/A/121, GLRO.

counting; Excise districts frequently changed their boundaries and evasion was widespread.[48] Nevertheless, together with evidence from parliamentary inquiries, they provide an unrivalled insight into the changing structure of a small sector of the Victorian economy.

The starting point is the annual returns of licences which, on a national basis, give the number of malting licences issued until 1880. These peaked in 1826 at 14,422 (of which 10,468 were taken out in England and Wales). By 1855–59, this figure had more than halved. By 1880 it had almost halved again (the sharpest falls coming in Scotland). Against this, however, the malt charged with duty rose sharply after 1830, stagnated through the 'Hungry Forties' and then maintained an upward trend until the late 1870s. (see Table 2.1)

These statistics underline two facts: first, the small *average* scale of malting in 1830; and secondly, the rapid concentration of the industry thereafter. In 1833–35, and again in 1862, the returns also give the number of maltsters within broad production bands and therefore provide some insight into the scale of malting firms (see Table 2.2).

Table 2.2

Maltsters' licences issued in Great Britain, according to production,
1833 and 1862 (quarters)

Quantity produced (quarters)	(i) 1833	(ii) (i) as percentage of total	(iii) 1862	(iv) (iii) as percentage of total
Not exceeding 5	1452	11.24	241	3.85
5– 50	2742	21.23	628	10.04
50–100	1012	7.84	561	8.97
100–150	1077	8.34	527	8.42
150–200	973	7.54	483	7.72
200–250	933	7.23	441	7.05
250–300	710	5.50	374	5.98
300–350	576	4.46	310	4.96
350–400	499	3.86	305	4.88
400–450	401	3.11	196	3.13
450–500	345	2.67	201	3.21
500–550	294	2.28	171	2.73
Over 550	1899	14.71	1818	29.06
Total	12,913	100.01	6256[1]	100.00

Note: 1833 figures are given for Great Britain only;
[1] Excludes 272 'beginners' who paid a surcharge according to quantity
(i) Year end 5 January 1834; (iii) Year end 31 March 1862.
Source: *Returns of Maltsters' Licences, PP* (1837), xxx, p. 10; (1862), xxx, p. 503.

[48] In the first year of use each individual malting required a separate licence; thereafter a producer covered all his maltings by a single licence, *PP* (1862), xxx, p. 503.

In fact, a large proportion of the licences issued in the early decades of the period were almost certainly for private use: in 1833, as many as 1452 maltsters (11.2 per cent) paid the 12½p. fee to make up to five quarters annually (to brew, at most, about twenty barrels of beer). A further 2742 (21.2 per cent) – probably beer house keepers, licensed victuallers, large institutions and estates – made up to fifty quarters; these two groups between them accounting for almost one-third of all licence-holders. However, by 1862, of 6256 licences, a mere 241 (only thirty-four in England and Wales) were in the smallest category, together with 628 for under fifty quarters. This marked, above all, the demise of private brewing, which declined sharply after 1830. In contrast, the number of maltsters taking out licences in the largest band (to make in excess of 550 quarters) remained steady over the thirty years (declining from 1899 to 1818), the proportion rising from 14.7 per cent to 29.1 per cent. Yet given that a 15 quarter malthouse could produce around 600 quarters annually, even at this level of production, there must have been enormous differences in scale, ranging from relatively small sales-maltsters to large brewers producing many thousand quarters a year. Bass, the largest of these, made 89,000 quarters in 1858–59.[49]

Unfortunately, we have no further evidence about production bands. But one issue which concerned the Select Committee on the Malt Tax in 1867 was the decline of the small maltster. Most of the witnesses were adamant that many still survived, but agreed with Manning Prentice that 'larger [maltsters] were becoming larger and the smallest going to the wall'.[50] Whereas those witnesses who claimed to the 1835 Excise Inquiry to be among the largest sales-maltsters were making 15–16,000 quarters annually, thirty years later it was 20–30,000 quarters.[51] Several reasons were suggested: changes in the excise regulations; the decline of publican brewing; and the coming of the railways which opened up national markets and stimulated a wave of capital investment in railside maltings. After 1880 there is every indication that the rate of concentration was maintained. Kelly's 1902 *Directory of the Wine and Spirits Trade* clearly confirms the continuing fall in numbers.[52] Against the background of a long-term decline in beer output (and, therefore, malt consumption), the concentration of the brewing industry in the late nineteenth century prompted a reciprocal trend in malting. Again it was the smaller maltsters who were squeezed hard. In contrast, the market leaders, Sutcliffes, Gilstrap Earp and R. & W. Paul, were all producing well in excess of 100,000 quarters annually by the outbreak of the First World War.[53]

---

[49] Owen, *Greatest Brewery*, p. 62.

[50] *Select Committee on the Malt Tax, PP* (1867–68), ix, p. 282.

[51] *Commission of Excise Inquiry, PP* (1835), xxxi, appendix 62; *Select Committee on the Malt Tax, PP* (1867–68), ix, pp. 293, 326, 331, 280.

[52] See p. 36.

[53] E. F. Taylor, 'Associated British Maltsters'; *Brewery Record*, 6 (September 1927); R. & W. Paul, Annual Cost Accounts.

How were these malting firms geographically distributed? What were the regional differences in their scale of production and pattern of growth? We have seen in Chapter 1 that the key factors influencing the development of malting were the regional specialisation of barley cultivation, proximity to markets and comparative transport advantages. A fourth variable, however, the changing structure of the brewing industry, was also of critical importance. Statistics based upon the brewers' annual returns to the excise can again be used to delineate the extent of these changes, their timing and geographical concentration. From these data we can deduce the scale and scope of the local market facing sales-maltsters. Excluding private brewers, the broad picture shows the steadily growing control over the industry of common (commercial) brewers. In 1831, they produced 54 per cent of beer output in England and Wales (in Scotland, it was already 90 per cent), with the licensed victuallers producing 34 per cent and the beer house keepers – the new class created by the 1830 Beer Act – around 11 per cent. By 1900, the proportions were 95 per cent, 3 per cent and 2 per cent respectively. Moreover, while the number of publican brewers was generally sustained until the mid 1860s, it fell rapidly thereafter. In 1870, 20,095 victuallers and 9735 beer house keepers still produced some 23 per cent of total output; twenty years later these numbers had fallen by over two-thirds and by 1900 had more than halved again.[54]

Yet, at the regional and even local levels, the rate and timing of these changes varied widely. Already in 1830 beer production in the eastern and southern counties, in London, Liverpool and Edinburgh, was controlled by common brewers; conversely, in the midlands, the west country and Wales, and in Manchester and Leeds, the publican brewer was predominant. While brewing historians have suggested a number of explanations, it is clear there is no simple answer. Several factors played a role: the size of local markets, regional transport developments and the competitive pull of the great London breweries. None of these, however, addresses the marked contrasts evident between Liverpool and Manchester or between Norfolk and Suffolk: in 1830, 90 per cent of output in the Norwich collection district was already in the hands of common brewers; in Suffolk only 32 per cent – 90 per cent concentration was not achieved in the county until the late 1870s. According to Richard Wilson, the answer may lie in demand rather than in supply side factors: 'the traditions and economy of the working class, the prime consumers, were also important considerations'.[55] Certainly in Birmingham, the stronghold of the small master, publican brewers retained their dominance until the final quarter of the century.

To what extent did these forces shape the structure of the malting industry? Unfortunately, the data are less complete than for brewing. Only for a brief

---

[54] For a more detailed discussion of these events see Gourvish and Wilson, *British Brewing Industry*, pp. 66–75.

[55] Ibid., p. 74.

period between 1855 and 1862 are the statistics for malting licences either broken down by collection or do they distinguish between brewer and sales-maltster. But, when considered in parallel with the brewing figures, a distinct pattern emerges. Generally, where the largest numbers of licences were issued and where a high proportion were taken out by sales-maltsters, mainly in the west (Chester, Gloucester, Worcester and Wales); and in the midlands (Birmingham, Coventry and Nottingham), publican brewing predominated. In the Stourbridge collection district, for example, 205 malting licences were issued in 1862, 160 (78 per cent) to sales-maltsters; and of the 1286 licensed victuallers in the district, 1228 (95.5 per cent) brewed their own beer as did 676 (95.3 per cent) of the 709 beer house keepers. They consumed between them over 91 per cent of the malt brewed. Conversely, in the south and east, in Cambridge, Norwich, Surrey and Sussex, the strongholds of the common brewer, far fewer licences were issued and there was a smaller proportion to sales-maltsters.[56] Of course, there were exceptions. The disparity between Norfolk and Suffolk is again evident; in Plymouth, unusually for the west country, the common brewer was already ascendant; Manchester was the only district without a single licence, while in Liverpool three out of four were held by brewers.[57]

After 1832 there is no further insight into malt production, other than on a national scale, to shed light on the average size of malting firms in different regions. There is, however, no indication of any significant shift from the trends discussed in Chapter 1: the growing concentration of malting in the east, with excess production over local demand; the reverse being the case in urban industrial regions. The figures suggest that, in the great malting counties of the east, the growing control of common brewers was matched by the rise of a relatively small number of sales-maltsters focused mainly on the national market. In contrast, the pattern of brewing in the west and midlands sustained an economy characterised by a large number of small producers selling within the confines of the local market.

When we examine more closely the structure of the malting industry, two features need to be stressed: the south–east versus north–west divide, determined by environmental factors; and more localised variations in the brewing industry. These trends are particularly evident in East Anglia, where the predominance of the region's companies coexisted with the contrasts between Norfolk and Suffolk. In each case, the regional specialisation in barley cultivation, access to waterborne transport and expanding urban populations

---

[56] The lowest levels were in the south: in Surrey, of thirty-eight licences issued, nineteen were held by sales-maltsters; in Sussex only fifteen out of a total of fifty-one.

[57] In Norwich, 32 (65 per cent) licences were held by sales-maltsters, in Suffolk, seventy-three (75 per cent), and in Plymouth, as many as 153 (81 per cent). It is notable that the pattern holds in Cumberland and Durham, districts where the common brewer predominated and which, therefore, were themselves exceptions to the north–west versus south–east divide.

underpinned a trade which reached far beyond the region. Yet, whereas in terms of total output there was little difference between the two counties (see Table 1.2), Kelly's 1846 *Directories* listed ninety-eight maltsters in Norfolk, but as many as 179 in Suffolk. The numbers in 1879 were seventy-six and 121, and in 1896, forty-nine and 108 respectively.[58] An analysis of the Poor Rate Books in the major ports of Great Yarmouth and Ipswich suggests a similar trend: an earlier and higher degree of concentration in Norfolk than Suffolk.[59]

How do we explain these different rates of change? Partly in terms of the key variables: environment, transport and local markets. Throughout the eighteenth century it was the Norfolk ports, particularly Yarmouth, which dominated the lucrative export trade in malt. Large corn merchants were encouraged to invest in malting so that by the 1740s five of the principal exporters owned over one-third of the malthouses in the town.[60] When, in the 1780s, the trade was destroyed by war, the focus shifted to the domestic brewing industry, both locally and in London. At a time of rapid population growth there were three centres, ripe for investment, in the thriving ports of Yarmouth (the east coast naval base) and Lynn and the great city of Norwich.[61] Almost at the same time, the London porter brewers, attracted by developments in agriculture and the ascendancy of Norfolk malt, began to shift their attention away from their traditional source of malt supply, Hertfordshire. By the close of the eighteenth century most were well established in Norfolk.

In comparison, the ports of Suffolk scarcely featured in the foreign trade; only during the first quarter of the eighteenth century did annual malt exports from Ipswich even approach 20,000 quarters.[62] The main reason, undoubtedly, was the neglected state of her ports. Conditions at Southwold were so bad that early in the nineteenth century Jacob Mealing, one of the largest corn merchants in the region, was forced to move his business to

---

[58] Kelly's *Directories* of Suffolk and Norfolk, 1846, 1879, 1888 and 1896.

[59] The Poor Rate Books show the extent of individual holdings and, because over the period considered the annual estimated rentals remain almost constant, provide a good indication of change of scale. The series is unfortunately incomplete for the counties as a whole. In Great Yarmouth in 1846 forty-two maltings were worked by twelve firms, all (with one exception), substantial concerns; by 1880 there were sixty-seven maltings (many of much greater capacity) but only ten firms. In Ipswich in 1854 forty maltings were operated by eighteen firms, of which nine worked single, small maltings; in 1880 there were forty-three maltings (including several larger and newly built) and fourteen substantial firms. Great Yarmouth Poor Rate Books, 1846–80, Y/LI/71–73, 175–77, 284, 228–31, 293, NRO; Ipswich Poor Rate Books, 1854–80, DC2/17/5, 300, 723, 21, 316, 739, 71, 326, 749, 526, 246.

[60] J. D. Murphy, 'The Town and Trade of Great Yarmouth, 1740–1850' (unpublished Ph.D. thesis, University of East Anglia, 1979), p. 46.

[61] In 1801 the population of Norwich was 36,000, Yarmouth 17,000 and King's Lynn, 10,000; by 1851 it had risen to 68,000, 31,000 and 19,000 respectively. Census Abstract of Eastern Counties, 1801–41, 1851.

[62] Ipswich Appendix, 1714–1823, HD 391/2, SRO, Ipswich.

Yarmouth. Subsequently, the entrenched attitudes of the harbour commission defeated even that stalwart Scotsman Patrick Stead.[63] More important was the steady decline of Ipswich from being a flourishing port where merchants had prospered on the wool and cloth trade. By the 1740s large ships were unable to reach the quays but were forced to load and discharge by lighter below the town. Sixty years later, even small vessels were often unable to reach the wharves.[64] The position improved in 1805 when the river commission was set up to levy tolls and improve the River Orwell, but not until 1837 did the Ipswich Dock Act empower the construction of the wet dock which subsequently breathed new life into the port. Shortly afterwards, the railways improved communications with the national market. This was vital for Suffolk, for, unlike her neighbour, she lacked thriving centres of urban growth. In 1801 the population of Ipswich, together with the next ten largest towns in the county, was 39,407 and scarcely exceeded that of Norwich alone, a local market which provided relatively few opportunities for the entrepreneur.[65] Clearly the industry lacked the advantages of Norfolk and remained for much longer fragmented and relatively underdeveloped. With improved communications, however, it went from strength to strength. There are many references to the great expansion of Stowmarket as a malting town; by 1870 it had more than twenty malthouses and was said to rank third in England.[66] A decade later, Ipswich had superseded Yarmouth as the largest exporter of grain to London.[67]

The remainder of the explanation rests with the different structure of the brewing industry in the two counties. While in both cases the mainstay of malting was the national trade, the Suffolk maltster faced a very different local market to his Norfolk counterpart. By the 1840s brewing in Norfolk was already concentrated in the hands of common brewers. The firm of Steward & Patteson, for example, owned around 250 public houses, no fewer than 183 in Norwich alone. Together with the next six largest brewers, they controlled three-quarters of the city's public houses.[68] Similarly, Lacons of

---

[63] His ships were delayed so frequently that he was forced to give up shipping corn. Twice he took his case to Parliament, but was never able to secure a Bill for the improvement of the harbour. In fact much of the malt made in Suffolk did not pass through the Suffolk ports but left, via Breydon Water, through Great Yarmouth; or from the Stour Valley via Harwich. R. Lawrence, *Southwold River: Georgian Life in the Blythe Valley* (1990), pp. 113–21; *First Report of the Tidal Harbours Commission, PP* (1845), xvi, pp. 337, 341.

[64] Ipswich Port Authority Records, SRO; W. G. Arnott, *Orwell Estuary: The Story of Ipswich River* (Ipswich, 1966), pp. 60–61.

[65] The population of the towns of Beccles, Bungay, Bury St Edmunds, Eye, Hadleigh, Lowestoft, Southwold, Stowmarket, Sudbury and Woodbridge in 1801 was 28,407. J. Glyde, *Suffolk in the Nineteenth Century* (London, 1851), p. 41.

[66] A. D. Bayne, *Royal Illustrated History of Eastern England*, i (1873), pp. 300, 351; W. White, *Directory* of Suffolk (1844), p. 582.

[67] M. J. Freeman and D. H. Aldcroft (eds), *Transport in Victorian Britain* (Manchester, 1988), pp. 190–219.

[68] Gourvish, *Norfolk Beers*, p. 32.

Great Yarmouth and Bagges of King's Lynn, and even small country brewers such as Bidwells at Thetford, had tied estates. Moreover, most of these brewers malted for themselves. Between them the common brewers in the Norfolk excise collection districts consumed almost 86 per cent of the malt brewed in the county.[69] In a similar fashion, the London brewers who owned maltings in Norfolk accounted for a significant proportion of the malt destined for the national market. Whitbreads, for instance, owned maltings at Yarmouth, Southtown and Whittington (Stoke Ferry) which by the 1820s were valued at the considerable sum of £18,800. Several of the larger sales-maltsters were also closely connected with brewers: Edward Combe malted on commission for Combe & Delafield; Jacob Mealing, Richard Marriott and Richard Dewing for Trumans. Others, like James Fison who employed fifty to sixty men in his Thetford maltings, sent malt to brewers in London and the north. In contrast, small sales-maltsters either relied upon the open market or the minority of licensed victuallers and beer house keepers who brewed for themselves (a mere 7 per cent and 13.5 per cent in 1840). Malting in Norfolk, like brewing, was already concentrated in the hands of large producers.

In several respects, the same features were evident in Suffolk. At Ipswich, a major brewer, John Cobbold, dominated brewing and malting through his tied estate and twelve maltings in the town.[70] Other brewers similarly owned public houses. When, in 1838, the executors of Samuel Alexander sold his small brewery in Woodbridge it had eighteen public houses scattered throughout the surrounding countryside.[71] Many brewers malted for themselves, although a smaller proportion than in Norfolk.[72] Again, several maltsters worked on commission for leading brewers: Patrick Stead for Bass and Trumans; Robert Burleigh of Woodbridge and Henry Dowson (who malted at Geldeston, Beccles and Oulton) for Trumans; and John Crisp of Beccles for Allsopps, Meux and Calverts. Other large maltsters, like Manning Prentice, sent malt to Guinness and the Liverpool brewers.[73] Yet it is equally clear that small-scale malting survived far longer in Suffolk than in Norfolk. Whereas in 1846 of twelve malting firms at Yarmouth only one could be described as small, at Ipswich, of eighteen firms, as many as eight worked a single small malting.[74] The reason, undoubtedly, was the parallel survival

69 *PP* (1842), xxxix, p. 518.

70 Cobbold's also owned two maltings at Woodbridge and three at Stowmarket. Articles of Agreement, John Cobbold to John Chevalier Cobbold, 12 November 1857, HA/231/1/1.

71 *Ipswich Journal*, 10 November 1838.

72 Of 179 maltsters listed in Kelly's 1846 *Directory*, only twenty-five (14 per cent) also brewed; in Norfolk, it was almost 38 per cent. Although an incomplete measure, in that some brewers who only malted for themselves were not listed as maltsters, it is probably representative of the two counties.

73 *Select Committee on the Malt Tax, PP* (1867–68), ix, p. 284.

74 Of an estimated rental between £14 and £36. Ipswich Poor Rate Books, DC2/17/5, 300, 723, 21, 316, 739, 71, 326, 789, 526.

of small-scale brewing in Suffolk until the end of the nineteenth century. In 1867 Manning Prentice told the Select Committee on the Malt Tax that, despite the general decline of small maltsters, his company competed 'side by side' with about half a dozen small firms based either in Stowmarket or the immediate neighbourhood. They sold mainly to publicans and private brewers, often undercutting the larger maltsters in order to attract their custom.[75] That year no less than 40 per cent of the malt brewed in Suffolk was consumed by publicans and beer house keepers.[76] Elias Amos, an agricultural labourer from Playford, near Ipswich, also described how he and his neighbours regularly brewed their own beer in their cottages. Most received malt as part of their harvest wages, but at other times they bought from small suppliers.[77] He was clearly well briefed to support the farming cause but, as late as the 1890s, the harvest brew was still an annual event in many Suffolk farmhouses and cottages.[78] Not for another decade did private and publican brewing in Suffolk virtually disappear and small-scale malting finally yield to the commercial strength of the leading malting firms.

Despite the structural differences, it was the preponderance of large-scale malt production – either by brewers or sales-maltsters – which characterised the East Anglian industry. As early as 1835 Patrick Stead was making 16–17,000 quarters of malt annually; in 1846–50 he sent an average of over 16,000 quarters to Trumans alone, as did Jacob Mealing of Norwich. During the 1850s and 1860s Bidwells often dispatched over 10,000 quarters, besides supplying their own Thetford brewery.[79] In 1867 Manning Prentice reckoned his firm was making in excess of 30,000 quarters annually, while little more than a decade later F. & G. Smith, the Great Ryburgh maltsters, manufactured as much as 80,000 quarters.[80] The Smiths, with their roots in farming, were relative newcomers to the industry, expanding rapidly during the buoyant 1860s and 1870s. It was a familiar pattern. At nearby Wells-Next-The-Sea, James Everitt also farmed and bought barley on commission for Bass and, as a young man in the 1820s, had been involved in the family brewery with its string of twenty-five public houses.[81] It was such links as these with the barley and malt trade which, according to Richard Wilson, underpinned the early progress made by common brewers in the eastern counties.[82] Certainly the wealth of Lacons and Cobbolds depended as much

[75] *Select Committee on the Malt Tax, PP* (1867–68), ix, pp. 282, 288.

[76] *PP* (1867–68), lxiv, p. 127.

[77] In contrast, James Everitt said that the tradition of harvest brewing in Norfolk had almost disappeared. *Select Committee on the Malt Tax, PP* (1867–68), ix, pp. 303, 412–14.

[78] W. Tye, 'Brewing Day in the Nineties', *Suffolk Review*, 1 (1956–58), pp. 156–60.

[79] Truman, Hanbury and Buxton, Barley Ledgers, B/THB/B/156, 157.

[80] *Select Committee on the Malt Tax, PP* (1867–68), ix, p. 319; Balance Sheet, F. & G. Smith, 30 October 1879, Crisp Malting Limited; unfortunately, it is the only one to have survived for this period.

[81] *Select Committee on the Malt Tax, PP* (1867–68), ix, pp. 300–5.

[82] Gourvish and Wilson, *British Brewing Industry*, p. 75.

on malting as upon brewing and other interrelated activities – their coastal trade, ship owning and banking.[83] Throughout the 1850s, for example, John Cobbold made in excess of 3000 quarters of malt for Trumans each year.[84] In the same way, the success of many East Anglian maltsters was founded upon a diversity of occupations, ranging from farming and corn merchanting to milling, brewing and shipping.

Pauls of Ipswich provide a classic example. The founder of the family's fortunes, George Paul (1740–1828), an ironmonger, settled in Bury St Edmunds in 1773. By the early decades of the nineteenth century George II (1776–1852), a thrusting entrepreneur, was also involved in the Suffolk grain trade. His son Robert (1806–64), owner of an Ipswich saddlery, had interests in the United Shipping Company, whose barges plied the coastal routes carrying wheat and barley and consignments of malt for the London brewers. The family also acquired a small brewery in Foundation Street, Ipswich, with a tied estate of fifteen public houses, private trade and wine and spirit business, which Robert managed. Then, in the early 1840s, the Pauls faced a financial crisis. The cause remains unknown, but these were years of deep depression when business failures were commonplace. Whatever the explanation, the family enterprises were sold and Robert continued as a wharfinger and maltster, initially renting a single 'corn-chamber' at the quay.[85] Nevertheless, his fortunes slowly recovered and on his death in 1864 he left a small, but thriving, malting and shipping business.[86] After a decade of administration by his executors, his young sons, Robert II (1844–1909) and William (1850–1928), inherited his business interests. The firm grew rapidly. In 1874 the brothers joined the Ipswich Corn Exchange and the Baltic Exchange in London and shortly afterwards became members of the London Corn Exchange in Mark Lane.[87] Expansion in malting and the corn trade was matched by diversification into the manufacture of animal feedstuffs and flaked maize for brewers – activities which earned for the brothers the title of 'Maize Kings of East Anglia'. The few coastal barges were transformed into an impressive fleet; a local shipyard followed in 1901. Unfortunately, few details of the firm's output have survived, but during the

---

[83] Ibid., p. 117; Mathias, *Brewing Industry*, pp. 322–23, 328–29.

[84] Made mainly at Woodbridge, some on commission, some on contract; Truman, Hanbury and Buxton, Barley Ledgers, B\THB\B\157.

[85] The brewery, which had an annual capacity of 10,000 barrels, was sold early in 1842. The saddlery was also in difficulty and, about the same time, George II and his second son, Thomas (a hosier, patten and clog manufacturer), also sold their Bury St Edmunds businesses. C2/7/2/2, SRO, Ipswich; *Ipswich Journal*, 30 April 1842.

[86] The eleven maltings, ranging from 12–25 quarters capacity, were valued at £3950; six barges and their stores at a further £1195. The total valuation, including stocks (mainly barley, malt culms and maize) was £7520. Valuation for Trustees of the late Mr Robert Paul, 1 July 1874.

[87] B. A. Holderness, 'Pauls of Ipswich' (typescript, 1980), chapter 4, pp. 13–16.

last pre-war season Pauls sold in excess of 144,000 quarters of malt and almost 100,000 quarters of flaked maize.

Other East Anglian firms grew similarly. Newson Garrett (1812–93), younger son of the well-known agricultural engineer Richard Garrett, spent seven years as a pawnbroker in London before in 1841 returning to his native Suffolk and purchasing a small corn merchant's business at Snape. Within three years he was sending 17,000 quarters of barley to the London brewers. He expanded into shipbuilding – he owned half the twenty-four ships in the port of Aldeburgh – and in 1848 was appointed agent for Lloyds. Large maltings were built at Snape and in the early 1850s Newson became a partner in the Bow Brewery, London.[88] When in 1882 the brewery company (one of the earliest to take company status) was registered with a capital of £450,000, Newson and his son Edmund (who managed the brewery) were among its first directors. Shortly afterwards the malting business of Newson Garrett & Son was incorporated, with Newson and his youngest son, George (the manager), as directors.[89] The firm of Thomas Prentice and Company of Stowmarket, with its origins in the early 1800s, likewise grew upon a diversity of interests. Initially, Manning Prentice (d. 1836) combined the role of general merchant with his partnership in Oakes Bank. His sons, Thomas (1796 – *c*. 1858) and William (1797 – *c*. 1868) were farmers, corn and timber merchants, brewers and maltsters; the firm was one of the first to test the Australian malt market and later sold malt, via their Copenhagen agent, to the celebrated Carlsberg brewery.[90] Several others followed the same pattern of merchant-manufacturing: Patrick Stead and J. & R. Marriott were corn merchants; F. & G. Smith and the Press brothers were millers; and James Fison combined malting and milling with the manufacture of artificial fertilisers. Many had their roots in farming, all had access to prime malting barley and a large proportion had shipping interests and exploited the region's river and coastal communications. While the drive and ambition of their owners was of course a further factor, it was these advantages which underpinned not only the regional specialisation of malting but the dominant position of malting companies in the eastern counties.

Similar factors, apart from involvement in the coastal trade, account for the early success of large malting firms in Lincolnshire and the east midlands. Typically, Sandars of Gainsborough were farmers and corn merchants, while at Newark the firm of James Thorpe & Sons began as millers in the mid 1700s. Much of their malt, as we have seen, was destined for the brewers

---

[88] The Snape maltings were subsequently converted into a concert hall and are better known as the home of the Aldeburgh Festival.

[89] J. Manton, *Elizabeth Garrett Anderson* (London, 1965), pp. 25–37; R. Simper, *Over Snape Bridge: The Story of Snape Maltings* (1967), pp. 6–8; *Brewers' Journal*, 15 August 1882; *East Anglian Daily Times*, 6 May 1893.

[90] C. A. Manning, *Suffolk Celebrities* (1893); J. Glyde, 'Materials for a History of Stowmarket', MS and cuttings, Stowmarket 9, SRO Ipswich; Holderness, 'Pauls of Ipswich', chapter 6, p. 6; *Select Committee on the Malt Tax*, PP (1867–68), ix, p. 284.

of Burton and the north. Indeed such was demand that, against the national trend, the number of maltsters in Lincolnshire rose sharply in the 1850s and 1860s.[91] But in Nottingham, the persistence of small-scale brewing late in the century also influenced the structure of the industry. In 1862 more than 85 per cent of the malt brewed in the Nottingham collection district was consumed by licensed victuallers and beer house keepers. As late as 1880, 70 per cent of all publicans still brewed for themselves, together with beer house keepers accounting for over 60 per cent of the malt consumed. As in Suffolk, small-scale maltsters worked side by side with nationally known companies like Gilstrap Earp. In both counties a third type of firm emerged, selling both to common brewers and (through tied estates) to brewing victuallers.

In the 1830s eleven of the fifty-four public houses in Bury St Edmunds, a noted malting centre, were owned by two maltsters, Henry McL'Roth and Robert Maulkin. Maulkin, the largest maltster in the town, owned six – and a further two in the surrounding countryside which had been acquired through the family's close links with brewing victuallers. In 1855 the malting business passed to Frederick King, Maulkin's son-in-law, who eleven years later began brewing, subsequently amalgamating with Edward Greene to form one of the leading provincial brewery companies, Greene King.[92] Joseph Pidcock, founder of the Nottingham firm of J. Pidcock & Company, began as a tavern keeper and spirits dealer before moving into malting.[93] When it was incorporated in 1893 (with a capital of £100,000), the company was malting at Nottingham, Ancaster, Retford and Tuxford. Several small maltsters also worked for Pidcocks, either on commission or contract. The company owned several public houses – six, situated in Nottingham and Stamford, were purchased in 1896–97. Malt and hops were supplied to the tenants.[94] The company also provided small loans to publicans and mortgages to a number of brewing victuallers who bought their own inns. In 1899, for example, £6000 was put up for six public houses, mostly in Wales. The tied estate was sold in 1902, shortly after the Nottingham magistrates, having convicted the tenant of the *Jolly Angler* of gambling offenses, revoked the licence. Pidcocks provided mortgages for the new owners, however, and continued to finance many small brewers well into the twentieth century.

These examples unfortunately raise as many questions as they answer. How early did Pidcocks acquire a tied estate? More importantly, were these isolated examples, or are similar cases to be found elsewhere? For it is clear

---

[91] Kelly's *Directories* of Lincolnshire list 89 in 1849, 141 in 1861, 120 in 1876, and 85 in 1888.
[92] R. G. Wilson, *Greene King: A Business and Family History* (London, 1983), pp. 98–99, 298.
[93] The evidence for this section is taken from Pigot's and White's *Directories* of Nottinghamshire, 1828–95; J. Pidcock & Company, Directors' Minutes, 1893–1910.
[94] Rents varied from £60 to £95. In 1899 the inns returned an average of just under 6 per cent of historic cost, ranging from 4½ to 6½ per cent (at the *Beehive*, where a new brewhouse had been installed) in Nottingham, to as much as 8½ per cent at Stamford.

that Pidcock's role of quasi-banker to publican brewers in Nottingham and Wales reflected both demand- and supply-side factors and was itself instrumental in sustaining small-scale brewing in these regions. One further example, and one which again emphasises the importance of market demand in shaping the character and development of malting companies, is that of Samuel Thompson & Sons. The business was founded in 1805 by Samuel Thompson of Oldbury, Worcestershire, who was later joined by his three sons. By the 1850s, the family were malting at Oldbury, Smethwick and West Bromwich; they had acquired a mill, two small local breweries and others at Wolverhampton and Uttoxeter, besides several public houses. The partnership was dissolved in 1872, with Samuel (1815–92), the second son, subsequently continuing the malting side of the business. His experience in brewing continued to influence the character of the enterprise. Expansion was rapid and by 1914 the company, producing 70–80,000 quarters of malt a year, was numbered among the leading sales-malting firms. But whereas Thompson's competitors in the eastern counties had invested in large, centralised maltings, growth was achieved simply through the acquisition of numerous small concerns scattered throughout the west midlands, the Welsh borders and the west country. Several hundred customers – small country brewers and home brew pubs – were supplied with local malt made from locally grown barley.[95] In their scale of production, Thompsons were the exception. For there were few maltsters of any size in these regions. Thomas Pitts of Plymouth reckoned he was one of the largest in 1867. Yet he produced only 6000 quarters annually, about a quarter as much as the other witnesses to the Select Committee on the Malt Tax.[96] As late as 1899, a remarkable 63 per cent of output was still brewed by publicans in the Shrewsbury collection district; correspondingly, Kelly's 1902 *Directory* lists no fewer than seventy maltsters in the county of Shropshire. Indeed, private and publican brewing persisted in the county long after the First World War; in 1919, there were twenty-one members affiliated to the newly re-formed Maltsters' Association, the third largest representation after Yorkshire and Suffolk, two of the leading malting counties.

A brief review of malting in Scotland again reveals the fundamental importance both of the eastern bias, in brewing and barley cultivation, and of the coastal trade. The early concentration of brewing and distilling were further factors instrumental in shaping the structure of the sales-malting sector. For as early as 1830, as Ian Donnachie noted, malting was 'overwhelmingly concentrated in the old-established centres of eastern Scotland and, like brewing and lowland distilling, had become an essentially urban industry'.[97] It was also an industry largely dominated by brewers and distillers. Already by this date, 90 per cent of beer output was controlled by common

---

95 Taylor, 'Associated British Maltsters', pp. 16–17; *Smethwick Telephone*, December 1949.
96 *Select Committee on the Malt Tax, PP* (1867–68), ix, p. 319.
97 I. Donnachie, *A History of the Brewing Industry in Scotland* (Edinburgh, 1979), p. 48.

brewers. In Edinburgh, Alloa and Falkirk, and in Glasgow where the industrial market grew quickly, brewers like William Younger, J. & R. Tennent
and George Younger penetrated the Scottish market and built up a thriving
export trade to London and the north, and, subsequently, to India and
Australia. Almost without exception, these brewers malted for themselves:
James Aitken of Falkirk built large maltings at Linlithgow, while several
Edinburgh brewers had premises at Dunbar and Haddington.[98] Even in
1825–26 (when there were still well over 200 brewers), Pigot's *Commercial
Directory of Scotland* listed a mere forty independent maltsters. During this
period, commercial distilling also grew substantially. Indeed, by the 1840s
four-fifths of all the malt made in Scotland was used in distilling.[99] Again,
most distillers malted for themselves and, like brewers, bought only marginal
supplies from sales-maltsters.[100] Thus by the mid nineteenth century the
independent sector faced both a limited and divided market, with little
apparent room for growth.

Yet it was during this period that several of the leading Scottish malting
companies were established. Hugh Baird, son of a wealthy Glasgow businessman, acquired the Canal Bank Maltings and Possil Road brewery in the
difficult 1820s and prospered. Until the 1860s he traded in partnership
with his younger brother Frank (who subsequently took over the brewery),
apparently with some success, for in 1837 the brothers received the royal
warrant. Malt was sold to local distillers and brewers, besides roasted malt
(the first to be made in Scotland) and hops. Malt was also sent, via the Forth
and Clyde Canal, to Guinness in Dublin and to brewers in the north of
England. The demand for malt rose steadily after 1850 as beer output
increased and many brewers were unable to satisfy their own needs. William
Younger, for example, made around 70,000 quarters of malt a year and
increased capacity by 40,000 quarters in the 1880s but was still forced to
buy extra malt.[101] Baird's Glasgow maltings were extended in the early 1890s
to meet the growing demand. A decade later, a pneumatic malting – one
of the few to be built by a sales-maltster and used mainly for the distilling
trade – was added. The company also encroached further into the English
market, finally acquiring in 1908 the Greenwich company of Corder &
Haycroft and, five years later, the Newbury firm of William Skinner.

The firm of Robert Hutchison of Kirkcaldy which, like Bairds, was
numbered among the leading sales-maltsters by the end of the period, was

---

[98] In 1862, of twenty-three licences issued in the Edinburgh collection district, all but three
were to brewers.

[99] The proportion fell after the introduction in the 1840s of the Coffey, or patent, still. Widely
adopted by the Lowland distillers for the production of grain whisky, it enabled 90 per cent of
cheaper, unmalted grain (including from the 1860s maize), and only 10 per cent of barley malt
to be used in mashing. R. B. Weir, *The History of the Distillers Company, 1877–1939* (Oxford, 1995),
pp. 7–18.

[100] A. Barnard, *The Whisky Distilleries of the United Kingdom* (London, 1887).

[101] Barnard, *Noted Breweries*, ii, p. 16.

also founded in the 1820s.[102] Initially a farmer and corn merchant, Robert Hutchison shipped barley and oats to Glasgow and speculated in Black Sea wheat and barley for the English market – a profitable but risky venture, which twice threatened the firm's finances. But the basis of growth was milling and malting. Again like Bairds, besides supplying the local market, Hutchisons sent malt to Guinness and to brewers in the north of England. The central importance of the coastal trade is illustrated most clearly by the firm of J. P. Simpson & Company of Alnwick, close to the Scottish border.[103] A late entrant, James Simpson settled in Alnwick in 1866 and also combined the roles of corn merchant and maltster, supplying small brewers in the north of England and southern Scotland, such as Rowell of Gateshead, J. Connell & Company of Edinburgh and the West Auckland Brewery. Further maltings were acquired at Berwick-upon-Tweed in 1888 and at Darlington in 1889 to cover north Yorkshire and County Durham. By then the company's main market was Ireland. Malt was sent to Jamesons of Dublin, but mainly to Guinness: in most years the great brewer took 10–15,000 quarters, around one-third of total production. As a consequence, maltings were built at Tweedmouth docks in 1902 specifically to handle Irish consignments and, subsequently, those to London brewers like Mann Crossman & Paulin. Success for a small number of sales-maltsters in Scotland and the north east was based, as elsewhere, upon exploiting the region's resources and, above all, upon securing a large, extra-regional market. Predominantly that market was Ireland or, more precisely, Guinness. Guinness, the largest brewer in the world by 1880, was increasingly influential in the malt market.

In several respects, brewing and malting in Ireland paralleled the Scottish experience: the early control of distillers and large brewers, like Beamish & Crawford of Cork and Guinness; and eastern location to gain the dual advantages of the nearby barley-growing counties and the eastern seaboard; for, as in Scotland, the success of Irish brewers depended on a thriving export trade, in this case to England. On the other hand, Guinness, through its unprecedented scale, dominated the barley and malt markets in a way no other brewer could. In 1878 the company consumed almost 220,000 quarters of malt (440,000 barrels).[104] This had risen to 350,000 quarters by the late 1880s and doubled again to 750,000 quarters by 1914 (when Guinness brewed 2.8 million bulk barrels of beer). In comparison, Bass, their nearest rival, consumed less than 300,000 quarters.[105]

---

102 This paragraph is based upon a typescript company history, 'The Hutchisons of Kirkcaldy: A History of the Family and the Firm'.

103 The evidence for this section is taken from a typescript company history, 'The History of the Family and Firm of J. P. Simpson and Company (Alnwick) Limited'.

104 In Ireland, the barrel was the standard measure for malt and barley; a barrel of malt consists of twelve stones and one of barley sixteen. These were roughly interchangeable, i.e. a barrel equals half a quarter.

105 Gourvish and Wilson, *British Brewing Industry*, p. 191.

Until the 1890s Guinness's policy was to secure its supply of malt at the cheapest rate consistent with quality.[106] As with other large brewers, this was achieved through an appropriate mix of malting, commissioning and contract buying. The first task, however, was to secure adequate supplies of good quality barley. By the 1880s the firm consumed over one-third of the Irish barley crop but, while its demands continued to grow rapidly, a number of factors combined to diminish both the acreage and quality of the native crop: the influx of imported grain; the decline in beer production in England in the early 1880s; and greater use of malt substitutes (although Guinness used none), which all depressed barley prices. Of course the cheap foreign grain eased supply problems, while the fall in prices was greatly to the company's advantage, but by the early 1890s the situation was serious enough to prompt direct intervention by Guinness. Through the auspices of the Irish Agricultural Organisation Society and, subsequently, the Irish Department of Agriculture, the company undertook a long-term programme of financial and practical support for farmers and research into seed quality, culminating in the development of a famed barley variety, *Spratt Archer*.[107] As a result, by the outbreak of the First World War, Guinness was able to satisfy 60 per cent of its increased needs with Irish barley, consuming in all in excess of half the native crop.[108]

Guinness's intervention in the barley market was matched by a determination to achieve greater control over malt supplies, both in Ireland and elsewhere. Until the 1870s the company relied substantially on commission malting, retaining, like Trumans, a string of agents scattered across the best barley lands. Marginal supplies were bought from sales-maltsters, including a number in England and Scotland. In 1877 the firm established its own maltings in Dublin and, partly to resolve problems of quality and partly to take advantage of low market prices, shifted away from commission malting.[109] The need to insulate the company from fluctuations in supply and price quickly took precedence, so that in 1899, in order to encourage the Irish industry, every effort was made to return to the commission system and a policy of 'non-commercial' buying adopted.[110] Instead of seeking

---

[106] This section is based upon P. Lynch and J. Vaizey, *Guinness's Brewery in the Irish Economy, 1759–1876* (Cambridge, 1960); and S. R. Dennison and O. MacDonagh's unpublished 'History of Guinness, 1886–1939', chapter 7.

[107] This followed a short-lived and unsuccessful scheme, financed by the Dublin brewers and distillers (including Guinness), to distribute subsidised seed to farmers. See also p. 71.

[108] Although the acreage under barley continued to decline, this was more than compensated for by rising yields. The Irish crop increased from an annual average of 1.3 million barrels in 1886–90 to 1.7 million in 1911–13.

[109] In 1878 Guinness made 31,500 quarters (14 per cent of its requirements) in the Dublin maltings. A further 91,500 quarters (42 per cent) were bought on commission and 95,000 quarters (44 per cent) from sales-maltsters.

[110] This was largely unsuccessful. In 1878 there were ten Irish commission agents, three in Dublin and seven in the country around Cork, Wexford and Dublin. Several maltsters were reluctant to return to the commission system, mainly because they found it uneconomic in their

'absolutely the lowest market price', maltsters were to be guaranteed a 'living profit'.[111] In return, all were required to improve and update their maltings and meet more exacting standards. To achieve greater control over Irish sales-maltsters and gain a better foothold in the English market, Henry Figgis, one of the leading Irish factors and suppliers, was also appointed as the company's agent and placed on the board of the Wakefield maltster Michael Sanderson & Son. Initially the policy worked smoothly, but a series of poor harvests was soon to test Guinness's commitment to the Irish industry and, no less important, to demonstrate its control over the malt market.

The problems began in 1908, when Irish barley yields fell sharply and competition from the Cork distillers pushed up prices. Guinness immediately bought 250,000 quarters of English malt, some through Figgis, from Sandersons. The same price was then offered to Irish maltsters. But Figgis, in his capacity as Irish agent and knowing the domestic situation, held out for a higher price. The situation could in fact easily have been resolved, for the English maltsters, feeling the full brunt of the fall in beer output, were desperately seeking extra contracts. It was a question of how far, and at what cost, Guinness was prepared to support the Irish industry. In the event the price paid, at a time when most of the maltsters were in financial difficulties because of the improvements enforced by the company, scarcely provided a 'living profit'.[112] The second crisis came three years later, when a poor harvest and unusually low stocks of malt and barley threatened production. La Touche, the managing director, quickly secured as much malt as possible from two of the main Irish suppliers. Only then was Figgis, as agent, brought into the negotiations. Although reluctant to accept his 'realistic' market price, La Touche had little choice but to give way. Figgis's success was short-lived as the company subsequently bought its malt without recourse to intermediaries. Indeed, the Irish maltsters were left in no doubt about their position in the following season: either they dealt 'uncommercially' or commissions would be taken up in England. Without exception, all accepted. Attempts that year by English maltsters to form a 'ring' were similarly dealt with. Foreign barley was bought on a large scale and the Irish agents given extra contracts. In fact, in 1913 English maltsters, having learnt their lesson, were offered five-year commission contracts. Guinness had achieved its objectives: it had fostered a strong, but compliant, Irish industry; it had gained a secure foothold in England and Scotland; and it had demonstrated to all the extent of its power.

---

small maltings. By the 1920s there were still three agents in Dublin, five in the country and one, E. S. Beaven, at Warminster, who also held the position of English consultant on barley matters.

111 Commission fees were calculated on the cost of the barley, plus cost of manufacture, interest on capital and an 'average' margin of profit; prices for sales-maltsters, 'provided the market was in Guinness's favour', were calculated on a similar basis.

112 One maltster was even refused credit by his bank to buy barley because of the large overdraft incurred through the required capital developments.

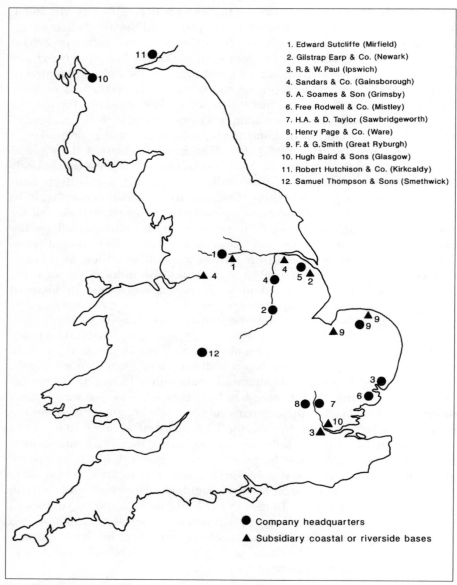

1. Edward Sutcliffe (Mirfield)
2. Gilstrap Earp & Co. (Newark)
3. R. & W. Paul (Ipswich)
4. Sandars & Co. (Gainsborough)
5. A. Soames & Son (Grimsby)
6. Free Rodwell & Co. (Mistley)
7. H.A. & D. Taylor (Sawbridgeworth)
8. Henry Page & Co. (Ware)
9. F. & G. Smith (Great Ryburgh)
10. Hugh Baird & Sons (Glasgow)
11. Robert Hutchison & Co. (Kirkcaldy)
12. Samuel Thompson & Sons (Smethwick)

● Company headquarters
▲ Subsidiary coastal or riverside bases

Figure 2.3 Twelve leading sales-maltsters (by production capacity), 1913.
Source: Company records, subscription lists, MAGB.

As the examples of Trumans and above all Guinness, illustrate, it was the changing structure of the brewing industry and its relationship with malting which were the key factors influencing the development of the independent sector. Brewers not only moved directly into malting but also enjoyed a range of viable options which yielded most of the benefits of integration: quality control, price stability, a guaranteed supply of malt and (not least) expertise and access to the invaluable information network of the most prestigious maltsters. Many were able to offset risk onto independent suppliers whilst minimising costs by an appropriate mix of partial integration and contract buying. On the other hand, there were frequent examples of close ties with malting firms which endured for several generations. Often there was trust and, certainly, respect for reputation. As in the case of Trumans, there were occasions when loyalty clearly overrode narrow economic interest. Overall the balance of power clearly rested with the parent industry. Similarly important, in determining the geographical concentration of the industry, were the environmental factors: the regional specialisation of barley cultivation, proximity to markets and comparative transport advantages. Access to the coastal trade, in particular, was of critical importance to Scottish maltsters, less favoured than their East Anglian counterparts, in securing wider markets. The influx of cheap imported grain after 1880, discussed in Chapter 3, further reinforced these trends. Lastly, the demise of private brewing and growing concentration of commercial brewing prompted a reciprocal concentration in malting. Only in strongholds of publican brewing, in Wales, the west country and in the heart of the midlands, did small maltsters survive into the twentieth century. It was a combination of these factors which determined the structure and location of the sales-malting sector. By 1914 the regional concentration in malt production was paralleled by a similar pattern of organisation. As Figure 2.3 illustrates, the largest sales-malting companies, in terms of output, were with one exception located in the east of the country. Only Samuel Thompson & Sons of Smethwick, unique in character, flourished upon the demands of small-scale brewers. It was a structure which reflected the ever tighter grip of common brewers after 1830.

3

The Free Mash Tun, 1880–1914

The Malt Tax [gives] an artificial preference to a particular commodity grown by the farmer ... and has practically the effect of a prohibition as between malt made from barley and every other material for the manufacture of malt. [The brewer] will brew from what he pleases, and he will have a perfect choice both of his material and of his methods ... our intention is to admit all materials whatever to perfectly free and open competition.[1]

The repeal of the malt tax in October 1880 marked a watershed in the history of the British malting industry. The consequences of the fiscal changes, the removal after almost two centuries of the constraints upon the maltster and the arrival of the 'Free Mash Tun', were in themselves far-reaching. Yet their impact is fully appreciated only when set in the context of other equally important developments: the influx of cheap foreign grain which transformed the market for malting barley; changes in the pattern of beer consumption; and increasing hostility from government towards brewers. In addition, a growing understanding of malt analysis and advances in technology, especially the adoption throughout Europe of pneumatic malting systems, meant the brewers' demands upon the maltster were becoming ever more exacting. These were years of unprecedented challenge and opportunity, with success for sales-maltsters dependent upon large-scale capital investment, a willingness to diversify and, above all, to adapt traditional methods to meet the demands of a new era.

When in 1880 Gladstone introduced the 'Free Mash Tun', he repealed the duty on sugar and replaced the malt tax with a beer duty of 6s. 3d. on each barrel of standard gravity.[2] This maintained government revenue, but provided the freedom for brewers to experiment with their raw materials. Not least, the repeal of the malt tax ended the lengthy campaign of the farming lobby whose objective was to boost the demand for barley of average quality. Previously, with the malt tax levied at a flat rate, brewers had little incentive to use any but the finest malts which yielded the greatest extract.

---

1 W. E. Gladstone, Budget Speech, 10 June 1880.

2 Standard gravity was defined as 1057°. An allowance of 6 per cent was also made for waste. Sugar duty was imposed in 1851 at 1s. 4d. per cwt, increased in 1856 to 6s. 6d., then the following year reduced to 3s. 9d.; it fluctuated around this level until its repeal in 1880, G. B. Wilson, *Alcohol and the Nation* (London, 1940), pp. 320–21.

Some second-grade barleys were used, especially for brown malt and by small rural maltsters who relied on local harvests, but the witnesses to the Select Committee on the Malt Tax, who supplied the London and Burton brewers, stressed that they always sought the best quality grain.[3] Any shortfall in the British crop was supplemented by fine, but costly, barleys imported from France and Denmark and by the Saale barleys grown in Moravia, Silesia and Bohemia. In years of relative harvest failure, the quantity could be substantial. In fact, Barnard claimed that in some years foreign grain was the mainstay of pale ale brewing at Burton.[4] As early as 1872–73, of 155,869 quarters of barley steeped by Bass 71.6 per cent were of foreign origin.[5] Similarly, after the disastrous harvest of 1879, when Beaven described much of the British crop as 'fit only for pig-food', three-quarters of the barley steeped in his Warminster malting business was imported.[6] Although these years were exceptional, several leading brewers and maltsters maintained agents in Hamburg, the main centre of the European grain trade, and in Copenhagen and southern France, underlining the importance of the constant search for quality grain.[7]

With the removal of the malt tax, farmers hoped that price and quality would be more closely related, thus increasing the demand for lower-yielding, cheaper malts. This is precisely what happened. It was not British barley, however, but cheap imported grain, which was already undermining the general profitability of cereal farming, to which brewers and maltsters turned (in spite of the patriotism so readily worn on their sleeves). Low world prices, an advance of duties and the sharply reduced freight costs encouraged the search for good foreign barleys. A further stimulus was the run of wet harvests which coincided with the repeal of the malt tax and highlighted the inadequacies of much of the British crop: poor yields, uneven ripening and therefore germination. Not surprisingly, farmers were soon campaigning as vigorously for the return of the malt tax as they had for its repeal.[8] The result, Sir Cuthbert Quilter's Pure Beer Bill, brought before Parliament in 1896, was designed to force brewers to use only barley-malt and hops. Yet support for the 1880 legislation was equally strong, prompting the formation of the Free Mash Tun Association, whose president was the engineer, consultant maltster and author Henry Stopes. With opposition from the brewers, the Pure Beer Bill was doomed to failure. However, as a concession to the

[3] *Select Committee on the Malt Tax, PP* (1867–68), ix, pp. 280, 300, 311.

[4] A. Barnard, *The Noted Breweries of Great Britain and Ireland*, iv (London, 1891), p. 534.

[5] C. C. Owen, *The Greatest Brewery in the World: A History of Bass, Ratcliff & Gretton* (Chesterfield, 1992), p. 73.

[6] E. S. Beaven, 'Barley for Brewing Since 1886', *Journal of the Institute of Brewing*, 42 (1936), p. 488.

[7] Barnard, *Noted Breweries*, iv, p. 538; Samuel Thompson & Sons of Smethwick maintained an agent at Le Mans, France, while Prentice Brothers of Stowmarket established a base at Copenhagen and imported considerable quantities of barley into Ipswich and Harwich.

[8] *Royal Commission on Agricultural Depression, PP* (1895), xvi, p. 232.

farming lobby, a departmental committee examined the raw materials used in brewing. Its final report brought little comfort to farmers, but the evidence of the witnesses provides a valuable insight into the changes wrought by the Free Mash Tun and the resulting developments in the production of beer.

To what extent did brewers and maltsters increase their reliance on foreign grain? Imports of barley rose significantly during the last quarter of the nineteenth century, but unfortunately the statistics do not distinguish between the quantities and varieties of barley used for malting or for animal feedstuffs.[9] Several contemporaries, however, spoke of a striking increase after 1880.[10] Richard Bannister of the Inland Revenue, in his evidence to the Departmental Committee on Beer Materials, suggested that whereas before 1880 about 10 per cent of the barley malted was of foreign origin, by the mid 1890s, the proportion had risen to around 30 per cent.[11] John Steele, the Chief Inspector of the Excise, also believed the figure to be between 25–30 per cent.[12] These estimates concur with the calculations made by Beaven, based on assumptions about the proportions of different varieties of foreign barley used in brewing. Beaven suggested that between 1881–85, and again between 1901–5, an average of approximately 25 per cent of the barley used in brewing was imported. For some individual years he found the proportion was as high as 30 per cent.[13]

From the maltsters' viewpoint, the real significance was not simply the greater use of imported barley but the decisive shift towards new varieties. Before 1880, most of the barley grown in England for malting was the two-rowed variety, *Chevalier*, which produced heavy crops of thin-skinned, plump corn, weighing on average between 54–56 lbs per bushel and yielding a high extract of sugars.[14] The characteristics of imported barleys were similar; indeed *Chevalier* barley was itself widely grown throughout Europe and, subsequently, in California and Chile. But from the autumn of 1884, the *Brewers' Journal* began to record the prices of barley from Smyrna (Turkey), Odessa, Persia and 'Danubian' barleys, a list which rapidly expanded to include the Ouchak barleys from Asia Minor, supplies from Algeria and India, and 'brewing' barley from California and Chile. By 1887 Henry Stopes could point to 'scores and scores of malthouses throughout Great Britain where thin foreign corn which nobody would have attempted to make into malt ten years ago' was the accepted raw material.[15] In contrast

9   B. R. Mitchell and P. Deane, *Abstract of Historical Statistics* (Cambridge, 1959), pp. 98–99.

10   J. L. Baker, *The Brewing Industry* (London, 1905), p. 166; R. Free, 'Barley from a Maltster's Point of View', *Brewers' Journal*, 15 November 1888.

11   *Report of the Departmental Committee on Beer Materials, PP* (1899), xxx, p. 257.

12   Ibid. (1899), xxx, p. 225.

13   Beaven, 'Barley for Brewing', *Journal of the Institute of Brewing*, 42 (1936), pp. 488–89.

14   Beaven suggested that at least 80 per cent of English malting barley was of this variety before 1880. Beaven, 'Barley for Brewing', p. 493; H. Stopes, *Malt and Malting* (London, 1885), pp. 70–72; Baker, *Brewing Industry*, pp. 14–16.

15   *Brewers' Journal*, 15 February 1887.

with the traditional malting barleys, these were six-rowed, narrow-eared varieties, pale and bright in colour, with thin kernels and light in weight, averaging as little as 34 lbs per bushel. They were sun-ripened and low in nitrogen, and the resulting malts were greatly valued for the sparkling brilliance which they imparted to the increasingly popular, light, running ales and bottled beers. Frequently they were mixed with fine quality English malts to counteract the latter's high nitrogen content. It was also claimed that they aided drainage in the mash tun and improved the stability of beer. Indeed, most brewers agreed with Barnard that 'all beers are cleaner, sounder and more brilliant when a portion of Smyrna malt is blended with heavier English grain'.[16] Finally, they were cost-effective. Although extracts were less than from English malts of average quality, the differential was outweighed by the lower price of foreign 'brewing' barley. Chapman, advocating the use of Smyrna or Danubian malt for the production of light, bottled beers, provided the following example:

> Good Danubian malt, cost 25s. per quarter of 336lbs, yields an extract of 83lbs per quarter. Cost per pound of extract: 3.6d.

> English malt of equal quality, cost not less than 35s. per 336lbs, yields an extract of 90lbs per quarter. Cost per pound of extract: 4.6d.

As he concluded, 'the advantage (apart from the ... increased stability of beer) is, therefore, obvious'.[17]

British and foreign barley continued to be purchased in proportions which depended upon harvest fluctuations, both domestic and foreign. Beaven's peak years are clearly explained by poor British harvests, such as the cold, wet summers of 1902 and 1903, when imports rose sharply and most brewers and maltsters relied heavily on foreign grain. Typically, Taylors, the Hertfordshire maltsters, who during the previous five years had malted an annual average of 31.7 per cent (31,627 quarters) of imported barley, increased the proportion to 49.6 per cent (53,240 quarters) and 57.4 per cent (48,367 quarters) respectively.[18] The underlying trend clearly marked an increasing shift away from the best quality grain, especially from France and the Saale, towards cheaper varieties. Initially the main supplies came from Smyrna. In his evidence to the Beer Materials Committee, Salamon presented statistics of the barley imports from the region for the decade before 1896, showing an annual increase from 84,259 quarters in 1887 to 668,180 quarters in 1896.[19] By 1914, however, the emphasis had shifted in favour of Californian barley, which was particularly valued because of its uniform

---

[16] Barnard, *Noted Breweries*, iv, p. 540; See also, *Departmental Committee on Beer Materials, PP* (1899), xxx, p. 37.

[17] A. C. Chapman, 'The Production of Light Bottled Beer', *Journal of the Institute of Brewing*, 2 (1896), p. 277; E. R. Moritz and H. Lancaster, 'The Economics of Brewery Malting', *Journal of the Institute of Brewing*, 11 (1905), pp. 491–507, also provide a range of similar examples.

[18] H. A. & D. Taylor Limited, Private Journals, PM.

[19] *Departmental Committee on Beer Materials, PP* (1899), xxx, p. 396.

character.[20] Consequently, during the season of 1910–11, a year when there was no shortage of good English malting barley, the *Brewing Trade Review* estimated that 12½ per cent of all barley steeped was Californian.[21]

The extent of the shift varied from brewer to brewer, depending upon the type of beers in which they specialised. Bass, renowned for their fine pale ales, had always used imported barley to supplement any shortfall in the supply of fine quality English grain. After 1900, however, Owen found that far less reliance was placed not only on English but also on good quality European barleys, while supplies from California, North Africa and the Middle East became of greater importance. Thus even during the season of 1912–13, after a disastrously wet harvest when only 14,325 quarters (8.76 per cent) of English barley were steeped, none was purchased from France or Moravia, the firm malting 50,142 quarters (30.65 per cent) of Californian and 68,876 quarters (42.10 per cent) of Turkish barley.[22] Producers of mild beer, like Trumans, continued to use a high proportion of English barley. In general, nevertheless, the pattern of change was unmistakable.

The second main element of Gladstone's Free Mash Tun was the increasing use of malt adjuncts. The use of sugar had been permitted since 1847 but the duty imposed upon it was intended to equate with the malt tax. As a consequence, therefore, it remained a relatively expensive material. Only in years such as 1867–69, when malt prices approached 70s. per quarter, did the amount of sugar used in brewing rise significantly.[23] The duty was repealed in 1880 and by 1886 it was estimated that sugar formed 9.9 per cent of the total raw materials used by common brewers in the United Kingdom. A decade later, the proportion had risen to 15.4 per cent.[24] After 1880, many brewers also began to include a proportion of unmalted grain in their grist. Unfortunately, between 1881 and 1896 the annual returns made by brewers to the excise do not distinguish between malt and adjuncts used in brewing. A special report was prepared for the Departmental Committee on Beer Materials for 1895, and from 1897 the quantities were recorded separately. In 1895, unmalted cereals, including raw and prepared grains, amounted to 3 per cent of the total. By 1900 the proportion had risen to 7.1 per cent, by 1914 to 9.6 per cent.[25] The most popular grains were rice and maize. Both were high in starch but, because of their tough outer husks and oil content, unsuitable for traditional malting. Typically, maize (the most popular) was pre-prepared either as 'grits' or 'flakes', rendering the starch easily convertible by the diastase of malt in the mash

---

20 F. Faulkner, 'Modern Malting', *Brewers' Journal*, 15 January 1891, p. 137; E. R. Moritz, 'The Alleged Deterioration of English Malting Barleys', *Brewers' Journal*, 15 June 1895, p. 329.

21 *Brewing Trade Review*, 1 December 1912; see also Beaven, 'Barley for Brewing', p. 489.

22 Owen, *Greatest Brewery*, p. 237.

23 *Return of Sugar Used in Brewing*, PP (1880), lxvii, p. 881; see below, Appendixes 1 and 3.

24 *Departmental Committee on Beer Materials*, PP (1899), xxx, pp. 318, 320.

25 Ibid., p. 314; *Brewers' Annual Returns*, PP (1901), lxix, p. 191; (1914–16), liv, pp. 412–13; see also below, Appendix 1.

tun. The germ (containing most of the unwanted oil) and the husk were first removed, a process initially perfected in America. The grain was then crushed, and either sold as grits, or gelatinised (subjected to steam heat which ruptured the starch cells), dried and finally rolled to form flakes.[26]

The main stimulus for brewers to use malt adjuncts was again twofold. First, most brewers considered that the addition of sugar and unmalted grain to the brewing grist, like sun-ripened barley, improved the stability, flavour and brightness of the lighter beers, and agreed with Salamon that 'it would be impossible for a brewer to brew the beer required today unless he used ... pre-prepared starch materials and sugar adapted for ferment-ation'.[27] Several contemporaries suggested a ratio of 75–80 per cent of malt to 20–25 per cent of malt substitutes, although the proportions varied according to the type of beer.[28] Chapman, for example, proposed for bottled beers a grist of 30 per cent English malt, 30 per cent foreign malt, 20 per cent unmalted grain and 20 per cent invert sugar.[29] For heavier beers, the proportion of English malt would be greater. Secondly, the use of unmalted grain substantially reduced unit costs of production. Chapman, comparing the cost per pound of extract obtained from the various unmalted grains, suggested 4.4d. for malt, 2.35d. for broken rice, the cheapest source of starch available, 2.8d. for maize grits and 3.7d. for prepared flaked maize.[30] Not surprisingly, few brewers of any size brewed only from malt and hops.[31]

What were the consequences of the Free Mash Tun? One positive aspect was the development of new varieties of malting barley. After 1880 many brewers and maltsters complained about the deterioration in the quality of barley offered for malting, a reflection not only of climate but of the straitened circumstances of the many farmers who economised on seed quality and fertilisers and grew barley on marginal land. This stimulated the research into barley cultivation and cross-breeding which gathered pace from the 1890s. The real breakthrough came with the production of the

[26] A. C. Chapman, 'Unmalted Grain and its Use as a Partial Malt Substitute', *Journal of the Institute of Brewing*, 1 (1895), pp. 149–52.

[27] *Departmental Committee on Beer Materials*, PP (1899), xxx, p. 54.

[28] Baker, *Brewing Industry*, p. 14; *Departmental Committee on Beer Materials*, PP (1899), xxx, p. 54; Stopes, *Malt and Malting*, p. 70.

[29] Chapman, 'Unmalted Grain', pp. 155–56.

[30] These figures relate to 1895 prices, which differ only slightly from those used in the previous example (see p. 68). At 1907 prices, J. C. Ritchie calculated a cost of 2.9d. per pound of extract from flaked maize, a saving of 1.7d. per lb. over malt. Chapman, 'Unmalted Grain', pp. 155–56; J. C. Ritchie, 'The Use of Flaked Malts', *Journal of the Institute of Brewing*, 13 (1907), p. 505.

[31] The *Annual Brewing Returns* for the year ended 30 September 1902 record that of 5750 brewers for sale, the 2970 (51.7 per cent) who used malt, unmalted cereals and sugar, used 89.9 per cent of the total raw materials used in brewing. The remaining 2780 (48.3 per cent), which included the largest single brewer, Guinness, used just over 10 per cent. With the exclusion of Guinness, their combined consumption represented only 4.2 per cent of the total. PP (1903), lxiv, p. 87.

first hybrid barley, *Standwell*, by the firm of Gartons of Warrington.[32] The main pioneers, however, were the Warminster maltster, E. S. Beaven, and Herbert Hunter, both of whom worked closely with Guinness. In 1902 Guinness initiated research into barley and malting; and shortly afterwards, in collaboration with the Irish Department of Agriculture, founded the barley research station at Ballinacurra, near Cork.[33] In 1908 their first barley breeder, Herbert Hunter, developed the hybrid *Spratt Archer*, first released in England twelve years later. E. S. Beaven malted exclusively for Guinness and, after his death, his family business was bought by the Irish brewers and continued to make their malt. In 1905 Beaven produced the hybrid *Plumage Archer*, which together with *Spratt Archer*, remained the most popular varieties of malting barley until the Second World War.[34]

Overall, the Free Mash Tun did little to boost the demand for British barley, although it must be emphasised that the demand for the best qualities was generally sustained. The increased supply of grain exerted a downward pressure on prices generally, especially from the early 1890s. By 1895 average prices for English barley had fallen sharply to 21s. 11d. per quarter.[35] Yet during that autumn the *Brewers' Journal* was quoting a price range of 36s. to 42s. per quarter for 'fine' English malting barley, 26s. to 35s. for 'secondary' quality and 18s. to 22s. for feed barley.[36] Rarely can average prices have been less meaningful. Moreover, as illustrated in Chapter 1, during the depression of the 1880s and 1890s more barley, not less, was grown on the light lands of Norfolk and Lincolnshire and proved critical to the survival of many arable farmers.[37] Nationally, however, the barley acreage declined steadily, and farmers whose land was unsuitable for the production of good quality grain were finally squeezed out of the market for malting barley.[38] The result, as Brown has illustrated, was further to reinforce the regional specialisation of barley cultivation.[39]

From the malting viewpoint, the picture was more complex. On the one hand, for those well-situated and with capital, there were opportunities to

[32] H. Hunter, *The Barley Crop* (London, 1952), pp. 58–59.

[33] T. Davies, 'Development of New Varieties of Barley', *Brewers' Guardian*, Centenary Issue (1971), p. 79.

[34] T. Davies suggests that *Spratt Archer* and *Plumage Archer* between them accounted for 80 per cent of the acreage of spring barley by the early 1940s. 'New Varieties', p. 80; For a detailed discussion of the development of new varieties of malting barley see E. S. Beaven, *Barley* (London, 1947); and Hunter, *Barley Crop*.

[35] Mitchell and Deane, *Historical Statistics*, p. 489.

[36] *Brewers' Journal*, October-December 1895.

[37] See Chapter 1, pp. 15–16.

[38] The barley acreage of Great Britain peaked in 1879 at 2,667,000 acres. By 1900 this had declined to 1,990,000 acres and by 1913 to 1,757,000 acres. Mitchell and Deane, *Historical Statistics*, pp. 78–79.

[39] J. Brown, *Steeped in Tradition: The Malting Industry in England Since the Railway Age* (Reading, 1983), pp. 88–89; see also Hunter, *Barley Crop*, p. 36.

exploit and several ports were confirmed as important centres of the malt trade. At Ipswich, for example, many of the vessels discharging cargoes of barley and maize were consigned to Pauls, the cheap grain providing the basis for rapid expansion and diversification into animal feedstuffs.[40] A brief account surviving from 1887 shows contracts struck with Gill & Fisher of Baltimore for 13,000 quarters of maize and over 20,000 quarters of barley.[41] The Albion Malting, Smart's Mill (a factory for dressing foreign barley), and No. 4 malting were all built during the 1880s, while the Stonham Maltings, capable of an annual output of over 16,000 quarters, were rented from the brewer E. P. Dawson and used almost exclusively for foreign grain.[42] Pauls also expanded their own shipping interests. In 1886 the first coastal steamship, the *Swift*, was acquired. By the early 1890s, their fleet comprised six steamships, ten 40–50 ton sailing barges, a number of lighters and steam tugs – including the *Merrimac*, which during the summer doubled as an excursion steamer taking parties to Clacton, Walton and Aldeburgh and around the Cork lightship. The company imported maize and barley from America and eastern Europe and shipped malt, barley and smaller quantities of wheat and oats outward, in all accounting for two-thirds of the grain exported from Ipswich.[43] The acquisition in 1902 of Gillman & Spencer of Rotherhithe, who had pioneered the manufacture of flaked maize, brought a London base and further diversification.[44]

Other maltsters were likewise involved in the foreign grain trade. Prentice of Stowmarket also received regular shipments of barley into the port of Ipswich.[45] Arthur Soames of Grimsby, suppliers of fine quality malt to the pale ale brewers of Burton, had by the late 1880s established agents in Smyrna, Algeria and Moldavia, and were directly importing cargoes in excess of 10,000 quarters of 'brewing' barley. The malt produced from foreign barley accounted for half the firm's output of some 100,000 quarters a year.[46] Similarly, many of the leading maltsters extended their businesses to provide access to major canals and the ports which were the focus of the foreign grain trade (see Fig. 2.3). Gilstrap Earp, despite their large maltings on

[40] For example, on 18 July 1885, the *Suffolk Chronicle* reported the arrival of the '*Ragusa* from Ibrail on the Black Sea, the largest steamship ever to enter the Dock, with 900 tons of maize for Messrs Paul'. See also Finch, *A Cross in the Topsail*, p. 12.

[41] R. & W. Paul, Private Ledger, 1887–88, PM.

[42] R. & W. Paul, Private Ledger, 1887–88, PM.

[43] Mostly barley and malt to London, although in 1885 the *Suffolk Chronicle* recorded 3000 quarters sent to Dublin. 7 February 1885; B. A. Holderness, 'Pauls of Ipswich' (1980), chapter 4, p. 7; Finch, *A Cross in the Topsail*, p. 43.

[44] *Brewers' Journal*, 15 August 1873; *Brewing Trade Review*, 1 May 1900; R. & W. Paul Limited, *Handbook* (privately printed, 1957), p. 16.

[45] Initially mainly from their agent in Copenhagen, but by the mid 1880s the focus was changing to southern Europe and Asia Minor. *East Anglian Daily Times*, 18 September 1879; *Suffolk Chronicle*, 10 January 1880, 17 January 1880, 7 February 1880, 22 May 1880, 17 January 1885, 18 July 1885.

[46] Barnard, *Noted Breweries*, iv, pp. 534–38.

the Trent, were quick to establish a base at Grimsby.[47] Edward Sutcliffe of Mirfield owned twenty maltings, on the rivers Aire and Calder, which used foreign barley imported by the company through Hull.[48] John Sandars not only improved his Grimsby maltings but also built two maltings on the Manchester Ship Canal which were worked exclusively for foreign grain.[49] Others, like S. Swonnell & Son, who moved from Nine Elms in London to Oulton Broad at the mouth of the port of Lowestoft, gained the dual advantages of good barley land and easy access to imported grain.[50]

On the other hand, the growing use of malt adjuncts clearly reduced the demand for malt. Of the forty-two quarters of raw materials required to make one gyle of Truman's country porter, only twenty were made by their commission maltsters; of these, four were made from foreign barley.[51] The shift to imported barley, while not affecting the aggregate level of demand, also called for adjustments to the old methods of purchase, handling and working. Maltsters, many of whom still received the bulk of their supplies by the waggon-load from local farmers, were suddenly faced with the need to handle and store large quantities of grain. Most foreign consignments also arrived well-mixed with seeds, stones and general rubbish, requiring the purchase of new machinery for screening and dressing. Foreign barley also needed different treatment in the steep, on the floor and in the kiln.[52] It even extended the working season, Pauls regularly malting Californian barley through June and July in their spacious maltings at Stonham.[53] In many ways it was a different world from the one in which most maltsters had learnt their trade as buyers of British barley and producers of quality British malt.

While the changes brought about by the Free Mash Tun were of great significance for the malting industry, the full implications are appreciated only when set in the context of the increasingly hostile climate facing brewers. This is best illustrated by the sharp reversal in the trend of beer output (see Fig. 3.1). After a long period of almost unbroken growth, beer output in the United Kingdom, at its peak in 1876, was more than 125 per cent above

[47] *Newark Advertiser*, 19 February 1896.

[48] 'Histories of Famous Firms: Edward Sutcliffe Ltd', *Brewery Record*, 6 (September 1927), p. 10.

[49] Letter to Inskipp & McKenzie, 11 December 1897, 2 Sandars 2/2, Lincoln Archives; *Brewers' Journal*, 15 May 1905.

[50] R. Simper, 'The Maltings of Suffolk', *Suffolk Fair*, 1, January 1972.

[51] The remaining ingredients were six quarters of crystal and black malt, eight quarters of flaked oats, two of caramel and six of sugar. Truman, Hanbury & Buxton, Monthly Reports, 28 September 1905, B/THB/A/211, GLRO.

[52] Good quality English barley required a steeping time of around fifty hours, average qualities, between fifty and sixty hours and light foreign varieties, as much as seventy hours. The latter also needed more space on the floor. Baker, *Brewing Industry*, p. 21; *Brewers' Journal*, 15 November 1916.

[53] Stonham Malt and Barley Ledgers, 1900–1904, PM. The *Brewing Trade Review* also noted that 'maltsters for sale not infrequently malt eleven months of the year and sometimes the whole year round', *Brewing Trade Review*, 1 July 1901.

its 1830 level.[54] Seven years later, at the trough of recession, it had fallen by 16 per cent. In the short term, the cause of concern was the onset of general recession, but recovery was slow and uncertain, with 1876 levels of production not surpassed until the final years of the century. Thereafter, except in Ireland, there was renewed stagnation; in England and Wales output in 1913 was barely higher than at the onset of initial recession. The pattern of per capita consumption was again a powerful indicator. Notable, in particular, was the breakdown after 1880 of the link between accelerating prosperity of the working classes and their expenditure on alcohol; as prices fell sharply and real wages and living standards rose, beer consumption no longer responded in the traditional manner. The explanation, widely debated by historians and social commentators, focuses mainly on changing patterns of working-class spending and on stable beer prices. Mass produced clothing and shoes, furniture, tobacco and tea, cheap travel and a host of leisure activities were increasingly counter-attractions for the working man's disposable income. The full impact of these developments was to be felt only after the First World War. Nevertheless, by the last quarter of the nineteenth century, they were the cause of great concern among brewers.

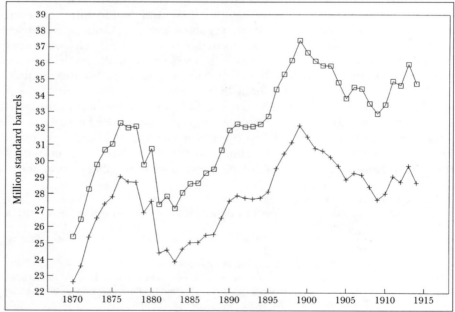

Figure 3.1 Beer production, United Kingdom and England and Wales, 1870–1914 (million Standard Barrels)
Key: □ United Kingdom   + England and Wales.
Source: Wilson, *Alcohol and the Nation*, pp. 369–70.

54 Wilson, *Alcohol*, pp. 369–70.

Several other factors underpinned the more permanent reversal of fortunes.[55] The licensing legislation of 1869 and the growing strength of the Temperance Movement had halted the growth in retail outlets, prompting brewers to protect their trade by costly discounts and by the purchase of public houses. Both entailed a heavy capital burden and led directly to the wholesale public flotation of brewery companies. In turn, as trade declined after 1900, many struggled to maintain interest payments to their debenture and preference shareholders. Finally, the Edwardian period was one dominated by the hostility of the Liberal government to the drinks trade and by the imposition of increased taxes. It was a combination which created intense competition among brewers and resulted in a wave of brewery amalgamations which reduced the number of smaller-scale brewers upon whom many small maltsters depended. All brewers became more cost-conscious and, with malt still the major element in production costs, they had every incentive to seek ways of using raw materials more efficiently. This led to improvements in the screening, dressing and milling of malt, but most notably to advances in mashing, draining and sparging which translated into a greater extract per quarter of malt. The 'hot-grist' mashing machine (which heated the brewing grist), patented in 1887 by Charles Clinch, enabling low grade malts to be used more effectively, was an important step forward: the system spread widely during the next twenty years.[56] Results were impressive. In 1894 the *Statist* claimed, with some exaggeration, that the average yield was 4–4½ barrels of beer per quarter of malt, in contrast to 2½–3 barrels fifty years earlier, a reflection both of the shift to lighter beers and of technical advance.[57] Using annual brewing returns, Hawkins calculated that almost all brewers continued to reduce their malt consumption. By 1900–1 average yields had risen to 5.26 barrels per quarter of malt, and by 1912–13 to 5.67 barrels per quarter.[58]

Against a background of stagnant beer output and the shift towards weaker beers, brewers were using a growing proportion of malt adjuncts and achieving a greater yield from the malt they used. It all added up, as Fig. 3.2 shows, to a steady decline in their demand for malt. At the peak of beer output in 1876, 7.6 million quarters of malt were consumed by brewers. In 1899, at the height of the recovery, when beer output in the United Kingdom

55 These events are discussed in detail by T. R. Gourvish and R. G. Wilson, *The British Brewing Industry, 1830–1980* (Cambridge, 1994), pp. 27–40; K. H. Hawkins and C. L. Pass, *The Brewing Industry: A Study in Industrial Organisation and Public Policy* (London, 1979), pp. 25–51; J. Vaizey, *The Brewing Industry 1886–1951: An Economic Study* (London, 1960), chapter 1.

56 *Brewing Trade Review*, 1 October 1877, 1 January 1888.

57 Quoted in K. Hawkins, 'The Conduct and Development of the Brewing Industry in England and Wales, 1888–1938: A Study of the Role of Entrepreneurship in Determining Business Strategy with Particular Reference to Samuel Allsopp & Sons Limited' (unpublished Ph.D. thesis, University of Bradford, 1981), p. 237.

58 By 1912–13, those brewers producing between 20–50,000 barrels annually achieved a yield of 6.45 barrels per quarter of malt. Ibid., p. 362.

was 15.9 per cent higher than in 1876, the consumption of malt, at 7.34 million quarters was 3.4 per cent lower. By 1909, at the trough of the brewing recession, demand had fallen by 18.3 per cent, to 6.21 million quarters. Even with the addition of the malt used in distilling, always of far less significance, 1876 levels of demand were surpassed only during brief periods between 1897 and 1899.[59]

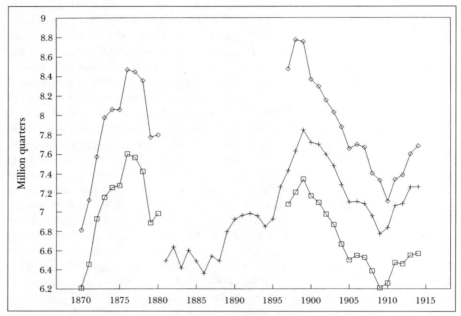

Figure 3.2 Malt consumed in brewing and distilling, United Kingdom, 1870–1914 (million quarters).
Key: □ Malt used in brewing   + Malt and adjuncts used in brewing;
  ◇ Malt used in brewing and distilling
Note: Between 1881–1896, brewers' annual returns to the excise do not distinguish between malt and adjuncts used in brewing.
Source: See Appendix 1.

When the relationship between the brewing and malting industries, discussed in Chapter 2, is recalled, the true scale of the maltsters' plight becomes apparent. After 1880, while the number of common brewers in the United Kingdom fell steadily (from 2162 in 1881 to 1111 in 1913), a greater proportion began to produce their own malt.[60] By 1914 around half of this

[59] Most distillers also produced their own malt. For the decade 1871–80, the annual average consumption of malt by brewers and distillers was 7.96 million quarters for the decade before the First World War 7.49 million quarters. See below, Appendix 1.

[60] Gourvish and Wilson, *Brewing Industry*, p. 111. Wilson defines a common or commercial brewer as one producing more than 1000 barrels a year.

1. The Sleaford maltings of Bass Ratcliff & Gretton, built in 1903–6. The block of eight, six-floor maltings had a frontage of 1000 feet and the capacity to produce 60,000 quarters of malt in a season. (*Brewing Trade Review*, October 1906, *BLRA*)

2. Fire: a common occurrence in the history of most malting companies. Pauls' No. 4 malting, built in 1890 at Eagle Wharf, Ipswich, was destroyed six years later. The 150 quarter malting was rebuilt the following year. (*Pauls Malt*)

3. 'Turning' malt on the working floor at Sandars' Paddock malting, Gainsborough, *c*. 1950. The process remained unchanged for centuries. (*Sandars & Company*)

4. Ploughing, or raking, malt at Associated British Maltsters Bath malting, *c*. 1977. (*Pauls Malt*)

5. Steward & Patteson's pneumatic malting, built at Norwich in 1908. The twenty-one drums were served by eight pneumatic steeping tanks. (*Brewing Trade Review*, August 1908, *BLRA*)

6. Key Street, Ipswich, 1912, the head office of R. & W. Paul from the company's formation until 1993. (*Pauls Malt*)

7. The work force of Robert Hutchison & Company, Kirkcaldy, *c*. 1900. (*Pauls Malt*)

8. King George V visiting Edward Sutcliffe's Belle Isle Maltings, Wakefield, in July 1912. The 400 quarter malting was the largest of the twenty-six owned by the firm before the First World War. (*The Brewery Record, Pauls Malt*)

9. The four-masted barque *Abraham Rydbury* unloading Australian grain into sailing barges at Ipswich Dock in 1934. (*Robert Malster*)

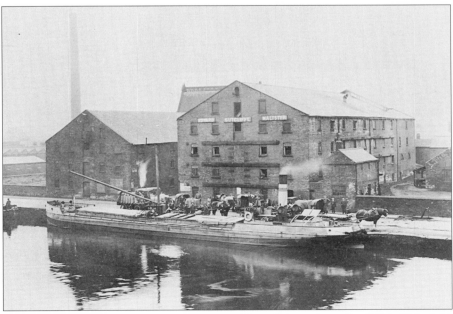

10. Loading the steam barge *Queen's View* with malt in sacks at Sutcliffe's Wakefield maltings in 1924. Typically, barges brought in a cargo of foreign barley before being reloaded. (*Eric Hepworth*)

11 (*left*). Robert Paul (1806–64), the founder of R. & W. Paul. (*Pauls Malt*)

12 (*right*). Robert Stocker Paul (1844–1909), partner (1874–93), joint managing director of R. & W. Paul (1893–1909), and responsible with his brother, William, for the company's rapid rise in the late nineteenth century. Known locally as the 'Maize Kings of East Anglia', the brothers were amongst the foremost grain importers in the region. (*Pauls Malt*)

13. William Francis Paul OBE (1850–1928), partner (1874–93), chairman and joint managing director of R. & W. Paul (1893–1927), surrounded by three of his sons (from left) Stuart (1879–1961), Russell (1875–1951) and Harry (1872–1950) at the company's head office, Key Street, Ipswich, *c.* 1915. (*George Paul*)

14. Henry Taylor (1822–76), son of Joseph Taylor. (*H.A & D.Taylor, Pauls Malt*)

15. Captain Charles Sutcliffe. (d. 1928) (*Edward Sutcliffe, Pauls Malt*)

16. Hugh Paul (1878–1947), director of R. & W. Paul (1906–47), and an expert barley buyer. He was drafted into the Ministry of Food in both World Wars, but was equally at home at the Royal Thames Yacht Club racing his J-class yacht, *Astra*. (*Pauls Malt*)

17. John Drysdale Sandars (1860–1922) who gave up the Bar to run the family firm. He was responsible for the company's rapid progress after the 1880s. (*John Burke*)

18. Pauls' cricket team, 1906, typical of many employees who enjoyed a wide range of sporting activities. (*Bob Woods*)

19. The staff of R. & W. Paul at The Boltons, the house of Robert Stocker Paul (seated, extreme left) for their annual garden party, *c.* 1908. (*Pauls Malt*)

much smaller number malted for themselves and made between them approximately half the malt consumed in brewing.[61] While many brewer-maltsters had traditionally bought a proportion of their supplies from sales-maltsters, some made their entire needs as recession bit. Others reduced the quantity purchased. Frequently they produced the best malts themselves and bought only the cheaper types, where profit margins were smallest. As John Sandars complained to a close adviser:

> The poor maltster has a hard time of it. The brewer always wants the best malt and the board and managers will not pay for it, and as a rule where a brewery makes part of the malt it uses, they always make the high class qualities and then grumble about the lowest which come from the maltster. And brewers now cut prices so low, we are quite unable to make up the material we should like ... One of the best maltsters in the county has lost a great deal of trade because he sticks to the fine qualities of old.[62]

In several ways, the demands upon the maltster steadily became more exacting. Brewers looked increasingly to those who could fulfil a single contract for upwards of 10,000 quarters delivered at the brewers' convenience. Most now produced a wide range of beers and demanded an equally wide range of malts. From the 1880s these were increasingly subject to detailed specifications, as brewers' chemists began developing techniques for malt analysis. The culmination, in 1906, was the Institute of Brewing's Malt Analysis Committee which defined standards and procedures for the evaluation of extract, moisture, colour, diastatic power and ready-formed sugars.[63] The power of analysis had been firmly underlined six years earlier by the arsenic scare of 1900, when around 3000 Manchester beer-drinkers were poisoned. The cause was found to be brewing sugar, but the subsequent Royal Commission closely examined all the raw materials used in brewing and (unexpectedly) found traces of arsenic in malt. A second, smaller incident in Halifax two years later was attributed to contaminated malt.[64] Extensive tests isolated traces of arsenic in coke and coal, which when burnt on malting kilns left small deposits of arsenic. This led to the substitution of the more heavily contaminated gas and oven cokes by expensive Welsh anthracite, modifications to malting kilns and the development of machinery to polish malt.[65] All were costly burdens on the already straitened maltster. Under the Sale of Food and Drugs Act, malt was required to contain less than 0.57 parts per million of arsenic. In fact almost all brewers demanded that every consignment, analysed according to the Marsh Test, was 'guaranteed pure'.[66]

[61] MAGB, Minutes of Executive Committee.

[62] Letter to Frank Faulkner, 11 March 1893, 2 Sandars 2/2, Lincoln Archives.

[63] *Report of the Malt Analysis Committee to the Council of the Institute of Brewing* (1906).

[64] *Report of Royal Commission on Arsenical Poisoning, PP* (1904), ix, pp. 2–10; *Brewers' Journal*, 15 December 1903.

[65] *Brewing Trade Review*, 1 July 1901.

[66] *Royal Commission on Arsenical Poisoning, PP* (1904), ix, appendix 227.

The extent to which the maltsters' livelihood in the 1900s depended on the brewers' chemist is clearly illustrated by the following contract for malt between the City of London Brewery Company and a Hertfordshire maltster, Henry Ward:

> Delivered to Brewery, as Briant's analysis No. 2583, 16th November 1908. Minimum extract, 95.5. Malt to be slowly grown, free from mould. Diastatic Power, 24–32; Colour 10–18; Matters Soluble 21 per cent maximum; Arsenic 1/500th. Moisture not above 2.5 per cent till 1st July, after that date, 3 per cent maximum; if above 3 per cent, deduct ¾d. per 0.1 per cent. If over 3.25 per cent, the Company have the right to refuse delivery.[67]

The years after 1880 were clearly ones of fundamental change for the malting industry. How did sales-maltsters respond to the many challenges they faced? First it is necessary to emphasise that the greater part of the industry, because of their limited scale and capital, probably made few conscious attempts to adapt to the changed climate. Many, as we have seen, disappeared. However, those companies which depended on the leading brewers for their livelihood felt the full force of the sudden decline in beer output after the late 1870s and the change in the pattern of demand for malt. John Sandars, who supplied many Manchester brewers, suffered an instant fall in sales from 38,000 quarters in 1879 to 30,000 the following year.[68] The Hertfordshire maltsters, Taylors, whose customers were the great London brewers, likewise watched their profits decline through the 1880s. Both were representative of large, old-established businesses, well-connected, closely aligned to brewers, acknowledged experts in their local markets, each with his own carefully nurtured network of farmers and merchants. For generations these families had prided themselves on producing nothing but the highest quality malt, using the finest barleys, both British and foreign. As such, they felt the full impact of change.

By the 1890s it was clear that anyone wishing to maintain a competitive position in the industry could do so only by adapting traditional methods to meet the demands of the day. The ability to fulfil single contracts of several thousand quarters of malt and to handle and store large quantities of grain, both British and foreign, was by now essential. Despite the hostile environment, new capital investment was unavoidable. Frequently the first step was to build a kiln for drying, or 'sweating', barley. In exceptionally wet years maltsters had always dried barley before steeping. During the run of wet harvests which marked the first phase of the Great Depression, the practice became commonplace. Not only the weather, but the fact that farmers, desperate for income, threshed and sold their barley as soon as possible, as well as a greater understanding of the benefits, made sweating necessary. The objectives were threefold: to overcome dormancy within the

---

[67] Henry Ward & Sons, Sales Book, D/E Wd B5, HRO.
[68] See below, Chapter 5, Table 5.4.

grain; to ensure evenness of germination; and to lengthen storage life. The grain was dried slowly, usually for one to two days, at a low temperature, never exceeding 110° F. A 'resting' time of six to eight weeks followed before malting, making ample storage space necessary. Frequently maltsters combined the erection of a sweating kiln with increased storage capacity.[69] Many also installed machinery for screening and dressing foreign grain. The experience of the Taylors was again typical. Their amalgamation with a local competitor, Barnard & Company, brought a group of maltings situated at Sawbridgeworth and a loan from the retiring partner which was used initially to build a separate barley drying kiln. Between 1890–94, screening and dressing machines were installed at each of the Sawbridgeworth maltings.[70] During the same period, a significant number of well-known maltsters, such as Gilstrap Earp and James Thorpe & Sons of Newark, acquainted their customers of similar improvements.[71]

Some maltsters were already incorporating these necessary improvements into new and larger maltings, but from the mid 1890s, as the recovery of trade became increasingly evident, investment in fixed capital was striking. The following decade witnessed a wave of construction unprecedented since the coming of the railways and unrepeated until the 1950s. Whereas during the 1830s most malthouses steeped 25–45 quarters, and thirty years later as much as 100 quarters, by the end of the century massive buildings dominated the ports and railheads. The Sleaford maltings completed by Bass in 1906 were in a class of their own; the huge block of eight floor maltings, each six stories high, had a total frontage of 1000 feet and the capacity to produce 60,000 quarters of malt a year.[72] The 300 quarter malting built by Pauls at the New Cut at Stoke, Ipswich, in 1904 was more typical of many built during this period. The total area of the seven working floors was 51,408 square feet. The malting also provided storage for 5000 quarters of malt and a separate silo for a further 14,000 quarters.[73]

Despite the great increase in the scale of production, there was little change in the production process itself. Indeed, one question which must be asked is why most British maltsters failed to adopt the only significant contemporary technological breakthrough, the system of mechanical or pneumatic malting, whereby grain is germinated in a controlled

---

[69] The malting engineer, James Saunders, suggested that each 100 quarter malting, steeping every four days, required 4500 quarters of barley storage. J. Saunders, 'Modern Malting from an Engineering Point of View', *Brewers' Journal*, 15 July 1905.

[70] H. A. & D. Taylor, Balance Books, PM.

[71] *Brewers' Journal*, 15 July, 15 September 1890.

[72] J. C. Lincoln, 'Sleaford Maltings: History of Architecture and Design, 1890–1939' (unpublished B.A. dissertation, Open University, n.d.), p. 11, Museum of Lincolnshire Life, Lincoln.

[73] In reality the malting steeped 325 quarters, i.e. 158 square feet per quarter steeped; 'best practice' advocated 180 square feet per quarter. *Brewers' Journal*, 15 December 1904; Hugh Philbrick's malting notebook.

environment. Pneumatic malting clearly had its origins in Britain. As early as 1844, White's *Directory* of Suffolk recorded that Patrick Stead of Halesworth had:

> lately obtained a patent for making malt by a new process and has erected a large kiln in the form of a tower, fifty feet high, divided into five storeys and heated by steam pipes and a hot air blast ... There is also a contrivance for regulating the temperature of the steep as well as the drying floors.[74]

Stead successfully made 'hot-air' malt for Trumans for four years until the steam apparatus failed, causing heavy losses and probably deterring others from similar experiments.[75] Although further patents were taken out in the 1850s by W. L. Tizard, there was little significant progress for another twenty years. During the 1870s extensive trials were conducted at Jacobsen's progressive Carlsberg brewery, but it was a French brewer, N. Galland, who in 1873 constructed the first mechanical malting at Maxeville, near Nancy, and developed the most popular of the pneumatic systems, drum malting.[76] In this process the grain was steeped in the traditional manner and then transferred to germinating drums. Usually of 30–50 quarters capacity, the drums were slowly revolved to aerate the grain and to prevent matting, each revolution taking between 40–50 minutes. Moist, filtered air, introduced by a fan via perforated pipes, maintained a temperature of 58–60° F and optimal levels of humidity. Waste gases were similarly withdrawn. After nine to ten days, moist air was replaced by dry air and the temperature slowly increased to 66–68° F to wither the green malt.[77] Subsequently, the contents of the drums were discharged onto a belt-conveyor, elevated to the kiln to be dried and cured in the conventional manner.[78]

The alternative to drum malting was the compartment, or box, system developed by Galland's assistant, M. Saladin. In this case the whole malting floor was enclosed from the external environment and the steeped grain placed in large germinating 'boxes' to a depth of two to three feet. Temperature and humidity were controlled by forcing air through the perforated

---

[74] W. White, *Directory* for Suffolk (1844), p. 371.

[75] R. Lawrence, 'An Early Nineteenth-Century Malting Business in East Suffolk', *Proceedings of the Suffolk Institute of Archaeology*, 36 (1986), p. 124.

[76] *Brewers' Journal*, 15 July 1881.

[77] Germination time varied according to the variety of barley. Briant suggested nine to ten days, plus withering, with the green malt transferred to the kiln on the fifteenth day; Hiepe, ten to fourteen days for germination and withering. No withering was required for malt made for distilling. Macey in 1971 estimated a total production time at this period of fifteen to seventeen days, compared to twenty to twenty-two days required for floor malting. L. Briant, 'Drum Malting', *Brewing Trade Review*, 1 February 1902, p. 41; W. L. Hiepe, 'The Establishment of Maltings on the Manchester Ship Canal', *Journal of the Institute of Brewing*, 4 (1898), p. 243; A. Macey, 'Advances in Malting Techniques', *Brewers' Guardian*, Centenary Issue, September 1971, p. 92.

[78] Drying and curing sometimes took place in drums similar to those used for germinating, but these were not generally considered successful. Briant, 'Drum Malting', p. 43.

floors of the boxes. During germination the grain was turned by mechanical screw turners. Again the green malt was transferred to a conventional kiln.[79]

Both systems appeared to offer several advantages over floor malting. Most significantly, malting ceased to be dependent on the weather and, for the first time, year-round production became a viable option. Substantial savings in space and labour were also claimed. Briant, for instance, estimated that a floor malting making 1500 quarters annually could produce 9–10,000 quarters when converted.[80] Similarly, labour could be cut by as much as two-thirds.[81] Moreover, most contemporaries suggested that while the construction costs of pneumatic maltings and equivalent floor maltings were similar, production costs in the former were considerably lower.[82] Finally, it was argued that the system was ideal for malting the cheaper varieties of barley and that the malt produced was more uniform and free from mould. Pneumatic malting was readily adopted in Europe, the United States and Australia, but in Britain its acceptance was comparatively slow.[83] Initially, the response was good, with three pneumatic maltings built during 1878–79: for Perry & Son at Roscrea in Ireland; the Beeston Brewery and Malting Company (Nottingham); and J. Nimmo & Son (Castle Eden, County Durham). After a lapse of five years, two more followed, for Flowers & Sons (Stratford-on-Avon) and Sedgwick & Company (Watford), and another in 1885 for J. Brutton of Yeovil.[84] It is notable that all were drum maltings and all owned by brewer-maltsters. Not until 1891 was the first Saladin box malting built, at Ditchingham in Suffolk, for the maltsters R. & W. Mann.[85]

Did this reflect the reluctance of sales-maltsters to accept technical change? The evidence suggests that the new technology was not dismissed lightly. In 1879 the *Brewers' Journal* noted 'a good deal of inquiry on the part of maltsters, and especially brewers who are their own maltsters, [into] the various systems of pneumatic malting'.[86] Subsequently, visits were made to Germany, France, even America, to inspect working maltings. Some, like the Taylors of Hertfordshire, returned to build their own.[87] Secondly, the benefits of the new system rarely matched the extravagant claims of some contemporaries. Savings in labour, as the head maltster of Bass's pneumatic

---

[79] Stopes, *Malt and Malting*, p. 234; Brown, *Steeped in Tradition*, p. 62.

[80] Briant, 'Drum Malting', p. 44.

[81] Stopes, *Malt and Malting*, p. 224.

[82] Briant, 'Drum Malting', p. 44; Stopes, *Malt and Malting*, p. 249; Saunders, 'Modern Malting', p. 762; Hiepe, 'Establishment of Maltings', p. 247.

[83] Stopes, *Malt and Malting*, p. 224; Briant, 'Drum Malting', p. 42.

[84] Stopes, *Malt and Malting*, p. 224; a second unit was also built at Beeston in 1884; *Brewers' Journal*, 15 October 1884.

[85] *Brewers' Journal*, 15 February 1906.

[86] Ibid., 15 October 1879.

[87] Ibid., 15 March 1891, 15 July 1896; *Brewing Trade Review*, 1 April 1891.

malting (erected in 1899) confirmed, were minimal.[88] Wages were low and labour costs, therefore, relatively unimportant. It could even be argued that this factor alone worked against technical change. Similarly, except for some urban brewers, a good supply of cheap land was rarely a problem, thus savings in space were also of little consequence. Expansion, even at major ports, was feasible. At Ipswich, for example, the Pauls purchased and demolished old buildings to provide sites for their maltings, while the Yarmouth malt trade mostly refocused from the crowded rows to the open spaces across the river at Southtown.[89] Of greater importance were the costs of construction and machinery, which again were greater than portrayed. When they went bankrupt in 1906, Robert and William Mann gave as the reason 'the heavy cost of the pneumatic malting erected in 1891'; the final cost, at £15,000, was almost double the estimated cost of £8000.[90] Jonathan Brown has stressed the high capital costs at a time of falling demand and overcapacity. The competitive climate clearly undermined business confidence and was a major determinant of future investment.[91] Nevertheless, such sums did not compare unfavourably with those invested in floor maltings of similar capacity.[92] While H. A. & D. Taylor's drum malting (with six 50 quarter drums) built in 1896 cost £18,000, Gilstraps invested £25,000 in floor maltings in 1895 and the same amount a year later to increase their annual capacity by 30,000 quarters.[93] Pauls sank almost £33,000 into their Stoke complex of two 300 quarter maltings and storage silo built after the turn of the century.[94]

At least as important as capital costs were the limitations of the pneumatic system. Early technical problems were mostly resolved during the 1880s by Julius Henning, but the withering process continued to cause difficulties resulting in the production of hard 'steely' malt.[95] This was ideal for distilling and the bottom-fermented lager popular abroad, but not for the infusion system of brewing favoured in Britain. Henry Taylor, for example, told the

---

88 The directors of Trumans after their visit to Burton also concluded 'these maltings are not built to work economically; there is more labour than there should be here'. Truman, Hanbury & Buxton, Monthly Reports, 13 March 1903, B/THB/A121, GLRO; Brown, *Steeped in Tradition*, p. 64.

89 Originally, the London brewers Combe & Company rented twelve small maltings in the Rows at Great Yarmouth. Subsequently, they built a complex of large maltings in Southtown, as did Robert Watling and Whitbreads. Yarmouth Poor Rate Books, Y/LI/175, 284, 293, NRO.

90 *Brewers' Journal*, 15 February 1906.

91 Brown, *Steeped in Tradition*, pp. 63–64.

92 For example, in 1894 Alexander Hunter built a pneumatic malting with eight 50 quarter drums (annual capacity 15–18,000 quarters), and claimed the cost was equal to erecting a 7000 quarter capacity floor malting. *Brewers' Journal*, 15 May 1894.

93 *Brewers' Journal*, 15 December 1895; 15 July 1896; H. A. & D. Taylor, Balance Books, PM.

94 R. & W. Paul, Capital Ledger, PM.

95 Hugh Baird told the Royal Commission on Arsenical Poisoning that 'we have found a difficulty in getting rid of the moisture. We cannot get our malt what we call freed properly'. *Royal Commission on Arsenical Poisoning, PP* (1901), ix, p. 289.

Royal Commission into Arsenical Poisoning he had 'never seen any malt ... made in Germany which would suit the London or Burton brewers ... It makes a different class of beer altogether'.[96] Similarly, Hugh Baird confirmed they only worked their drum malting to make distillers' malt; it could not produce the high quality malt demanded by brewers.[97] It is notable that, whereas Gough & Sons of Bury St Edmunds built a pneumatic unit at their branch in Melbourne (Australia), they worked only floor maltings in England.[98] An analysis of those who invested in pneumatic maltings reveals a substantial proportion were distillers or Scottish maltsters likely to supply the distilling trade.[99] Finally, Robert Free (one of the most technically innovative of all maltsters), Taylors and Bass, built large floor maltings *after* investing in pneumatic units, suggesting the latter were either not completely successful or served only part of their needs.[100] The evidence illustrates that the comparatively slow acceptance of the new technology is explained not only by high capital costs but also by its failure to meet the particular requirements of British brewers. From the maltster's viewpoint this was critical. While his customers remained sceptical, the risks in adopting the new process outweighed potential gains. That the majority continued to build floor maltings was clearly a rational response to the prevailing economic climate and to the specific market they faced.

Far from being as unprogressive as the brewing trade press often portrayed them, the leading maltsters were concerned to maintain the momentum of growth. Thomas Earp, for instance, was engaged in long-running experiments with electricity and gas as alternatives to coke and anthracite. In 1901 he told the Royal Commission he had tried drying-drums 'long before malting drums were in practical use'.[101] For several years, John Sandars worked closely with Dr Edward Moritz, consulting chemist to the Country Brewers' Association. Under the latter's guidance, he conducted comparative trials of steeping times, kiln temperatures and yields and adopted Hayne's 'patent kilns'.[102] Robert Free, who designed his own maltings, worked extensively on kilns and patented the conical steeping

---

[96] *Royal Commission on Arsenical Poisoning, PP* (1901), ix, p. 283.

[97] The firm of Robert Hutchison & Company, of Kirkcaldy, also found that 'brewers had a certain prejudice against [pneumatic] malt'. *Royal Commission on Arsenical Poisoning, PP* (1901), ix, p. 283. *Brewers' Journal*, 15 February 1898.

[98] *Country Brewers' Gazette*, 23 July 1879.

[99] Of the thirty-two companies identified which built pneumatic maltings before 1914, eighteen were brewers, nine distillers and five sales-maltsters. Twelve were Scottish, another three located in the far north of England and four more in Ireland, a striking proportion given the comparative scale of the English brewing industry.

[100] *Brewers' Journal*, 15 January 1897.

[101] *Royal Commission on Arsenical Poisoning, PP* (1901), ix, p. 284.

[102] Letter to Edward Moritz, 4 April 1897, 2 Sandars 2/2; Diaries of John D. Sandars, 28 March–2 August 1893, 3–5 March 1894, 2 Sandars 1/14, 15, Lincoln Archives.

cisterns which became popular after the repeal of the malt tax.[103] While there was little change to the work on the malting floors and kilns, there was great concern to handle barley and malt more efficiently. Previously the entire malting process, from unloading barley from farmer's waggon, barge or railway truck to the dispatch of malt, had relied almost exclusively on manual labour. With the introduction of power-driven elevators (known as Jacob's ladders), belt and worm conveyors and pneumatic intake plant, it was soon feasible for barley to be delivered, rough dressed, stored, screened, graded and conveyed to the cisterns (preferably self-emptying conical cisterns) by machinery. After the malt was unloaded from the kiln, the processes of screening, dressing, polishing, weighing and sacking could be similarly mechanised. Few, perhaps, went to quite the same lengths as William Paul, who in 1899 travelled across America with his son Stuart to inspect at first hand the latest developments. At Buffalo, and elsewhere, 'Electric and Export Elevators' and silos were carefully inspected.[104] The detailed plans obtained were subsequently put to good use when the company developed the wharf at Rotherhithe and a silo 'on American lines' was built beside No. 5 Malting at Ipswich.[105] The malting itself was typical of the many described by the *Brewers' Journal*. A gas engine powered conveyors, elevators and machinery for dressing, screening and weighing barley and malt. The seven working floors featured conical steeping cisterns and the drying kilns, automatic reversible turners. The malting was lit throughout by electricity, significant progress from the hazardous use of oil lamps and candles.[106]

These maltsters also responded to the advances in science upon which their trade increasingly depended. Gilstrap Earp, in the early 1880s, were probably the first to build their own laboratories. By 1896 John Sandars could also advise prospective customers:

> Having been working to analysis for the last few years I can safely undertake to work any malts within a few points of a given diastatic capacity, percentage of ready-formed sugars and albuminoids ... Next year I am starting a laboratory

[103] Before 1880, the excise regulations required steeps to be flat-bottomed, rectangular and shallow to allow accurate gauging. This meant emptying the cisterns by shovel (which damaged the corns) and, usually, hoisting to the working floors. Free's hopper-bottomed cisterns were located at the top of the malthouse and emptied by gravity onto the working floors, thus saving both damage and labour. *Brewers' Journal*, 15 October 1888; Saunders, 'Modern Maltings', p. 448; I. A. Peaty, *Essex Brewers and the Malting and Hop Industries of the County* (Brewing History Society, 1992), p. 132. For a discussion of developments in drying kilns, see Brown, *Steeped in Tradition*, p. 67, and Stopes, *Malt and Malting*, pp. 197–211, 359–89.

[104] Diary of William Paul, 1 May, 16 May 1899. Everywhere time was spent at the Produce Exchange and Board of Trade; typically at Chicago: 'We called on Mr Seckel, agent for the Atlantic Transport Line from New York. They recommended us to do business with Bartlett, Frazier & Company ... They deal in everything in the Corn Trade ... I arranged for future business', 25 April 1899.

[105] Gillman & Spencer, Directors' Minutes, 26 April–15 July 1904.

[106] *Brewers' Journal*, 15 December 1904.

with a man specially trained to malt analysis by way of checking the working of the different maltings and keeping deliveries as regular as possible.[107]

His claim that he had 'done as much as I can to bring my own malting business thoroughly up to date' was clearly justified. Similarly, the acquisition of Gillman & Spencer by Pauls in 1902 brought a well-established laboratory where the previous owners, Alexander Gillman and Ernest Spencer (who were also the proprietors of the London School of Brewing and Chemistry), had developed a range of brewers' additives and pioneered the production of flaked maize.[108] The site became the focus for Pauls' own research and development which was further consolidated in 1907 by the appointment of Dr Marcus Wechsler, a chemist who patented several caramels suitable for the brewing and food trades. By the early years of the new century, Taylors, Free Rodwell of Mistley, R. & D. Mann of Wakefield and the Scottish maltsters Bairds and Hutchisons were all employing their own chemists to carry out routine analysis of malt and, after the arsenic scare, anthracite. From the evidence of witnesses to the Royal Commission on Arsenical Poisoning, it is clear that many maltsters regularly submitted samples to consulting chemists for analysis. Sometimes family members received a scientific education: Manning Prentice III studied at University College, London, while Charles Sutcliffe, like Manning a Fellow of the Chemical Society, joined the family business in 1909 and was by the 1920s chairman of the Yorkshire and North Eastern Section of the Institute of Brewing. Others, like John Sandars, took advantage of the courses in malting chemistry taught by Edward Moritz.

This is not to suggest that to any extent maltsters initiated the major technological and scientific developments affecting both brewing and malting. Progress, never widespread, was more frequently a direct response to the pressures from the parent industry. For the familiar reasons of limited scale, to which must surely be added a significant element of conservatism, the 'rule-of-thumb' practical maltster continued to outnumber those who accepted the latest developments. Even though brewing led the way, it was itself in many respects one of the most conservative of industries, and the source of many traditional practices which spilled over into malting. It included such rituals as the post-breakfast parade at Sutcliffes of bowler-hatted foremen – the insignia of management – with their kiln samples, awaiting judgement and grading by the principals. The firm was the largest

---

[107] Letter to Threlfalls Brewery Company, 21 April 1896, 2 Sandars 2/2, Lincoln Archives.

[108] The London School of Brewing and Chemistry was advertised for several years in the *Brewers' Journal*, although there are no details of its ultimate fate. Henry Stopes (who became vice-chairman of Gillman & Spencer on its incorporation in 1887) described the school as one where: 'Both Theoretical and Practical Brewing and Malting can be studied side by side. The Course comprises Elementary, Inorganic and Organic Chemistry, the Chemistry of Brewing, Qualitative and Quantitative Analysis'. *Brewers' Journal*, 15 January 1885; 15 August 1888; Stopes, *Malt and Malting*, p. iii.

in the industry by the First World War.[109] Yet, while qualifications about technical progress are clearly essential, the evidence does illustrate that even this small section of the British economy could boast its share of forward-looking businessmen.

The competitive climate after 1880 encouraged maltsters to diversify or seek alternative markets for their products. Some maltsters, like the Prentices and Fisons, fostered interests which, while fully integrated into the rural economy, were outside the parameters of brewing and the malt trade. Others focused on the specialist products increasingly demanded by the brewery and grocery trades. The manufacture of flaked maize and rice, as we have seen, proved a viable option for those located at ports. A few, like Pauls, through their subsidiary Gillman & Spencer, developed a range of brewers' additives: caramels, finings and preservatives. Others, encouraged by the repeal of the malt tax and the growing popularity of health foods, began the production of malt extract, a demand previously met by German and American imports. Robert Free led the field. By the late 1880s the Standard Malt Extract Company, established close to his Mistley maltings, was supplying both the brewing and grocery trades. Registered and renamed in 1897 as the English Diastatic Malt Extract Company Limited (better known as EDME) the company continues to trade.[110] By the turn of the century, Macadams of Belhaven, Dunbar (subsequently British Malt Products Limited), the St Neots brewers, Paine & Company, with their 'John Bull' brand, and from 1903 Edward Fison of Ipswich with 'Fiona' malt products, were also established.[111] Likewise Robsons of Leeds began producing malt flours, as did Sutcliffes, under the none too catchy brand name 'John Barleycorn in the Bakery'.[112]

A number of maltsters endeavoured to establish a viable export trade. Since the end of the eighteenth century, when war had ended the lucrative exports to the Dutch gin distillers, the malt trade had been almost entirely domestic.[113] Imports, with the malt tax providing an effective tariff, were always minimal. There remained a small reciprocal trade with Ireland for many years, and Guinness provided an important market for several British companies. Some maltsters, like John Sandars, maintained a Dublin agent. But by 1860 total United Kingdom malt exports amounted to 36,389 quarters

---

[109] E. F. Taylor, 'History of the Formation and Development of Associated British Maltsters Limited, 1928–78' (typescript, 1978), p. 2.

[110] *Brewers' Journal*, 15 November 1888.

[111] Muntona Limited and Edward Fison Limited, *Notes for Employees* (1956), p. 16.

[112] Overall, the quantities are unlikely to have been substantial. The first *Census of Production*, in 1907, refers to 'a comparatively small portion [of malt] sold to ... manufacturers of malt extract'. By 1924, production of malt extract and flour was valued at £177,000, against a total malt production valued at £5.95 million. *Census of Production* (1907), Final Report, pp. 475–76; *Census of Production* (1930), Final Report, p. 175.

[113] See above, Chapter 1, pp. 25–26.

(97 per cent destined for Australia), and in 1880, some 52,611 quarters; compared to the 6,981,375 quarters consumed by British brewers and 815,000 quarters used by distillers.[114] Traditionally, export malt was handled by the London factors, but during the 1880s Gilstrap Earp began shipping malt direct to Australia and John Sandars was making plans to develop a similar trade.[115] Likewise, every year between 1895 and 1914, Pauls shipped consignments of malt from Ipswich.[116] On several occasions, however, the result was a net loss. The largest profit of £271 was recorded in 1899, but thereafter the amount steadily dwindled to a mere £16 in 1913. Although there is no indication of the quantities involved, the minute profits mirror the small scale of national malt exports. Total British exports peaked in 1902 at 162,603 quarters, three-quarters of which was shipped to Australia and Africa. The following year, trade almost halved and then remained virtually static until the outbreak of the First World War.[117]

Why were attempts not more successful? One factor was the general return to protectionism after 1880, prompted by the collapse of world grain prices and industrial recession. Australia, the main focus of malt exports, illustrates the problems clearly. On the one hand, the rapidly expanding market for beer and the poor quality of native barleys, and therefore malts, offered attractive opportunities. On the other hand, after 1880 Australia carefully cultivated her own infant industry behind protective tariffs. With the ending of British preference in the 1850s, individual states followed their own commercial policies, Victoria favouring protection and South Australia revenue tariffs.[118] Both were important centres of brewing. In 1881 a duty of 2s. per cental was levied on imported barley 'for the encouragement of the home grower';[119] by the 1890s a prohibitive duty of 36s. per quarter on malt imports was in place.[120] New South Wales, Queensland and Western Australia encouraged free trade until the passing of the Commonwealth of Australia Act in 1902. Thereafter a universal tariff of 24s. per quarter levied on all malt imports effectively killed the trade with Britain.[121] Somewhat ironically the *Brewers' Journal* congratulated the Tankard Malting Company

---

114 Of which 46,920 quarters were exported to Australia, 89.2 per cent of total malt exports; *PP* (1881), lxxxvii, p. 85.

115 Unfortunately there are no further details. Letters to J. Edwards, 22 June 1889, 15 July 1889; 2 Sandars 2/2, Lincoln Archives.

116 R. & W. Paul Limited, Private Ledgers, PM.

117 Trade with Australia peaked in 1898 at 65,611 quarters; by 1903 it had fallen to 19,889 quarters and by 1913, to 8294 quarters. Similarly, African exports peaked in 1902 at 68,862 quarters, fell sharply and averaged 27,386 quarters in the decade before the First World War. Annual Statement of the Overseas Trade of the United Kingdom, 1880–1914.

118 A. G. Kenwood and A. L. Lougheed, *The Growth of the International Economy, 1820–1990* (3rd edn, London, 1992), chapter 4, pp. 60–77.

119 A measure of volume, 1 cental was equivalent to 100 pounds. *Brewers' Journal*, 15 October 1881.

120 *Brewers' Journal*, 15 January 1891.

121 Ibid., 15 May 1907.

of Melbourne on its new pneumatic maltings and pointed to 'the enterprise
of our Colonial friends in developing ... a comparatively new industry'.[122]
Against the general downward trend in malt exports, it is notable that
increasing quantities of malt were exported to Holland, one of the few
European countries to maintain free trade, again suggesting that protection
was an important determinant of export policy. It is also clear that freight
costs and the risks of damage to malt in transit were high. Not surprisingly,
in 1907 the *Brewers' Gazette* concluded that exports were 'unworthy of further
consideration'.[123]

How successfully did sales-maltsters adjust to the challenges they faced? This
is most accurately judged when the structure of the industry is recalled.
Traditionally, the sector was not only fragmented, comprising several thousand small firms, and product and market specific, it was also partially
integrated into brewing. As such, it was subject to a significant degree of
control from its parent industry. Between 1880–1914, however, against a
radically changing and generally hostile climate, a clear group of market
leaders emerged, equal in their scale of production to all but the very largest
of the brewer-maltsters, such as Guinness and Bass. Several were producing
around 100,000 quarters of malt annually: Arthur Soames of Grimsby,
Sandars & Company, Henry Page & Company, H. A. & D. Taylor and Free
Rodwell Limited. Pauls, Gilstrap Earp and Sutcliffes made considerably
more. Because of the dearth of company records, the figures probably
understate the true position. Fig. 2.3 shows the market leaders of 1913. It
illustrates the continuing importance of markets and location; the proximity
to the industrial centres of London, Scotland and the north; and the prime
barley lands of the eastern counties. It also demonstrates the renewed
emphasis on the ports. Equally important, however, was the response of the
leading maltsters to the challenges of the new era. All had invested heavily
in fixed capital; and all had assessed and adopted appropriate technology
and remained abreast of scientific advances. Many had also endeavoured,
by diversifying, to extend their trade, but these companies were in the
minority. The greater part of the industry, because of limited scale and
capital, and doubtless a degree of conservatism, made few attempts to adapt
to the changed climate. The evidence nevertheless demonstrates that the
leading maltsters reacted rationally to the specific market they faced and
went to considerable lengths to establish a position at the forefront of the
trade.

[122] Ibid., 15 July 1891; in 1902, the *Brewing Trade Review* reported that 'owing to the recent
imposition of the tax on malt imported into Australia the brewers there ... are erecting
malthouses and importing barley', and, by 1908, that 'very large and increasing quantities of
good malting barley are grown [in Australia]', *Brewers' Journal*, 1 December 1902, 15 November
1908.
[123] *Brewers' Gazette*, 11 April 1907.

4

Entrepreneurs and Companies, 1830–1914

Because there were in 1830 several thousand licensed maltsters, it is difficult to generalise about the typical maltster or the typical malting firm. At one end of the spectrum were Bass and Allsopp making tens of thousands of quarters in their numerous maltings, at the other were 'handicraft' producers, farmers and licensed victuallers whose activities were of little commercial consequence. Many of the small malting firms which litter the pages of early trade directories were also short-lived affairs. But there were a minority of maltsters who through tenacity and dynamism sustained their businesses over successive generations to make names for their companies in the malting and brewing industries.

Despite the malting industry's diversity, two factors determined entry to the trade. First, much of the capital brought into the industry came from related occupations. As we have seen in Chapter 2, many of the leading maltsters were also farmers and corn merchants or had brewing interests. John Sandars (1826–90), who inherited his grandfather's Gainsborough malting business, typically came from a family deeply involved in agriculture and the national grain trade. Among the witnesses in 1867, James Everitt also rented 1200 acres of Lord Spencer's land at South Creake in North Norfolk, while Richard Hunt was a miller owning a thousand acres of which he farmed a quarter himself.[1] In each case, malting was a natural progression, exploiting established networks, maximising expertise and absorbing surplus capital.

Secondly, it required only a small capital to establish a malting firm. Joseph Branston (1778–1861), for example, son of a Lincolnshire farmer, was first apprenticed to a Newark grocer before setting up on his own account and subsequently expanding into malting. When in 1836 he brought his eldest son, Joseph William (1811–59) into partnership, the 'Stock, Capital and other effects' of his entire business were valued at £4210.[2] Yet in his obituary in 1861 he was described as 'one of the most opulent and extensive merchants in the locality'.[3] Similarly, Patrick Stead (1788–1869) traded for several years as a corn merchant and factor with Thomas MacKenzie before they were joined by a third partner, John Robinson, in 1817. Stead and Robinson were

---

[1] *Select Committee on the Malt Tax, PP* (1867–68), ix, pp. 326, 311.

[2] G. Hemingway, 'The Branston Family of Newark' (typescript, 1980), p. 2; Articles of Agreement, 21 October 1836, DDH 180/3, Nottingham Archives.

[3] *Newark Advertiser*, 22 May 1861.

each to bring in £2000, with MacKenzie to make his contribution 'when sufficient profits had accumulated'.[4] Fixed capital investment, for the purchase of land, buildings and machinery, was modest. When Stead retired in 1851 (he was by then the sole proprietor), he sold his entire business, including the seven maltings he had built at Halesworth, cottages and shares in the Blythe Navigation, to Trumans for £18,000, a surprisingly small sum to secure the most prestigious malting company of its day.[5] A decade later, the 120 quarter malting built at Newark by Henry, the younger son of Joseph Branston, and described as 'the largest kiln in the county', cost £3745.[6] The witnesses in 1867 similarly spoke in terms of £30–35 per quarter steeped (i.e. £3000–3500 for a 100 quarter malting) for a new railside malting. In comparison, Pauls' 180 quarter malting built in 1885 cost £8723 (£48 per quarter).[7] Although costs were beginning to rise, there was no radical change until the end of the century. Many maltsters continued to rent their premises, rentals ranging from as little as £30–40 a year for small, older properties to a few hundred pounds for modern maltings.[8]

Estimates of working capital are less clearly defined. Before 1880 the malt duty, together with the seasonal purchase of barley, accounted for the majority of working capital. The witnesses in 1867 reckoned that to make 10,000 quarters of malt without duty required £10,000, with duty £15,000. This probably erred on the side of generosity: much depended on the rate of turnover and the credit extended to brewers; the custom was three to four months, but one witness gave discounts to those who settled within the month – before duty became liable – thus substantially reducing his outlay.[9] These estimates placed the total capitalisation of the largest sales-malting companies, producing around 30,000 quarters annually, between £40,000–55,000 (allowing a generous £10,000 for fixed capital).[10] After 1880, the burden of tax shifted from malt to beer. But where malt was made on commission, both the cost

---

[4] Robinson, son of a Banff merchant whose interests included shipping and brewing, was also to obtain credit of at least £2000 with a London bank or mercantile house. Articles of Partnership, 31 July 1817, D51/1978, NRO; R. Lawrence, 'An Early Nineteenth-Century Malting Business in East Suffolk', *Proceedings of the Suffolk Institute of Archaeology*, 36 (1986), p. 115.

[5] Truman Hanbury & Buxton, Thursday Private Memoranda, 2 April 1849, B/THB/A/129, GLRO.

[6] *Lincoln and Stamford Mercury*, 21 August 1863.

[7] The malting provided storage for 4000 quarters of malt and 10,000 quarters of barley. Statement of Account, Messrs Grimwood & Sons, 13 April 1886; *Suffolk Chronicle*, 2 January 1886.

[8] Generally rents were calculated at around £3 per quarter steeped; Simpsons paid £190 a year for a new 60 quarter malting built by the Duke of Northumberland in 1884 and £620 for the 205 quarter malting rented in 1890 from the brewers, Plews & Sons.

[9] *Select Committee on the Malt Tax, PP* (1867–68), ix, pp. 282–83.

[10] It is impossible to gauge the real impact of the repeal of the tax. Every 10,000 quarters of malt produced involved an outlay of £10,833 for duty from six weeks after production until payment was received from the customer. Any savings were partly offset, at least in absolute terms, by the rising scale of output and fixed capital costs after 1880.

of barley and the duty were normally met by the brewer. Capital requirements, therefore, varied considerably across the period and between maltsters whose output and position in the industry may have been very similar.

Two examples, both of old-established, respected companies already in the hands of at least the third generation of founding families, serve to illustrate this aspect of the industry's capitalisation. First, and reasonably close to the model suggested by the witnesses, was the partnership between Joseph Taylor (1810–91) and Henry Taylor (1822–76), grandsons of the great Hertfordshire factor, John Taylor (1765–1826).[11] By 1871 the brothers were malting at Stansted, Ware and Saffron Walden, producing in excess of 30,000 quarters annually. The total value of the firm's assets was £42,029, of which freehold property accounted for £4221, including a railway malting valued at £2447. Partners' capital and retained profits amounted to £27,028. The business declined for several years after Henry's death as his widow slowly withdrew his capital. Then in 1886 his sons, Henry Algernon (1855–1935) and Douglas (1856–1940), acquired the business of Barnard & Company and entered into partnership with its junior partner, Charles Richardson; Henry brought in £20,000, Douglas £11,500 and Charles Richardson £5000, while a loan of £26,000 was secured with the retiring senior partner and Richardson's father-in-law, Edmund Barnard. Thereafter the firm's assets increased steadily. By 1900 they were valued at £139,966, of which fixed capital accounted for £48,702, partners' capital totalled £105,598 and loans another £25,720. During that season 90,832 quarters of barley were steeped.[12] At the other end of the spectrum were Lee & Grinling of Grantham, Allsopp's long-standing commission maltsters. As late as 1894, when Robert Lee (1862–1905), who had previously worked the business inherited from his father and grandfather as sole proprietor, entered into partnership with Edward Grinling, each brought in a mere £1000.[13] Over the next decade, partners' capital grew to £18,000. Loans and mortgages of £9000 were raised from family members which, with a bank overdraft, financed the building of the Gonerby maltings at a cost of almost £13,000. During the season of 1903–4, when the firm's assets totalled £32,327, almost 36,000 quarters of malt were produced, of which more than 17,000 quarters (47 per cent) were made on commission.[14] Similarly, when

---

11 See Mathias, *Brewing Industry*, pp. 457–63; H. A. & D. Taylor Limited, *200 Years of Malting*; a third brother, William, in partnership with Joseph Lecaud, owned the Anchor Brewery, Saffron Walden. It was acquired in 1897, with eighty licensed houses, by Reid's Brewery Company. *Brewers' Guardian*, 1 March 1891.

12 J. L. & H. Taylor and H. A. & D. Taylor, Balance Books, PM.

13 The maltings owned by Robert Lee were rented to the firm; others were rented or leased locally. Lee & Grinling, Private Ledgers Nos. 1 and 2, PM.

14 Previously, the quantity made on commission for Allsopps had been greater, as much as 30,270 quarters during 1889–90. The decline reflected the brewer's falling trade. Weekly Malt Returns, C/T/35, Allied Breweries Archives; Lee & Grinling, Statement of Capital and Profits, 1894–1904; Balance Sheet 29 September 1904; Private Ledgers Nos. 1 and 2, PM.

in 1909 John Crisp, Allsopp's other commission maltster, converted his business to limited liability status, the total valuation (including goodwill) amounted to only £18,731.[15]

How much capital did new entrants bring into the trade? Almost certainly it was equally varied. In 1867 Thomas Prentice reckoned a maltster entering the trade, renting maltings and producing 10,000 quarters a year, 'working quickly for a small profit and quick returns', needed a working capital of £4000.[16] For a total investment of perhaps £12,000 another witness, James Everitt, who began malting in the late 1850s, had built two 60 quarter maltings at Wells-Next-The-Sea to produce 6000 quarters of top quality malt.[17] Likewise, Frederick and George Smith built maltings at Great Ryburgh in the 1860s and then at East Dereham and Wells-Next-The-Sea rapidly to join those at the forefront of the trade;[18] while in 1869, the partners of the London brewery company, Courage, provided the capital to finance their brother, Alfred, in malting, the partnership of Tomkins and Courage subsequently supplying all their malt.[19] There were also many men of modest origins who, by the plough-back of profits and the support of family and friends, established thriving firms. Typically James Simpson (1841–97), son of a Leeds butcher, first worked for a corn factor before setting up on his own account at Alnwick, Northumberland; while Richard Peach (1855–1918) began as a workman in the grain department of Bass, Ratcliff & Gretton and then in 1885 founded his own malting company.[20]

Until the end of the nineteenth century, the majority of malting firms were owned by sole proprietors, families or partners. Many were short-lived affairs, for which a brief entry in the *Gazette* or trade directories is all that remains. As in brewing, there were a striking number of successful and enduring family businesses: Pauls of Ipswich, Sandars of Gainsborough, John Crisp of Beccles, H. A. & D. Taylor of Sawbridgeworth, Simpsons of Alnwick and two Scottish maltsters, Hugh Baird and Hutchisons, to name but a few. The usual route was for sons to enter the family firm after completing their education. Robert and William Paul, for example, were educated privately and then, after their father's premature death, learnt the complexities of the trade from a trusted manager. William Gilstrap (1816–96) similarly received a basic commercial education and then immediately joined his

---

[15] John Crisp & Sons, BT 31, 18818/102663, PRO.

[16] *Select Committee on the Malt Tax, PP* (1867–68), ix, p. 283.

[17] Ibid., pp. 300–10.

[18] B. Wharton, *The Smiths of Ryburgh: 100 Years of Milling and Malting* (Crisp Malting, 1990), p. 11.

[19] G. H. Hardinge, *The Development and Growth of Courage's Brewery 1787–1932*, (London, 1932), p. 12.

[20] 'The History of the Family and Firm of J. P. Simpson', *Brewing Trade Review*, 1 October 1913.

father's Newark business.[21] By the later decades of the century, however, many maltsters sent their sons to the by now popular public schools. Richard Simpson (1872–1905) went from Barnard Castle School to Malvern, beginning a family tradition that survived to the 1990s, while Robert Lee (1862–1905) attended the Magnus School, Newark and Tonbridge. A spell in Germany followed before he was articled to the respected maltsters Clarkes of Derby.[22]

Although there are few details, malting apprenticeships in many respects probably mirrored those provided by brewers.[23] Instruction included the practical aspects of the business, in this case the purchase of barley and the intricacies of malting, accountancy and perhaps, by the end of the century, malting analysis. Apprenticeships were often arranged with family friends, and several well-known maltsters, Clarkes, Lewis Meakin and James Thorpe, for example, were noted for their training skills. Robert Lee and his partner, Edward Grinling, trained a long procession of pupils, usually two or three together, being paid premiums of £200 for the two years spent at Grantham.[24] Among them was William Paul's son Hugh (1878–1947), beginning not only the family tradition of training but a link which eventually united two families in business and marriage. In 1907 Pauls acquired a financial interest in the newly incorporated company of Lee & Grinling, with Hugh's cousin, Robert Harold Paul (1872–1950), becoming a director. His nephew, Joseph (Jock) Causton (1905–87), after Harrow and two years spent with a grain company in Antwerp, completed his training in Grantham and then in 1930 married Nancy, Edward Grinling's only daughter.[25]

The uncertainties of succession meant that frequently sons received a less conventional training. Joseph Gilstrap Branston (1838–1926) went from the Magnus School to Leamington College and then spent five years on the London Stock Exchange before returning to Newark on the premature death of his father. He admitted he 'did not know barley from oats'. His son, Walter (1872–1952), sent to Charterhouse and Trinity College, Cambridge, was called to the Bar before joining the family firm. Henry (1878–1934), his cousin, also followed to Charterhouse, but subsequently received a more appropriate training at the Leigh Brewery in Lancashire.[26] This interchange between the two industries was common. Brewers sent younger sons to train with maltsters, like Alfred Yeomans (1868–1935), who went from Burton

21 *Newark Advertiser*, 14 August 1987.

22 *Grantham Journal*, 2 June 1905.

23 T. R. Gourvish and R. G. Wilson, *The British Brewing Industry, 1830–1980* (Cambridge, 1994), p. 244.

24 Lee & Grinling, Private Ledger No. 1, PM.

25 Pauls held 3000 of the 23,000 £1 ordinary shares issued. The company was acquired in 1928; Lee & Grinling Limited, Private Ledger No. 3, PM; Pauls & Whites, *Pauls & Whites: Background Note* (privately printed, 1972), pp. 17, 19. I am grateful to Mrs Nancy Causton for information about the Grinling family.

26 Hemingway, 'Branston Family', p. 69.

Grammar School to Lewis Meakin as a malting pupil. Several maltsters also trained with brewers.[27] Hugh Baird (1800–90), son of a wealthy Glasgow businessman, was apprenticed to an Edinburgh brewer, then completed his training with a Ware maltster and with Hoare & Company, the big London brewers. His eldest son, Hugh, also trained with an Edinburgh brewer before joining the family firm; while his second son, Montagu, more unusually, studied chemistry 'with a view to becoming a practical maltster'. Subsequently, he was elected to the council of the Institute of Brewing and was its president in 1906–7.[28]

After completing their training, sons usually became partners in the family firm. Not all partnerships, especially those between fathers and sons, involved formal arrangements. There is no evidence, for example, of partnership articles between the Pauls. Even where partners were unrelated, as in the case of Thomas Gentel and Richard Dawber, they might trade substantially for many years without legal ties.[29] Where sons were admitted to the family firm on a more formal basis, agreements ranged from five, seven to ten years or even for the joint lives of the co-partners; when dissolved prematurely the reason was usually the death or debts of one of the partners. In general, where the business was small, sons quickly assumed an equal share of responsibility and profits; in more established firms, similar progress and its rewards accrued more slowly. Typically, Joseph Branston 'desirous of making provision for the future advancement of his eldest son', twenty-five-year-old Joseph William, gave him an equal share of the stock, capital and profits of his business. Nine years later, the entire business was assigned to Joseph William and his younger brother, Henry. The capital, unfortunately unspecified, was to be brought in equally by the two partners with any additions to receive interest at 5 per cent. Again, profits were to be equally shared.[30]

The great majority of partnerships were family concerns, but on rare occasions, usually to fill a void in succession or enable a senior partner to devote himself to social pursuits or politics, outsiders or salaried managers were introduced. The career of Thomas Earp provides an instructive example. Thomas (1830–1910) was of humble origin. The son of a gardener, he progressed via the patronage of the local vicar to Derby Grammar School, before becoming junior clerk to a Newark wine and spirits merchant and maltster, George Harvey. Within two years, he had replaced the firm's Manchester malt agent and began steadily transforming the business.[31] In

[27] *Journal of the Institute of Brewing*, 26 January 1935.

[28] A. Barnard, *The Noted Breweries of Great Britain and Ireland*, ii (London, 1889–1891), p. 464; *Brewing Trade Review*, 1 January 1915; 'Annals of a Scots Family' (Anon.), Bairds Malt.

[29] SE 13, MSS 238/127, Lincoln Archives.

[30] Deed of partnership, Joseph and Joseph William Branston, 21 October 1836, DDH 180/3; Deed of Partnership, Joseph William and Henry Branston, 30 July 1845, DDH 180/4, Nottingham Archives. See also articles of partnership between Joshua Miller and Frederick and Thomas Miller, 31 January 1868, D/ET B38, HRO.

[31] *Newark Advertiser*, 23 February 1910.

1872 he became a partner and, until Harvey's death seven years later, enjoyed a third share of the company's profits.[32] At no time, however, did he contribute more than a tiny fraction of the firm's capital: by October 1878 only £600 to George Harvey's £38,416.[33] This was all the more remarkable because from 1864 he was a partner in the Trent Brewery with Joseph Richardson (manager of Marfleets, another Newark maltster) and a Mr Slater.

In October 1880, after Harvey's death, Thomas became a co-partner with William Gilstrap in the firm of Gilstrap Earp & Company. Again it was a partnership of convenience, a response to the problems of succession and administration which had plagued the Gilstraps for years.[34] Of the two surviving sons of Joseph Gilstrap, William died childless. His younger brother George (1822–64) produced three daughters then, at the early age of forty-two, was tragically killed in a railway accident. Two years previously William had left Newark on the purchase of the Fornham Park Estate near Bury St. Edmunds. Although he remained until his death the senior partner, from that time onwards he ceased to play an active role in the firm. His time was divided, doubtless more pleasurably, between his country estate, shooting from his lodge at Herringswell, a favourite haunt of the Prince of Wales, and travelling abroad. At Newark the manager accepted much of the routine responsibility, but the vital task of fostering contacts with brewers fell to Arthur Soames, who in 1852 had married Joseph's youngest daughter, Anna Amelia. By the late 1870s, however, Arthur and his son had set up on their own account at Grimsby and William was searching for a replacement.

The family network exhausted, William turned instead to a business alliance, the amalgamation of Gilstrap & Sons with the firm of Harvey & Earp. While the deed of partnership between William Gilstrap and Thomas Earp has not survived, it is clear from the subsequent partnership agreed in 1889 between William, Thomas and John MacRae, the husband of William's niece Isabella (a daughter of George Gilstrap), that again Thomas enjoyed favourable terms. The huge capital of £100,000 was supplied by William, 'except for sums not greater than £40,000 as Thomas Earp and John MacRae may between them choose to bring in'. Yet Thomas received half the profits, William nine-twentieths and John MacRae the remaining one-twentieth. Nevertheless, the agreement was tightly worded, illustrating the control maintained by William. Thomas's role was clearly defined: he was 'to manage the business, instruct John MacRae and introduce him to customers so by 1895 he may be able to assist or succeed Thomas Earp'

---

[32] Deed of Partnership, George Harvey and Thomas Earp, 13 August 1872, DDH 154/306, Nottingham Archives.

[33] Balance Sheet, Harvey & Earp, 31 October 1878, DDH 154/318, Nottingham Archives.

[34] The evidence for this paragraph is taken from G. Hemingway, 'The Gilstraps of Newark' (typescript, 1982); *Newark Advertiser*, 19 February 1896.

(who would be sixty-five years old). John MacRae 'was to retire from any other activity, to engage in the business and reside within ten miles of Newark'.[35] The last point, in particular, was a bone of contention between the two. William, however, was adamant:

> The man who arrives late is behind all day ... How can you, who have everything to learn, expect to be effective in the concern if you are not there when the machinery is set going? You will always be behind. Unless you put your head into the collar for the first seven years at least, others will be your master.[36]

We are left wondering about MacRae's commitment to business. Thomas remained in effective control until his retirement in 1905, aged seventy-five. His death five years later brought to an end an impressive career, and not only in business; a local philanthropist, and three times mayor, he was returned between 1874 and 1885 as Liberal MP for Newark, evidence indeed of his talents and ascendency in other spheres. His role in the business was filled by Hubert Cherry-Downes. A pupil of James Thorpe and co-founder of Yeomans Cherry & Curtis, the Burton maltsters, Cherry-Downes returned to Thorpes as barley buyer before assuming command at Gilstraps. Nevertheless, the Gilstrap name and financial control continued after Sir William's death. John MacRae, on condition that he adopted the family name and arms of Gilstrap of Fornham Park, became heir to his business interests.[37] Family succession was all important.

Succession was one of the main problems facing family partnerships and, as in the case of Gilstrap Earp, was often resolved by recourse to personal networks and the extended family.[38] Both were similarly instrumental in providing business finance and in generating trading links. Mark Casson has argued convincingly that networks, based on shared values and beliefs, played a crucial role in limiting the uncertainly of business dealings. The all important determinant was the quality of business culture, and the extent to which it promoted trust. 'Trust facilitates cooperation between entrepreneurs and cooperation is just as important as competition in achieving efficiency.'[39] For sales-maltsters, weak sellers in a partially

---

[35] Indenture of Partnership between Sir William Gilstrap, Thomas Earp and John MacRae, 6 December 1889, DDH 178/27, Nottingham Archives.

[36] Letter from Sir William Gilstrap to John MacRae, 7 August 1890, DDH 178/27a, Nottingham Archives.

[37] *Who Was Who*, 3, *1929–40*, p. 886.

[38] See M. B. Rose, 'Beyond Buddenbrooks: The Family Firm and Management of Succession in Nineteenth-Century Britain', in J. Brown and M. B. Rose (eds), *Entrepreneurship, Networks and Modern Business* (1993), pp. 127–43; P. L. Payne, *British Entrepreneurship in the Nineteenth Century* (London, 1985).

[39] M. Casson, 'Entrepreneurship and Business Culture', in Brown and Rose (eds), *Entrepreneurs*, p. 30.

integrated industry, facing more uncertainty than most entrepreneurs, this was all important. While the balance of power clearly rested with brewers, they were themselves paternalistic and bound by an informal code of conduct which emphasised loyalty to their small suppliers – precisely the characteristics of a high-trust culture. To what extent were sales-maltsters able to exploit this situation? How important were networks of trust in the formulation of business strategy?

It is possible to identify two main groups for whom kinship and religious networks played an important role in long-term growth and survival. First, many East Anglian maltsters were part of the far-reaching dissenting network which touched so much of the region's life. The Pauls are a case in point. The family originated from Burwell in Cambridgeshire. When in 1773 George Paul I (1740–1828), an ironmonger, brought his young bride, Sarah, to Bury St Edmunds they were welcomed into the close-knit circle of the Independent (later Congregational) Church.[40] Subsequently, the church accounts record 'the sum of Twenty Pounds, Cash lent to Mr George Paul on his note, at five per cent'.[41] In time, George became deacon and one of a small caucus of businessmen who led the church. His son, George II (1776–1852) followed closely in his footsteps. Also a deacon, for more than twenty years he was instrumental in spreading the faith to villages throughout the rich corn-growing belt of south west Suffolk. Here he met and worshipped with like-minded friends and businessmen: the Prentices, Fisons, Nathaniel Byles and John Crisp of Beccles (whose daughter, Mary Ann, married George's fourth son, William), all leading corn-merchants and maltsters. Almost certainly, it was these connections which fostered the family's interests in the grain trade and, subsequently, brewing and malting. George's sons, Robert (1806–64) and William (1808–90), who both lived and worked in Ipswich from the early 1830s, were similarly involved in chapel life. William moved to Norwich in 1843 to follow his profession of schoolmaster, but Robert, his wife Elizabeth and young family remained at the heart of the close community at Tacket Street.[42] In turn, each of the children was accepted as a teacher in the flourishing Sunday School and

---

[40] George was born in Burwell. When his uncle, John South, an ironmonger, died childless in 1768, he left his premises and £200 to his eldest nephew John and £200 each to John's brothers, George and Robert. They continued the business until 1772, when Robert died. Shortly after, George married and moved to Bury St Edmunds, where he set up as an ironmonger. *Ipswich Journal*, 2 October 1773. I am grateful to Geoffrey Paul for information about the Paul family; see also B. A. Holderness, 'Pauls of Ipswich' (typescript, 1980).

[41] Whiting Street Chapel, Subscriptions and Accounts, FK 3/502/28, SRO, Bury St Edmunds.

[42] After the death of his wife, Mary Ann, in 1836, William married her younger sister, Jane Crisp; in September 1843 they were 'dismissed to Mr Read's church in Norwich'. He first ran a boarding establishment at Hill House, Ber Street Gate, which formed the nucleus of Bracondale School which survived until the 1990s. Tackett Street Church Records, FK 3/1/2/7, 3/1/3/22, SRO, Ipswich.

served upon its many committees.[43] When, during the critical years after their father's death, Robert II (1844–1909) and William II (1850–1928) shouldered the responsibility of the family business, support was again forthcoming from the extended family of the church. In 1877, when the brothers acquired their first substantial malting, the purchase was financed by a £3000 mortgage from Robert's father-in-law, William Hewitt.[44] The latter, who for many years traded in partnership with William Prentice, a relative through marriage of the Pauls, was a man of some substance, owning four maltings and the Victoria Mill at Stowmarket, a timber yard at Bury and three Suffolk farms. By 1882 he had loaned the Paul brothers a total of £9000. Subsequently, this was redeemed by a gift to his daughter Emily, Robert's wife.[45] Further support from Robert, and William's mother and their sisters, Selina, Elizabeth and Ellen, and her husband George Thompson, underpinned the rapid expansion of the business.

The brothers were an able team. William, in particular, proved a thrusting entrepreneur in the classic Victorian mould. Uncompromising and hasty – he resolved a dispute over the repair of barges by purchasing his own shipyard – he was determined to remain at the forefront of progress. In 1899, with his son Stuart, he undertook an extensive tour of America.[46] Business travel was combined with religious observance and every Sunday William and Stuart attended a local church.[47] Not least, William's diary gives a fascinating insight into his perceptions of American business and businessmen:

> The New Yorker, as far as the businessmen are concerned, are much more open than we are in England, and not so reticent, talking more freely of their business before each other. Many of them will tell you their business, and the extent, after knowing you only a short time. They are quick as lightening, and many of them extremely smart. Life seems shorter here, businessmen continue active a very short time comparatively, and commence young. The leading men in the Corn Trade are mostly about thirty, and I have heard of some wonderful quick advancement for young men. Heads of

[43] On 20 July 1865, for example, William (aged fifteen) was accepted 'in full as a teacher having passed the usual term of probation'. Typically, in 1869 he was responsible for organising the flags and transporting the copper and provisions to the field for the Summer Treat, enjoyed by 180 teachers and visitors and 500 scholars. Ibid., FK 3/1/2/10, SRO, Ipswich.

[44] This was the 'Oliver Prentice' malting in Fore Street, Ipswich. It had a 100 quarter steep and was worked until the 1912–13 season.

[45] Robert married Emily, William's younger daughter, in 1870. Before his death William gave £9000 each to Emily, his son William and elder daughter Katherine Partridge. On her father's death, Emily inherited the Childer malting at Stowmarket and two farms in the Ringshall area and, on the subsequent death of her mother, the family home and a further £4000. Accounts and Will of William R. Hewitt; Executors' Accounts (Robert Stocker Paul).

[46] The Dock End Shipyard was purchased from H. Shrubshall in April 1901. R. & W. Paul, Private Journal.

[47] At Chicago, for example, the Episcopal Church was recorded as 'High', but the singing 'very good'. Diary of William Francis Paul, 23 March 1899.

firms make a great point in recognising ability in their servants and do not stand much on long service. The survival of the fittest seems to be the principle.[48]

William's observations were doubtless followed by much reflection. On the one hand, he was as ambitious and forward-looking as the smartest American; a self-made man, he preached the values of personal effort.[49] On the other hand, the harshness and pace of life clearly repelled him. He valued his long-serving and loyal workforce, 'my old servants and fellow helpers in business', and sought to reward them.[50] From an early age, he was active in civic life; a justice of the peace, member of the Ipswich Dock Commission, the Museum and Library Committee and a Trustee of Ipswich Municipal Charities. A staunch Liberal, he served as town councillor (1890–1908), alderman (1909–28) and mayor (1900–1). Notably, during his term of office, he refused to participate in the ceremonies or services of the established church. Wealth brought comfort, not personal extravagance; a growing involvement in agriculture – by the turn of the century he was farming at Freston and Kirton; and a commitment to improve the welfare of the town's citizens. For many years chairman of the public health committee, he instigated the public refuse system and the TB sanatorium.[51] For his work at Broadwater, an auxiliary hospital for wounded servicemen which he both donated and administered for the duration of the war, he received the OBE and Order of St John. In 1914 the William Paul Housing Trust built its first tenements for the poor and aged. Shortly before his death he created Bourne Park in one of the most densely populated districts of the town. His obituarist, with much justification, described William as the greatest benefactor in the history of Ipswich. In the words of the Revd Patten: 'He regarded position and influence as a stewardship for which he would be called to give account'.[52]

Robert was similarly a respected and competent businessman. Like William, he was a magistrate, member of the Dock Commission, alderman and mayor: a shy, reticent man, he nevertheless regarded public office as a duty. From an early age he served on numerous committees at Tacket Street

---

[48] Diary, 30 March 1899.

[49] His speech in 1920, when the Freedom of Ipswich was conferred on several citizens, emphasises his strong opinions: 'For all your new-fangled political theories, you will find you will come back to the efforts of individual men, if Ipswich and England, is to take its place in the future'. *Suffolk Chronicle and Mercury*, 13 April 1928.

[50] Will of William Paul, proved 16 May 1928; William left his personal and estate servants £10 for each year of service up to ten years, and £20 for each year beyond ten; long-serving members of staff received bequests of between £300 and £500.

[51] He offered the borough council an addition of 50 per cent upon any donations from other sources up to £10,000 for the building of the Sanatorium. Holderness, 'Pauls of Ipswich', chapter 3, p. 15.

[52] *Suffolk Chronicle*, 13 April 1928; see also 'A Parish at War', *Suffolk Review*, Autumn 1991, pp. 10–13.

and worked for many of the town's charities. The next generation of the family followed closely in their fathers' footsteps. Two of Robert's sons, Robert Harold (Harry) and Russell (who with William's sons, Stuart and Hugh, joined the business), and their sister, Mabel, all married members of the Pretty family who were drapers and corset manufacturers and worshipped with the Pauls at Tacket Street. They all were renowned for their welfare work. Harry continued as superintendent of Tacket Street Sunday School long after he succeeded William as chairman of R. & W. Paul; he founded and was captain of the Boy's Brigade and was treasurer of the church for over forty years. His brother, Russell, was treasurer of the Suffolk Congregational Union, 1921–49, while Mabel set up a creche, soup kitchen and blanket club for the women employed at her husband's corset factory.

The Pauls were therefore part of a close-knit, dissenting network. During the formative years of the business it was instrumental in providing trading links and financial support. There is little doubt that the dissenting tradition also shaped a business philosophy based on hard work, thrift and discipline which fostered a philanthropy that exceeded even the convention of the time. In the same way, the Prentice family, consisting of Manning (d. 1836), his sons, Thomas (1796–c. 1853) and William (1797–1869), and grandchildren Manning II (1823–75), Eustace (1832–84), Edward (1838–71), Oliver (b. 1821) and Catherine (b. 1823), were the pillars of the Independent Church at Stowmarket. Their involvement was equally remarkable in its commitment and continuity.[53] The same was true of the Crisps at Beccles and Wrentham, while James Fison (1785–1844) and his brother, Cornell (1793–1880), were the mainstays of the Wesleyan Chapel at Thetford.[54] They were united by marriage, religion and politics.[55] Between them, they occupied a dominant position in the East Anglian malt trade.

In contrast, the trade in Newark was controlled by the Gilstraps, Branstons and Thomas Earp. Of the town's brewers, Richard Warwick and James Hole, the latter was himself a maltster until in 1870 he founded the Castle Brewery.[56]

---

[53] C. A. Manning, *Suffolk Celebrities* (1893), p. 200; John Glyde, 'Materials for a History of Stowmarket', Miscellaneous and cuttings, Stowmarket 9, SRO, Ipswich.

[54] J. L. Smith-Dampier, *East Anglian Worthies* (1949), p. 77. For details of the Crisps' involvement with chapel life, see R. Lawrence, *Southwold River: Georgian Life in the Blyth Valley* (Exeter, 1990), pp. 76–83.

[55] The church records and census returns illustrate how close their relationships were. Marriages between the families were common. Of the ten children of William Prentice, maltster, timber, iron and corn merchant of Stowmarket, Catherine married James Fison, brother of Edward, the Ipswich maltster. Oliver married Mary Ritchie, great-granddaughter of William Crisp of Wrentham, and Samuel married Ellen Crisp Paul, daughter of William and Mary Ann Paul, and aunt of Robert Stocker and William Francis Paul. Records of Tacket Street Church, FK 3/502/28, 3/502/52–3, SRO, Ipswich; Records of Northgate Street Chapel, SRO, Bury St Edmunds; Census returns of Ipswich and Stowmarket.

[56] The evidence for this section is taken from Hemingway, 'Branston Family' and 'Gilstraps'; *Newark Advertiser*, 10 December 1879, 20 July 1887, 19 February 1910, 14 August 1987; Barnard, *Noted Breweries*, iii, pp. 349, 365.

These same families held sway in local politics and religion. All were committed churchmen. If in their politics they were less united – William Gilstrap, somewhat surprisingly broke with family tradition and supported his Liberal partner – in the main they were like Joseph Branston 'emphatically Conservative and zealous supporters of the farming interest'. Together they administered the town charities and the Trent Navigation, were school governors, magistrates and generous philanthropists. Their families were central to the social life of Newark and, not surprisingly, they intermarried. Joseph William Branston married Elizabeth, eldest daughter of Joseph Gilstrap. More significantly, his brother, Henry, saw three of his daughters, Emily, Florence and Eliza, married to the three sons of Richard Warwick. All the sons followed their father into the brewery.[57] The last example is important because it underlines the close relationship between these wealthy maltsters and the brewing fraternity.

The diaries of another of the Trent Valley maltsters, John Sandars, illustrate the importance of such connections in securing trade. John Sandars (1826–90) was a third-generation maltster. His grandfather, Samuel (1763–1835), began malting in Gainsborough in around 1780.[58] John's father, Edward (1794–1852), continued the Lincolnshire business, while his uncle, George (1805–79), with whom John trained, malted in Manchester. Besides his malting interests, George was a director of the Manchester and Birmingham and Trent Valley Railways, Deputy Lieutenant for the West Riding of Yorkshire and MP for Wakefield (1847–57). Another uncle, Joseph (1780–1857), a Liverpool corn merchant, was one of the promoters of the Liverpool and Manchester Railway. John therefore moved among the region's elite, establishing a network of brewing contacts which were to prove invaluable when he succeeded to his father's business. A wealthy man in his own right, he divided his time between malting and farming; he served as JP for Lindsey, captained the local company of Volunteers and, in later years, was Deputy Lieutenant of Lincolnshire.[59] By his death, his portfolio of investments exceeded £100,000. He regularly loaned capital to the smaller brewers and, in turn, supplied their malt.[60] John's eldest son, George II, was destined

---

57 Richard Warwick bought the Town Wharf Brewery in 1856. In 1888 he acquired the business of Richardson, Earp & Slater and the company was registered as Warwick & Richardson Limited. His three sons all became directors.

58 Samuel Sandars was the sixth son of John Sandars (1729–1800), a leading Derby corn merchant. His brother, Cornelius, was a maltster and sacking manufacturer at Owston, near Gainsborough. During the French Wars, Samuel gained lucrative contracts to buy corn for the government; on one occasion he had fifty vessels confined by bad weather at Hull. He also bought barley on commission for Benjamin Wilson, 'Family History Written by a Daughter of Samuel Sandars' (typescript), 2 Sandars 10/9, Lincoln Archives; E. Sandars, *The Sandars Centuries* (privately published, 1972); Mathias, *Brewing Industry*, p. 452.

59 *Lincolnshire Chronicle*, 14 February 1890.

60 Typical was Foster's Brewery mortgage of £4000 and £18,000 lent to a Liverpool brewer, R. G. Gatehouse; Executors' Accounts, 1890–91, 2 Sandars 4/12.

to enter the business but turned instead to farming. His brother, John Drysdale (1860–1922), was educated at Wellington College and Trinity College, Cambridge, then called to the Bar. As a young man, his life revolved around the many pursuits of a country gentleman: hunting and shooting; militia training in June; Aintree, Henley and the London season. When in 1886 he took his brother's place in the family firm, little changed. Business replaced the Northern Circuit; social life continued. Indeed, it is difficult to know where one ended and the other began. Apart from the shooting parties at Gate Burton, he frequently joined his brewing friends at the theatre and races. Easter 1887, for example, was spent around Manchester: at the Timperley Chases with Hubert Wilson (future chairman of Wilson's Brewery Limited); and hunting with Yates' (of the Castle Brewery) otter hounds at Beeston Castle.[61] Many of his friends, who of course were his customers, were also in his debt. Typically, when George Tickner and Philip Lascelles decided to buy a new business in Guildford, it was to John that they turned.[62]

Sandars was not alone in combining business and pleasure effectively. William Gilstrap took great pains to impress upon John MacRae the need to integrate the two. Militia training was enjoyed only at a cost:

> You would miss the opportunity of meeting friends and clients in London that month, Marylebone Cricket etc. etc. Arthur Soames worked that little game for his own pleasure and profit with other things of the season.[63]

More formal ties which provided a brewing connection also became increasingly common. When Robert Lee, like his Newark colleagues a staunch Conservative, mayor of Grantham, magistrate and freemason, took as his partner Edward Grinling, he gained not only an expert at his trade. Edward's father, James Church Grinling, was a partner and later director of Samuel Allsopp & Sons, the great Burton brewers. Edward had been their head maltster.[64] Lastly, when James Hole converted his business to limited liability status in 1890, among the first directors was Arthur Gilstrap Soames, the Grimsby maltster and nephew of Sir William.[65]

Like their East Anglian counterparts, the Trent Valley maltsters were clearly part of a business network based on common values: of religion, politics and inter-marriage. Whereas the first were part of a close-knit and

---

[61] Diaries of John Drysdale Sandars, 1880–94, 12–15 April 1887, 2 Sandars 1/8, Lincoln Archives.

[62] John Sandars' Letter Book, 30 May 1894; 2 Sandars 2/2, Lincoln Archives.

[63] Letter from Sir William Gilstrap to John MacRae, 7 August 1890, DDH 178/27a, Nottingham Archives.

[64] James Church Grinling joined Allsopps in 1865. Previously he was chief accountant with the Great Northern Railway Company. Edward joined the grain department after completing his education. His brother, Arthur, was a corn merchant. *Brewers' Journal*, 15 January 1894, 15 November 1899.

[65] *Brewers' Guardian*, 1 April 1890.

self-supporting circle, the second fostered links which tied them closely to brewers. While both were effective in self-preservation, in each case their companies followed a pattern of growth closely defined by their comparative social status. On the one hand, John Sandars, the Branstons and the Gilstraps focused almost exclusively on malting. In contrast, the East Anglian maltsters diversified more widely. The three sons of Manning Prentice (Manning II, Eustace and Edward) inherited their father's malting business but also began manufacturing chemical fertilisers. Manning II's eldest son, Manning III (b. 1846), also diversified into paper-making and explosives. He became managing director of Prentice Brothers (registered in 1891 with a nominal capital of £50,000 to acquire the chemical and fertiliser interests) and of Thomas Prentice & Company, maltsters, registered in 1909 with a capital of £20,000.[66] Malting was by then clearly the smaller part of the business. At Thetford and Ipswich, an almost identical pattern of development was followed by the Fisons, who again extended their malting and milling interests to the production of chemical manures: the two companies of James Fison (Thetford) and Joseph Fison of Ipswich continued into the 1990s, as Fisons plc.[67] The rapid expansion of Pauls was likewise underpinned both by diversification and specialisation. Such decisions were based on several factors. Pauls' diversification into animal feedstuffs was clearly influenced by transport developments, location and the flood of cheap imported grain. More significant, however, was their expansion within the parameters of brewing, where specialisation into the production of low-cost, high-volume, foreign malt, flaked maize and a range of brewers' additives were strategic moves which enhanced their bargaining power. Only through their financial interest in Lee & Grinling, which for many years remained a closely guarded secret, was there any attempt to consolidate links with brewers.

During the closing decades of the nineteenth century most sectors of the British economy experienced significant changes in organisation, as many partnerships were converted to joint stock limited liability companies. The trigger was the sale of Guinness to the public in October 1886; wildly successful, the authorised capital was twenty-eight times oversubscribed.[68] Not surprisingly, many other companies, often facing unprecedented capital demands, followed suit. The brewing industry was itself transformed.

66 *Brewers' Journal*, 15 August 1891, 15 November 1909.

67 In 1919 James Fison (Thetford) Limited amalgamated with Edward Packard & Company of Ipswich, also manufacturers of chemical fertilisers, to form Packards & James Fison (Thetford) Limited, renamed Fisons Limited in 1942. The malting business of James Fison & Sons Limited of Thetford was acquired in 1944 by R. & W. Paul Limited. Similarly, Edward Fison Limited of Ipswich (founded by the brother of James, Cornell and Joseph) was acquired in 1935 by Muntona, currently trading as Muntons. Munton & Fison, *A Brief History of Munton & Fison Limited to Mark Their Fiftieth Anniversary, 1921–1971* (privately printed, 1971), p. 7; Fisons Limited, *This is Fisons* (privately printed), pp. 5–7.

68 For a detailed discussion see Gourvish and Wilson, *British Brewing Industry*, p. 250.

Whereas in 1881 only seven brewery companies were listed on the London Stock Exchange, by 1900 there were 326.[69] Even small industries, like malting, felt the impact. While the great majority of smaller firms remained aloof from any change in organisation, between 1890 and 1914 a total of seventy-six were registered as limited liability companies (see Fig. 4.1).[70]

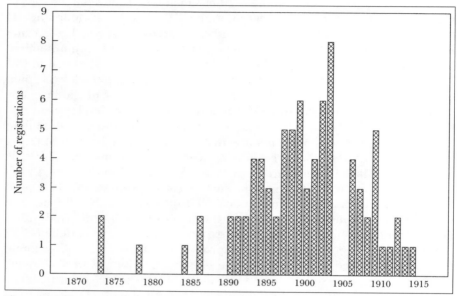

Figure 4.1   Incorporation of sales-malting companies, 1870–1914.
Source: See below, Appendix 5.

Although the main thrust of the shift to corporate status occurred after the mid 1880s, the necessary developments in company law had taken place several decades earlier. The Joint Stock Companies Act of 1844 extended the benefits of incorporation, previously enjoyed by overseas traders and public utilities, or secured by Private Act of Parliament, to manufacturing industry. Subsequently, the Act of 1856 removed the main hurdle of unlimited liability. Thereafter, simply by filing with the Registrar of Joint Stock Companies a memorandum of association signed by seven shareholders, firms

[69] K. Watson, 'Industrial Finance in the UK: The Brewing Experience, 1880–1913' (unpublished D. Phil. thesis, University of Oxford, 1990), pp. 94, 106.

[70] Because almost all malting firms remained essentially *private* companies, this undoubtedly understates the scale of the movement. Most vendors inserted a brief notice in the brewing trade press listing directors and details of capitalisation. Directors' minutes and files of dissolved companies, where available, have also been consulted. However, for a number of companies listed in trade directories no further information is available.

gained the benefit of limited liability.[71] Incorporation offered several other advantages: as the growing capital requirements of industry stretched the resources of partners, their families and friends, it allowed access to new sources of capital; it enabled vendors to realise their assets and it resolved many of the problems of continuity which had hindered partnerships. Previously, the death of a partner had made a restructuring of the firm essential. Retirement, when the withdrawal of capital could destabilise the finances of the firm, caused similar problems. Yet, despite the benefits of the new legislation, its adoption progressed slowly and by the mid 1880s limited companies accounted for less than 10 per cent of all business organisations.[72] The Act of 1856 had transformed company law, but its liberal terms did little to instil confidence in the new companies. Fraud and speculation persisted. Shannon found as many as a third of the companies registered between 1856 and 1883 were abortive or failed within the first five years of their existence.[73] Not surprisingly, many industrialists viewed the early companies with great suspicion. The handful of malting companies which registered under the Acts before 1890 certainly did little to commend the transition to other members of their trade. Two were capitalised at a mere £10,000. The largest, the North Lincolnshire Farmers Malting and Manure Company, registered in 1873 with a capital of £125,000, was quickly restructured with no further mention of malting.[74] The Birmingham Malting Company of the same year was restructured twice, failed to attract new subscribers when it doubled its capital to £100,000 and then was wound up voluntarily in 1884.[75] Similarly, S. Stanbridge of Camberwell led a chequered existence. Registered in 1884 with a capital of £40,000 'chiefly required to take over the freeholds and complete the erection of malting kilns and stores', it raised its capital in 1887 to £100,000 of which 8000 £5 shares were offered (with only partial success) for public subscription. The following year a further prospectus was issued, but the maltings were never built and by 1893 the business was in the hands of the official receiver.[76] Only the Cardiff Malting Company, registered in 1886, was established on a sound basis and survived into the twentieth century.

During the 1880s, several factors underpinned the gradual acceptance of the corporate form: the trend towards lower share denominations, developments in promotion and underwriting, and the impending reform

---

[71] The reforms of company law are discussed in detail in A. B. Levy, *Private Corporations and their Control*, i (London, 1950); H. A. Shannon, 'The Coming of General Limited Liability', *Economic History*, 2 (1931), pp. 358–79, and his 'The Limited Companies of 1866–1883', *Economic History Review*, 4 (1933), pp. 380–405; P. L. Cottrell, *Industrial Finance, 1830–1914: The Finance and Organisation of English Manufacturing Industry* (London, 1980), pp. 39–79.

[72] P. L. Payne, 'The Emergence of the Large-Scale Company in Great Britain, 1870–1914', *Economic History Review*, 20 (1967), p. 520.

[73] Shannon, 'Limited Companies', p. 405.

[74] *Brewers' Journal*, 15 January 1873; BT31/1694/6070, PRO.

[75] Ibid., 15 August 1873, 15 April 1884; BT31/1881/7496, PRO.

[76] Ibid., 15 April 1884, 15 June 1887, 15 April 1893.

of company law. At the same time such incidents as the failure of the City of Glasgow Bank in 1878 highlighted the risks of unlimited liability.[77] One of the main reasons, however, for the increase in new registrations, was the growth of the 'private' company. Somewhat belatedly, private companies were defined under the 1907 Act as those, with fewer than fifty shareholders, which restricted the transfer of their shares and raised no public capital. But in 1890 one-third of all registrations were already effectively 'private'. By 1914 the proportion had risen to four-fifths.[78] In most cases, the assets of the partnership were simply sold to the new limited company and the shares allotted between the former partners – who now became directors – and their families and friends. The vendors gained all the benefits of incorporation, but retained their privacy and control of their businesses.

Not surprisingly, as in general they were family firms and their capital requirements modest, the vast majority of malting companies remained private. Of the seventy-six companies which registered between 1890 and 1914, it is possible to identify only eight which sought a quotation for any class of their shares. In many cases, the entire capital was retained in the hands of founding families. The incorporation of R. & W. Paul in 1893 provides a classic example. The initial capital of £250,000, divided into 5000 £10 preference and 20,000 £10 ordinary shares, was held in equal parts by Robert and William Paul, who became joint managing directors. Similarly, in 1907, they were allotted the further issue of 5000 preference shares. When in 1913 6000 preference and 4000 ordinary shares raised the capital of the company to £400,000, it was divided between William, Robert's widow, and four sons who were also directors.[79] The same pattern was followed in 1902 when the company made its first major acquisition. Gillman & Spencer, previously a public company, was re-registered and assumed private status, with the 10,000 preference and 40,000 ordinary shares initially issued divided equally between Robert and William. They also held a quarter of the original £40,000 debentures (the only occasion when capital was raised from a wider sphere). The two brothers were managing directors and were joined on the board by their sons. Likewise, when in 1919 William and two sons became the first directors of the Hull Malt Company, the entire share capital remained in family hands.[80] Many other firms, such as Sandars & Company, F. & G. Smith, Henry Page & Company, J. Pidcock & Company and William Jones & Son, were similarly converted into limited companies simply by a paper transaction between the former partnership and the new enterprise.[81]

---

[77] Cottrell, *Industrial Finance*, pp. 162–63.

[78] Ibid., p. 163.

[79] R. & W. Paul Limited, Directors' Minutes and Balance Sheets.

[80] Directors' Minutes, Gillman & Spencer (1902) Limited; the Hull Malt Company Limited, PM.

[81] Directors' Minutes, F. & G. Smith, Crisp Malting Limited; Sandars & Company, J. Pidcock & Company, PM; *Brewers' Journal*, 15 September 1903, 15 August 1909.

Table 4.1 illustrates the registration and capital structure of the few malting companies which offered shares for public subscription. All eight companies issued non-voting capital, six offering preference shares and the remaining two debentures. In four cases, all the ordinary shares were retained by the original partners, who became directors of the new company. When in 1893, for example, the well-known partnership of Robert Free and William Rodwell was incorporated, the entire 8000 ordinary and 5000 6 per cent preference shares of £10 each were taken by the directors and their friends. But within two years the new company raised £75,000 in 4½ per cent debentures to finance the building of new maltings and grain elevators at Mistley; and a further £30,000 5 per cent debentures in 1898. Both were quoted on the London Stock Exchange.[82] Similarly, when the firm of Hugh Baird & Sons of Glasgow was registered in October 1894, all the 6600 £10 ordinary shares, issued and one-third of the 8000 preference shares, 'being the largest amount allowed by the Stock Exchange', were taken by the vendors in part payment of the purchase price. The remaining shares were almost five times over-subscribed.[83]

Table 4.1

Flotation and capital structure of public malting companies, 1890–1914

Year	Company	Issued capital	Stock Exchange	Ordinary shares	Preference shares	Debentures
1893	Free Rodwell	130,000	London	—	—	75,000 [1]
1894	Hugh Baird	146,000	London/ Glasgow	—	53,330	—
1895	Thomas Bernard	150,000	Edinburgh	—	75,000	—
1896	White, Tomkins & Courage	360,000	London	120,000	120,000	—
1897	Michael Sanderson	120,000	Leeds	30,000	50,000	—
1897	J. & C. H. Evans	60,000	Birmingham	—	30,000	15,000 [2]
1898	E. Bailey & Son	35,000	Bristol	23,330	—	35,000
1900	W. J. Robson	95,000	Leeds	35,000	30,000	—

Note: [1] Issued in 1895; [2] Issued in 1899.

Source: Company Prospectuses

[82] *Brewers' Journal*, 15 November 1893; *Stock Exchange Yearbook*, 1900.

[83] *Brewers' Journal*, 15 November 1894; *Stock Exchange Official Intelligence*, 1910, p. 572. The rules of the London Stock Exchange required that at least two-thirds of any capital had to be publicly traded to receive an official quotation. However, several of the provincial stock exchanges did not enforce this rule: see the examples of W. J. Robson and Michael Sanderson & Son, both quoted at Leeds. W. A. Thomas, *The Provincial Stock Exchanges* (London, 1973), pp. 138, 143, 197.

Of the four companies which issued equity, two were extending their interests beyond traditional malting. The incorporation of White, Tomkins & Courage in 1896, the largest of all the companies in terms of capitalisation, merged two firms which specialised in the production of flaked malt: T. H. White & Company Limited (already registered in 1893 with a capital of £140,000) and the partnership of Tomkins, Courage & Cracknell. According to the prospectus: 'the demand for the special classes of flaked malt ... has grown so large, [the] present works are not sufficient to execute orders. It is intended to employ part of the capital ... in the erection of new works in the North of England'.[84] The nominal capital was registered at £360,000 and the purchase price set at £335,000. The vendors, who became the directors of the new company, received as payment 6000 ordinary and 6000 preference shares of £10 each and the balance in cash. The remaining 12,000 ordinary and 12,000 5 per cent preference shares were offered to the public.[85] The vendors also retained the maximum share capital allowable under the Stock Exchange rules. The prospectus of E. Bailey & Son of Frome similarly portrayed a flourishing malting business and gave as the reason for the flotation the desire to raise capital for further expansion, notably the purchase of a factory at Avonmouth for the production of flaked maize. Again, of the 3500 £10 ordinary shares 'the Vendor agrees to take as large a holding ... as Stock Exchange rules allow, thus retaining a most substantial interest in the concern'. Both the ordinary shares and £35,000 4½ per cent debentures were listed at Bristol.[86] On the other two occasions when maltsters issued equity, both were diminishing their interests in the enterprise. The conversion of W. J. Robson of Leeds, registered with a capital of £120,000, followed the death of George Robson in 1900. The vendor, his elder son, William, wishing to devote himself to the large estates he had inherited in Yorkshire, retired from the business. He received a purchase price of £75,000 (including £45,000 for the goodwill of the business), paid in 4000 ordinary and 2000 preference shares of £5 each and £45,000 in cash. Although he ceased to play an active role in the business, he remained the largest shareholder. Another 5000 ordinary shares were unissued 'reserved to provide for building new kilns and further increase the business'. The remaining 7000 ordinary and 6000 preference shares were offered and fully subscribed.[87] The partners of Michael Sanderson & Son of Wakefield, registered in 1897, also wished to realise some of their wealth. Although the two elderly vendors, Thomas Sanderson and his brother Michael, remained involved in the business until their deaths, they had no heirs to succeed them. Registered with a nominal capital of £150,000, the assets of the business, mainly ten

[84] White, Tomkins & Courage, Prospectus, July 1896, Guildhall Library.

[85] *Brewers' Journal*, 15 June 1893, 15 July 1896.

[86] E. Bailey & Son, Prospectus, October 1898, Guildhall Library.

[87] W. J. Robson & Company, Directors' Minutes, PM; *Stock Exchange Yearbook, 1901*; *Brewers' Journal*, 15 May, 15 July 1900.

maltings at Wakefield and Nafferton, were valued at £55,936 and the purchase price, including goodwill of £40,000, set at £95,000, to be paid as 3000 ordinary and 1000 £10 preference shares together with £55,000 in cash. A further 5000 preference and 3000 ordinary shares were offered and a listing obtained on the Leeds Stock Exchange.[88]

What motivated maltsters to seek company status? Because of the limited evidence it is difficult to draw firm conclusions, but in the first instance they were clearly influenced by the general trend throughout British industry. For some maltsters family reasons – death, lack of succession, the desire to realise assets – were deciding factors. After the death of George Wheeldon of Derby in 1899 his elderly brother and former partner, William, administered the business in his capacity as executor. His own death, three years later, and the subsequent withdrawal of Harvey Whitson, George's son-in-law, and another partner, prompted George's son to convert the business in to a limited company.[89] The firm of R. Peach & Sons was likewise registered in 1913 as a private company 'for family reasons and owing to a large extension of trade', only months before the death of its founder.[90] Few maltsters raised public capital, and those who did retained all or a large proportion of the equity: illustrating, on the one hand, their reluctance to relinquish family control and, on the other, suggesting the benefit of limited liability may have been a key factor and incorporation therefore a defensive move. Nevertheless, the first and most significant wave of registrations occurred during the decade after 1890, when the climate overall was more optimistic than that of preceding years.[91] Of seventeen companies capitalised at £100,000 or more between 1890 and 1914, fourteen were registered in 1890–1900 and only three in 1901–14, again a period which included some very difficult trading years. Not only was the average capitalisation of the thirty-six companies registered before 1901, at £83,144, more than double that of the thirty-eight companies registered after (average capitalisation, £37,921), those which offered capital for public subscription did so during the first period.[92] Their prospectuses naturally presented a buoyant picture, but on almost every occasion one of the reasons given for the flotation was

[88] Michael Sanderson & Son Limited, Directors' Minutes, PM; *Country Brewers' Gazette*, 22 July 1897.

[89] *Brewers' Guardian*, 25 April 1899, 29 April 1902; *Brewers' Journal*, 15 August 1903.

[90] *Brewing Trade Review*, 1 April 1913, 1 October 1913.

[91] This was well after the brewers' first surge of 1886–90; in 1891–94 brewers' flotations were relatively inactive.

[92] Fig. 4.1 (above, p. 104) illustrates seventy-six companies identified as adopting company status in 1890–1914. The capitalisation of Robert Hutchison & Company is unknown; T. H. White & Company (registered in 1893), which merged and was re-registered in 1896 as White, Tomkins & Courage, has been counted only once. Harrison, in his study of the cycle, motor-vehicle and related industries (although mainly concerned with public companies) found a similar correlation between the buoyancy of trade and incorporation. A. E. Harrison, 'Joint-Stock Company Flotation in the Cycle, Motor-Vehicle and Related Industries, 1882–1914', *Business History*, 23 (1981), pp. 165–90.

to raise finance for expansion. Offers were fully or oversubscribed – and most vendors stated that no money had been spent on promotion – again suggesting that incorporation was seen in positive terms. Probably the most accurate interpretation therefore is that, before 1900, incorporation was viewed by large and often innovative and well-managed companies as a progressive step. After 1900, for many smaller firms feeling the full impact of falling demand, it represented a defensive move.

Despite its limitations, the data also provides further evidence of the growing links between brewing and malting companies. As the environment became increasingly hostile after 1880, many maltsters placed informal, often long-standing, relationships on a more formal basis. Several attracted directors of brewery companies to their boards. Quite how effectively such links could be established is clearly illustrated by the example of S. Swonnell & Son. The company was registered in 1898 to amalgamate the old-established maltsters and malt roasters and the similar interests of Tomkins, Courage & Cracknell (who had previously merged their flaked malt interests with T. H. White). Of the original board of five, Alfred Courage was the brother of Henry and Edward Courage of the brewers, Courage & Company. His joint managing director, Henry Tamplin, was both a director of Tamplin & Sons Brewery Limited, Brighton, and of Farnham United Breweries. A third member, George Garrett, youngest son of Newson Garrett, managed his father's malting business at Snape. His father and two brothers were directors of Smith, Garrett & Company Limited, the Bow brewers, as was George Swonnell, the vendor.[93] Similarly, the board of the Cardiff Malting Company could boast three directors of brewery companies: Samuel Brain of S. A. Brain & Company, E. Davies and J. J. Griffiths, both of Rhondda Valley Breweries Company, the latter also a director of William W. Nell.[94] Few malting boards could perhaps claim between them so many brewery connections but, to a lesser extent, such links were achieved by a significant number of companies. The initial board of Free Rodwell included J. A. Ind, director of the Colchester Brewery Company; subsequently E. M. Ind, of Ind Coope & Company, stood as trustee for their debenture stock.[95] W. J. Robson attracted H. J. Buckmaster of J. & J. Yardley & Company and the Albion Brewery Company, Burton-upon-Trent.[96] Alfred Yeomans served the boards of Yeomans, Cherry & Curtis and the brewers Marston, Thompson & Evershed, while the Derby maltster, Unwin Sowter, became a director of the brewers Z. Smith & Company.[97]

[93] S. Swonnell & Son Limited, Directors' Minutes, PM; *Brewers' Journal*, 15 August 1882, 15 September 1898.

[94] Barnard, *Noted Breweries*, iii, p. 467; *Stock Exchange Yearbook, 1900*, p. 1297.

[95] Free Rodwell, Prospectus, Guildhall Library; *Brewers' Journal*, 15 November 1893.

[96] W. J. Robson & Company Limited, Directors' Minutes, PM; Duncans' *Brewery Manual* (1910), p. 35.

[97] *Brewers' Journal*, 15 August 1890, 15 October 1900; Kelly's *Directory of the Wine and Spirit Trades, 1902*; *Brewing Trade Review*, 1 June 1910.

On occasions the initiative came from brewers, as when Guinness, after several complaints about malt quality, placed their agent, Henry Figgis on the board of Michael Sanderson & Son. Subsequently, the company introduced several outsiders with the clear objective of enhancing its reputation. In 1903 Edward Moritz, consulting chemist to the Country Brewers' Association, was retained as consultant analyst. The following year, John Westrope, senior partner of the Hull barley import merchants, was invited to join the board, the first of several 'men of experience who would have influence among brewers'. He was joined in 1911 by Richard Simpson of J. P. Simpson & Company, the Alnwick maltsters, and two years later by Charles Sutcliffe, senior partner of Edward Sutcliffe of Mirfield, and Thomas Fawcett, chairman of Thomas Fawcett & Company of Leeds.[98] Sometimes the boards of malting companies were dominated by a single brewery enterprise. In 1889 Frome United Breweries was formed from the amalgamation of three local firms. Previously, two of its directors, Alfred and Edmund Bailey, had registered their old-established malting business. Alfred continued to serve as chairman and managing director of both concerns.[99] Similar arrangements existed between the Hertford brewers McMullen & Sons and the malting company A. McMullen & Company;[100] and between the Leith brewers, Thomas & James Bernard and Thomas Bernard & Company.[101] Lastly, in a few cases, maltsters found security by merging their firms with one or more breweries to form a new limited company. The North Worcestershire Breweries, for instance, registered in 1896, brought together four breweries, a wine and spirit business and the Stourbridge malting business of Thomas Taylor, who became a director of the new enterprise.[102]

One further development in business organisation, underpinned by the widespread adoption of corporate status, was the merger movement of the late nineteenth century.[103] In contrast to the buoyant mid-Victorian period, the cycle of falling output and overcapacity (often made worse by improved technology), falling prices and profits affected most industries, prompting widespread attempts to stabilise prices and reduce competition. The initial

---

[98] Michael Sanderson & Son Limited, Directors' Minutes, 26 October 1903, 12 December 1904, 15 September 1911, 28 March 1913, PM.

[99] *Stock Exchange Yearbook, 1900*, p. 1297.

[100] *Brewing Trade Review*, 1 May 1897; *Brewers' Journal*, 15 September 1902.

[101] Thomas Bernard & Company, Prospectus, Guildhall Library; *Brewers' Journal*, 15 April 1895.

[102] *Brewing Trade Review*, 1 June 1896.

[103] For a discussion of these events see L. Hannah, 'Mergers in British Manufacturing Industry, 1880–1918', *Oxford Economic Papers*, 26 (1974), pp. 1–20; M. A. Utton, 'Some Features of the Early Merger Movements in British Manufacturing Industry', *Business History*, 14 (1972), pp. 51–60; H. W. Macrosty, *The Trust Movement in British Industry: A Study of Business Organisation* (London, 1907); H. Levy, *Monopolies, Cartels and Trusts in British Industry* (London, 1927).

response was often an informal agreement between competing firms to fix minimum prices, followed by more formal trusts or cartels, regulated by trade associations, which allocated production quotas, markets or pooled profits. However, despite signed agreements and penalties, enforcement proved a major problem, for under British common law such agreements to restrain trade were illegal and not therefore enforceable through the courts. A more lasting solution was legal consolidation through merger, and during the final years of the century the creation of substantial firms was increasingly evident. Here, brewing led the way. Between 1898 and 1914, as brewers sought to protect their trade by the acquisition of public houses, as many as 284 brewery companies were absorbed.[104] Yet, despite the direct impact on the malting industry, there is little evidence of a reciprocal trend. Throughout the period the commonest form of merger remained the absorption of the many unregistered firms, in particular the small rural partnerships which owned perhaps a handful of malthouses. The Pauls acquired maltings in this way at Woodbridge, Stowmarket, Stonham and Ipswich, while Edward Sutcliffe of Mirfield, still a partnership in 1914, purchased a number of small local concerns to become the largest sales-maltster in the industry.[105]

After 1900, the acquisition of smaller competitors by the leading companies became increasingly evident. Hugh Baird, for example, acquired Corder & Haycraft of London in 1906 and the Newbury business of William Skinner in 1913,[106] while Samuel Thompson & Sons of Smethwick purchased Bishop & Butt of Bristol and the Wiltshire business of J. H. Knight & Sons in 1913.[107] There were, however, no multi-firm mergers of any significance as in other sectors comprising a large number of small firms. To a large extent, this reflected the relationship between malting and its parent industry: brewers preferred to spread their interests widely and, as the founders of Associated British Maltsters were to discover in later years, were not prepared to countenance a large-scale malting merger. It is certainly notable that, of the sample companies, only two were formed as a direct result of merger and both manufactured 'specialist' products: White, Tomkins & Courage, where the stated objective was to reduce competition and effect economies in management and freight costs; and S. Swonnell & Son, registered in 1898, which merged the coloured and roasted malt business of the same name with that of Tomkins, Courage & Cracknell.[108] Indeed, among the flaked malt producers merger was relatively common. Within a year of

[104] K. Hawkins, 'The Conduct and Development of the Brewing Industry in England and Wales, 1888–1938: A Study of the Role of Entrepreneurship in Determining Business Strategy with Particular Reference to Samuel Allsopp & Sons Limited' (unpublished Ph.D. thesis, University of Bradford, 1981), p. 223.

[105] *Brewery Record*, 6 September 1927, p. 10.

[106] *Brewers' Journal*, 15 October 1907; *Brewers' Gazette*, 6 November 1913.

[107] E. F. Taylor, 'History of the Formation and Development of Associated British Maltsters Limited, 1928–78' (typescript, 1978), p. 16.

[108] *Brewers' Journal*, 15 September 1898.

incorporation, White, Tomkins & Courage had acquired the Liverpool business of Frederick Dresser,[109] while in 1902 Pauls purchased another flaked malt producer, Gillman & Spencer, who themselves had previously acquired the Torrified Grain Company. While Gillman & Spencer, the Hull Malt Company and the Cereals Company – all flaked malt manufacturers – became acknowledged subsidiaries of R. & W. Paul, it was felt necessary to conceal the owners' financial interests and subsequent acquisition of the maltsters Lee & Grinling.

It was only in the more specialist areas of production that maltsters were able to regulate their trade by restrictive practice. The attempt to form a 'ring' against Guinness in 1911–12 was, as we have seen, quickly dealt with. In contrast, the manufacturers of flaked maize colluded successfully for several years before the outbreak of the First World War. From the annual reports of White, Tomkins & Courage, the largest producer, it is plain that the main determinants were intense competition and violent fluctuations in the price of raw materials. In 1902, however, shareholders were informed that 'their competitors had shown a disposition to concerted action and they had therefore been able to raise the price of the manufactured article'.[110] No details of the arrangement survive, the subsequent complaints about rivals attempting to take trade suggesting it was not lasting.[111] On 1 July 1908, the eight surviving companies entered into a more enduring agreement, 'which may render the trade of a profitable nature'. The association closely resembled the class identified by Macrosty as a 'pool' or syndicate, where both minimum prices and production quotas were determined. Meetings were held monthly to set the ruling price for the sale of flaked maize and rice to brewers. In addition, the total trade of the association was estimated and, in accordance with the following schedule (Table 4.2), each member's annual production quota was calculated to reflect its current percentage.

Each signatory of the schedule contributed £5 for every 1000 quarters of their annual quota. If this was exceeded, a fine of 5s. per additional quarter delivered was levied, while any shortfall attracted a rebate of 4s. per quarter.[112] Initially, the agreement was to expire in December 1911, but in October 1910 it was extended for a further period of three years. The following March, John Shaw, the chairman of Shaws Hull Malt Company, told his shareholders that 'owing to the present combination between Manufacturers, the trade are getting a fair return for their capital'.[113] He was,

[109] *Brewing Trade Review*, 1 May 1898.

[110] *Country Brewers' Gazette*, 27 March 1902.

[111] *Brewers' Journal*, 15 April 1904.

[112] The London accountants, Fairbairn & Wingfield, were appointed secretary to the Association with powers to inspect members' books and to administer the system of fines and rebates, while all disputes were referred to the president of the London Chamber of Commerce for arbitration; Agreement between the Manufacturers of Flaked Maize and Flaked Rice for Brewing Purposes, 1 July 1908, PM.

[113] Shaws Hull Malt Company Limited, Directors' Minutes, March 1912, PM.

Table 4.2

Production quotas agreed by the manufacturers of flaked maize and rice for brewers, 1908

Name	Trade in quarters of flaked maize and rice for brewing purposes	Present percentage of total trade
White, Tomkins & Courage (London)	120,000	33.477
R. & W. Paul and Gillman & Spencer	93,000	25.941
Manbre Saccharine Company (London)	39,000	10.878
Cereals Company (Greenock)	38,000	10.599
Liverpool Malt Company	29,770	8.304
Liverpool Saccharine Company	20,000	5.578
Shaws Hull Malt Company	9830	2.741
E. Bailey & Son (Frome; Bristol)	8900	2.482
Total Production	358,500	100.000

Source: Pauls Malt Archives.

however, also concerned that there were 'signs that one or more Mills may break away ... and in such an event we are almost certain to go back to the disastrous competition of four years ago'. The agreement, nevertheless, was renewed. John Shaw's comments in 1914, a relatively prosperous season, probably present a fair assessment:

> It is true that we are working in agreement with the other seven maize manufacturers in the UK. It might be possible to obtain a higher price for our flakes, but our united policy has always been to earn a reasonable living profit without it in any way unduly exploiting the Brewer or exhorting an unfair price from him. Furthermore, owing to the free trade policy of this country and the dumping tactics of other nations, we are constantly in contact with Belgium and American competition and a certain amount of trade is secured by them ... the cost of the raw material is one of the great factors in our business, and we cannot for obvious reasons raise our price to the Brewer above a certain level.[114]

The Association endured at least until war interrupted production. During its period of operation, the profits and dividends of the Hull Malt Company, White, Tomkins & Courage and Gillman & Spencer all recovered substantially. It was clearly viewed by the members as beneficial.[115]

The second example of collusion, more local in nature, illustrates the

114 Shaws Hull Malt Company Limited, Directors' Minutes, March 1914, PM.
115 In 1911 a further agreement was signed between White, Tomkins & Courage and Gillman & Spencer relating to the sale of flaked rice and tapioca to the grocery trade; Gillman & Spencer (1902) Limited, Directors' Minutes Book, 10 April 1911, PM.

attempts of four of the leading East Anglian maltsters, Free Rodwell, J. Gough & Sons, the Ipswich Malting Company and R. & W. Paul, to regulate the price and supply of imported barley to other maltsters and brewers. From the terms of the agreement, it is clear that the main incentives were protection against a similar arrangement operated by the barley shippers and the reduction of competition and protect profits. The agreement was renewed annually for the next seven years, when the correspondence ceases. Apart from minor disputes regarding the sharing of port dues, it appears to have operated smoothly and must, therefore, again have been viewed as beneficial. It is unlikely that such agreements were common. In a few cases, they enabled maltsters to reduce the intense competition of the period and protect their profits. For those unable, or less inclined, to diversify, there remained the benefits of limited liability and, probably the most effective strategy until well into the twentieth century, the security provided by personal networks and close ties with and within the brewing fraternity.

5

Costs, Prices and Profits, 1830–1914

William Ward's comment that 'selling matches ... could easily be more profitable than trying to sell malt' was a sentiment frequently echoed throughout the malting world.[1] Witnesses to parliamentary inquiries either bemoaned the intense competition characteristic of the industry or, like the Norfolk maltster, James Everitt, contrasted his more prosperous years in brewing.[2] Henry Stopes, writing in 1885, reckoned 'malting is a declining industry', while twenty years later Julian Baker similarly believed 'the margin of profit is becoming smaller each year'.[3] Adding substance to these impressions is another matter. We know little about the thousands of small maltsters who drifted in and out of the trade during the nineteenth century, or about the many problems they faced with farmers and brewers. Men like John Hyde of Gainsborough, who in the 1860s produced around 1200 quarters of malt annually, relied on publicans and private customers purchasing only a few bushels to brew at home. Like many others, brick makers, coal merchants and insurance agents for example, Hyde extended his trade, dealing in soap and soda, suggesting the need to supplement his malting income.[4] Generally, the evidence relates to more substantial maltsters but, even among the sector's leading firms, financial records are rarely complete. There were few *public* malting companies and, therefore, as the *Brewers' Gazette* noted, 'no glimpse by the outside public ... of this essentially private trade'.[5] Most contemporary authors focused on the practicalities, rather than the economics, of malting. The exception was Hugh Lancaster, who wrote in some detail about financial matters. His work, together with evidence from parliamentary inquiries, provides the basis for the first section of this chapter, a discussion of malting costs after 1830.[6]

Any consideration of malting costs is complicated, first, by the difficulty

[1] Letter to C. Long from W. S. Ward, 8 December 1914, Letter Book, DE WD B20, HRO

[2] For which he said he 'was very well paid ... It is a [decidedly] better business than malting', *Select Committee on the Malt Tax, PP* (1867–68), ix, p. 303.

[3] H. Stopes, *Malt and Malting* (London, 1885), p. 35; J. L. Baker, *The Brewing Industry* (London, 1905), p. 30.

[4] Malt and Trading Account, 1859–64; Brace 3/22, Lincoln Archives.

[5] *Brewers' Gazette*, 11 April 1907.

[6] H. Lancaster, *Practical Floor Malting* (1906), pp. 171–86, and his 'The Probable Effect on the Increased Beer Duty on the Malt Trade of the United Kingdom', *Brewing Trade Review*, January 1915, pp. 10–12.

of evaluating the out-turn, or yield, of malt per quarter of barley steeped. Calculations were based not simply on the quantity of barley steeped but on the malt obtained, with the malt quarter of 336lbs, and not the barley quarter of 448lbs, as the standard unit. The out-turn was influenced by two factors: the increase or loss during malting, itself determined by the moisture content of the barley and the ease with which it modified on the working floor; and the weight loss from screening. Both varied considerably according to the variety and quality of the barley. On the one hand, consignments of imported 'brewing' barley usually contained a high proportion of rubbish but were well dried (containing around 10 per cent moisture), recording a heavy screening loss but frequently a considerable malting increase. On the other, good quality British barley was cleaner but was of much higher moisture content (possibly 15 per cent or more) and therefore more susceptible to weight loss during sweating and malting. The importance of the out-turn and the way in which maltsters calculated their costs is clearly illustrated by Lancaster's two examples:

Table 5.1

Examples of calculating the cost per quarter of malting

Damp English Barley requiring Sweating		Dirty, Foreign Barley such as Syrian Tripoli	
1. Sweating		**1. Sweating**	
100 quarters of barley at 28s.	2800s.		
Cost of sweating at 6d. a quarter	50s.		
Loss of 10 quarters		———	
90 quarters dried barley	2850s.		
Cost per quarter dried barley,	31s. 8d.		
2. Screening		**2. Screening**	
90 quarters at 31s. 8d.	2850s.	100 quarters barley at 25s.	2500s.
1 quarter broken sold at	20s.	1 quarter broken sold at 15s.	
1 quarter thin sold at 15s.	−35s.	5 quarters thin sold at 10s.	−65s.
½ quarter dust		2 quarters stones and dirt	
87½ quarters screened barley	2815s.	92 quarters screened barley	2435s.
Cost per quarter screened and dried	32s. 2d.	Cost per quarter screened nearly.	26s. 6d.
3. Malting		**3. Malting**	
87½ quarters barley 2815s.		92 quarters barley	2435s.
92 quarters malt at 6s. a quarter	552s.	100 quarters malt at 6s. quarters	600s.
92 quarters malt cost	3367s.	100 quarters malt cost	3035s.
Cost per quarter of malt	**36s. 7d.**	**Cost per quarter of malt**	**30s. 4d.**

Source: Lancaster, *Floor Malting*, pp. 182–83.

The second problem is the division between malting-for-sale and com-mission malting. In the former, the sales-maltster purchased his own barley and saw a return on his capital some three to four months after the malt was delivered to his customers, perhaps a year, or even two years, later. In the latter, the brewer provided the capital to buy barley, paid all freight costs and where necessary an extra fee for drying barley (usually 1s. per quarter). Production costs were therefore lower than when malting-for-sale.[7] For example, Lee & Grinling's costs for commission malt for the year ending September 1904 were 3s. 8.3d. a quarter, compared to 5s. 9d. for malting-for-sale.[8] Most maltsters received a fee of around 5s. per quarter (6s. for brown malt), an amount which, remarkably, remained unchanged through-out the nineteenth century. In the 1830s Trumans paid their commission agent, J. & R. Marriott of Narborough, 5s. (plus an extra 6d. for freight to Lynn); sixty years later Lewis Meakin of Burton received the same amount. Guinness paid their commission agents 3s. a barrel of malt (6s. a quarter); Allsopps paid Lee & Grinling 4s. 9d., while in the 1890s Pauls made commission malt for the Commercial Brewery Company of London for the exceptionally low fee of 4s. 3d. a quarter.[9] The details of arrangements varied considerably: some brewers covered insurance, loaned machinery or rented their maltings to the maltster. Unfortunately surviving records are incomplete, but the following letter from John Sandars to a prospective customer, the Burton & Lincoln Brewery Company, underlines the substan-tial benefits to be gained from commission contracts:

Our terms are 5s. quarter reckoned on the Barley steeped which covers the cost of making, rent and all our personal expenses. We take the culms as against the coke ... and for sack hire we charge at ½d. sack. We stand legally in the position of warehousemen and as such do not insure stock which is at owner's risk. Barleys bought in these markets are paid for at fourteen days and we expect remittance to meet payments.

Our ordinary course is to forward you every Saturday samples and particulars of each parcel of Barley bought on your account during the week and also to furnish you with a statement of the money we have to pay for you during the following week, for which we like to receive a remittance on Tuesday mornings. In case of large payments, we ask you to send a special cheque or Banker's Draft so as to save on bank commission.[10]

7 For further details of commission malting see pp. 38–40.
8 Lee & Grinling, Cost Accounts, PM.
9 Private Ledgers, Lee & Grinling and R. & W. Paul Limited, PM; Truman, Hanbury & Buxton, Monthly Reports, 9 May 1899, B/THB/A/120, GLRO.
10 Letter to the Burton & Lincoln Brewery Company, 8 September 1890, 2 Sandars 2/2, Lincoln Archives. Some maltsters, like John Sandars, initially calculated the malting fee and their manufacturing costs on the quantity of barley steeped, and subsequently adjusted for the out-turn. Others, like Swonnells and Henry Page, followed Lancaster's procedure. Because most records are fragmented, it is not always clear which method companies adopted.

Frequently, maltsters divided their production between commission malting and malting-for-sale, although by the end of the nineteenth century malting-for-sale usually dominated. In most cases the purchase of raw materials represented the greatest element of the maltster's costs followed, until 1880, by excise duties. Other costs were relatively insignificant. James Everitt, in his evidence to the Select Committee on the Malt Tax in 1867, gave his total costs as 40s. a quarter for barley, 21s. 8d. for duty and 3s. 6d. for production, a figure which included interest on working capital of 5 per cent, and a notional return on fixed capital, calculated as a rent of £2 per quarter (i.e. £100 for a 50 quarter malthouse).[11] Other witnesses likewise suggested 3s. to 3s. 6d. a quarter for production costs, including labour, fuel, carriage and rent.[12] The 1880s brought not only the repeal of the malt tax and falling barley prices but a wider choice, which to some extent diminished the sharp annual fluctuations of earlier years. Lancaster, writing in 1908, suggested a ratio of around 80 per cent for raw materials to 20 per cent for production costs.[13] The latter he divided into fixed and variable costs. Fixed costs he calculated should be 3s. 6d. per quarter of malt. These included rent at 5 per cent of capital cost, depreciation at 2 per cent for buildings and 7–10 per cent for machinery, plus provision for rates and taxes. Variable costs were calculated at between 3s. and 4s. per quarter of malt. His calculations included interest on working capital reckoned at 1s. per quarter, 9d. to 1s. 3d. per quarter for both wages and fuel, 1d. to 3d. for power for machinery and general expenses of around 2d. Sales of malt culms and kiln dust raised 6d. a quarter, leaving a net total manufacturing cost of between 6s. and 7s. per quarter.[14]

How accurate were Lancaster's calculations? One further factor influencing malting costs was the *type* of malt made. Henry Page's projections for malting costs for season 1905–6 highlight the considerable differential, notably in fuel and labour, between the production of pale (giving a ratio of 88.3 per cent for barley to 11.7 per cent for manufacturing) and brown malt (82.0 per cent to 18.0 per cent; see Table 5.2).[15]

[11] *Select Committee on the Malt Tax, PP* (1867–68), ix, pp. 303–08.

[12] Between 1866 and 1874, the Norwich brewers Steward & Patteson recorded annual average production costs of 3s. 1d., ranging from a low of 2s. 3d. in 1870 to a high of 4s. 9d. in 1874. Steward & Patteson barley book, BR 1/118, NRO.

[13] His estimates were based on an average price of 28–30s. for English, and 25s. for foreign barley, against manufacturing costs of 6–7s. per quarter of malt. Lancaster, 'Floor Malting', pp. 181–82.

[14] These estimates were based on an output of 12,000 quarters of malt.

[15] The figures, which formed the guidelines for negotiating the new season's contracts, are further complicated because it was assumed that 100 quarters of screened barley would produce 100 quarters of pale malt but 120 quarters of brown, thus reducing the cost of the latter to approximately 32s. a quarter.

Table 5.2

Henry Page's 'Formulae for Making Pale Malt and Brown Malt',
October 1905

Cost per quarter	Pale malt		Brown malt	
	s.	d.	s.	d.
Labour	1	2	1	8
Coal	1	0		—
Faggots		—	3	0
Delivery		1	3	0
Cartage/Meterage		5		9
Charges and 'Oddments'		6		3
Screening		1		—
Making and delivering	4	2	6	11
Screened barley *	31	6	31	6
Total cost per quarter	35	8	38	5

Note: * Calculated on the basis of unscreened barley at 30s.
quarter, and a screening loss of 10 quarters for every 110
quarters, purchased. Screenings were sold for 15s. per quarter.

Source: Henry Page & Sons, Miscellaneous Papers; Pauls Malt
Archive.

Generally, by the end of the nineteenth century the balance of production
had shifted towards pale malt. From 1905, Pauls' cost accounts provide a
more comprehensive and representative picture. While no records of barley
purchases have survived to complete the analysis, Table 5.3 illustrates the
meticulous care with which many maltsters calculated their costs. Pauls did
not allow for interest on working capital, nor is it clear whether they included
depreciation for buildings and machinery. On the other hand, they included
provision for repairs, cartage and freight to outlying malthouses, fire insurance, and a substantial increment to cover 'general expenses'; in this case
embracing fifteen separate items such as salaries, commission, discounts,
bad debts and costs of analysis. During 1905–6 the company worked seventeen maltings, including those at Stonham, Stowmarket and Woodbridge.
By 1910 they had also acquired 'Cobbold's' malting in Ipswich, while two
years later No. 6 at Stoke was worked for the first time in place of five of
the small, old maltings. The following year 6907 quarters were also produced
in 'outside' maltings belonging to other companies (Eve & Co, Maldon,
Edwards of Woodbridge, Singer & Lord of Ipswich, C. H. Ayres of King's
Lynn and Catchpoles of Ipswich), at an average cost of 4s. 3d. per quarter,
to which was added the general expenses of 1s. 1¼d., making a total cost
of 5s. 4¼d. a quarter.[16]

[16] R. & W. Paul, Cost Accounts, PM.

Table 5.3

R. & W. Paul Limited, manufacturing cost per quarter of barley steeped,
seasons 1905–6, 1910–11 and 1913–14

Season	1905–6			1910–11			1913–14		
Quantity steeped	93,030 quarters			108,746 quarters			136,000 quarters		
Cost per Quarter	s.	d.	%	s.	d.	%	s.	d.	%
Rent – Buildings	1	3.1	24.5		11.2	16.5		10.8	17.5
Rent – Machinery		2.4	4.0		2.3	3.4		2.2	3.6
Rates		0.4	0.6		3.0	4.5		2.9	4.7
Wages		11.5	18.7		11.3	16.8		11.6	18.8
Porterage		2.2	3.6		2.6	3.2		2.2	3.6
Coal		11.9	19.3		11.9	17.6		11.8	19.1
Water		0.7	1.1		0.9	1.3		1.1	1.8
Power for Machinery		1.2	2.0		1.0	1.5		0.8	1.3
Repairs		2.8	4.6		2.8	4.1		2.9	4.7
Fire Insurance		0.6	1.0		0.5	0.7		0.6	1.0
Freight/Cartage		1.9	3.1		2.3	3.4		1.6	2.6
General Expenses		10.8	17.5	1	6.3	27.0	1	1.2	21.4
Total cost per quarter	5	1.4	100.0	5	7.7	100.0	5	1.8	100.0
Less sales of malt culms and kiln dust		6.0			6.5			6.0	
Net cost per quarter	4	7.4		5	1.2		4	7.8	

Source: R. & W. Paul, Cost Accounts, PM.

Pauls' costs were almost certainly below the average achieved by many maltsters, especially brewer-maltsters. There was probably some substance in Lancaster's contention that many brewers were completely ignorant of the real cost of malting. He quoted one successful brewer, regrettably anonymous, who charged nothing for rent simply because his maltings had been built out of brewery profits and the capital subsequently written off.[17] Others, such as Bass, clearly analysed their costs as carefully as Pauls, and Owen provides a breakdown of the cost per quarter of malt made at Burton for four sample years between 1889 and 1911.[18] During this period Bass worked twenty-two malthouses at Burton, including the huge Shobnall Maltings, built in the 1870s at a cost of nearly £100,000, and the Plough Maltings, converted in 1899 to a pneumatic malting with fifteen 28 quarter

[17] Although Lancaster accepted that large scale production reduced costs, he thought it 'most improbable that malt [could] be made in any modern house for 5s. per quarter'. Lancaster, 'Floor Malting', pp. 178, 185.

[18] C. C. Owen, *The Greatest Brewery in the World: A History of Bass, Ratcliff & Gretton* (Chesterfield, 1992), p. 236.

drums.[19] Production during this period averaged 206,130 quarters annually. Thus there was clearly scope to maximise scale economies. During 1910–11, however, when 197,839 quarters of malt were made at Burton, the average cost was 39s. 11.2d., of which barley accounted for 31s. 11d. (79.9 per cent), and manufacturing, 8s. 0.2d. (20.1 per cent) – a ratio extremely close to that suggested by Lancaster.[20] In comparison, Pauls' manufacturing costs during the same season were as low as 5s. 7.7d. (net cost 5s. 1.2d.). The composition of the two series varied considerably but the differential between labour costs, in particular, was substantial. Labour costs at Burton, always above those in Suffolk, rose steadily from 2s. 1.2d. per quarter in 1888–89 to 3s. 1.3d. by 1910–11. In contrast, Pauls' labour costs were always under 1s. a quarter before the outbreak of the First World War.

This striking consistency was underpinned, first, by malting wages which, in the rural eastern counties, remained low and stable throughout the period. Typically, John Sandars of Gainsborough paid 18s. to 20s. a week in the 1860s, and the same amount thirty years later.[21] In addition, there was 1s. a week 'back money', paid as a bonus at the end of the season, plus allowances for specific tasks, such as unloading barley and coal, night 'ploughing' and 'putting up' malt. At Sandars, each man received 6d. for putting up half a ton of culms, while at F. & G. Smith's Wells-Next-The-Sea maltings, seven men shared 2s. 6d. per ton for carrying twelve-stone wicker baskets of coal across the quay and into the fire-hold. Some paid allowances in beer (one pint for catching a rat), while Swonnells of Snape gave beer tokens, redeemable at the nearby Plough and Sail. Others made a daily beer allowance. Pauls provided cottages for many of their workers, and at F. & G. Smith's there was Christmas beef (seven pounds for floormen and nine for firemen) and the summer outing to Great Yarmouth. Hours were long, including Sunday working, with some firms operating a system of fines: Sandars penalised anyone late, 3d. for the first quarter of an hour, 6d. for half an hour. The work was also seasonal, with all but a handful of men laid off at the end of the season. But overall, malting wages and the various allowances compared favourably with the 12s. to 13s. paid to agricultural labourers and, especially at a time of widespread depression, were sufficient to attract an adequate supply of labour.

In the midlands and north different conditions and agricultural rates of pay prevailed. Official statistics quote wages of maltsters in Newcastle as ranging from 22s. to 24s. by the late 1860s.[22] Similarly, at Burton the rapid

[19] Ibid., pp. 74, 111.

[20] Similarly, during 1903–4, total production costs were 37s. 7.2d. per quarter. Barley, at 30s. 5.9d. represented 81.1 per cent and manufacturing, at 7s. 1.3d., 18.9 per cent of total costs.

[21] The evidence for this paragraph is taken from recordings of maltsters (1972), tapes 50 – 54, Museum of East Anglian Life, Stowmarket; Diaries of J. E. Sandars, 1849–76, 1 Sandars 1 and 2 Sandars 1/2–15; Sandars & Company, Ferry Cash Book, PM; M. Manning, 'Great Ryburgh Maltings', *Norfolk Industrial Archaeology Society Journal*, 2 (1976–80), pp. 15–20.

[22] No figures are given for the eastern counties. In 1866, rates in Edinburgh were 19s. a week, in Dublin, as low as 12s.; in Belfast in 1874, 18s. a week. *PP* (1887), lxxxix, pp. 613–17.

growth of the brewing industry and resulting labour shortage saw wages rise to 23s. 4d. (plus 2s. 'back money' and allowances) in the 1880s.[23] Thereafter trends closely reflected the fortunes of the brewing trade: during the prosperous years of 1898 and 1899, strikes at Newark and Burton secured further increases bringing weekly wages to an average 28s., while in the depressed conditions of 1906, employers forced cuts of 4s. a week.[24] By the outbreak of war both trade and wages had recovered, with 1913 marked by strikes at Burton, Kirkcaldy and in Yorkshire with the National Union of Gas and General Workers, who organised maltsters pressing for a minimum weekly wage of thirty shillings.[25] Strikes were not common throughout the industry but they clearly reflected the greater bargaining power of maltsters in these industrial regions.[26] Somewhat ironically, many of those who fought for higher wages and better conditions were in fact Suffolk men, part of the annual migration of East Anglian workers to Burton for the malting season.[27] Underpinned by the well-established links between brewing and agriculture, the movement reconciled the Burton brewers' demand for labour and the excess supply of agricultural labour in the eastern counties. During the 1890–91 season, 126 East Anglians found work with Bass, Ratcliff & Gretton in their Burton maltings, as many as 256 six years later. Other Burton firms were almost certainly involved and Owen estimated that, by the mid 1890s, some 300–400 migrant workers were employed in the town.[28] Even this may understate the true scale of the movement: the *Brewers' Gazette*, for example, reporting the 1906 strike, quoted '800 men, principally from Norfolk and Suffolk'.[29] The migration, which continued until the depression of the 1930s encouraged the employment of more local labour, was clearly substantial.

[23] *Brewers' Journal*, 15 December 1889; official statistics quote 1886 wages for maltmen at: Burton 21s. 3d., Lancashire 23s. 1d., London 26s. 3d., Kent, Surrey and Sussex, 23s. 2d.; *PP* (1893–94), lxxxiii, p. 107.

[24] *Brewers' Journal*, 15 December 1889, 27 September 1906; *Grantham Journal*, 30 December 1899.

[25] In Yorkshire the union organised 1000 maltsters to press for a package which included a fixed minimum wage of 30s., 2d. per quarter for drying, 2s. extra for special work on Sundays, and an end to the system of 'back-money', with wages paid in full every week. The outcome overall is unknown, but Wilson confirms that at Burton maltsters wages were increased to 30s. in 1913. *Brewers' Journal*, 15 February, 15 May, 15 December 1913; T. R. Gourvish and R. G. Wilson, *The British Brewing Industry, 1830–1980* (Cambridge, 1994), p. 199.

[26] There is little evidence of strikes in East Anglia and it is notable that companies such as Pauls and Sandars did not permit union membership.

[27] G. E. Evans, *Where Beards Wag All: The Relevance of the Oral Tradition* (London, 1970), chapters 21–26; C. C. Owen, *The Development of Industry in Burton upon Trent* (1978), pp. 97–98; See also *Gone to Burton*, produced by Dick Joyce for Anglia Television, East Anglian Film Archive, Centre of East Anglian Studies, University of East Anglia.

[28] Owen, *Development of Industry*, pp. 97–98.

[29] Although no details have survived, Bass also employed East Anglian workers at their Sleaford maltings. Russell Button (1905–1991), of Helmingham, Suffolk, was employed for five seasons, from October 1926 to May 1931. He joined Pauls in 1932 and completed forty years service. I am grateful to Brian Seward of Pauls Malt for this information.

Estimates of labour productivity varied widely and comparisons are difficult. While Bass's eight 120 quarter malthouses at Sleaford were worked by a total of forty-eight maltsters (i.e. one man per 20 quarters steeping capacity), more than this number were employed in addition for barley handling, as firemen and as general labourers.[30] At the other extreme, old-fashioned 'one-man maltings', with a steeping capacity ranging from ten to twenty quarters, were worked by a single man who did everything, from fetching coal to dispatching malt. The *Brewers' Gazette* reckoned one man to every 13 quarters of steeping capacity, but managing as much as 20 quarters where labour-saving machinery was employed. Several malt-sters agreed that 15–20 quarters (approximately 600–800 quarters per man per year) was a typical workload, depending on the malthouse and material.[31] At F. & G. Smith's Ryburgh maltings, however, each maltster worked an average of 25 quarters of steeping capacity, while Russell Button recalled that at Pauls' Stoke maltings two men handled as much as 55 quarters of capacity between them (approximately 1100 quarters per man per year).[32]

Pauls' high labour productivity clearly reflected the steady modernisation of the business, mechanised handling of barley and malt, and the use of labour-saving machinery such as kiln-turners. The directors of Trumans, on their visit to Ipswich in the spring of 1903, were particularly impressed by the conveying and screening plant.[33] During the last pre-war season, 49,595 quarters of malt were produced at the Stoke Maltings at an average wage cost of 9d. per quarter; at the old Wash Maltings, where 2583 quarters were made, this figure was almost doubled.[34] Given that 9d. per quarter was the figure suggested almost eighty years earlier by the Select Committee on Agricultural Distress, this was no mean achievement.[35] Doubtless it also indicated a greater concern for labour costs among sales-maltsters than among brewer-maltsters. For the latter, labour costs were minimal in com-parison with the cost of raw materials and distribution. Wilson concluded that before the 1890s brewers made little effort to economise on labour.[36]

---

[30] J. Brown, *Steeped in Tradition: The Malting Industry in England Since the Railway Age* (University of Reading, 1983), p. 61. At F. & G. Smith's Great Ryburgh maltings approximately sixty men were employed, of whom thirty-five were maltsters. The remaining twenty-five worked in the 'day gang', fetching coal etc., or as storemen, carpenters, bricklayers and engineers. Manning, 'Great Ryburgh Maltings', p. 16; Arthur Riches, tape 52, Museum of East Anglian Life.

[31] *Brewers' Gazette*, 6 July 1905; tapes 50–54, Museum of East Anglian Life, Stowmarket; P. Stephens (ed.), *Newark: The Magic of Malt* (1993), p. 39.

[32] Manning, 'Great Ryburgh Maltings', p. 16.

[33] Hanbury Truman & Buxton, Monthly Reports, April 1903, B/THB/A/121, GLRO.

[34] R. & W. Paul Limited, Cost Accounts, PM.

[35] *Second Report of the Select Committee on Agricultural Distress, PP* (1836), viii, p. 189; Lancaster also suggested 1s. a quarter for labour by mid century. Lancaster, 'Effect on Increased Beer Duty', p. 10.

[36] Gourvish and Wilson, *British Brewing Industry*, p. 197.

For maltsters, facing falling demand and rising competition, paring labour costs was one way of protecting profit margins after 1880.

In comparison with the bigger brewer-maltsters, most sales-maltsters were not substantial employers of labour. In 1887, Bass employed 420 men in their Burton maltings; two years later, their neighbours, L. & G. Meakin – sufficiently prestigious to be included in Barnard's volumes – employed seventy maltsters and six foremen. F. & G. Smith, the Norfolk maltsters, similarly employed around sixty men; Pauls, between 120 and 150.[37] It was in the size of their salaried staff, however, that the greatest differences were evident. Barnard noted a dozen clerks plus the cashier at Baird's Glasgow maltings,[38] whereas Sandars relied upon two travellers and two clerks who ran the Gainsborough office. The appointment in 1889 of a general manager at a salary of £350 a year was a short-lived affair; besides an obvious clash of personalities, there was simply insufficient work to justify the post. His replacement was employed at a mere £120 a year.[39]

In comparison with most brewery companies, salaries were modest. The younger generation of the Pauls, Russell, Hugh and Stuart, who joined the company in the 1890s, received £150 a year at age twenty, rising to £400 five years later.[40] Typically, in 1881 James Garnham, one of the Ipswich clerks, was paid £114 per annum, while the general manager, Charles Raffe, received £300 (plus a £10 Christmas box), rising to £360 by the time of his retirement twenty years later. It was the travellers, upon whom much of the company's success depended, who were the elite of the staff. One of the company's first (and most valued) representatives, Robert Thompson, was paid £400 a year in 1899 plus a Christmas bonus of £100 'as Extra Good Year'. By the early 1900s, most received £300 plus commission, although the amount varied according to the importance of the territory: F. R. Harris received £600, while Douglas Smith, appointed to cover the north east, only got £200 plus railway fares and 3s. a day expenses.[41] Many members of staff received bonuses, depending on merit and the state of the company's profits, and there were also numerous gifts, such as the £50 paid to F. R. Harris, 'on account of illness of wife and child', followed by £54 5s. 4d. to settle the doctor's bill.[42] Pauls' most important benefit, and the one which underlines their deep commitment to workers' welfare, was the staff superannuation fund. Set up in 1908, this pioneering scheme was comparable to those of

---

[37] Estimated from a total wage bill of £4439; R. & W. Paul, Cost Accounts; Owen, *Greatest Brewery*, p. 77; A. Barnard, *The Noted Breweries of Great Britain and Ireland*, ii (London, 1889–1891), p. 483; Manning, 'Great Ryburgh Maltings', p. 18.

[38] Barnard, *Noted Breweries*, ii, p. 483.

[39] Letters to James Edwards, 7 March 1889, 15 July 1889, 15 March 1890, 2 Sandars 2/2.

[40] Subsequently, as directors, 'arrangements' were agreed with their respective fathers, Ledger 'B' Revenue.

[41] Private Ledger; Ledger 'B' Revenue; B. A. Holderness, 'Pauls of Ipswich' (1980), chapter 10, pp. 15.

[42] December 1909 and 1910; Salaries Ledger, 1899–1925.

such nationally known companies as Cadburys, providing a pension at the age of sixty of at least three-fifths of final salary. Sixty-one members joined immediately; by 1914 there were 119.[43] On the one hand, Pauls' standards were exacting and the demands made of staff considerable but, on the other, the rewards guaranteed a comfortable middle-class standard of living and security of employment. Not surprisingly, posts were keenly sought and long service, often extending to forty or fifty years and continuing from one generation to another, was a marked feature of the company.

A discussion of malt prices faces several problems. While Truman's records provide an exceptional series of malt prices from the 1740s to 1914, no complete series of *maltsters'* prices has survived before the twentieth century.[44] Frequently, sales were recorded in ledgers simply by the coloured sack 'ties' traditionally used to distinguish between different malts and contracts.[45] Market reports quoted prices for 'Norfolk Pale' and 'Hertfordshire Brown', while from the 1860s the *Brewers' Journal* listed the prices of English, Scotch and Saale, the special amber, crystal and roasted malts, and distinguished between 'old' and 'new' season's malt. Twenty years later, the range was extended to include Smyrna, Ouchak, Indian and Californian malts. While this underlined the growing range of malts produced, it failed to provide an accurate guide to the prices at which most malt was sold. As John Taylor had told the Select Committee on Public Breweries many years earlier: 'Nobody knows the prices of malt but those houses to whom we sell. The *County Chronicle* [price series] has nothing in the world to do with the prices of the malt ... I sell'.[46] At the heart of the problem was the secrecy which surrounded the negotiation of malt contracts. While most maltsters sold a range of malts of varying qualities, prices were never advertised. Typically, Swonnells, who specialised in roasted and crystal malts, offered three qualities of crystal, five of roasted (ranging from 28s. to 38s. a quarter), besides amber and two brown malts. The list of eleven prices, and the names of the 'special

[43] Employees joined at age twenty and contributions were paid equally by employees and company. In 1919 William Paul made a personal contribution of £3440 to bring the entitlement of older employees into line with those whose service was fully covered. Minutes of Superannuation Fund.

[44] See P. Mathias, *The Brewing Industry in England, 1700–1830* (Cambridge, 1959), p. 547, for Truman's average prices, 1741–1830; these are based not on average buying prices but the price of stocks at their annual valuation. Most malt was bought on contract or commissioned and therefore would not directly reflect market prices. *Parliamentary Papers* provide average prices, with a few omissions, between 1830 and 1880; the sales-maltsters, Lee & Grinling, from 1903 to 1948.

[45] One contract for Savill Brothers included: 600 quarters Saale (white tie) at 53s., 600 quarters Best English (plain tie) at 47s., 500 quarters Ouchac (red tie) at 43s., 500 quarters French (green tie) at 38s., 4000 quarters Pale (black tie) at 39s., 1500 quarters Coloured (string tie) at 39s., 4000 quarters coloured (yellow tie) at 36s. and 1000 quarters Coloured (blue tie) at 33s. Henry Ward & Sons, Sales Book, 2 January 1893, D/EWd B5, HRO.

[46] *Select Committee on Public Breweries, PP* (1819), v, p. 453.

firms' who received a discount of 6d. a quarter were known only to the directors and their agents.[47]

Securing contracts was the task of principals and, in bigger firms, their agents and travellers. Reputation and quality were critical. John Sandars, for instance, spent much of his time visiting and socialising with brewers, who were as much friends as customers. Similarly, agents and travellers cultivated the head brewers who in many companies controlled the purchase of malt. Good connections were invaluable: Sandars' Manchester agent, Herbert Foster, had previously owned the Swan Brewery at Ardwick,[48] while Frank Shutes, Pauls' northern salesman, was the son of Bass's head barley buyer. His brother, Leslie, subsequently became London salesman and another brother was second brewer for Greenall Whitley at St Helens.[49] Each contract was negotiated individually. Agents offered their samples and, within prescribed limits, agreed a price. But the extent to which not only prices but credit, delivery terms and discounts varied is evident from the sales ledgers of the Ware maltster, Henry Ward. Sometimes delivery times were specified; Morgans of Norwich drew 150 quarters a month, whereas in the case of Bass, Ratcliff & Gretton contracts were open-ended, with 'delivery to be at their option'.[50] Credit reflected both the size of contracts and the rating of customers. Thus terms for small quantities purchased by the Forrest Hill Brewery were 'cash one month', for the Welch Ale Company, cash on delivery, while a highly-rated customer, such as the London brewers Hoare & Company, received three months credit with 5 per cent discount for early payment.[51] Also notable was the general tightening of credit terms over the period. During the 1880s and 1890s, three to four months was the norm for trusted customers; by the early years of the new century one month was typical. By the end of the decade, discounts were offered for prompt payment.[52] Conversely, fewer contracts specified delivery times.

What is evident, both from published market prices and from Truman's records, is the underlying trend across the century. After the peak years at the end of the French Wars, when malt prices exceeded £5 a quarter, prices fell sharply then fluctuated quite markedly until the 1860s, when they

[47]   S. Swonnell & Son, Price List, 9 November 1913, PM.

[48]   A. Gall, *Manchester Breweries of Times Gone By* (Manchester, 1978–80), p. 3.

[49]   I am grateful to Bill Nelson of Pauls Malt for this information.

[50]   Henry Ward & Sons, Sales Book, 31 January 1884, 22 July 1908, D/E Wd., HRO.

[51]   Henry Ward & Sons, Sales Book, 7 February 1891, 7 March 1891, 10 February 1893, 5 December 1907, HRO.

[52]   Throughout the period, Henry Ward's main customer was Saville Brothers Limited, which every year purchased around 12–13,000 quarters of malt. For years they were given four months credit from delivery. By the season of 1909–10, they were offered 4 per cent discount for cash. After the outbreak of war, when the demand for malt exceeded supply, their terms were cash, plus 5 per cent interest on any malt not delivered by the following 31 December. 1 January 1885, 1 January 1910, 17 April 1916. B5, D/E Wd, HRO.

stabilised around £3 a quarter.[53] Then, from the 1880s, prices collapsed, a function both of falling barley prices and of the greater use of malt adjuncts. Trumans, for example, paid an average 38s. 5d. a quarter in 1880–89 and 31s. 1d. a decade later. Only from 1909 was there a sustained recovery; even then, prices never exceeded £2 per quarter before the outbreak of the First World War.[54]

Were such trends indicative of falling profits across the century? Actually, there is much to suggest the *early* period was one of hardship. Most witnesses to the 1835 Excise Inquiry emphasised low returns and poor profits – with malt sold at less than cost price. Henry Aldrich of Ipswich bemoaned that:

> For the whole of last season, there were one third of the malthouses in our town not put to work ... one building which cost £2500 only a few years ago has been taken down, as well as others.[55]

These were years of deep depression in rural Suffolk. The surge in malting licences after the 1830 Beer Act against a background of slowly growing beer output and falling malt prices all suggest intense competition in the industry.[56] Witnesses to the Select Committee on the Malt Tax in 1867 still did not think malting a good trade (although poor weather made 1867 a difficult year). Yet, in these middle decades of the century, it is harder to reconcile the rising demand for malt as beer output rapidly increased with this pessimistic picture (see Table 2.1). While there is some insight into profits, evidence remains fragmented and unclear, not least because of the natural caution of witnesses intent on presenting their case to its best advantage. James Everitt reckoned his profit ranged from 10d. to 2s. 10d. a quarter (based on a selling price of 66–68s.), depending on credit or cash discounts. How precise these figures were is questionable because, in common with most witnesses, he allowed for a malting 'increase' (or out-turn) of 4 per cent, which he acknowledged could in reality be a 'decrease'. Generally, 2s. 6d. a quarter was considered 'acceptable' (although it is unclear whether this relates only to the 'bad' year of 1867).[57] Yet, as shown in John Sandars' accounts, some maltsters clearly exceeded these margins (Table 5.4).

---

[53] The peak year was 1813; Mathias quotes 105s. 7d. paid by the London brewers Meux Reid. Official prices fluctuated more than those of Trumans, indicating the greater price control achieved by commission and contract buying. P. Mathias, *Brewing Industry*, p. 471.

[54] See Appendix 3.

[55] The following spring several maltings in the town were also offered for sale or demolition. *Commission of Excise Inquiry, PP* (1835), xxxi, pp. 140–47, 392; *Ipswich Journal*, 21 May 1836.

[56] In 1827, 10,494 malting licences were issued in England and Wales; by 1830 numbers had fallen to 8993 but the following year increased to 10,376. Licences peaked in 1833 at 10,598 then fell steadily thereafter. G. B. Wilson, *Alcohol and the Nation* (London, 1940), pp. 385–86.

[57] *Select Committee on the Malt Tax, PP* (1867–68), ix, pp. 303–9.

Table 5.4

John E. Sandars, total production of malt, net profit and average profit per quarter, 1867–85

Year	Malt produced (quarters)	Net profit (£)	Average profit per (s. d.)	
1867	14,703	3699	5	0
1868	15,856	4526	5	8½
1869	19,039	4689	4	11
1870	21,259	Loss – bad debts		
1871	22,715	3785	3	4
1872	30,228	3880	2	7
1873	30,956	7790	5	0½
1874	33,163	3737	2	3
1875	32,670	5431	3	4
1876	26,120	3119	2	4
1877	29,073	5924	4	1
1878	31,011	5559	3	7
1879	38,577	8239	4	3
1880	30,486	9002	5	10
1881	33,455	6486	4	8
1882	27,629	4216	3	1
1883	31,740	5092	3	2½
1884	32,488	5237	3	3
1885	40,830	6431	3	2

Source: Lincoln Archives, 2 Sandars 2/4/6.

In this case, the difference is explained in terms of revenue, a reflection of Sandars' fine reputation. During the season of 1866–67, most malt sold for between 68s. and 73s. per quarter, but 'fine malt' fetched 78s. 0d. and 'extra fine' 80s. a quarter. The following year, the bulk of Sandars' sales ranged between 70s. 6d. and 74s. 8d. per quarter. Even so, Sandars' profits fluctuated sharply from year to year. On the one hand, this reflected specific problems: bad debts in 1870 and again two years later, while the loss of several rented kilns in 1876 affected both output and profits.[58] On the other, the improved margins the following year reflected the fine quality of the domestic harvest and underlined the constant problems faced by all malt-sters: the oscillations in the quality of barley (which in turn determined the yield) and in its price. It was these factors, more than any other, which explain the sharp *annual* fluctuations in profits which were such a marked feature of the industry and probably account for much contemporary

[58] 2 Sandars 4/4/6, Lincoln Archives; Sales Ledger, Pauls Malt.

pessimism.[59] Equally important was the downward *trend* in profits in the years after 1880. The sudden fall in the demand for malt, as beer output declined and brewers turned increasingly to malt adjuncts, left the industry with a legacy of excess capacity and fierce competition.

From the 1880s maltsters' records provide a clearer picture of the profits achieved. There remain a number of pitfalls for the unwary historian, not least the many variations in accounting practice; and the difficulty in defining consistent measures of profitability.[60] While any conclusions must be viewed with caution, the evidence suggests that brewers, facing falling consumption and, after 1900, increasing duties, squeezed profit margins.

The best surviving profit series, which runs from 1880 to 1951, is that of the small Fakenham maltster Richard Dewing. From 1837 until the 1960s, the Dewings made malt on commission for Truman, Hanbury & Buxton. To some degree they were therefore insulated against sharp fluctuations in demand. Indeed, there is little doubt that without the support of this major brewer, the business would not have survived the adverse climate after 1900. Nevertheless, the pattern of profits provides some guide to the changing fortunes facing the malting industry. In 1871–75 an annual average of 7000 quarters of malt were commissioned by Trumans, rising in 1876 to a peak of 9181 quarters. By 1881–85 the average had fallen to 4535 quarters. It recovered slowly by the end of the century and then, between 1906–10, declined to a low of 3775 quarters.[61] Throughout the period the commission fee of 5s. a quarter remained unchanged, so that the firm's net profits closely mirrored production, declining from an average £1179 between 1881–85 to £866 a decade later; then recovering slowly only to slump to an average £547 between 1906 and 1910. In other cases, production was maintained but only at the expense of profit margins. Henry Ward's sales averaged 12,357 quarters in 1881–85, more than doubled to 26,086 quarters in 1896–1900, then averaged 32,362 quarters throughout the following decade. A slight decline between 1910–12 was followed by record sales of over 36,000 quarters during the last pre-war season.[62] In contrast, profits followed a downward trend: declining from an annual average of £5576 in 1896–1900 to £5272 between 1906–10 and falling to £2910 the following year. Profit

---

[59] Despite the wider choice of barleys after 1880 and depressed prices, the *Brewers' Gazette* thought annual fluctuations in profits undermined public confidence in malting companies and was one reason why so few sought public flotations. *Brewers' Gazette*, 11 April 1907.

[60] See R. Church, B. Baldwin and B. Berry, 'Accounting for Profitability at the Consett Iron Company before 1914: Measurement, Sources and Uses', *Economic History Review*, 47 (1994), pp. 703–24, for some of the problems.

[61] Unfortunately there is a break in Truman's barley records after 1877. It is likely that the quantity commissioned remained the same or continued to increase up to the end of the decade. The figures after 1880 are calculated from the records of Richard Dewing, Truman Hanbury & Buxton, Stock Book, Fakenham, and Account Book, FG 190.991 and FG 189.991, Fakenham Gasworks Museum.

[62] Henry Ward & Sons, Sales Book, 1880–1919, D/EWd B5, HRO.

The British Malting Industry

margins, which peaked at 4s. 10d. per quarter in 1896 and reached a low of 2s. 2¼d. in 1911, were clearly being squeezed.[63] Several of the larger companies, notably those which had invested heavily in fixed capital, such as Pauls, Sandars and Taylors, similarly sustained or increased production. Lancaster thought this was often at the expense of profit margins and Table 5.5 tends to confirm this suggestion.[64]

Table 5.5

Average profit per quarter of selected malting companies, 1899–1913
(shillings and pence)

	Henry Ward		S. Swonnell		R. & W. Paul		H. A. & D. Taylor	
	s.	d.	s.	d.	s.	d.	s.	d.
1899	3	7¼	3	5	—		1	10
1900	4	4¾	3	4½	—		2	5¾
1901	2	7½	2	1	—		1	6½
1902	4	1¾	2	2¼	—		2	6
1903	4	2¼	2	10¼	—		1	7
1904	4	7¼	2	11¼	—		2	1
1905	3	6	2	3¾	—			
1906	2	6¾	1	11	2	5¼	—	
1907	4	1¼	1	7½	3	7¼	—	
1908	3	6		0½	1	11	—	
1909	3	6¼	1	10	2	3	—	
1910	2	4¾	2	6¼	2	4¼	—	
1911	2	2¼	3	5¾	2	0	—	
1912	3	9½		1	3	9¾	—	
1913	3	6¾		0¾	2	8	—	

Source: Henry Ward & Sons, Sales Book and Statements of accounts, D/EWd B1, B4 and B5, HRO; S. Swonnell & Son, Miscellaneous Papers; R. & W. Paul, Accounts; and H. A. & D. Taylor, Balance Books. All PM.

Some further insight into the profitability of the sector may be gained from an analysis of the ordinary dividends paid by fourteen representative companies between 1895 and 1913 (see Table 5.6). The unweighted annual average fell from 9.42 per cent in 1895–98 to 5.00 per cent in 1909–13, while the weighted average (by ordinary share capital), reflecting the strength of the larger companies, fell less steeply, from 9.85 per cent to 7.11 per cent.

---

[63] Henry Ward & Sons, Summaries of Annual Accounts, 1895–1913, and Annual Statements of Accounts, 1898–1915, D/EWd B1 and B4, HRO.

[64] Lancaster, 'Effects on Increased Beer Duty', p. 11. These figures also compare unfavourably with the profit per quarter earned before the 1880s by John Sandars, see p. 130.

Table 5.6

Company profitability (ordinary dividends, per cent), 1895–1913
(annual averages)

Company	Ordinary dividends (per cent)			
	1895–98	*1899–1903*	*1904–08*	*1909–13*
Hugh Baird	12.50	7.90	5.90	3.20
F. & G. Smith	10.00	7.00	3.90	5.60
R. & W. Paul	10.06	9.35	11.40	16.45
Thomas Bernard	7.13	7.00	3.30	3.60
H. A. & D. Taylor	12.22 [2]	10.46	7.00	5.60
J. Pidcock	9.00	10.00	6.33	6.00
Cardiff Malting Company	5.00	—	6.25	3.30
J. & C. H. Evans	—	7.50	0	0
S. Swonnell & Son	—	7.40	4.50	4.00
E. Bailey & Son	—	9.50	9.90	8.40
M. Sanderson & Son	—	5.80	0.50	0.50
W. J. Robson	—	5.17	4.10	5.90
14 Company av. (unweighted) [1]	9.42	7.91	5.49	5.00
14 Company av. (weighted) [1]	9.85	8.13	6.08	7.11

Notes:
[1] See Appendix 9 for full sample details.
[2] Calculations from 1895–1901 based on profits paid on partners capital as proxy for ordinary dividends.
Source: See Appendix 9.

These conclusions must be viewed with caution for, at best, dividends represent an imperfect measure of profitability. The practice of financing dividends from capital reserves, in particular, was far from uncommon.[65] In 1908, for example, Bairds of Glasgow saw net profits, which during the previous five years had averaged £9717, fall to £1919. They transferred £5000 from reserves to write down investments, cover the dividend on preference shares and a dividend of 2½ per cent on the ordinary shares.[66] This, however, was the exception. That year, when uncertainty over the Licensing Bill overshadowed the entire drinks trade, no fewer than four of the sample companies passed dividends. Yet over the long term, almost all maintained a steady stream of income to shareholders, indicating they were soundly financed.[67] A second measure, the return on capital employed, illustrates a trend very similar to that of the distribution of dividends (see

[65] R. Church et al., 'Accounting for Profitability', pp. 709–10.
[66] *Brewing Trade Review*, 1 December 1908.
[67] See Appendix 9.

Table 5.7).[68] It is notable that these returns were well below the 8–12½ per cent suggested by the witnesses in 1867, again reinforcing the impression of falling profits after 1880.[69]

Table 5.7

Company profitability (return on capital employed, per cent),
1895–1913 (annual averages)

Company	1895–98	1899–1903	1904–08	1909–13
R. & W. Paul	8.88	6.80	7.36	8.90
J. Pidcock & Company	5.51	7.56	3.31	4.33
S. Swonnell & Son	—	7.39	6.63	6.99
W. J. Robson	—	7.08	5.61	7.53

Source: Company Accounts and Directors' Minutes.

The exception, both in terms of dividends and return on capital, was Pauls. Apart from a slight decline in 1899–1903, the company went from strength to strength. Pre-tax profits, which increased from an annual average of £29,328 in 1895–98 to £58,349 in 1909–13, were equally buoyant. This clearly reflected both the diversity and the capable, far-sighted management underpinning the rapid expansion of the enterprise. Was it also evidence of financial policies which, in the view of Alfred Chandler, were symptomatic of the weaknesses of British family firms? According to Chandler, their goal was 'to provide a steady flow of cash to owners who were also managers'.[70] Unlike American managerial firms, they preferred short-term income – demonstrated by a pattern of high and stable dividends – to long-run asset growth. Pauls indeed seems a classic example of Chandler's thesis. Every year, 5 per cent of net profits were allocated to reserves. Interest on the 6 per cent preference shares accounted for £3000 and a 6 per cent ordinary dividend, a further £12,000. Of the remainder, half was distributed as a bonus on the ordinary shares and the other half divided equally between the joint-managing directors, Robert and William Paul. In 1902, for example, 72.7 per cent of the pre-tax profit of £29,704 was paid in dividends; 95 per cent when the additional bonus to Robert and William is included – a ratio

[68] Return on capital employed represents net profits as a percentage of capital. See below, Appendix 8 for fuller definitions. Again, the partnership of Henry Ward of Ware fared comparatively well, achieving a return on capital of 15.83 per cent, 15.26 per cent and 11.63 per cent over the same periods. Comparisons are difficult because in some cases information is taken from directors' minutes or ledgers which do not provide a complete picture of the firm's capital structure.

[69] Manning Prentice put his return on capital as high as 15–20 per cent. These estimates were based on a capital investment of £10–15,000 to produce 10,000 quarters of malt; *Select Committee on the Malt Tax, PP* (1867–68), ix, pp. 282–26.

[70] A. D. Chandler, Jr, *Scale and Scope: The Dynamics of Industrial Capitalism* (Cambridge, Massachusetts, 1990), p. 390.

of dividends to earnings on a par with the examples cited by Chandler.[71] However, from the company's private ledgers it is evident that the amounts appropriated were reloaned to the company at an interest of between 4 and 5 per cent. Admittedly, this approach guaranteed greater financial security for the Paul family. Yet retained profits were clearly central to financial policy. Thus in 1902, of the £226,220 shown on the balance sheet under 'sundry creditors', only £26,684 was attributable to 'Bills Payable'. Of the remainder, which 'practically represents the working capital of the company', £66,000 came from overdrafts, £41,000 from two substantial mortgages, while £82,570 was lent by Robert and William. An additional £9775 from small loans brought the family contribution up to 46 per cent of total borrowing.[72] As the scale of business increased, the company steadily raised its borrowing powers with the Capital and Counties Bank, but retained dividends and family funds remained major sources of capital for many years. Thus, during the course of 1914, £7876 was paid as interest on family loans. Taking an average of 4½ per cent as the rate of interest, this implies a principal of over £175,000, approximately 70 per cent of the 'sundry creditors' shown on the balance sheet. There can be little doubt that growth took precedence over short-term income.

Most malting firms were similarly concerned with survival. This was evident even among the less successful firms. Throughout this period, for instance, Michael Sanderson & Son paid the price for belated modernisation. In turn, its chairman, Henry Figgis, blamed the cost of coal and wages, poor harvests and the depression in brewing. Finally in 1908 he despaired of the 'intense competition which prevailed amongst Maltsters to secure business at any cost. It really looks', he concluded, 'as if it will become a question of the survival of the fittest'.[73] In order to restore the company's finances, the managing director, Michael Sanderson, made a gift of the 3000 £10 ordinary shares he and his deceased brother had a decade earlier received on the sale of their business to the public. Subsequent dividends were credited to the company.[74] Elsewhere, companies like W. J. Robson, F. & G. Smith, Taylors and Pidcocks hardly faltered through these testing years; all paid modest dividends and built up healthy reserves. For Bairds, the problems of 1908–10 proved but a temporary setback. It is difficult to generalise across the industry but, among the leading companies, there is little evidence to support Chandler's thesis.

Were contemporaries justified in their belief that malting was not a prosperous trade? Of course, fortunes varied widely. The brewing journals

---

[71] Ibid., p. 390 n. 161.

[72] R. & W. Paul Limited, Balance Sheet and Auditors' Report, Private Ledgers.

[73] Michael Sanderson & Son, Directors' Minutes, 16 December 1901, 17 December 1903, 18 December 1908.

[74] Ibid., 18 December 1907; Duncan's *Manual of British and Foreign Brewery Companies* (1910), p. 259.

and local press record those who after a lifetime's endeavour faced bank-ruptcy or whose estates could be counted in hundreds, not thousands, of pounds.[75] Many more left only a modest fortune, such as Charles Evans (1849–1929), chairman of the troubled firm of J. & C. H. Evans, whose estate was valued at under £11,000.[76] Nevertheless, others achieved a level of wealth which, by the standards of the day was quite substantial: John Crisp (1840–1917), Robert Free (d. 1928), Henry Ward (1832–1908) and Henry Taylor (1855–1935) all left around £100,000; George Branston (1812–93) of Newark and Jesse Gough (1831–1900) of Bury St Edmunds £150,000.[77] Many served as aldermen, mayors and magistrates, administered local charities and were mainstays of churches and chapels. Many farmed and enjoyed a range of country pursuits. A few, like George Robson, owned large estates. George Sandars, Thomas Earp and Henry Page-Croft were Members of Parliament; and, for their services to malting, Edmund Barnard received a knighthood and William Gilstrap a baronetcy. In some cases, success was based on the progress of preceding generations: John Sandars and Henry Page were as well connected as the brewers they served. The latter left in excess of one million pounds on his death in 1894. There were also self-made men such as Sir William Gilstrap (1816–96), Robert Paul (1844–1909) and William Paul (1850–1928), who from modest beginnings created impressive fortunes. Sir William purchased the Fornham Park estate near Bury St Edmunds, became High Sheriff of Suffolk and divided his time between his shoot and travelling in Europe. Like the Pauls, he gave unstintingly to his native town.[78] The latter maintained their commitment to business, Robert leaving an estate valued in excess of £300,000 and William £700,000.[79] These were the exceptions. If their fortunes failed to match those of the elite brewers, they are nevertheless not compatible with the pessimistic picture which pervades contemporary literature.

[75] Although bankruptcy was not common in malting, significant cases include Dawber & Gentel (Lincoln), with liabilities over £100,000; James & Henry Randell (Randells Maltsters Limited, Grays), over £75,000; Richard Wilson & Son (Shropshire), £52,682; *Brewers' Journal*, 15 August 1873, 15 January 1910, 15 July 1919.

[76] Ibid., 15 July 1929.

[77] Ibid., 15 March 1901, 15 January 1929, 15 December 1935; *Brewing Trade Review*, 1 December 1908, 1 December 1917.

[78] *Newark Advertiser*, 19 February 1896.

[79] *Brewers' Journal*, 15 February 1909, 15 April 1928, 11 February 1928; Will of William Paul, proved 16 May 1928, Somerset House.

6

War and Depression, 1914–1945

The Great War had an enormous impact on the British malting industry. Wide-ranging government controls quickly brought production to a standstill while, even more seriously, proposals to nationalise the brewing industry threatened the sector's long-term survival. The Maltsters' Association of Great Britain, refounded after a lapse of almost forty years, provided a much-needed industry voice whose full value was to be realised in the difficult years ahead. The brief post-war boom quickly gave way to deep depression: 'an acid test' in the graphic words of Charles Sutcliffe – 'a fight for the survival of the fittest'.[1] The Second World War brought renewed prosperity for those who had weathered the storm. It also, however, created its own problems which finally swept away many of the traditions and practices which for so long had characterised the malting industry.

Although during the course of the First World War government controls were imposed on most sectors of the British economy, few experienced such all-embracing intervention as brewing and malting.[2] First, in November 1914, beer duty was increased from 7s. 9d. to 23s. per standard barrel (i.e. of 1055° gravity); by April 1920 it stood at £5, almost thirteen times the 1913 level. Secondly, steps were taken to reduce the brewers' demand for raw materials. Beer production was limited, in December 1916 to 70 per cent of the 1913–14 output of 36.2 million standard barrels and by the following March to 28 per cent, a mere 10 million standard barrels.[3] In addition, the strength of beer brewed and its price were restricted, with the aptly named 'Government Ale' (beer of under 1036° gravity) becoming the standard beverage after

---

[1] C. E. Sutcliffe, *Brewery Record*, 7 (July 1928), p. 9.

[2] For a detailed discussion of the war-time controls imposed on the brewing industry, see T. R. Gourvish and R. G. Wilson, *The British Brewing Industry, 1830–1980* (Cambridge, 1994), chapter 8; G. B. Wilson, *Alcohol and the Nation* (London, 1940), pp. 127–133; D. H. Aldcroft, 'Control of the Liquor Trade in Great Britain, 1914–21', in W. H. Chaloner and B. M. Ratcliffe (eds), *Trade and Transport: Essays in Economic History in Honour of T. S. Willan* (Manchester, 1977), pp. 242–57; J. Turner, 'State Purchase of the Liquor Trade in the First World War', *Historical Journal*, 23 (1980), pp. 589–615; W. Beveridge, *British Food Control* (Oxford, 1928); and L. M. Barnett, *British Food Policy during the First World War* (London, 1985).

[3] This reduction was never achieved. Actual output for 1917–18 was 13.8 million standard barrels, additional output being sanctioned for military canteens and as a response to industrial unrest. The standard barrelage fell to 12.9 m. barrels in the year ending March 1919, but because of reductions in gravity, 23.3 million bulk (i.e. selling) barrels were produced. Gourvish and Wilson, *British Brewing Industry*, p. 320.

1917. Thirdly, the supply of raw materials, barley, malt and hops, was controlled. Other measures, however, culminating in proposals to nationalise the brewing industry, were not dictated simply by the demands of war, for Lloyd George perceived in alcohol an even more deadly foe than Germany.[4] Thus in June 1915 the Central Control Board (Liquor Trade) was established to secure state control over the sale and supply of intoxicating liquor. Opening hours of public houses were cut and, in January 1916, after reports of drunkenness in the key munitions area of Carlisle, the town's breweries and public houses were taken into public ownership.[5] In 1915 and again two years later, advisory committees were appointed to examine the feasibility of state purchase of the entire UK liquor trade. Their final reports, published in 1918, revealed no valid barriers to nationalisation. But escalating costs, estimated by 1920 at £1000 million, and a powerful brewing lobby, ensured that Lloyd George was not to achieve his goal.[6]

If Britain's brewers saw the First World War as 'an unqualified misfortune',[7] the position of the malting industry was critical. Lancaster reckoned the initial increases in beer duty alone would cost the industry some £350,000 in lost profits and interest while leaving maltings to the value of £3 million redundant.[8] The control of raw materials was equally serious. On average the brewing industry used 1,500,000 tons of barley, maize and rice annually. The 1916 restriction on beer output, which aimed to save 150,000 tons of imports, therefore made only a minimal contribution.[9] With German submarines exacting a growing toll on cereal imports, further measures to protect bread supplies were inevitable. In October 1916, the Wheat Commission took effective control of buying, selling and distributing all cereals and, subsequently, the import of maize, rice and barley. The following spring maximum prices were fixed for home-grown barley.[10] From January 1917 the Food Controller, Lord Devonport, restricted malting itself. Maltsters

---

[4] 'We are fighting Germany, Austria and Drink; as far as I can see, the greatest of these three deadly foes is Drink', David Lloyd George, speech at Bangor, 28 February 1915; see *Brewers' Journal*, 15 March 1918.

[5] Weekday opening hours were reduced from 16–17 hours to 5½ hours, with a compulsory afternoon break and evening closing at 9–9.30 p.m. Wilson, *Alcohol*, p. 130.

[6] Aldcroft, 'Control of the Liquor Trade', p. 249.

[7] Gourvish and Wilson, *British Brewing Industry*, p. 317.

[8] Lancaster based his calculations on a 35 per cent reduction in malt consumption from the 62 million quarters produced in 1913 and an estimate of £10 million for the fixed capital of the UK malt trade. H. Lancaster, 'The Probable Effect on the Increased Beer Duty on the Malt Trade of the United Kingdom', *Brewing Trade Review*, January 1915, pp. 11–12.

[9] Barley imports alone averaged 978,500 tons in 1912–14, *Brewing Trade Review*, 1 November 1915.

[10] Maximum prices for the 1916 crop were set at 65s. per quarter, for the 1917 crop at 62s. 9d. per quarter and for 1918 at 67s. per quarter. Because malting required good quality barley, maltsters were permitted to pay up to 5s. 3d. per 448lbs above the standard price. Grain (Prices) Orders, 16 April and 14 August 1917, 31 August 1918; Maize, Barley and Oats Restriction Order, 2 May 1917.

were first requested to make returns of all stocks of malt and barley and their steeping capacity; then, under the Malt (Restriction) Order of 20 February, further malting was prohibited.[11] Distilling of raw spirits was stopped and all barley stocks were requisitioned. Even before the drastic restriction of beer output to ten million barrels, itself reducing the demand for malt to a mere two million quarters, the malting industry was at a standstill.

Maltsters were, of course, deeply concerned about the proposed nationalisation of brewing. In common with many brewers, they were not opposed to state purchase provided compensation was adequate but, like the other allied trades, were excluded from the proposed schemes.[12] Given that brewery maltings could produce four million quarters of malt annually (double the amount apportioned for war-time beer production), any permanent restriction of beer output meant that state-owned maltings would supply the total demand for malt.[13] Without compensation, sales-maltsters would lose their livelihood and face financial ruin.

Not surprisingly, the combination of these problems turned maltsters' thoughts towards collective action. Since its formation in 1907 most maltsters had been members of the Allied Brewery Traders' Association. Following the first malting restriction, however, they appointed their own committee and asked the Food Controller to set up a Malt Clearing House to handle the distribution of stocks. A joint committee of brewers and maltsters was appointed and a deputation to the Prime Minister, Lloyd George, secured the promise that if the state purchased the brewing industry, the maltsters' case would be considered.[14] On 14 May 1917 Edmund Barnard, a leading Hertfordshire maltster, addressed the representatives of over ninety malting companies. Their industry, he told his audience, was under grave threat and the time had come to establish an independent trade association.[15] The

[11] Regulation 2F of DORA (Defence of the Realm Act), Return of Malt Stocks (26 January), Brewers (Malt Purchases) Order 1917 (3 February), Malt (Restriction) Order 1917 (20 February) and Malt (Restriction) No. 2 Order 1917 (12 April).

[12] The *Brewers' Journal* thought that 'The position of the Allied Trades appears not to have received from the Government the attention it warrants'. Despite a membership of nearly 2000 firms which to some extent were dependent on the brewing industry, their request for a representative on the Home Office committee, which included brewing representatives, was ignored. *Brewers' Journal*, 15 April 1917; Gourvish and Wilson, *Brewing Industry*, p. 328 n. 42.

[13] Statement of the Maltsters' Association of Great Britain, July 1917.

[14] The committee comprised the following brewing representatives: J. Gretton (Bass, Ratcliff & Gretton), T. S. Manning (Southdown & East Grinstead Breweries), W. Hall Walker (Peter Walker & Sons), James Younger (George Younger & Sons) and E. S. Beaven (Guinness's barley consultant and maltster); and for the malting industry, H. D. Cherry-Downes (Gilstrap Earp & Company), R. V. Reid (Hugh Baird & Sons), J. D. Sandars (Sandars & Company), Edward Sutcliffe (Sutcliffes) and H. Stanley Taylor (James D. Taylor & Sons), Hon. Secretary. MAGB, Minutes of Executive Committee, 28 February, 16 April 1917.

[15] MAGB, Minutes of Executive Committee, 14 May 1917.

Maltsters' Association had first been formed in 1827, when the burden of excise regulations weighed so heavily upon the industry.[16] Little is known about its work and it appears to have lapsed in 1880 when the malt tax was repealed. Now, support for its refoundation was overwhelming; within a year 226 companies had affiliated, encompassing all but a tiny minority of the trade and indicating the insecurity of sales-maltsters at this time.[17]

How effective was the Association in protecting its members' interests? With regard to state purchase, the advantage of having an official voice was soon apparent. In accordance with Lloyd George's promise, each of the three advisory committees appointed in June to examine the financial aspects of the question listened to representatives of the Association. Its secretary, Edmund Barnard, in his evidence to the English committee, stressed the unique position of the industry, maintaining that 'we stand alone'.[18] He argued that the state should therefore acquire the assets of the malting industry in conjunction with those of brewing, suggesting a figure of £6 million as fair compensation.[19] Although the final reports of the three committees (with the exception of the Scottish one) recommended that maltsters should be excluded from purchase and compensation, they agreed that they were a 'special' case and proposed that for a given period the government should supply its needs from state-owned maltings and those of sales-maltsters in the same ratio as at nationalisation.[20]

While the threat of state purchase failed to materialise, the Association was also instrumental in alleviating many of the restrictions which continued to plague the industry. Several key members were drafted into the Ministry of Food: Charles Sutcliffe, E. S. Beaven and H. Stanley Taylor (secretary of the Malt Clearing House Committee) were all members of the Control Committee for Brewing Materials; Owen Wightman served on the Home Cereals, Brewing and Distilling branch of the Wheat Commission, while Hugh Paul was appointed honorary Commercial Private Secretary to the Food Controller, Lord Devonport, and his successor, Lord Rhondda. Hugh Paul subsequently became a member of the Royal Commission on Wheat

---

16 See Chapter 1, p. 29.

17 After six months 203 companies had affiliated to the Association. By September 1918 it was thought that only thirteen small firms were not members.

18 *Liquor Trade Finance (England and Wales) Committee, PP* (1917–18), xxvi, Minutes of Evidence, pp. 15–22.

19 Statement of the Maltsters' Association of Great Britain, July 1917. A value of £5,191,000 was estimated for England and Wales, £407,000 for Scotland and £402,000 for Ireland. Malting buildings accounted for £3,600,000, machinery £400,000, directors and technical staff £200,000 and goodwill £1,800,000. The latter was calculated on five years' purchase of the average net profits of sales-maltsters (2s. per quarter on 3.6 million quarters) between 1901–14.

20 The Irish committee went so far as to suggest that if no such scheme could be agreed, then, as a matter of equity, the sales-maltsters should be purchased upon the basis of the value of their buildings, machinery, stock and goodwill. *Report on Proposals for State Purchase of the Licensed Liquor Trade: Reports of the English, Scottish and Irish Committees, PP* (1918), xi, p. 72.

Supplies and Chairman of the Bread Committee.[21] The Brewers' Society was also lobbied, for one of the main concerns of the Association, given that any resumption of malting would be strictly limited, was the *balance* of production between sales- and brewer-maltsters. The society was fully supportive and throughout the summer of 1917 Edmund Barnard worked closely with John Gretton (chairman of Bass, Ratcliff & Gretton) in formulating a joint proposal regulating malting fees and production quotas.[22] Unfortunately, the York-shire brewers refused to ratify the agreement.[23] The problem was effectively resolved by Hugh Paul in his role as Private Secretary to Lord Rhondda. Under his guidance, a system of malting licences, based on average output during 1914–16 (thus allowing each company to make an equivalent pro-portion of the limited output), was approved and in place by the autumn. The season was again cut short in February, mainly to satisfy the American Food Administrator, Herbert Hoover, and to ensure the release of grain exports. But the licensing system, together with the support of their cus-tomers, enabled sales-maltsters to deliver around 40 per cent of their 1914–16 average.[24] In contrast, Bass, Ratcliff & Gretton demonstrated their support by reducing their Burton output to one-third of its pre-war level, and that at Sleaford to a mere quarter, and by purchasing malt from a number of independent traders and commission maltsters.[25]

The problems caused by the shortage of labour proved more intractable. As early as January 1916, the *Brewing Trade Review* thought it impossible to make even the limited output sanctioned by government.[26] Many companies extended malting into the summer, but when the following season ended abruptly more men enlisted or found essential war work so that by the

[21] Food Files, ii and xii, Beveridge Papers, BLPES; E. F. Taylor, 'History of the Formation and Development of Associated British Maltsters Limited, 1928–78' (typescript, 1978), p. 11.

[22] The agreement provided for sales-maltsters to make two-thirds of any quota; to cover increased unit costs of production, commission fees were to be fixed at 10s. per quarter plus up to 2s. for profit and 1s. for kiln drying, with margins for sale-malting determined by adding a further 6d. a quarter for each month from the date of contract. The Malt Clearing House Committee also fixed maximum malt prices for season of 1917–18. MAGB, Minutes of Executive Committee, 19 June, 3 and 5 July 1917; Brewers' Society Minute Book, 5, 9 July 1917; *Brewers' Journal*, 15 May 1918.

[23] The Brewers' Society 'owing to the ... precarious position of the malting trade', continued to urge their members to order as much of their malt as possible from sales-maltsters, Brewers' Society Minute Book 5, 12 September 1917.

[24] Pauls sold 62,320 quarters of malt in 1917–18, against an average of 125,296 quarters in 1914–16; Lee & Grinling 11,098 quarters against 22,137. Some companies, like Pidcocks of Nottingham, were given extra quotas to make malt for the Navy and Army Canteen Board. R. & W. Paul, Cost Accounts; Lee & Grinling, Accounts; J. Pidcock & Company, Directors' Minutes, 17 September 1918, PM.

[25] C. C. Owen, *The Greatest Brewery in the World: A History of Bass, Ratcliff & Gretton* (Chesterfield, 1992), p. 147–48.

[26] The *Brewing Trade Review* estimated that with the available staff it would only be possible to make 60 per cent of normal output; working throughout the summer could increase production by a further 20 per cent. *Brewing Trade Review*, 1 January 1916.

resumption of malting in the autumn the situation had worsened.[27] Despite pressure for malting to be classed a reserved occupation, until the summer of 1918 skilled workers such as foremen and kilnmen were not exempted from national service.[28] The only solution therefore, as in many other sectors, was the employment of women. Unfortunately, there is little evidence to shed light on the numbers enlisted, but it is clear that most companies relied on women and a few elderly retainers to carry them through the war.[29] Generally, women were seen as effective workers, the manager of Michael Sanderson of Wakefield typically reporting that the twenty females working two maltings were 'proving satisfactory'.[30] When the government order allowing the use of female labour was revoked, in July 1919, the Maltsters' Association, with the support of the Brewers' Society, gained an extension of the order until the summer of 1920.[31]

Other aspects of deregulation soon followed the return to peace. Licences remained in force but were increased by a quarter in January 1919. Brewers were once more allowed to use flaked maize. Distilling was also resumed. On 1 March, the Royal Commission on Wheat Supplies decontrolled the purchase, sale and distribution of Californian and Chilean barleys. Restrictions on beer output ceased in July, although the average gravity of 1044° remained in force. This last measure, which meant that the demand for malt would not regain its pre-war level, revived fears about loss of market share to brewer-maltsters. A deputation to the Ministry of Food had already urged the retention of malt quotas as long as any restriction remained on beer production.[32] John Gretton was also approached.[33] Both thought that the continuation of any system during peacetime not only impractical but unwarranted and on 28 August all malt restrictions were revoked. Given that Pauls' sales during the following season recovered to 89 per cent of the 1914–16 average, while Lee & Grinlings' exceeded them, their conclusions would seem justified.

How did war affect the viability of malting firms? Almost certainly there were small ones unable to withstand the many pressures which ceased trading or sold their businesses. Nevertheless, somewhat paradoxically given the

---

27 MAGB, Minutes of Executive Committee, 26 November 1917.

28 Those exempt were foremen, kiln foremen or drier-men over thirty-eight years of age; carters, lorrymen or draymen over thirty-three years and other classes, including floormen, over forty-three years. Military Service (Exemptions) Order (No. 2) 1918; MAGB, Minutes of Executive Committee, 14 May, 1 July 1918.

29 See the plates in P. Stephens (ed.), *Newark: The Magic of Malt* (1993), pp. 13, 37 and 41; *Newark Advertiser*, 3 February 1968; Owen, *Greatest Brewery*, pp. 147 and 149; and J. Brown, *Steeped in Tradition: The Malting Industry in England Since the Railway Age* (University of Reading, 1983), p. 55.

30 Michael Sanderson & Son, Directors' Minutes, 7 April 1916, PM.

31 MAGB, Minutes of Executive Committee, 7 April 1919; Brewers' Society Minute Book, 7, 15 April 1919.

32 MAGB, Minutes of Executive Committee, 11 March 1919.

33 Ibid.

threat of state control, reduced output and labour shortage, there is little evidence of financial hardship. For the majority of companies, the war restored profits and the short post-war boom took them to levels not experienced since the turn of the century. Increased malting fees agreed with the Brewers' Society protected profit margins while exports of malt, much to the annoyance of British brewers, rose substantially.[34] Separate licences were issued for the manufacture of malt foods; thus some companies like Robsons increased their production of malt flour.[35] Others, such as Pidcocks, supplemented their income by drying grain and storing wheat and flour for the government.[36] John Parnell Tucker profited from astute barley buying during the early phases of the war.[37] For those with diverse interests there were also windfall profits which more than compensated for any problems with malting. Pauls' fleet of steamers and barges, for example, proved an invaluable asset. By 1917 the toll of merchant shipping was such that coastal barges (which were shallow enough to sail over mines) were used increasingly to ferry supplies to the northern ports of France. Roger Finch quotes instances of barges carrying coal from Goole to Dieppe at freight rates fourteen times those in peacetime, yielding a profit of £800 per voyage to be shared between crew and company.[38] Not surprisingly, during 1917–18 trading profits on shipping exceeded £12,000 against the customary £1000 to £2000. More significantly, the corn trade brought unprecedented returns; a trading profit of £172,733 in 1917 which, with a further £50,645 from malt, £43,715 from the flake mills and various sundry accounts, brought pre-tax net profits of £267,362. When adjusted for war-time inflation, this still amounted to a massive £154,544.[39] While such figures were probably exceptional, most companies enjoyed a substantial improvement in earnings. H. A. & D. Taylor saw net profits, which between 1909 and 1913 had averaged £4745, rise to an annual average of £6952 between 1914 and 1916, then

---

[34] From March 1915 exports of malt were prohibited, except to British possessions. However, the Board of Trade continued to issue licences and during 1915 more than 403,000 quarters of malt were exported and 176,000 the following year, against approximately 90,000 quarters in pre-war seasons. Most exports were of lager malt; in December 1916, Edward Fison Limited, were given a licence to send 200 tons to Italy. This trade gave rise to a protracted and often bitter disagreement between the two industries. Brewers accused maltsters of unpatriotic behaviour, but their real concern was clearly the impact on the price of malt. *Brewing Trade Review*, 1 March, 1 July, 1 September, 1 November and 1 December 1915, 1 July and 1 November 1916, 1 November 1917. Food Files, 2, p. 12, Beveridge Papers, BLPES.

[35] W. J. Robson & Company, Directors' Minutes, 25 June 1917, PM.

[36] J. Pidcock & Company, Directors' Minutes, 25 September 1917, 8 April 1818, PM.

[37] John Parnell Tucker, 'Commerce, Public Life and Sport', p. 21, typescript autobiography kindly loaned by Edwin Tucker & Sons Limited.

[38] R. Finch, *A Cross in the Topsail* (Ipswich, 1979), p. 49.

[39] R. & W. Paul Limited, Accounts, PM; Excess Profits Duty was initially set at 50 per cent on profits earned above pre-war levels, raised to 60 per cent in 1916 and 80 per cent in 1917. In 1919 the rate fell to 40 per cent and was set at 60 per cent in 1920. Most companies provided for Excess Profits Duty by building up substantial income tax reserves.

reach £19,813 between 1917 and 1920.[40] Likewise, the small firm of Richard Dewing & Company recorded net profits of £4343 and £4532 in 1920 and 1921 respectively, sums which even when adjusted for inflation, were unmatched in the years after 1880.[41]

An analysis of the ordinary dividends declared by a sample of sixteen companies reinforces this picture. The unweighted average showed an increase from 5.00 per cent in 1909–13 to 6.58 per cent in 1914–16 and 9.94 per cent in 1917–20. The annual average, weighted by the size of ordinary share capital, increased from 7.11 per cent to 10.28 per cent and 14.09 per cent.[42] Even those companies which had struggled during the previous years returned to profitability. J. & C. H. Evans & Company, for example, made their first distribution in 1919, following a lapse of fifteen years.[43] Michael Sanderson & Son, after a decade when dividends on cumulative preference shares were passed on three occasions and on ordinary shares on all but two, also resumed payments in 1915 and between 1917 and 1920 distributed an unprecedented 10 per cent. The following year, £15,000 of reserves were capitalised and distributed as bonus shares, with one new ordinary share offered for every four held.[44] Sandars of Gainsborough, registered as a private company in 1915 with issued capital of £150,000, acquired the Grimsby business of Arthur Soames & Son in 1916, then in 1919 almost doubled its capital, making two bonus issues of preference shares: one for one in September and one for two in December.[45] Between 1919 and 1921 fifteen partnerships, with a total capital of £763,000, were also registered as limited liability companies, the most significant wave of activity since the previous peak around the turn of the century. Among them were such market leaders as Gilstrap Earp & Company (capitalised at £325,000) and J. P. Simpson of Alnwick (£70,000).[46] The climate of optimism tempted others to invest for the future. Late in the war, the Nottingham firm of J. Pidcock spent £9000 on three maltings at Grantham, thus increasing its steeping capacity by more than 200 quarters.[47] Frederick Cooke, a director of W. J. Robson, was the driving force behind a similar expansion: between May 1919 and the following February maltings were bought at Pontefract and Brentwood and the firm's barley stores extended.[48] The evidence

---

[40] H. A. & D. Taylor Limited, Balance Books, PM.

[41] Richard Dewing & Company, Balance Books, FG 189.991, Fakenham Gasworks Museum.

[42] See Appendix 9.

[43] *Duncan's Manual of British and Foreign Brewery Companies* (1946), p. 122.

[44] Michael Sanderson & Son, Directors' Minute Books, PM.

[45] Sandars & Company, Directors' Minutes, 26 September 1916, 2 October 1919, 9 February 1920. A loan of £40,000 from Arthur Soames was also repaid by 1919.

[46] See Appendix 5.

[47] J. Pidcock & Company, Directors' Minutes, 17 September 1918, PM.

[48] W. J. Robson & Company, Directors' Minutes, 6 May, 22 July, 9 September, 16 December 1919, 3 February 1920, PM.

suggests that, despite their many difficulties, maltsters emerged from the war more prosperous than before and with a new confidence.

The brief post-war boom ended abruptly during the winter of 1920–21. With the recovery of world production grain prices tumbled, prompting the repeal of the Corn Production Act with its guarantees of farmers' prices.[49] British barley, which during 1920 had averaged 89s. 4d. per quarter, fell to 52s. 2d. the following year.[50] Maltsters involved in the grain trade or caught with large stocks immediately felt the impact. Pauls, for example, saw trading profits on malt fall in one year from £95,868 to a mere £182, and on their corn trade from £80,010 to £9732. Only the transfer of £120,000 from Income Tax reserves transformed a net loss into a reasonable profit.[51] Of greater long-term significance was the fall in beer production (see Fig. 6.1).

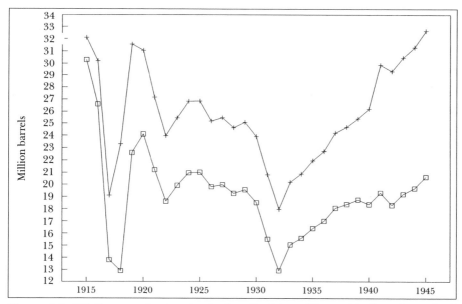

Figure 6.1 UK Beer production (excluding Eire) in millions of bulk and standard barrels, 1915–45.
Key: □ Standard barrels; + Bulk barrels.
Source: Gourvish and Wilson, *British Brewing Industry*, pp. 320, 618.

[49] For a detailed discussion of these events see C. S. Orwin, *A History of English Farming* (London, 1949), pp. 82–85.

[50] B. R. Mitchell and P. Deane, *Abstract of British Historical Statistics* (Cambridge, 1959), p. 489.

[51] R. & W. Paul Limited, Accounts, PM.

Between March 1920 and 1923, United Kingdom beer production fell by almost a quarter, from 31.5 million bulk barrels to under 24 million. After a modest recovery, output stabilised to 1930 then, at the trough of the depression in 1932, fell to less than 18 million barrels: expressed as standard barrels, the 12.9 million barely equalled the war-time low of 1918. Despite the steady recovery thereafter, average output remained lower than in the 1920s and well below pre-war levels.[52] Several factors underpinned an equally sharp decline in beer consumption: a lost generation of young men; unemployment, which devastated the industrial north, Scotland and Wales, the major centres of working class demand for beer; and the price of beer, pegged by high levels of excise duty, which Gourvish estimated was 40 per cent higher in real terms in 1931–33 than in 1920–23.[53] Finally, alternative leisure pursuits (sports, the cinema, radio and dancing) and social factors (the housing boom and rise of suburbia) indicated a permanent change in the lifestyle of the nation. For all of these reasons, Britain was becoming a more sober country: in 1913, per capita consumption of beer was 27.5 gallons: in 1931–38, it fell to 13.1 gallons of standard gravity.[54]

The long-term fall in beer output, as in earlier years, determined the demand for malt. The only significant change was that malt represented a progressively smaller proportion of brewers' total costs. Vaizey estimated that whereas in 1914 malt accounted for 40 per cent of total costs and excise duty around 15 per cent, by 1920 the figures were 25 per cent and 40 per cent respectively; and by 1935 10 per cent and 60 per cent.[55] Sharp falls in barley and therefore malt prices after 1920 indeed did much to cushion brewers from the heavy burden of excise duty. Nevertheless, there was every incentive to protect profit margins, and by manipulating beer gravity it was possible to reduce both elements of cost.[56] While average gravity rose slowly from 1039.4° in 1919 to peak at 1043.17° in 1928, the 1930–31 increases in excise duty, imposed by the Labour Chancellor of the Exchequer Philip Snowden, stimulated a fall to 1039.52° in 1932. Taking the entire period from 1919–38, Gourvish calculated that beer production in bulk barrels fell by 1.65 per cent per annum and in standard barrels by 1.82 per cent,

[52] Output of 18.4 million standard barrels in 1938 was less than half the 38.1 million standard barrels brewed in 1913.

[53] Apart from a rebate of £1 per bulk barrel from April 1923, excise duty remained at £5 per standard barrel until April 1930 when it was increased to £5 3s. 0d. From September 1931 until April 1933 it reached a peak of £6 14s. 0d. per standard barrel. Gourvish and Wilson, *British Brewing Industry*, p. 340. These issues are also discussed in detail by K. Hawkins, 'The Conduct and Development of the Brewing Industry in England and Wales, 1888–1938: A Study of the Role of Entrepreneurship in Determining Business Strategy with Particular Reference to Samuel Allsopp and Sons Limited' (unpublished Ph.D. thesis, University of Bradford, 1981), pp. 413–41.

[54] Gouvish and Wilson, *British Brewing Industry*, p. 339.

[55] J. Vaizey, *The Brewing Industry, 1886–1951: An Economic Study* (London, 1960), pp. 25–26.

[56] The *Brewing Trade Review* reckoned that each degree of gravity added 1s. 9d. in duty and 5d. in raw materials to the cost of each barrel. *Brewing Trade Review*, 1 February 1923; quoted in Hawkins, 'Conduct and Development', p. 533.

confirmation that the sharp fall in malt costs as a proportion of total costs reflected not only the relative importance of duty but a further reduction in the consumption of malt per barrel, especially after 1930.[57]

The full impact of these developments on the malt trade is illustrated in Fig. 6.2.

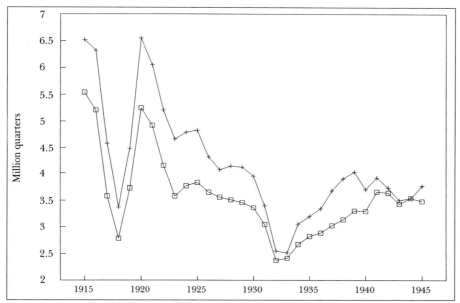

Figure 6.2 Malt used in brewing and distilling, UK, 1915–45 (million quarters).
Key: □ Malt used in brewing; + Malt used in brewing and distilling.
Source: See Appendix 2.

Between September 1920 and 1923, the consumption of malt by brewers fell by almost one-third, from 5.25 million quarters to 3.58 million. After a modest recovery to 1926, consumption fell slowly to 1930 and then collapsed to 2.37 million quarters in 1932, a fall of 54.9 per cent from 1920. Recovery thereafter was steady, but by September 1939 demand was still below the 1930 level. The demand for distilling malt exhibited a similar decline, falling during 1933 to 96,000 quarters. Indeed, during that year the total consumption of malt by the two industries, some 2.51 million quarters, represented a mere 28.6 per cent of the 1898 peak of 8.77 million quarters.[58]

[57] Gourvish and Wilson, *British Brewing Industry*, p. 337.

[58] In addition, the 1935 Census of Production recorded that 43,000 quarters of malt (1.24 per cent of the total 3,456,000 million quarters produced) were used in vinegar making and 191,667 quarters (5.55 per cent) in the manufacture of malt extract and malt foods. *Census of Production* (1935), Final Report, p. 178.

Furthermore, the problems of falling malt consumption were compounded because brewer-maltsters produced a greater proportion of their own malt. The many brewery amalgamations of the period proved particularly damaging. Many brewer-maltsters acquired firms which had previously bought malt and subsequently used their spare capacity to meet the needs of the new company. Unfortunately, there are no accurate statistics which distinguish between the two sectors, but the Maltsters' Association estimated that, whereas in 1913 sales-maltsters had produced approximately half the 6.5 million quarters of malt consumed by brewers, by 1930 their members made scarcely one million, less than one-third of the 3.36 million quarters then demanded.[59] Moreover, only the conservatism and loyalty of some brewers, reluctant to terminate long-standing agreements, had maintained trade at these levels.[60] The further increases in beer duty in April 1930 and September 1931 were the final straws. The subsequent sharp decline in beer consumption meant that brewers, forced to protect their own profits, could no longer lend their support. Maltsters' production was decimated, and the industry threatened with its 'final and complete ruin'.[61]

How did the Association react? In 1922, when most firms within it were thought to be working at about half their capacity, Hubert Cherry-Downes, its chairman, outlined a scheme for cooperative trading and the closure of redundant maltings involving a profits pool and compensation for those wishing to leave the industry. His proposals were perhaps too radical; they met with little support from either the Brewers' Society or some of the major malting companies and there were no further developments.[62] Instead attention was focused on maintaining a strong lobby to government, a campaign led by the wealthy maltster and MP for Christchurch, Sir Henry Page-Croft.[63] Besides the decline in output, he had ample evidence of real hardship. Several companies, such as Edward Fison and Austin Brothers, were in arrears with their annual subscriptions to the Association. The directors of George Wheeldon considered 'the present trading conditions did not warrant continuance of membership'; J. Gough of Bury St Edmunds

---

[59] Statement of the Maltsters' Association of Great Britain, 7 December 1931.

[60] The Maltsters' Association thought 'Brewers generally [had] treated the Sale Maltsters well and in some cases generously', MAGB, 7 December 1931.

[61] MAGB, 7 December 1931 and 23 February 1933.

[62] MAGB, Minutes of Executive Committee, 13 February, 8 May and 2 October 1922.

[63] Sir Henry Page-Croft was instrumental in organising the maltsters' lobby; in 1922 he urged the Association and other Allied Traders to organise petitions from their employees and working men's clubs and to collect statistics for unemployment in the industry. In 1932–33 he served as chairman of a committee of MPs and proposed the industry-wide survey which provided the evidence to present to the Chancellor in 1933. MAGB, Minutes of Executive Committee, 27 April, 8 May 1922, 5 February 1923, 14 November 1932.

resigned.[64] By October Sir Trustram Eve, the expert retained to represent members at urban rating panels was:

> appalled at the position of maltsters who are not also brewers ... Messrs Guinness are not [buying] any barley and have sufficient malt for more than one season's trade ... From enquiries amongst English brewers, I hear much the same tale.[65]

That winter alone, twenty-seven rating appeals brought reductions ranging from 23–80 per cent of pre-war assessments; 75 per cent at Newark, 62 per cent at Bishop's Stortford and 66 per cent at King's Lynn.[66] In March 1933, after undertaking an industry-wide survey, Sir Henry Page-Croft took the maltsters' case to the Chancellor, Neville Chamberlain. The survey results demonstrate the full scale of the downturn. Members were asked to provide comparative statistics for 1930–31, 1931–32 and the current season to 1 December. Each company was weighted to reflect its output.[67] Taking 1930–31 as 100, the evidence showed an aggregate decline of 25.6 per cent in labour employed, 12.6 per cent in the quantity of British barley purchased, 29.2 per cent on expenditure on transport, and a massive 82.6 per cent fall in net profits. The figures to December 1932 were worse: 42.5 per cent, 20.6 per cent and 41.7 per cent respectively (no details of profits were requested). Two-fifths of UK maltings were standing idle.[68] Table 6.1 shows the problems at the level of the individual firm.

Of the fifty companies analysed,[69] fourteen recorded a loss during 1931–32, including such substantial firms as the Scottish maltsters Hugh Baird and Thomas Bernard, Henry Page (Ware), William Jones (Shrewsbury), R. S. Watling (Great Yarmouth) and Sandars & Company (Gainsborough and

---

[64] Initially, members selected a subscription, between the minimum 5s. and maximum 10 guineas to reflect their scale of production, and no detailed breakdown of subscriptions was given. An additional, voluntary, levy of 1d. per quarter of the 1917 steeping licences was first requested during 1918–19. By 1920–21 this provided the official basis for subscriptions which were divided into seven categories, ranging from £50-100 to under £3. From 1923, in order to maintain membership levels, subscriptions were reduced to one-quarter of these levels. Minutes of Executive Committee, Membership Lists and Cash Accounts, MAGB, Newark-upon-Trent.

[65] Letter from Sir H. Trustram Eve to the Executive Committee of the Maltsters' Association, 1 October 1923.

[66] MAGB, Minutes of Executive Committee, 5 February 1923.

[67] Companies were weighted according to their subscriptions to the MAGB, based on steeping licences issued in 1917. Allowance was made for amalgamations but some margin of error, reflecting changes in market share, persisted. MAGB, Survey 1932, 'Beer Tax and the Malting Industry'.

[68] The percentage decline in profits was slightly understated because five firms recorded a loss but gave no further details. The unweighted averages were: 1931–32 – decline of 27.6 per cent in labour, 23.4 per cent in quantity of barley, 30.0 per cent on expenditure on transport, 77.3 per cent in net profits; 1932–33 – 47.7 per cent, 40.9 per cent and 51.1 per cent respectively. MAGB, Survey 1932, 'Beer Tax and the Malting Industry'.

[69] This includes Associated British Maltsters (see Table 6.1 below). There is no separate breakdown of the nine companies involved.

Table 6.1

Net profits, barley purchased and labour employed during season
1931–32, as a percentage of season 1930–31

Company	Net profits	Barley purchased	Labour employed	Labour employed to end of 1932
		1931–32 as a percentage of 1930–31		
ABM [1]	48.8	84.3	81.3	62.7
R & W Paul	75.0	217.0	68.0	27.0
Sandars & Company	loss	71.6	63.5	74.2
H. A. & D. Taylor	75.0	107.0	82.6	72.6
Free Rodwell	24.4	52.9	64.8	29.9
Hugh Baird	loss	97.0	71.0	54.0
Henry Page	loss	70.0	56.0	40.0
R. Peach	38.2	50.5	51.4	43.7

Note: ABM [1] (Associated British Maltsters) comprised: John Crisp, G. & W. E. Downing, Gilstrap Earp, Thomas Haigh, W. J. Robson, Michael Sanderson, Edward Sutcliffe, J. D. Taylor and Samuel Thompson.

Source: MAGB Survey, 1932, 'Beer Tax and the Malting Industry'.

Manchester). The impact was universal, but those who supplied the north, Scotland and Wales were notably hard hit. Bairds, for example, saw a net profit of £7020 in 1930–31 transformed into a loss of £2341,[70] while Sandars, who also specialised in top quality malt, suffered a massive decline. In contrast, Taylors, who supplied the south, and Pauls, who made cheap 'foreign' malt, maintained profits at 75 per cent of 1930–31 levels. It was the small firms, however, many of whom had struggled for years to survive, which suffered most. At best their profits fell sharply. Some, like the Yorkshire maltsters Austin Brothers and Smiths of Pontefract, and W. Thomas & Company of Wolverhampton, made losses. Others finally gave up. Frederick Wilkinson of Micklethwaite in Yorkshire completed his return: 'Before the extra Beer Tax came out, I kept one man and myself. Now we are both out of work'.[71]

The turning point was the budget of April 1933 when the Chancellor reduced beer duty to levels which, for many brewers, were below those of 1923–30.[72] In return, brewers were asked to reduce the price of beer by 1d. a pint, to increase gravity and, as an alternative to higher duties on imported

[70] *Brewers' Journal*, 15 December 1932. It is unclear how these figures relate to their response to the industry's survey.

[71] MAGB, Survey 1932, 'Beer Tax and the Malting Industry'.

[72] Beer duty was reduced to £1 4s. 0d. per barrel of 1027° gravity or less, plus 2s. for each degree above. Gourvish and Wilson, *British Brewing Industry*, p. 352.

barley, to use as much home grown barley as possible. Further pressure from the National Farmers Union in 1934 led to a commitment by brewers and maltsters to buy at least 7½ million cwts of the domestic crop annually. The target was surpassed during each subsequent pre-war season.[73] This gentleman's agreement, when combined with economic revival, proved successful, on the one hand providing support for British agriculture, and on the other underpinning the steady recovery of beer output and the demand for malt.

These sustained pressures had severe consequences for the malting industry, most significantly, the continued rationalisation of the sector. Figs 6.3 and 6.4 illustrate the decline in membership of the Maltsters' Association between 1918–19 and 1938–39, from 245 companies to ninety-one. Two clear trends emerged. First, the number of small firms contracted sharply, those producing less than 3000 quarters annually falling from 108 in 1920–21 to fifty-five in 1924–25 and only eighteen in 1938–39. Notably in Yorkshire (where total numbers fell from forty-nine to eighteen), in Shropshire (twenty-one to six) and in Suffolk (twenty-eight to twelve), this was largely accounted for by the loss of small firms. Many, like E. R. Gayford of Hadleigh, Walter Betts of Eye, Suffolk, and the three Yorkshire maltsters, W. Sheard, P. A. Taylor and Musgrave & Sagar, simply ceased trading.[74] The second factor was the marked increase in merger activity which affected most sectors of the British economy.

In the period between 1920–29 Hannah found as many as 1884 manufacturing firms disappeared by merger, a further 1414 in 1930–39.[75] More significantly, in 1915–35, 283 quoted brewery companies acquired 261 firms, 227 of them in 1919–32.[76] The loss of so many of their customers clearly provided a stimulus for maltsters to rationalise their own productive capacity. As Charles Sutcliffe saw it: 'even if twenty of the largest maltsters in the country were to go clean out of business, the requirements of brewers could easily be satisfied by the remainder'.[77] Yorkshire, where several small and medium-sized concerns were absorbed by major competitors, was the focus of much activity. The Wakefield & South Elmsall Malting Company, Dan

---

[73] In December 1924, the NFU twice lobbied the Import Duties Advisory Committee to increase the duty on imported malting barley to 20s. a quarter plus equivalent duties on sugar, maize and rice grits and flakes. To prevent this, the Brewers' Society, fully supported by the Maltsters' Association, agreed to increase their use of domestic barley. During 1936 7,729,484 cwts. were purchased, rising to 9,526,604 cwts during 1939. MAGB, Minutes of Executive Committee, 17 October 1936; *Brewers' Almanack* (1946), p. 127.

[74] MAGB, Minutes of Executive Committee, 8 May, 29 May 1922, 29 March 1926, 9 May 1927 and 9 October 1933. See below, Appendix 10.

[75] L. Hannah, *The Rise of the Corporate Economy* (London, 1976), p. 178.

[76] Overall, between 1920–39, the total number of brewery companies fell from 941 to 428. K. H. Hawkins and C. L. Pass, *The Brewing Industry: A Study in Industrial Organisation and Public Policy* (London, 1979), p. 48; Gourvish and Wilson, *British Brewing History*, p. 346.

[77] C. E. Sutcliffe, *Brewery Record*, 7, July 1928, p. 9.

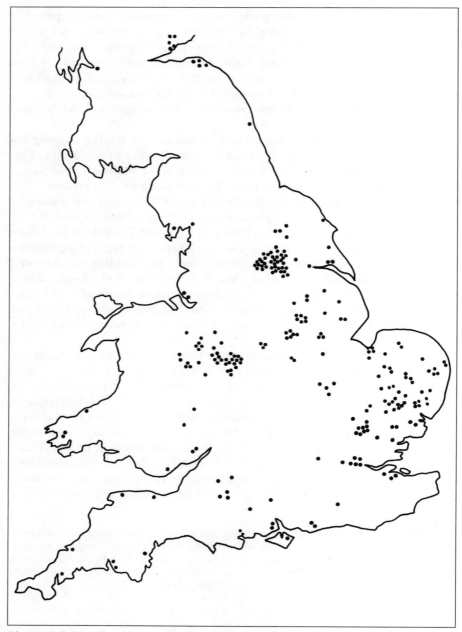

Figure 6.3 Membership of the Maltsters' Association of Great Britain, 1918–19.
Source: Memberships lists, MAGB.

Figure 6.4 Membership of the Maltsters' Association of Great Britain, 1938–39.
Source: Memberships lists, MAGB.

Byass of Scarborough and Alfred Messenger of Cleckheaton were all bought by Edward Sutcliffe.[78] In 1922 Michael Sanderson acquired Haworth Brothers of Wakefield; five years later, W. J. Robson amalgamated with John Crisp of Beccles; and in 1935 Thomas Fawcett of Castleford merged with their neighbours, Austin Brothers. Elsewhere the Burton firm of R. Peach acquired J. Gough of Bury St Edmunds and in 1937 R. Bishop & Son of Newark; while Hugh Baird & Sons of Glasgow bought Harrison Gray of Chelmsford and Tuckers & Blakes of Bristol in 1924 and 1931 respectively.[79] In Suffolk, Pauls finally gained control of Lee & Grinling of Grantham in 1928, while six years later Thomas Prentice & Company of Stowmarket was taken over by the brewers Greene King.[80] All, however, were overshadowed by the amalgamation in 1928 of Gilstrap Earp, Edward Sutcliffe, Samuel Thompson and W. J. Robson (with its subsidiary John Crisp), to form Associated British Maltsters.[81] The merger was masterminded by Hubert Cherry-Downes and reflected his earlier determination to minimise the industry's problems through cooperative trading.[82] The motives were again defensive. According to the company's official history:

> Competition in the industry was the real reason for the formation of ABM, hoping some form of rationalisation would lead to sufficient savings for modernisation of plants.[83]

Annual subscriptions to the Maltsters' Association, which were related to members' output, provide the best indication of the changing level of concentration in the industry. The measure has its shortcomings. By 1920–21, subscriptions were based on the steeping licences issued by the Ministry of Food in 1917.[84] Unfortunately, these were not adjusted to reflect changing market shares until 1943, but thereafter they were related directly to annual output.[85] During 1920–21, eight companies were included in the largest

[78] MAGB, Minutes of Executive Committee, 7 May 1923; *Brewery Record*, 7 (July 1928), p. 9.

[79] *Brewers' Journal*, 15 October 1922, 15 August 1927; J. P. Tucker, 'Commerce, Public Life and Sport' (typescript), p. 33; I. A. Peaty, *Essex Brewers and the Malting and Hop Industries of the County* (Brewing History Society, 1992), p. 130; Stephens (ed.) *Newark*, pp. 29, 48.

[80] L. Richmond and A. Turton (eds), *The Brewing Industry: A Guide to Historical Records* (Manchester, 1990) p. 159; R. & W. Paul, Directors' Minutes, 31 July 1928.

[81] Initially the new company traded under the name of Gilstrap Earp. To avoid confusion, it will be referred to throughout as Associated British Maltsters (ABM).

[82] Correspondence between Hubert Cherry-Downes, Douglas Taylor and the Charterhouse Investment Trust Limited, January-February 1928, PM. See below, Chapter 8.

[83] Taylor, 'Associated British Maltsters', p. 6.

[84] See n. 64 above.

[85] Between 1920–43 the level of subscriptions changed several times but no other adjustment was made, except to allow for merger and for the few companies who specifically asked to have their rate altered. The figures for 1943–44 are unlikely to differ significantly from those for 1938–39. Membership of the MAGB scarcely changed during these years, from ninety-one members to eighty-nine, and there is little evidence of merger activity. The only known merger of any significance was the acquisition in 1941 of Richard Dobson of Leeds by Pauls.

category defined by the Association (those who had received licences to steep more than 48,000 quarters of malt). Between them they accounted for 33.6 per cent of total output volume. At the other end of the spectrum, 108 firms (those which made less than 3000 quarters) produced 6 per cent of the sector's output. In 1943–44, the fifteen firms who made less than 3000 quarters accounted for a mere 1.1 per cent of production, while the eight largest companies, together with their subsidiaries, controlled 58.7 per cent of output volume. The three largest concerns, Associated British Maltsters, R. & W. Paul and H. A. & D. Taylor, alone produced 42 per cent of sales-maltsters' output. Yet as they stand these statistics create a false impression, not least because more than half of all the malt made was produced by brewers themselves. It is also necessary to appreciate the true nature of most malting mergers, for only rarely did subsidiaries lose either their identity or autonomy. Typically, when Muntona acquired Edward Fison of Ipswich, the company, although supervised from Bedford, continued to be run as a separate concern.[86] The reasons were twofold. First, brewers still preferred to spread their interests widely. As the newly amalgamated firm of ABM discovered, despite their insistence that each business was to be worked exactly as before by the same managing directors, 'the merger ... was in many cases unpopular and virtually meant we had to compete against each other'.[87] For the same reason, Lee & Grinling continued to operate as a separate company and its links with Pauls were not disclosed. Secondly, there was the reluctance of partners and directors to lose control of firms which usually had been owned by their families for generations. Brigadier Jack Grinling continued to run the family firm with little interference from the parent company. Generally, it is difficult to perceive either significant economies of scale in terms of production, transport or marketing or in the more negative aspects of monopoly power. It is perhaps more accurate therefore to measure the level of concentration in terms of those who competed against one another in the market. Counting each company which paid a separate subscription to the Maltsters' Association as the basis for this calculation reveals a more modest level of concentration: in 1943–44 the eight largest companies controlled 37.7 per cent of total production, while the three largest, Gilstrap Earp, Edward Sutcliffe and R. & W. Paul, accounted for 18.5 per cent.

Small companies that did survive were either secure in a niche market or enjoyed the protection of a major customer, as in the case of Richard Dewing and Trumans. Markets and location, as Figs 6.3 and 6.4 illustrate, also remained important. But in general, prosperity during the inter-war years demanded a sound strategy. Merger was one option. Many companies also diversified, either building on earlier ventures or by moving into new activities. Pauls, for example, besides their acquisition of Lee & Grinling,

86 'Notes For Employees', Muntona Limited and Edward Fison Limited (*c.* 1956), p. 16.
87 Taylor, 'Associated British Maltsters', p. 6.

purchased the Stonham Maltings which had been rented since the 1890s, the Creeting Road Maltings at Stowmarket and, in 1937, maltings at Blyton in Lincolnshire worked under the umbrella of Lee & Grinling.[88] Growth also continued through horizontal integration and diversification into related products. The latter, in particular, by maximising production, distribution and research capabilities, exploited Chandler's 'economies of scope' and took full advantage of new opportunities.[89] Within the parameters of brewing, the Hull Malt Company, manufacturers of flaked maize, was acquired in 1918. In 1929, as a joint venture with White, Tomkins & Courage, the Albion Sugar Company, producing invert sugars for the brewing trade, was registered. Russell Paul and Alexander Gillman (of Gillman & Spencer) became directors of the new company.[90] The main emphasis, however, was on the expansion of the animal feeds sector. The production of maize grits, meals and flakes continued and in 1925 the Cereals Company (1925) was registered in Edinburgh with William, Harry, Russell, Hugh and Stuart Paul as its first directors.[91] With farmers increasingly aware of the benefits of scientifically formulated and balanced rations, Pauls also decided in 1929 to enter the new growth area of compound feeds, concentrating mainly on poultry. Despite the uncertainty of these years, mills were built at the Manchester Ship Canal in 1931, at Avonmouth Docks in 1934 and at Faversham the following year. Those already in operation at Ipswich, King's Lynn, Hull and London were extended and re-equipped, involving a total investment in excess of £400,000 between 1931 and 1938. Initially profits were small, a reflection both of intense competition and the worsening agricultural depression, but in 1933 sales of poultry foods returned £49,168; six years later, the figure was £236,464. Throughout these years the mills contributed on average almost 40 per cent of total trading profits and did much to minimise fluctuations in malting and the international grain trade.[92]

Diversification, if on a more modest scale, was a key strategy for several other successful companies. Some, like ABM and H. A. & D. Taylor expanded their production of malt extract and malt flour.[93] Similarly, Muntona Limited, founded in 1921 by Munton Baker-Munton, introduced a range of branded products: 'Muntona Malted Soap', 'Yeaso', a high-protein yeast food and 'Maltona' cattle food. Then, in 1935, Muntona acquired the Ipswich

[88] R. & W. Paul, Capital Expenditure Ledger, PM.

[89] A. D. Chandler, Jr, *Scale and Scope: The Dynamics of Industrial Capitalism* (Cambridge, Massachusetts, 1990), pp. 38–42.

[90] R. & W. Paul, Directors' Minutes, 18 June 1929, PM.

[91] *Brewers' Journal*, 15 March 1925.

[92] R. & W. Paul Limited, Accounts; B. A. Holderness, 'Pauls of Ipswich' (1980), chapter 8, pp. 12–13, chapter 9, p. 8.

[93] In 1931 ABM registered a subsidiary company, Sunvi Limited, using the brand name of Edward Sutcliffe's malt flours in an attempt to increase sales. H. A. & D. Taylor acquired Diamalt Limited, manufacturers of malt extract, in 1920. ABM, Directors' Minutes, 10 August, 5 October 1931. *Stock Exchange Yearbook* (1945), p. 686.

business of Edward Fison.[94] Not surprisingly, given the close alignment between the two industries, the main alternatives were to be found within agriculture. The Agricultural Marketing Acts of 1931 and 1933, with their promise of support for ailing farmers, persuaded the ABM directors that the time was opportune for diversification into poultry and pig foods.[95] Begun at Bristol early in 1932 under the direction of John Crisp, the venture initially sustained heavy losses. But with bleak prospects in malting, it was felt necessary to persevere and two years later Gilstrap's Grist Mill was successfully established at Newark.[96] The second major growth area of the inter-war years, canning and bottling fruit and vegetables, was the avenue selected by Bairds. Building on links built up through the hop trade with Wolton & May (who were also substantial fruit growers), a subsidiary company, Baird, Wolton & May Limited, was registered in 1932 and a canning factory employing a workforce of 250 opened in Barming, Kent.[97]

As in earlier years, maltsters continued to strengthen brewing links. John Parnell Tucker, who became chairman of the Heavitree Brewery at Exeter, was one of several maltsters who secured seats on the boards of brewery companies.[98] Richard Simpson of J. P. Simpson & Company of Alnwick, who in 1911 had joined the board of the Wakefield maltsters, Michael Sanderson, became a director of the Alnwick Brewery Company in 1924 and of John Rowell & Son, the Gateshead brewers, in 1937.[99] Similarly, Henry Hutchison of Robert Hutchison & Company of Kirkcaldy served the boards of the Scottish Malt Distillers' Company and James Calder & Company (Brewers) Limited.[100] One problem was the frequent brewery mergers which terminated established links. In 1920, for example, J. Stanley Taylor of James D. Taylor of Bath secured a seat on the board of the Bath Brewery Company, only for the business to be acquired three years later by the Bristol Brewery Georges & Company.[101]

There were also companies like F. & G. Smith who, perceiving the fall in demand for malt to be permanent, responded by disinvesting. The 1920s saw the disposal of the Burnham maltings and the closure and sale for demolition of the Ryburgh mill.[102] By 1929 a further decline in sales persuaded

---

[94] Originally registered as Munton & Baker (Bedford) Limited, the company was soon renamed Muntona Limited; it trades today as Muntons. Munton & Fison, *A Brief History of Munton & Fison Limited to Mark Their Fiftieth Anniversary, 1921–1971* (privately printed, 1971), p. 6.

[95] ABM, Directors' Minutes, 7 December 1931, 9 January 1933.

[96] Ibid., 4 January, 15 February 1932, 27 March 1933, 10 September 1934.

[97] *Brewers' Journal*, 15 April 1932.

[98] Tucker, 'Commerce, Public Life and Sport', p. 30.

[99] *Brewers' Journal*, 15 March 1924, 15 June 1937.

[100] Ibid., 15 January 1924.

[101] Ibid., 15 December 1920; Richmond & Turton (eds), *Historical Records*, p. 81.

[102] F. & G. Smith Limited, Directors' Minutes, 24 February 1923, 2 May 1925, 30 January 1926.

Russell Pearce Gould, the company's accountant and financial adviser, that 'it is questionable that the Company would ever be called upon to utilise the full capacity of its steeps again'.[103] On his recommendation, the Wells branch was closed and the capital of the company written down from £200,000 to £100,000 by exchanging the £10 ordinary shares for £5 in cash, three £1 7 per cent cumulative preference and two £1 ordinary shares. In 1932 the company's capital was further reduced to £40,000 by the repayment of the 60,000 preference shares.[104] Despite an appeal from the chairman, E. R. Hill, for suggestions for profitable sidelines, a proposal to start a canning factory for fruit and vegetables was rejected. Instead, the 1930s saw a steady disposal of the firm's assets. There was, however, no shortage of competitors willing to purchase redundant maltings.[105]

Despite the difficulties of the early 1920s and the crisis of 1931–33, the period was not one of undiluted hardship. Several companies achieved consistent profits. Pauls returned an average trading profit on malt of £53,106 between 1924–28, £27,976 between 1929–33, rising again to £43,072 in 1934–38. Record pre-tax profits of £329,714 in 1937 indicate the strength of this diverse enterprise. Pauls' subsidiary, Lee & Grinling, with its reputation for high quality malt, was equally sound. Net profits fell significantly only between 1922 and 1924, in the year of the General Strike (1926) and in 1931–32. After the turning point of the 1933 budget, profits were quickly restored with annual average net profits in 1934–38 at £8513, previously surpassed only in the record years of 1920–21.[106] Similarly, Pidcocks and Swonnells both saw their profits dip during 1923–24, and in particular after 1930, but overall achieved sound results,[107] while Bairds, badly hit in 1932–33, quickly recovered to return average net profits of £8440 in 1934–36.[108] Douglas Taylor, chairman of H. A. & D. Taylor, was perhaps typical when in 1936 he reported to his shareholders a successful year underpinned by an excellent harvest, increasing contracts and deliveries and flourishing malt extract and roasting trades.[109]

[103] Ibid., 9 February 1929.

[104] Ibid., 7 February 1929, 18 July 1932.

[105] Vynne & Everitt purchased Wells No. 7 malting in 1932 and Chapman's Granary seven years later; Pauls purchased Wells No. 18 in 1939, while in 1934 Ryburgh No. 5 malting and barley kiln was leased to Ipswich Malting Company. The remaining maltings and other property at Wells-Next-The-Sea were sold in 1937–39.

[106] Annual average profits for the period were: 1921–23, £8196; 1924–28, £6393; 1929–33, £7052; 1934–38, £8513; Lee & Grinling, Accounts and Miscellaneous Papers.

[107] Annual average profits were:

	1921–23	1924–28	1929–33	1934–38
J. Pidcock	£28,514	£18,502	£10,180	£12,546
S. Swonnell	£21,978	£15,951	£13,871	£12,761

J. Pidcock & Company, Directors' Minutes; S. Swonnell & Son, Private Journal.

[108] J. Pidcock & Company, Yeomans, Cherry & Curtis, Directors' Minutes; S. Swonnell & Son, Private Journal; Lee & Grinling, Accounts; *Brewing Trade Review* (1935).

[109] H. A. & D. Taylor Limited, Directors' Minutes, 20 November 1936, PM.

There were, of course, exceptions. From 1927 the Birmingham maltsters J. & C. H. Evans, returning to former ways, passed ordinary dividends on all but two occasions until the outbreak of war.[110] And in 1933 Thomas Bernard & Company of Leith wrote down their capital from £150,000 to £56,000, returning £5 per £10 preference share and writing £7 10s. 0d. off the value of the 7500 £10 ordinary shares. The arrears on preference shares, accumulated since 1926, were cancelled and the next ordinary dividend paid in 1944.[111] Nevertheless, the unweighted annual average ordinary dividend declared by sixteen representative companies (allowing for capitalised bonuses), which fell from 13.52 per cent in 1921–23 to 11.15 per cent in 1929–33, recovered to 12.96 per cent in 1934–38 while the weighted average fell only marginally from 14.02 per cent to 13.77 per cent before rising to 14.19 per cent (see Table 6.2). These figures clearly reflect the problems of the early 1930s and, not surprisingly given the degree of partial integration between brewing and malting, are less positive overall than Gourvish's results for brewing.[112] Over the long term, however, the weighted average, reflecting the strength of the larger companies, displayed an upward trend.

It is essential to re-emphasise the limitations of the measure. Variations in accounting conventions doubtless continued. In addition, diversification was widespread and usually, as in the case of Pauls, net profits and ordinary dividends relate to the entire enterprise. The inter-war years also saw important developments in the taxation of private companies, with the provision of special powers to the Inland Revenue whereby under certain circumstances they could influence the level of dividends paid by profitable private companies.[113] The directors of French & Jupp's, for example, were advised by their auditors that to reduce the liability for Supertax it was necessary to distribute a larger proportion of the company's profits as dividends. Ordinary dividends, previously maintained at 5 per cent, were thus increased to 15 per cent.[114] A degree of caution is therefore needed in the interpretation of the statistics. While in the short term fluctuations in profits and dividend payments may be smoothed by the manipulation of reserves and depreciation, in the long run the flow of income to service

---

[110] *Duncan's Brewery Manual* (1946), p. 122.

[111] Thomas Bernard & Company, *Stock Exchange Yearbook* (1945), p. 833.

[112] Gourvish and Wilson, *British Brewing Industry*, p. 343.

[113] To minimise the ability of shareholders to avoid Supertax, Section 21 of the Finance Act 1922 gave the Inland Revenue powers whereby they could influence the dividend payments of some private companies – basically if controlled by five or fewer persons. The Revenue could decide what dividend *ought* to be paid in relation to profits and apportion the company's profit in excess of *actual* dividends paid amongst its shareholders for the purposes of surtax. This could be avoided by maintaining dividends at a level which allowed retentions at a rate no more than the Revenue would regard as reasonable to finance the company's trade. I am grateful to John Barney for this information.

[114] This conflicted with the directors' opinion that, to safeguard the long-term future of the company, it was advisable to build up substantial reserves and pay a dividend of no more than 5 per cent. French & Jupp's, Directors' Minutes, 24 January, 28 November 1922.

Table 6.2

Company profitability (ordinary dividends, per cent), 1921–38 (annual averages)

Company	1921–23	1924–28	1929–33	1934–38
Hugh Baird	10.00	6.00	2.00	2.60
F. & G. Smith	8.67	8.20	10.30[3]	19.50
R. & W. Paul	18.92	22.20	23.90 [27.23][1]	20.60
Thomas Bernard	3.33	0.00	0.00[4]	0.00
J. Pidcock	38.33	30.00	22.00	28.00
Cardiff Malting	5.00	15.20[2]	11.20	14.00
J. & C. H. Evans	10.00	7.20	2.00	0.50
S. Swonnell	15.00	16.40	17.40	16.10
Lee & Grinling	7.50 [9.38][1]	10.00	19.00	21.00 [23.00][1]
Gilstrap Earp/ABM	20.00	19.50	9.00	11.00
16 Company av. (unweighted)[5]	13.52	12.33	11.15	12.96
16 Company av. (weighted)[5]	14.02	13.81	13.77	14.19

Notes:
[1] Takes account of capitalisation of bonus shares
[2] Takes account of cash bonus of 30 per cent paid from reserves
[3] Capital written down by 80 per cent
[4] Capital written down by 62.5 per ent
[5] See Appendix 9 for full sample

Source: Appendix 9, below.

dividends must be provided by trading profit. The ability of several companies to sustain, or in some cases increase, ordinary dividends over a number of decades indicates their financial strength. A second measure, the rate of return on paid-up capital, confirms this picture. Pauls, for example, saw a return on capital of 11.6 per cent in 1921–23, a low of 10.6 per cent in 1929–33, rising to 12.7 per cent in 1934–38; Pidcocks, 17.1 per cent, 7.3 per cent and 10.2 per cent respectively.[115]

How is the apparent contradiction of financial soundness reconciled with the many problems of the period? First, the role of the Maltsters' Association in providing a collective voice for the industry should not be underestimated. Their success in such areas as rating assessments, their constant pressure on government and above all perhaps their ability to work fruitfully with the Brewers' Society were clearly significant. But to a large extent, the answer is to be found in the concentration of the industry and, in particular, the

[115] See below, Appendix 8; J. Pidcock & Company, Directors' Minutes; for Paul's subsidiary company, Lee & Grinling, whose profits related exclusively to malting, the figures were 14.2 per cent, 8.8 per cent and 8.3 per cent.

demise of the smaller companies. Moreover, from financial records it is evident that even those which survived fared badly in comparison with larger competitors. Richard Dewing, who made malt exclusively for Trumans, enjoyed their support throughout the 1920s, returning annual average net profits of £3460 for the decade after 1921; between 1932–39, however, average profits slumped by 67 per cent to £1136 and in real terms were comparable with the difficult years before the war. Similarly, the small firm of Alfred Gough, registered in 1918 with issued capital of £6000, struggled throughout the entire period to maintain consistent profits, recording losses on no fewer than five occasions. It is possible that only their close link with Swonnells ensured their survival.[116] In marked contrast, several larger companies prospered and enhanced their market share. Most diversified, particularly in the manufacture of malt extract or patent foods. A few progressive firms also moved into the new growth areas of compound feeds and fruit and vegetable canning, sectors closely related to agriculture which maximised existing expertise, production and distribution resources. Mergers added a further dimension while the emphasis on strong personal networks continued. Although markets and location remained important, with those who served the industrial north, Scotland and Wales feeling the full force of recession, the quality of entrepreneurship was clearly critical. As Charles Sutcliffe suggested, 'only the soundest and best concerns emerged from this acid test'. His words, written in 1928 before the crisis of the early 1930s, proved even more appropriate a decade later. Much of the 'dead wood' was cut out of the industry. But a nucleus of enterprising companies emerged sounder and fitter than at one time might have been expected.[117]

The outbreak of the Second World War in September 1939 saw the rapid return of pervasive controls and high taxation. Beer duty was immediately doubled to £2 8s. 0d. per barrel of 1027°, then repeatedly raised until in April 1944 it stood at £7 0s. 8d.; the incremental duty for each degree above 1027° increased from 2s. to 5s. 2d.[118] Despite unprecedented levels of taxation, there was no attempt to reduce output. Beer consumption and the incidence of drunkenness had fallen sharply since the previous war and, in

---

[116] Results for Alfred Gough Limited were (in per cent):

	1921–23	1924–28	1929–33	1934–38
Average Dividends	0.2	5.0	5.5	11.0
Return on Capital	0.4	9.5	6.5	5.9

William Sylvester, chairman of S. Swonnell & Son, was a director of Alfred Gough from its incorporation in 1918. Like Swonnells, the firm produced coloured and roasted malts. In 1955 it became a wholly owned subsidiary. Subsequently the Saffron Walden maltings were closed and the business transferred to Snape. Alfred Gough Limited, Accounts and Directors' Minutes, PM.

[117] C. E. Sutcliffe, *Brewery Record*, 7 (July 1928), p. 9.

[118] Gourvish and Wilson, *British Brewing Industry*, p. 356; *Brewers' Almanack* (1958), pp. 114–15.

contrast to Lloyd George's hostility towards the drinks trade, beer-drinking was seen as important in supporting morale and industrial productivity. Beer production in bulk barrels increased by 32 per cent between 1938 and 1945 and in standard barrels (i.e. 1055°) by 12 per cent.

There was no fall in the demand for malt, the annual average consumption by brewers in 1940–45, at 3.51 million quarters, showing an increase of 18.1 per cent over the previous six years. The only decline was in the demand for distilling malt, mostly produced by distillers for their own use and therefore scarcely affecting sales-maltsters.[119] The main problem for malt-sters, given the restricted supply of barley, labour shortage and the destruction of maltings, was to satisfy brewers' needs. Purchases of home-grown barley, under the terms of the agreement negotiated in 1933, were already the subject of limited control. From November 1938 a sub-committee of the Maltsters' Association, representatives of the Brewers' Society and Ministry of Agriculture, had also tackled the problem of price support. The resulting agreement, introduced in July 1939, was quickly made redundant by the wartime embargo on imported barley for malting and the consequent increase in domestic prices.[120] Most maltsters entered the war with good stocks of kiln-dried barley carried over from the abundant harvest of 1938. Nevertheless, by December 1939 the domestic price had risen 50 per cent.[121] It had been hoped to leave barley prices to the free market but, while the acreage of barley increased by almost 46 per cent during the first two years of war, this was offset by poor yields, especially for the 1941 crop.[122] Prices reached record levels, the *Brewers' Journal* quoting £15 per quarter by the following spring.[123] The government was forced to intervene and from July 1942 fixed maximum prices for malting barley: £7 per quarter for the 1942 crop, falling to £5 by 1944.[124]

Similarly, purchases of malt and barley were subjected to more compre-hensive regulation. The appointment in September 1939 of Hugh Paul as Director of the Cereals Department at the Ministry of Food was, however,

---

[119] Distillers' supplies of grain were limited to one-third of 1938–39 purchases. R. J. Hammond, *History of the Second World War: Food*, i (London, 1951), p. 84.

[120] The 1939 Barley Scheme, brought into force under the Agricultural Development Act, introduced a levy of 1s. per standard barrel brewed if the price of home-grown barley did not exceed 32s. 4d. per quarter, plus a subsidy of 30s. per acre paid by the government; both levy and subsidy fell as barley prices increased. The MAGB sub-committee comprised H. D. Cherry-Downes, Hugh Paul and Colonel Grinling. MAGB, Minutes of Executive Committee, November 1939; Brewers' Society Annual Report (1944), pp. 6–7.

[121] MAGB, Minutes of Executive Committee, 20 December 1939. The weighted average price for the year ending August 1940 increased to 57s. 4d. a quarter against 33s. 4d. a quarter the previous year. *Brewers' Almanack* (1946), p. 54.

[122] The UK barley acreage increased from 1,013,000 acres for the year ending 31 May 1939 to 1,475,000 in 1941; by 1945 it had more than doubled. *Brewers' Almanack* (1960), p. 64.

[123] *Brewers' Journal* 18 March 1942; Brewers' Society Annual Report (1942), p. 4.

[124] Barley (Control and Maximum Prices) (Great Britain) Order, 1942, 1943 and 1944.

one which pleased both brewers and maltsters.[125] Indeed, with his experience at the Ministry during the First World War and acknowledged expertise in the grain markets, few were better qualified for the task. His proposals for the distribution of barley were outlined in April 1940 and a joint advisory committee of brewers and maltsters, under the chairmanship of Hubert Cherry-Downes, appointed to oversee the scheme.[126] Designed to maintain beer output at pre-war levels, the scheme allowed brewers to purchase sufficient barley and malt to meet their demand, provided aggregate beer production did not exceed that of the previous year. Each September, maltsters received preliminary permits to buy 70 per cent (60 per cent in 1941 and 80 per cent in 1942) of the quantity of barley steeped in 1938–39; supplementary licences were subsequently issued to cover any additional sales.[127] With supplies of flaked maize exhausted by the spring of 1940, manufacturers were also licensed to produce 'flaked barley malt' which could satisfactorily constitute 10 per cent of brewers' grist.[128] Then, early in 1943, when the supply situation worsened and the decision was taken to use barley in bread, Hugh Paul asked brewers to reduce their barley consumption by 10 per cent by using substitutes, notably flaked oats and dried potato 'cosettes'.[129] The assistance of maltsters was also requested in buying, kiln-drying and storing barley for milling, the Ministry of Food guaranteeing to purchase all kiln-dried barley at 162s. 6d. per quarter.[130] After the abundant harvest of 1943, however, the position quickly eased and thereafter brewers and maltsters experienced little difficulty in obtaining all the barley they were licensed to buy.

With the gradual appearance of the combine harvester on Britain's farms, one problem was solved only for another to take its place.[131] Traditionally, barley had been harvested, stored in the stack then threshed throughout

---

[125] The Brewers' Society reported that 'he has occupied [the position] with outstanding knowledge and ability, and ... holds the complete confidence of the Society and trade', Brewers' Society, Annual Report (1939–40), p. 7. Jock Causton, also of R. & W. Paul, was appointed Executive Officer for Control of Barley under the Cereals Control Board.

[126] Apart from Hubert Cherry-Downes, the Advisory Committee comprised: Philip Grinling (Lee & Grinling), Robert V. Reid (Hugh Baird) and Cuthbert T. Taylor (H. A. & D. Taylor); and the brewers S. O. Neville (Whitbread), F. Nicholson (Vaux), E. L. D. Lake (Greene King), F. A. Simonds (H. & G. Simonds), Sir Richard Wells (Charles Wells) and C. J. Newbold (Guinness). MAGB, Minutes of Executive Committee, 3 June 1940; Gourvish and Wilson, *British Brewing Industry*. p. 361.

[127] Maltsters were also licensed to export malt to British Dominions to maintain existing trade. MAGB, Minutes, 6 August 1940, 3 November 1941, 20 July 1942.

[128] MAGB, Chairman's Speech, 3 November 1941, 19 January 1942.

[129] The saving was achieved within six months. Hammond, *History of the Second World War: Food*, iii (1962), pp. 265–69; Brewers' Society Annual Report (1944), pp. 7–8.

[130] Maltsters were to use their judgement to buy at market value within the controlled price. The guaranteed price (ex maltings or store) included 142s. 6d. per quarter for barley and 20s. per quarter to cover all other costs up to 31 May 1943; thereafter, 12d. per quarter per week was paid to cover interest and storage charges to date of delivery. MAGB, Minutes, March 1943.

[131] It was estimated that by the 1942 harvest there were 950 at work; by the 1944 harvest 2500.

the winter months, ensuring a steady flow of grain onto the markets. In contrast, large quantities of barley requiring drying and storage now flooded the markets immediately after harvest. With maltsters already committed to storing and drying milling barley, the position was critical. Indeed, only the dry harvest of 1943 saved the situation. Government proposals to build communal grain driers and bulk storage at railheads followed, but were successfully opposed by maltsters who needed to work each parcel of grain according to its quality.[132] Nevertheless, the long-term implications for large-scale capital investment in drying plant and storage facilities were clearly evident.

Of even greater concern was the shortage of labour and loss of malting capacity. The outbreak of war saw the immediate requisition of a number of maltings for the storage of food: Pauls lost two of their Ipswich maltings, H. A. & D. Taylor six maltings at Sawbridgeworth representing 20 per cent of total capacity.[133] Every company was affected by the loss of labour as employees were called up for military service.[134] In industrial areas especially, men were attracted to alternative employment by higher wages and year-round work. In response, the Maltsters' Association appointed a labour sub-committee to survey members' needs and negotiate with the Ministry of Labour for malting to be classified an essential industry.[135] The arrival of large numbers of US and Empire troops during the summer of 1942 intensified the problem. The Association readily agreed to the government's request for extra malt to meet their needs, but this was subject to an improvement in the labour position, a second survey undertaken in September showing the immediate need for 800 floormen to maintain maximum output.[136] Nevertheless the position continued to deteriorate: by September 1943 the Brewers' Society considered the shortage of labour their principal problem and subsequently a number of maltings remained idle forcing some brewers to reduce output.[137] F. & G. Smith, unable to find sufficient labour for their Great Ryburgh malting, were forced to cut contracts for future deliveries by 20 per cent.[138] Concessions were made. A certain amount of unskilled labour was made available and skilled workers aged between thirty and thirty-four given a period of deferment of call up. A few key men were released from the forces. When in March 1943 the foreman at Pauls' Stonham maltings, James Wicks, suddenly died, his son Leslie returned to take his

---

[132] W. H. Bird, *A History of the Institute of Brewing* (London, 1955), pp. 76–77.

[133] F. & G. Smith, Directors' Minutes, 9 December 1939; H. A. & D. Taylor, Directors' Minutes, 8 November 1939, 10 December 1940.

[134] By November, H. A. & D. Taylor reported two directors and twelve employees called up for military service. Director's Minutes, 28 November 1939, PM.

[135] Initially, only malting managers and foremen over the age of twenty-five were exempt from military service. MAGB, Minutes of Executive Committee, 27 July 1940, 3 November 1941.

[136] Ibid., 20 July 1942, 28 September 1942.

[137] Brewers' Society, Annual Reports (1943), p. 5; (1945), p. 5.

[138] F. & G. Smith, Directors' Minutes, 27 June 1945.

place. The position at Stonham illustrates just how difficult conditions were: pre-1939 and again after 1945, on average twenty-five to twenty-eight men were employed during the malting season; for the majority of the war, only thirteen to fourteen.[139]

As in the First World War, many companies eased their labour problems by employing women. At Dobsons of Leeds three women replaced every two men (and received two-thirds the pay), while the Bedford maltings, owned by the brewers Mitchell & Butlers, with the exception of a few male foremen, were worked entirely by women.[140] On every occasion, both employers and male colleagues spoke highly of their work.[141] In marked contrast, there were numerous complaints regarding the quality of much of the unskilled labour made available to the industry. Typically, Hutchison's found it 'required at least two men of the present type to make up for one good man previous to war. It would appear impossible to make floormen out of the labour that has been sent to us'.[142] In some areas even unskilled labour was unavailable. ABM encountered few problems at Louth, whereas at Newark they were forced to let maltings stand idle.[143] One solution, although again not without problems, was to hire labour from the Irish Republic, while by the latter stages of the war a few companies like Pauls were using Italian prisoners of war.[144]

The supply problem was further exacerbated by bomb damage to numerous maltings. During the initial onslaught of 1940, ABM's Bridgehill Malting at Louth, capable of an annual output of 10,000 quarters, Sandars' Manchester maltings and two of F. &. G. Smith's Great Ryburgh maltings (together with 10,000 quarters of malt and barley) were all destroyed. The loss caused Smiths to cancel 60 per cent of all outstanding contracts with further cuts in 1942, when the company's remaining 200 quarter malting at Ryburgh was badly damaged and stock valued at £108,000 destroyed. Sandars' production was similarly devastated when in June 1943 the largest of the Soames maltings at Grimsby was lost. Between them, the Manchester and Grimsby maltings had accounted for 50 per cent of the firm's output.[145]

---

[139] Stonham Maltings, Wages Book; interview with Leslie Wicks, 20 August 1991.

[140] The evidence for this paragraph is taken from recordings of maltsters (1972), tapes 48–55, Museum of East Anglian Life, Stowmarket.

[141] For example, 'after short training it was found that, taking everything into consideration, their work was very satisfactory', C. T. Taylor, 30 September 1942.

[142] Letter from Captain A. Hutchison of Kirkcaldy to the MAGB, 19 January 1942.

[143] ABM, Directors' Minutes, 14 July 1941.

[144] The scheme to bring over Irish workers was organised through Guinness in Dublin, some companies like ABM providing hostels for the men. But while their work was generally satisfactory, there were complaints about drinking and fighting. Pauls used Irish labour but, by 1945, twelve to fourteen Italians eased the shortfall at Stonham. MAGB, Minutes of Executive Committee, 6 December 1943; ABM, Directors' Minutes, 13 April 1942; Stonham Maltings, Wages Book.

[145] ABM, Directors' Minutes, 9 December 1940; *Of Malt and Men, 1865–1965*, Sandars & Company Limited; 'One Hundred Years of Malting, 1890–1990', Anglia Maltings Group Review (1989), pp. 6–7.

Faced with the urgent need to restore production, each company maximised existing capacity by installing air-conditioning plant at their remaining maltings, thereby making year-round malting possible. The introduction of air-conditioning had been discussed by some companies before the war and early in 1939 ABM had commenced work at Whitley Bridge and Bath. Generally, however, the uncertain climate had deterred investment in new technology. But after the destruction at Louth, ABM commissioned further plants at Leak's Row, Louth and Barton-on-Humber, followed in 1944 by a second plant at Bath. Sandars installed air-conditioning at one of the remaining Grimsby maltings and at Carr Lane and Paddock, Gainsborough, while F. & G. Smith invested £10,000 on plant at Dereham.[146] Other companies followed suit: H. A. & D. Taylor invested at Sawbridgeworth, Bishop's Stortford and Cambridge and, by the end of the war, Pauls' Stoke maltings (Nos 5 and 6) were both air-conditioned, followed shortly after by Nos 2 and 4.[147]

By malting through the summer months and utilising all available labour most companies did their utmost to maintain production. Given the situation of excess demand, there was every incentive to do so. Taylors, despite reduced capacity through requisition and a major fire at Bury St Edmunds plus an acute shortage of labour, achieved deliveries throughout the war of more than 90 per cent of the 1937–39 average.[148] Pauls' average deliveries exceeded those of 1937–39 by almost 20 per cent, while the 157,400 quarters sold in 1940–41 and 1943–44 broke all earlier records. Likewise, during the last two years of war when conditions were at their most difficult, ABM achieved record deliveries some 40 per cent above pre-war levels.[149] Despite higher wages and raw material costs, record sales translated into higher pre-tax profits. Typically, between 1939–45 Lee & Grinlings' labour costs increased from 4s. 8d. to 9s. 5d. per quarter and barley costs from £1 18s. 3d. to peak at £7 10s. 11d. per quarter, but these were matched by average malt prices which rose from £2 18s. 1d. to £9 3s. 0d. a quarter. Net profits, which between 1934–38 averaged £8513, peaked in 1944 at £43,885.[150] Pauls' trading profit on malt averaged £173,687 between 1943–45, reaching £193,454 in 1944, more than double the 1920 peak. Similarly, Taylors reported 'exceptional' trading profits, averaging £103,713 for the three years ending September 1945.[151] The government imposed an Excess Profits Tax (set initially at 60 per cent of average profits between 1935–37

---

[146] ABM, Directors' Minutes, 20 December 1937, 6 February 1939, 8 November 1943, 14 February 1944, 18 December 1944; *Of Malt and Men*; F. & G. Smith, Directors' Minutes, 26 June 1943.

[147] H. A. & D. Taylor, Directors' Minutes, 3 February 1942, 25 January 1945; R. & W. Paul, Capital Expenditure Ledger, PM.

[148] H. A. & D. Taylor, Directors' Minutes, 18 December 1945, PM.

[149] ABM, Chairman's Report, 18 December 1944, 31 December 1945.

[150] Lee & Grinling, Accounts and Costs, PM.

[151] H. A. & D. Taylor, Directors' Minutes, 15 June 1943, December 1945, PM.

and subsequently raised to 100 per cent) which effectively absorbed war-time profits, although a 20 per cent post-war credit was promised for reconstruction. Nevertheless, most companies built up substantial reserves and maintained healthy dividends, the unweighted average of ordinary dividends of sixteen representative companies (including bonus distributions) increasing from 12.96 per cent in 1934–38 to 16.87 per cent in 1939–45, the weighted average rising from 14.19 per cent to 16.06 per cent.[152] Even J. & C. H. Evans, whose finances were always fragile, maintained a steady 5 per cent after 1940, while Thomas Bernard & Company paid their first dividend on ordinary shares for more than twenty years in 1944.

Encouraged by the return to prosperity much thought was given to post-war reconstruction, the Maltsters' Association appointing sub-committees to consider the three critical areas of labour, buildings and raw materials. For not only were men and maltings exhausted and in disrepair, the advent of the combine harvester heralded permanent change. Capital investment in plant and storage facilities would inevitably be substantial. Equally important were changes in the labour market. Traditionally, wages set marginally above those in agriculture had secured an ample supply of labour. In the late 1930s economic recovery and rearmament brought higher wages to many industries and marked the initial drift from malting. The war only emphasised this situation. In response, the Association suggested radical change: higher wages, including a national minimum rate, overtime for weekend work, year-round employment and a general improvement in working conditions.[153] The proposals were widely adopted. Even more significant, for the first time in the history of the industry, escalating labour costs stimulated technical change. Long before the war had ended, many companies had made plans for mechanisation.[154] At the industry level, the old fears about overcapacity remained, but the proposed committee to oversee the closure of old floors and construction of new plant did not materialise. It was time, as the Maltsters' Association advised its members, 'to bury the past'.[155] Malting, the most traditional of industries, stood poised on the brink of change.

---

[152] See Appendix 9.

[153] MAGB, Labour Sub-Committee Report, 27 March 1944.

[154] By the end of 1943 Taylors had obtained government permits to proceed with further air-conditioning, electrification and the installation of kiln-turners, while the ABM directors visited America to survey the latest technology. H. A. & D. Taylor, Directors' Minutes, 22 January, 11 May, 7 December 1943; ABM, Chairman's Report, 1943, 1944, 1945.

[155] MAGB, Chairman's Speech, 30 August 1943, 27 March 1944.

7

The Malting Revolution, 1945–75

The maltster of today is a very different individual to his namesake of 10, 20, 50 or even 100 years ago, but most of the change [has] occurred in the last decade ... One can only wonder whether the maltster of 1975 will be recognisable as such, and not just a white coated automaton seated in front of a huge control panel, selecting his barley by some electronic device and controlling the whole of a vast malt factory by the pressure of a finger.[1]

So wrote Jock Causton in 1965 in his review of 'One Hundred Years of Malting', his prophetic words capturing the pace and scale of change facing the industry. For, despite the progress after 1880, by the outbreak of the Second World War empirical methods still prevailed and most malt was made in floor maltings built before the turn of the century.[2] The war marked the turning point, the arrival of the combine harvester and the destruction of capital stock prompting the first significant advances in technology. The return to peace brought further problems. As elsewhere, maltsters soon felt the impact of the escalating costs of labour and fixed capital; the first stimulated technical change, but the second proved prohibitive for all but the largest companies. More specifically, sales-maltsters faced radical changes in supply and demand. Until the late 1950s, government controls depressed all aspects of the malt trade. Thereafter, the surge in whisky production and world beer output underpinned the penetration of new and growing markets. Lastly, the industry felt the full force of the widespread merger movement, as rapid rationalisation of the British brewing industry transformed the pattern of supply and brought to an end the centuries-old relationship between the two sectors.

The return to peace brought little relief to either brewers or maltsters from the controls and restrictions of wartime. Indeed, in many ways, the late 1940s and early 1950s proved more difficult. Beer duty increased, to peak in April 1948 at £8 18s. 10d. per barrel of 1027°, 645 per cent above the pre-war duty. Even after reductions in the budgets of 1949 and 1950,

---

[1] J. W. F. Causton, 'One Hundred Years of Malting: Some Notes on its Growth and Development', *Brewers' Journal*, Centenary Number (1965), p. 134.

[2] A. Macey, 'Advances in Malting Techniques', *Brewers' Guardian*, Centenary Issue, September (1971), pp. 89–93.

it remained above the 1944–47 level.[3] In addition the world grain shortage
prompted restrictions in beer output. In May 1946 production was limited
to 85 per cent of the standard barrelage of the previous year (ending 30
September 1945); and in January 1949 to 78 per cent. Cereals were similarly
controlled. Maltsters' steeping licences were immediately cut to 90 per cent
of their 1945–46 quotas, with 1946–47 preliminary licences issued for 60
per cent, rather than the usual 80 per cent, of estimated requirements.[4]
Consequently, there were shortages of beer in many areas. The fuel crisis
of 1947, the relatively high price of beer and delays in the much-needed
refurbishment of public houses were further factors exacerbating the situation. Even after 1950, when many restrictions eased, the demand for beer
remained sluggish and by 1958 output had fallen by 27.2 per cent of the
1945 level to 23.7 million bulk barrels (see Fig. 7.1).

Figure 7.1 United Kingdom beer production, 1945–75 (million bulk barrels).
Note: 1945 = Year to 31 March 1946, *et seq.*
Source: Gourvish and Wilson, *British Brewing Industry*, pp. 618, 630.

[3] Average gravity was also cut by 10 per cent between August 1946 and May 1947. The
incremental duty for each degree above 1027° also rose from 5s. 2d. to 6s. 7d. These measures
are discussed in detail by T. R. Gourvish and R. G. Wilson, *The British Brewing Industry,
1830–1980* (Cambridge, 1994), pp. 356–57, 364–68.
[4] Restrictions on buying and steeping remained in force until the 1950–51 season. Ministry
of Food Direction to Maltsters, 3 June 1946; Brewers' Society, Minutes of Brewing Materials
Committee, 23 October 1947, 14 July 1948; MAGB, Chairman's Address, 23 October 1950.

In contrast, recovery after 1958 was demand-led. Greater prosperity and population growth stimulated a general increase in alcohol consumption.[5] New products, such as keg beer and lager, and the liberalisation of licensing which led to a growing number of supermarket outlets, underpinned a deepening of the market to include new groups of beer-drinkers, especially the middle class, women and the young. After a long downward trend, beer consumption rose from a low point of 137 pints per head in 1958 to 203.7 in 1975.[6] As Fig. 7.2 illustrates, the demand for malt for brewing followed a similar pattern.

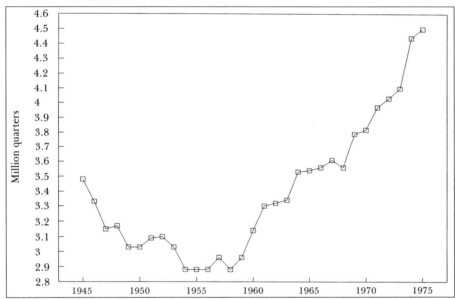

Figure 7.2 Malt consumed in brewing, UK, 1945–75 (million quarters).
Note: Year end = 30 September to 1970; 31 March thereafter.
Source: See below, Appendix 2.

The steady decline to 2.88 million quarters by 1958, a fall of 17.2 per cent of the 1945 level, was less steep than the corresponding fall in beer output. This reflected both an increase in average beer gravity of some 7 per cent in 1945–50 and a fall in the use of adjuncts from the exceptional levels of wartime. In particular, further restrictions on the use of sugar saw consumption decline by a third of the pre-war level.[7] Conversely, after 1958

[5] In 1958–70 beer consumption grew by 3.5 per cent per annum, spirits by 4.5 per cent. Brewers' Society, *UK Statistical Handbook* (1976), pp. 16, 32.

[6] Brewers' Society, *UK Statistical Handbook* (1976), p. 32

[7] Sugar was first rationed in April 1940 to 70 per cent of the 1939 level. This was pegged at 90 per cent in September 1945 and further reduced to 74 per cent in January 1948 and 71.7 per cent in January 1950. Brewers' Society, Annual Report (1949–50), p. 21. See Appendix 2.

the demand for malt rose less rapidly than beer production. The growing popularity of light beers and fall in the relative price of alternative cereals such as maize again encouraged the greater use of adjuncts. These ranged from the traditional flaked maize and rice to new products such as wheat flour. In particular it was feared that barley syrups would prove an effective substitute for malt.[8] Advances in brewing technology, such as the lauter tun, also enabled a further improvement in the extraction rate. This was increasingly sacrificed, however, by the use of barleys of higher nitrogen content, shorter germination times and the reduction of mashing time in order to obtain faster throughput in the brewery.[9] While the proportion of malt in the brewing grist declined from 80.6 per cent in 1950–54 to 77.3 per cent in 1970–74, overall the total weight of malt and adjuncts per gallon of beer increased.[10]

Of far greater importance were changes in the pattern of supply. In the quarter century after 1950, brewing experienced a wave of amalgamation and acquisition which radically restructured the industry. This prompted an equally far-reaching rationalisation of malting which is discussed below. In addition, for many brewers their involvement in costly acquisition programmes, and investment in new production plant and retail outlets, took precedence over extending malting capacity. Most continued to operate their own maltings to full capacity but, as demand increased throughout the 1960s, brewers' production failed to keep pace.[11] In 1963 (the first year for which the Maltsters' Association collected statistics), 55.0 per cent (1.8 million quarters) of all the malt consumed in brewing was produced by sales-maltsters. By 1975 the proportion had risen to 64.9 per cent (2.9 million quarters), demonstrating a significant reversal of the trend which, for more than a century, had seen sales-maltsters produce a falling share of the malt used in brewing.

The second major post-war development was the rapid expansion after 1960 of the demand for malt for distilling. Traditionally, the Scotch whisky distillers had been virtually self-sufficient in the supply of malt. Most worked their own maltings and the small quantities purchased were supplied by Scottish sales-maltsters. From the beginning of the Second World War, a number of factors combined to transform the industry. First, from December 1939 distillation was restricted and for six years whisky stocks were steadily depleted by continuing supplies to home and export markets.[12] Secondly,

---

[8] See pp. 189–90.

[9] I. M. Burgess and C. J. Knell, *British Malting Barley: Supply and Demand* (London, 1978) p. 75.

[10] Ibid., pp. 74–75, 356, 359.

[11] Several brewers either closed capacity or ceased malting in the early 1970s: Vaux, Camerons, Newcastle Breweries, Jennings and Greenalls, while in 1972 the sales-maltsters, J. P. Simpson, acquired Bernard's Haddington maltings.

[12] Only minimal quantities of new whisky were produced and home market supplies sharply curtailed. Exports were maintained as far as possible, especially to the USA, to finance arms

like brewing, the industry was constrained by the post-war shortages of grain, the 1945 distilling licences limiting production to 45 per cent of the 1938–39 make.[13] Thirdly, from 1 May 1947, the government decreed that 75 per cent of all production was to be exported (the majority to hard currency markets). Against a background of growing economic prosperity, restrictions on domestic sales remained in force until the late 1950s.[14] The result was a pent-up demand for whisky which was only partially satisfied by the steady increase in production from 29.5 million original proof gallons in 1950 to 41.1 million in 1956. Thereafter (apart from a sharp decline in 1968), expansion, underpinned by rising exports to the USA, Japan and Europe, and by buoyant domestic demand, was rapid, output rising to an all-time peak of 183.6 million gallons in 1974.[15]

Total production is divided between grain and malt whisky. The former, representing the greater part of the industry, is produced by the patent, or 'Coffey', still process, where around 85 per cent of the mash is unmalted grain, usually maize or (in modern times) locally-grown wheat. The remaining 15 per cent is diastatic malt, either imported from Finland or made from imported barley.[16] In contrast, malt whisky (produced by the pot still process) is made only from malted barley and this, although the smaller part of the industry, has tended to define the malt market.[17] In 1950 malt whisky output, at 12.8 million original proof gallons, represented 43.3 per cent of total production. Output rose steadily, but more slowly than the growth of grain whisky production, to 1964, then increased at an annual average rate of growth of 9.7 per cent to 1974 against 2.7 per cent for grain whisky, thereby increasing its market share to 45.0 per cent (82.7 million gallons) at the peak in 1974.[18] This trend was reflected in the malt consumed in distilling (see Fig. 7.3), which, apart from the sharp fall in 1968,

purchases. M. S. Moss and J. R. Hume, *The Making of Scotch Whisky: A History of the Scotch Whisky Distilling Industry* (Edinburgh, 1981), pp. 162–65; see also J. House, *Pride of Perth: The Story of Arthur Bell & Sons Limited, Scotch Whisky Distillers* (London, 1976); B. Spiller, *The Chameleon's Eye: James Buchanan & Company Limited, 1884–1984* (London, 1984).

[13] No distilling licences were issued for 1946.

[14] The domestic allocation was reduced to 20 per cent of production in May 1948 and duty increased to £10 10s. 10d. per proof gallon. Formal government restrictions ended in 1953 but, because of the shortage of mature stocks, rationing persisted until 1959. Moss and Hume, *Scotch Whisky*, p. 167.

[15] An annual average growth rate of 8.10 per cent in 1952–56, 10.70 per cent in 1956–67 and 5.56 per cent in 1967–74; exports rose by an average 9.6 per cent annually in 1951–75, Burgess and Knell, *British Malting Barley*, pp. 52, 113.

[16] Ibid., p. 38; the majority is now made by British maltsters.

[17] On average, most brands of blended whisky contain about 35 per cent of malt whisky to 65 per cent of grain, the higher quality brands normally having a higher malt content. Ibid., p. 39.

[18] An average annual growth rates between 1952–64 of 8.33 per cent for malt whisky and 13.19 per cent for grain, Ibid., pp. 49–50.

rose steadily from 826,000 quarters in 1950 to a peak of 4.54 million in 1974.[19]

Figure 7.3 Malt used in distilling, UK, 1945–75 (million quarters).
Note: Year end to 1969 = 30 September; from 1970 = 31 March
Source: See Appendix 2.

The rapid growth in whisky output was accompanied by a corresponding expansion in productive capacity. Many long-disused distilleries, such as Glenturret and Benriach, were reopened. In 1957 MacDonald & Muir doubled the capacity of their Glenmoray Distillery, as did the Canadian firm of Hiram Walker at Glenburgie the following year. In 1959–67 Scottish malt distilleries increased the number of their stills by more than half.[20] Overall, the number of distilleries in operation rose from ninety-five in 1950 to 102 a decade later and 122 in 1975 (of which 108 were malt whisky distilleries), while in 1960–69 a total of 113 new stills were built (all but eight of which were malt stills) with a further 115 malt stills added in 1970–74.[21] A few of the leading companies also expanded their malting capacity. The Distillers' Company, which dominated both malt and grain production, built large centralised maltings to supply the group. Similarly,

---

[19] See Appendix 2.
[20] Moss and Hume, *Scotch Whisky*, pp. 168–72.
[21] Ibid., p. 223; Burgess and Knell, *British Malting Barley*, p. 42; K. Marsden, 'Technical Change in the British Malting Industry' (unpublished Ph.D. thesis, University of Salford, 1985), p. 149.

the international corporations which penetrated the growing market ensured their self-sufficiency, Hiram Walker acquiring the Kirkcaldy
sales-maltster, Robert Kilgour & Company, and the American Publicker
Industries (who in 1965 converted an old paper mill into Inver House
distillery), forming a separate subsidiary, Moffat Malting.[22] For most companies, investment in new stills took precedence. A growing number closed
small, outdated floor maltings, which were neither cost effective nor able to
support their growing needs, and for the first time bought their supplies
from English sales-maltsters.

The resulting penetration of the distilling market developed in two phases.
Initially, English sales-maltsters supplied home produced malt, often selling
through a Scottish agent. ABM were represented by the Leith grain merchants Herdman & McDougall,[23] while in 1961 Pauls began an enduring
relationship with the Kirkcaldy maltster Robert Hutchison & Company.[24] In
the first season, Hutchisons sold 30,000 quarters on behalf of Pauls, 60,000
quarters in 1963–64 and 170,000 quarters three years later. Pauls also sold
directly to William Grant: 11,000 quarters in 1961–62 and 77,000 quarters
the following season, again demonstrating the rapid growth of the market.[25]
By 1966–67 Pauls' distilling trade stood at 260,000 quarters, while that for
the entire industry, some 1.5 million quarters, was of sufficient scale for the
Maltsters' Association to commission a special malt train to transport consignments north.[26]

Until the mid 1960s, climatic limitations prevented any significant increase
in barley production and therefore further development of the malting
industry on Scottish soil. The nearest any English maltster ventured was to
Bridlington in Yorkshire, where in 1963 Munton & Fison, in partnership
with Highland Distilleries and Invergordon Distillers, built a 300,000 quarter
capacity malting.[27] But four years later, the culmination of researches into
barley breeding and technology discussed below prompted the first penetration into Scotland when four of Pauls' former employees, led by their

---

[22] Marsden, 'Technical Change', p. 135.

[23] Herdman & McDougall worked with Geoffrey Cherry-Downes to establish ABM's distilling
trade. E. F. Taylor, 'History of the Formation and Development of Associated British Maltsters
Limited, 1928–78' (typescript, 1978), p. 25.

[24] Pauls' links with Robert Hutchison, who enjoyed the highest reputation in Scotland,
developed from the personal friendship of Jock Causton and Sandy Hutchison, who for many
years worked together on the executive of the MAGB and the Home Grown Cereals Authority.

[25] Correspondence between R. & W. Paul and Robert Hutchison & Company, 1962–73.
Information supplied by Hugh Philbrick.

[26] Other major suppliers were ABM, approximately 500,000 quarters; and Munton & Fison,
who specialised in the production of diastatic malt for the grain whisky distillers, 300,000
quarters. Taylor, 'Associated British Maltsters', p. 25; Munton & Fison, *A Brief History of Munton
& Fison Limited to Mark Their Fiftieth Anniversary, 1921–1971* (privately printed, 1971), pp. 11–12.

[27] The new company, Edward Fison Limited, became a wholly-owned subsidiary of Munton
& Fison plc in 1968.

research chemist, Oliver Griffin, formed the Moray Firth Malting Company. The venture proved successful, tempting others to follow suit: ABM in 1970 and two years later, Pauls (who acquired their long-standing agents, Robert Hutchison & Company). These developments underpinned a further significant increase in market share. Whereas in 1963 British sales-maltsters produced 643,000 quarters of malt for distilling, 34.9 per cent of the total quantity consumed by the industry. By the peak of 1974, the quantity had increased to 2,572,000 quarters, representing 56.7 per cent of total distilling consumption. A market which for centuries had been of minimal significance had, in the space of thirty years, assumed an importance almost equal to that of the brewing industry (see Table 7.1).

The final development of the period, after a lapse of almost two centuries, was the revival of a viable export trade. During the inter-war years, several of the leading companies had attempted to penetrate overseas markets. ABM, after considering the purchase of a European firm, in 1939 formed their own subsidiary company, ABM Exports Limited, under the management of a Prague maltster, Bedrich Lorenz.[28] Similarly, Pauls secured contracts in Switzerland and with the South African brewers Ohlsens. But generally, the high import duties imposed by many European and South American countries proved an effective barrier. At their peak in 1930, total UK malt exports amounted to 118,807 quarters, 83.8 per cent of which was sent to Ireland (effectively to Guinness) against the 3.9 million quarters consumed by the domestic brewing and distilling industries.[29] After the Second World War, there was every incentive to increase exports. While UK beer output declined by 18.7 per cent in 1946–58, world production increased by 53.4 per cent over the same period and, in 1946–75, by 217 per cent.[30] Unfortunately, statistics for world malt exports are not available before 1965. Thereafter, the market grew rapidly, reflecting the significant increase in beer production in Africa, Central America and Asia, regions unsuited to barley cultivation and, therefore, with little malting capacity.[31] Between 1965 and 1975 the world trade in malt grew from 5.44 million quarters to 14.7 million quarters, an annual average growth rate of 11.5

[28] A Jewish refugee, Lorenz had previously been a partner in the Prague malting firm of Klatscher & Lorenz, which ceased trading in April 1939. ABM, Directors' Minutes, 6 July 1931, 3 April, 3 July, 14 August 1939.

[29] ABM examined the feasibility of establishing an agency in Argentina, but Arthur Cherry-Downes (son of the joint managing director), who lived in Buenos Aires, concluded the combination of transport costs and import duties would render the trade unprofitable. ABM, Directors' Minutes, 11 February, 8 April, 13 May 1929; Annual Statement of Overseas Trade; see Appendix 4.

[30] World beer production increased from 251 million hectolitres in 1946 to 385 million in 1958 and 796 million in 1975; Pollock and Pool Limited, *The Malting Industry, 1995–2002*, table 1.1.

[31] Burgess and Knell, *British Malting Barley*, p. 350; Pollock and Pool, *Malting Industry*, section 7.

per cent which far outstripped the 2.4 per cent annual growth of the UK market.[32]

Nevertheless, the post-war increase in UK malt exports (see Fig. 7.4), to an all-time peak of 866,471 quarters in 1974, was achieved against a difficult climate.

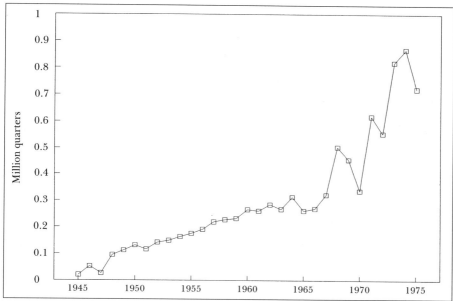

Figure 7.4 UK malt exports, 1945–75 (million quarters).
Source: See Appendix 4.

Initially, the continuation of war-time controls hindered progress. With the exception of small quantities sent to British possessions such as Malta and Singapore, malt exports were prohibited until 1947, when a quota of 60,000 quarters, allocated according to pre-war exports, was introduced.[33] Increased to 131,200 quarters the following year, it remained in force until 1952–53.[34] In the event, the quota was mainly academic because the restrictions on the supply and price of raw materials ensured that the export ceiling was rarely threatened. In particular, the maximum and minimum prices for home-grown barley, first imposed in 1942, continued for eleven

[32] United Nations, *Food and Agriculture Organisation: Trade Yearbook*, 25, 29; Appendix 4.

[33] Export licences were allocated by the chairman (Colonel Grinling) and an advisory committee of the MAGB.

[34] A condition was that a substantial proportion was exported to dollar-earning countries; exports to some 'soft' currency areas were prohibited (for example, to Holland until 1949). Initially the largest importer of British malt was Switzerland. Minutes of the Cereals and Exports Sub-Committee, MAGB, 18 July 1949.

years. British maltsters, unlike their foreign counterparts, therefore purchased barley at well above the world price. Foreign brewers accepted a small premium for the high quality of British malt, but in November 1949 the MAGB estimated a gap of 15 per cent between the average continental price of 150 shillings a quarter and the lowest price their members could achieve.[35] Orders were repeatedly lost to Denmark, France and Belgium, and to the most serious competitor, Czechoslovakia. The Czechs traded through their well-established national export agency, Koospool, and, with the benefit of government subsidies, sold high quality malt at near dumping prices.[36] Requests to the Ministry of Food for similar support brought no response.[37] In fact the lowering of the statutory minimum price of barley merely prompted a gentleman's agreement between the National Farmers' Union and the Brewers' Society, whereby, in order to ensure an adequate supply of good quality malting barley, brewers agreed to pay not less than 10 shillings per quarter above the minimum price. With some reluctance the MAGB together with the National Association of Agricultural Merchants (NACAM) and Flaked Maize Manufacturers' Association (FMMA), accepted a scheme resulting in the formation in March 1950 of the Barley Panel, with representatives from each industry.[38] The agreement was sustained until early in 1953 when the Maltsters' Association informed the Brewers' Society that they could no longer support minimum prices.[39] The decision, however, coincided with the introduction, under the 1947 Agriculture Act, of deficiency payments for cereals. This finally shifted the burden of support onto the British taxpayer and allowed maltsters to operate in a free market.

By the end of the decade attention was focused on the newly-created European Common Market. Despite initial uncertainty, the industry looked with increasing optimism towards Britain's prospective membership. Throughout 1962 the Maltsters' Association held informal talks with Euromalt, the association of EEC maltsters, who extended a warm welcome to

---

[35]   MAGB, 15 November 1948.

[36]   The 1950 unofficial agreed UK minimum price for Pilsener malt to Switzerland was 69.25 SF; the Danish price, 67SF and the Czech, 61SF, which was subsequently reduced to 55 F. Minutes of the Cereals and Export Sub-Committee, MAGB, 18 September, 23 October 1950.

[37]   Of particular annoyance were imports of cheap Polish malt into the UK and the numerous bilateral trading agreements, such as the 1949–50 Anglo-Italian Trade Agreement, which excluded malt. Minutes of the Cereals and Exports Sub-Committee, MAGB, 15, 29 November 1948, 17 January 1949, 27 March 1950.

[38]   It was also agreed that brewers would use at least 90 per cent of home grown barley (80 per cent for export beer). The Barley Panel, which served between 1950–56, initially comprised Colonel H. D. Wise and J. W. F. Causton (MAGB), Lord Gretton and N. B. Smiley (Brewers' Society), L. M. DuPre and G. C. Williams (NFU), Colonel E. P. Clarke and H. B. Watkins (NACAM) and W. S. H. Paul and R. Wallace (FMMA). The Scotch Whisky Association joined in 1951.

[39]   The gentleman's agreement continued, but from 1954 applied only to maximum prices; MAGB, Chairman's Report, 20 September 1954.

their British counterparts.[40] After de Gaulle's veto, the Association was instrumental in setting up a similar Eftamalt Committee. But the EFTA members were neither well organised nor were they such important players in the world market.[41] The benefits were slight and, at best, did little to alleviate the growing problems facing British maltsters: the internal customs union and third-party tariffs erected by the Common Market; subsidies and grants enabling member countries to expand their malting capacity at low cost; and export restitutions, which compensated for the high internal price of malting barley and allowed members to sell cheaply in the new high-growth markets of Africa and Asia.[42] The benefits can be seen most clearly in the rapid growth of the French industry. In 1960, French malt exports totalled 439,520 quarters; twelve years later, 2.29 million quarters, an average annual growth rate of 14.7 per cent. In contrast, over the same period, British exports increased from 264,013 quarters to 554,727 quarters, a growth rate of 6.4 per cent per year. Moreover, between 1965 and 1972, the French share of the world malt trade rose from 15.3 per cent to 22.7 per cent; Britain's, from 5.3 per cent to 5.5 per cent. Equally significant, in 1973, the first year of Britain's membership of the EEC, exports rose to 818,688 quarters, an increase of 47.6 per cent over the previous year (7.1 per cent of world trade).[43]

With virtually no support, in real terms, from government, the progress made was considerable. Overall, the changing pattern of British exports closely paralleled those of world trade, although the falling share of West German imports clearly reflected the problems associated with the Common Market. In 1960 West Germany alone accounted for 45.3 per cent of all British exports, by 1970 only 7.8 per cent. Over the same period, the emphasis had shifted to the great growth markets of Africa and Asia, with Nigeria taking 19.7 per cent and Japan 25.9 per cent of British exports.[44]

[40] MAGB, Chairman's Report, 17 September 1962, 16 September 1963.

[41] The European Free Trade Association, formed in 1960, initially comprised Austria, Denmark, Norway, Portugal, Sweden, Switzerland and the UK. A major problem was that some countries were not organised through national associations equivalent to the MAGB. MAGB, Chairman's Report, 16 September 1963, 19 September 1966.

[42] Restitutions, calculated on the basis of 1.33 tones of barley/1 tonne of malt, took into account the premium paid for malting barley as against the world price of barley.

[43] French maltsters received government subsidies, grants for the provision of grain storage facilities and concessional interest rates from the Crédit Agricole. The Belgians, who received similar benefits, increased their share of world trade from 13.8 per cent to 18.5 per cent over the same period. United Nations, *Food and Agriculture Organisation: Trade Yearbook*, 25, 29; Burgess and Knell, *British Malting Barley*, p. 350.

[44] In 1960, Europe accounted for 56.9 per cent of British exports, Africa 8.3 per cent and Venezuela, 9.0 per cent. By 1970, while West Germany still accounted for 8.8 per cent of world imports, second only to Japan at 13.4 per cent, Europe as a whole took only 14.7 per cent of British exports, South America 15.3 per cent, Africa 27.5 per cent and Asia 31.6 per cent. Annual Statement of the Overseas Trade of the UK, 1960, 1970; United Nations, *Food and Agriculture Organisation: Trade Yearbook*.

Three companies, in particular, dominated these developments, ABM, Pauls, and Munton & Fison, who by 1965 were responsible for 50 per cent, 25 per cent and 12½ per cent of exports respectively.[45] Pauls' first post-war consignments, some 2620 quarters of malt, left Ipswich in 1947; by 1960 the quantity had risen to 52,480 quarters. Three years later, their first Wanderhaufen malting was built to supply the growing trade and the following season 78,720 quarters were sent to more than twenty-five countries, notably West Germany, Africa and Venezuela. The majority went direct from Ipswich to the Port of London or to Europe in the firm's own barges and was sold through two agents, Eric Briess and Alex Schindler. As in the domestic market, much depended on reputation and personal contacts, and in 1968, on Schindler's retirement, the business of Schindler Stein was purchased for £110,000. Three years later, to gain experience of the Common Market and the system of restitutions, a quarter stake was taken in a Belgian company, Malteries Huys NV; while in 1973 an Alsace company, Usines Ethel SA, situated in the heartland of French beer production, was

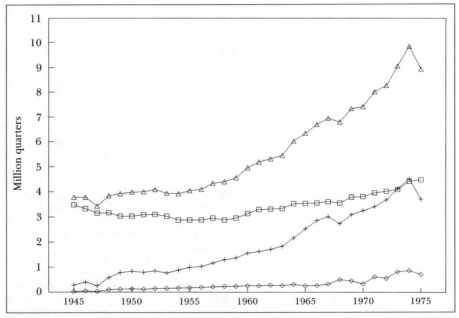

Figure 7.5 Total malt consumed in brewing and distilling and exported, 1945–75 (million quarters).

Key: □ malt used in brewing   + malt used in distilling
         ◇ malt exported   △ total malt consumed.
Source: Appendix 2 and 4.

[45] *East Anglian Daily Times*, 26 January, 9 October 1965.

purchased.[46] That year, Britain's first as a member of the European Community, 265,680 quarters of malt were exported from Ipswich alone.[47] The full impact of the post-war changes in the demand for malt is illustrated in Fig. 7.5.

The total consumption of malt used in brewing and distilling, together with that exported, rose from a post-war low of 3.42 million quarters in 1947 to a peak of 9.84 million quarters in 1974. That year the quantity used by distillers (4.54 million quarters) exceeded for the first time that consumed in brewing (4.44 million quarters). In addition, 866,471 quarters (8.8 per cent) were exported. Equally notably, the previous year had seen the long-established peak of 8.91 million quarters produced in 1898 finally surpassed. Not least, as Table 7.1 demonstrates, the period had witnessed a decline in the self-sufficiency of both brewers and distillers, with much of the growing demand for malt met by sales-maltsters.

Table 7.1

Total UK malt production, percentage produced by brewers, distillers and sales-maltsters, 1963–75

Year	Total malt production	Brewers		Distillers		Sales-maltsters	
	Thousand quarters	*Thousand quarters*	*%*	*Thousand quarters*	*%*	*Thousand quarters*	*%*
1963	5688	1500	26.4	1200	21.1	2988	52.5
1964	5758	1433	24.9	1300	22.6	3025	52.5
1965	6285	1333	21.2	1347	21.4	3605	57.4
1966	6368	1379	21.7	1378	21.6	3611	56.7
1967	6278	1410	22.5	1522	24.2	3346	53.3
1968	6606	1397	21.2	1535	23.2	3674	55.6
1969	6914	1449	21.0	1640	23.7	3825	55.3
1970	7439	1483	19.9	1725	23.2	4231	56.9
1971	7478	1509	20.2	1771	23.7	4198	56.1
1972	8370	1620	19.3	1863	22.3	4887	58.4
1973	9000	1778	19.8	1909	21.2	5314	59.0
1974	9590	1620	16.9	1968	20.5	6002	62.6
1975	9099	1640	18.0	1476	16.2	5983	65.8

Note: Figures for production, based on members' returns are consistently below those for consumption (see Appendix 2).

Source: MAGB, Annual Statistics.

[46] And in 1977, the German company Malzfabrik Schragmalz GMBH.

[47] See Appendix 6; I am grateful to Peter Simmonds for information regarding the development of Pauls' export trade.

The thirty years after the Second World War were to witness a technical revolution unprecedented in the history of the malting industry. Despite the advances of the last quarter of the nineteenth century, the malting process had changed little. In particular, the years of falling demand and overcapacity after 1920 had brought few further developments. Progress was limited to minor advances; such as improvements to malt bins and barley-intake; and although most firms maintained laboratories, these were more concerned with routine analysis than research and development.[48] The major contribution of the period was the research conducted by the Institute of Brewing, in conjunction with the government-sponsored National Institute of Agricultural Botany (NIAB), the Plant Breeding Institute and some of the leading brewers, notably Guinness, on the quality and selection of malting barley. Field trials held at Rothamsted Experimental Station in 1922–31 also led to a better understanding of fertilisers and underpinned a significant increase in barley yields, while a series of annual conferences held during the 1930s were instrumental in bringing together farmer, merchant and maltster, laying the foundations for a closer working relationship in the post-war era.[49] Such work stands out in these otherwise bleak years.

The war marked the turning point: the loss of malting capacity, the advent of the combine harvester and, not least, the labour shortage all made change inevitable. Most significantly, with the return to peace it was soon evident that the cheap and ready supply of labour, which for so long had inhibited technical change, was not to return. Despite higher wages, men were no longer prepared to work irregular hours, seven days a week, on a seasonal basis.[50] Before the war, for example, the Burton maltster Yeomans, Cherry & Curtis employed a labour force of ninety; by 1951 this was reduced to seventy-one; despite the provision of employee housing, the position deteriorated steadily into the 1960s.[51] More positively, war-time demand had brought healthy profits and enabled many companies to build up the substantial reserves necessary to invest in labour-saving capital equipment, thereby encouraging modernisation and technical change.

Undoubtedly the most pressing problem facing the industry was the rapid spread of the combine harvester. Two and a half thousand were at work in Britain's fields in 1944, more than 10,000 six years later, when around a half of all cereal crops were cut by them.[52] Hence the barley crop, which

[48] H. M. Lancaster, 'Advances Made During the Last Fifty Years in Malting', *Journal of the Institute of Brewing*, 42 (1936), pp. 497–98.

[49] W. H. Bird, *A History of the Institute of Brewing* (London, 1955), pp. 40–42, 76–77; 'History of the Guinness Barley Research Station' (typescript, 1987).

[50] At Pauls, labour costs per quarter of malt at the Stoke Maltings increased from 2s. 3d. in 1938 to 5s. 3d. in 1950 and 8s. 1d. in 1960. R. & W. Paul Limited, Annual Costings.

[51] Yeomans, Cherry & Curtis, Directors' Minutes, 19 March, 12 November 1951, 29 December 1954, 18 November, 30 December 1960.

[52] B. Seward, 'Developments in Harvesting Technology: A History of Reducing Labour Requirements', *Brewing Room Book, 1998–2000* (Pauls Malt, 1997), p. 45.

traditionally had been stored in the stack and threshed throughout the winter months, providing a steady flow of grain, was increasingly harvested and marketed in little more than eight weeks. In practical terms, older varieties of malting barley were not ideal for combine harvesting because their long straw made them prone to 'lodging'.[53] The brief period of marketing also placed new demands on working capital.[54] Most importantly, existing storage and drying facilities were totally inadequate. By 1952 it was estimated that a further 500,000 tons of storage capacity were urgently needed.[55] Despite other demands on their capital resources, maltsters were forced to spend huge sums on the provision of drying and storage capacity, such as the 40,000 quarter silo built by Pauls at Ipswich in 1951.[56]

The situation was made more difficult by the post-war reliance on the domestic crop. From the 1880s maltsters had used substantial quantities of imported barley. Estimates for the late nineteenth century suggest between 25–30 per cent of all barley malted was foreign. By the 1924 *Census of Production*, the proportion was 39 per cent and, despite the pressure put on brewers to use more home-grown barley, by 1939, of the 9.5 million cwts of barley malted, 30 per cent were still imported.[57] This was partly because insufficient barley was grown in the UK to satisfy maltsters' requirements. In addition imported grain was ideal for malting during the summer months and until the new crop was ready, thus avoiding the costly carry-over of stocks from the previous season to the end of October.[58] However, with the wartime embargo on imported barley, the position changed irrevocably. Six years of dependence on the domestic crop, together with the post-war

[53] Lodging, or flattening by wind and rain; it was also essential that the grain was properly dry before harvesting. J. S. Hough, *The Biochemistry of Malting and Brewing* (Cambridge, 1985), p. 15.

[54] It was estimated that, by early November 1951, as much as £10 million of maltsters working capital had been deployed in purchasing the new season's barley. Letter from H. A. & D. Taylor to the MAGB, 10 November 1951.

[55] Muntona Limited, *Drying and Storage*, p. 30.

[56] Despite constant pressure from the MAGB for a coordinated policy, there was no effective response from the government. A repeated complaint was that the planned production of combines was never matched by the issue of building licences for grain storage. There was also little consensus of opinion between farmers, maltsters and merchants. While in Europe the problem was resolved by the provision of co-operative farm storage, in Britain the burden fell heavily on the malting industry. MAGB, Chairman's Report, 20 October 1947, 18 October 1948, 17 October 1949; I. R. Murrell, 'Malting History' (typescript, no date), p. 8; *Ipswich Evening Star*, 30 January 1951; Taylor, 'Associated British Maltsters', p. 22.

[57] See p. 67; *Census of Production (1924)*, Final Report, pp. 162–63; Causton, 'One Hundred Years of Malting', p. 131.

[58] Barley, which ripens in cool, damp conditions such as those common in Britain, experiences a period of dormancy which prevents germination immediately after reaching maturity. Therefore the domestic crop had to be stacked for at least four to six weeks before it was threshed and ready for malting. Causton, 'One Hundred Years of Malting', p. 131; Macey, 'Advances in Malting Techniques', p. 93; O. P. Hudson, 'Malting Technology', *Journal of the Institute of Brewing*, Centenary Review, 92, March-April 1986, p. 116.

restrictions, and the gentleman's agreement whereby brewers guaranteed to use at least 90 per cent of home-grown barley, meant that British maltsters were never again to rely heavily on imported grain. At the extreme, Pauls, who before the war had relied mainly on foreign, principally Californian, barley, subsequently used almost 100 per cent English.[59]

More positively these developments gave a new stimulus to the work of the NIAB, in particular the breeding and selection of more suitable varieties of malting barley. Before 1939, *Spratt Archer* and *Plumage Archer*, developed early in the century, had accounted for 80 per cent of the spring barley acreage.[60] Two Danish varieties, *Kenia* and *Maja*, although not classed as malting barleys, subsequently became popular because of their higher yields and resistance to lodging. The real breakthrough came in 1953 with the release of *Proctor*. Bred at Cambridge by Dr G. D. H. Bell, Director of the Plant Breeding Institute, *Proctor* was low in nitrogen, highly responsive to fertiliser and short-strawed, and quickly became the dominant variety south of the Humber. It retained its popularity until the early 1970s when it was challenged by higher yielding, disease-resistant but lower quality varieties such as *Zephyr* and *Wing* and by the near feed varieties *Julia* and *Maris Mink*. Its final demise was brought about by *Maris Otter*, a variety which spearheaded the revolution in winter barley growing that led to the rapid decline in availability of spring varieties from 1975.[61] Lastly, the 1964 Plant Varieties and Seeds Act, which enabled barley breeders to claim royalties, stimulated further progress. Most notably, the first variety to qualify, *Golden Promise*, an exceptionally short-strawed, early ripening variety, highly resistant to lodging, transformed the potential for growing malting barley in Scotland.[62]

The pressing need to increase grain storage, combined with building restrictions and the shortage of raw materials, meant that initially most companies tackled the problem of replacing their malting capacity in a piecemeal way. For many, this simply meant installing conveyors or elevators, mechanical turners and kiln loaders. The greatest benefits came from air-conditioning, which enabled year-round production. By 1950 around 100 maltings had been converted.[63] For those with no option but to replace lost capacity, the choice lay between a fully mechanised floor malting or one of

[59] This comprised approximately 90 per cent of *Spratt Archer* to 10 per cent of *Plumage Archer*, all spring-sown except for a small amount of winter-sown *Spratt* and *Pioneer*. Information supplied by Hugh Philbrick.

[60] T. Davies, 'Development of New Varieties of Barley', *Brewers' Guardian*, Centenary Issue, September 1971, p. 80.

[61] Davies estimated that by 1962 *Proctor* accounted for 80 per cent of the spring barley acreage, Ibid., p. 80. See also A. Douet, 'Norfolk Agriculture, 1914–1972' (unpublished Ph.D. thesis, University of East Anglia, 1989), p. 377.

[62] Relative straw lengths were: *Spratt Archer* and *Plumage Archer*, 40 inches, *Proctor*, 32 inches and *Golden Promise* (bred by Dr Palmer for Milns of Chester), 28 inches. Davies, 'New Varieties of Barley', p. 81.

[63] Marsden, 'Technical Change', p. 185.

the available pneumatic systems. The former was developed in Germany before the First World War but, despite further advances during the 1930s, never became popular in Britain because of its high capital costs. Only two were built: one at Grimsby by Sandars & Company, to replace maltings destroyed by enemy action, and one for Worthington, the Burton brewer. In comparison with conventional floor maltings of similar size, both achieved substantial labour savings and increased output, but still contrasted unfavourably with a Saladin box (compartment) or drum malting.[64] These latter systems were first adopted in Europe during the late nineteenth century, but neither found favour in Britain, mainly because the malt produced was not of the quality considered right for the infusion system of brewing. However, the post-war era brought major improvements with the Saladin system, improved fans enabling the box length and depth of grain, and therefore batch size, to be increased.[65] Similarly, the addition of a perforated floor inside drums solved the air-flow problems which had previously resulted in poor quality malt.[66] Both systems achieved labour savings of up to three-quarters. Practically, drums had several advantages but were more costly to install and to maintain.[67] There was no consistent pattern of adoption: one emerged which reflected the needs of specific firms. In 1950 Munton & Fison installed four Swedish-designed drums in their new Stowmarket maltings. Eight years later, however, they added six Saladin boxes which proved to be more cost-effective for the production of low-margin export malt.[68] Conversely, ABM's first mechanical malting, a Saladin box, was completed at Louth in 1952. It was again found to be ideal for the high volume production of lager malt which was exported from Immingham. Those ABM built at Knapton (Yorkshire) in 1958, and Wallingford (Berkshire) in 1961 were also based on the compartment system. Subsequently drums were installed at Abingdon and Pontefract in 1964 and at Bury St Edmunds two years later.[69]

[64] Sandars' Grimsby malting, completed in 1952, had an annual capacity of 40,000 quarters. The huge cost of £998,000 was met by war compensation, but was secondary to Colonel Sandars' belief that only floor maltings made top-quality malt. Worthington's malting, built in 1955, had an annual output of 48,750 quarters and a labour force of eighteen, but proved less economical than Bass's drum malting built three years later. Sandars & Company, *Of Malt and Men, 1865–1965;* C. C. Owen, *The Greatest Brewery in the World: A History of Bass, Ratcliff & Gretton* (Chesterfield, 1992), pp. 175, 190. H. A. D. Cherry-Downes, 'Mechanisation of Maltings', *Journal of the Institute of Brewing*, 54 (1948), p. 211.

[65] Marsden, 'Technical Change', p. 189.

[66] Designed by F. A. Reddish, head maltster and chemist at the brewers Greene King, the improved drums were patented by the Bury St Edmunds engineer Robert Boby. R. G. Wilson, *Greene King: A Business and Family History* (London, 1983), p. 218.

[67] Drums were not prone to the constant condensation which affected boxes but ultimately the limitation of capacity compared unfavourably with box systems which were capable of taking batches of 1500–2000 quarters. Hudson, 'Malting Technology', p. 115; Cherry-Downes, 'Mechanisation of Maltings', p. 212; Taylor, 'Associated British Maltsters', pp. 22, 24.

[68] Munton & Fison, *A Brief History*, pp. 10–11.

[69] In 1959–60 Louth produced 91,850 quarters of malt and Knapton 103,340 quarters, of

The third pneumatic system, the Wanderhaufen or 'moving piece', was invented in 1878 by Jacobsen, the founder of the Carlsberg brewery. A modification of compartment malting, it represented the first system of semi-continuous production. Unlike the Saladin box, the germinating 'streets' were divided into evenly spaced sections containing batches of differing age (physically unseparated from each other). The turners gradually moved each batch of grain further along the street, leaving the first section clear for a new batch to fill. Again it was post-war improvements, particularly the mechanical turning developed by the German engineer Ostertag, which led to the system's wider adoption.[70] Popular in Europe, the first to be built in England was completed by Pauls in 1962. Six years earlier, the company had installed two Saladin boxes in a fire-damaged floor malting, thereby increasing production at Ipswich by 20,000 quarters a year. The Wanderhaufen offered several advantages, especially in the effectiveness of its turning, in its minimal labour requirements and, not least, in maximising the limited space at the dock-side. The four streets, together operated by six men, were capable of producing 60,000 quarters of malt a year. In comparison, Pauls huge seven-storey Stoke maltings, even with air-conditioning, had an annual capacity of 50,000 quarters and a labour force of thirty-four, while their country maltings at Thetford, Wells-Next-The-Sea and Stonham, between them producing around 27,500 quarters, required a total of forty men.[71]

While the savings in labour and space achieved by mechanised malting were critical to successful modernisation, so too were the gains accrued from a greater understanding of the fundamentals of the malting process. Here the key development was the establishment in 1951 of the Brewing Industry Research Foundation (BIRF) at Nutfield in Surrey.[72] A joint venture between the Brewers' Society and the Institute of Brewing, its main objective was to promote independent research for the benefit of the sector as a whole.[73] From the malting viewpoint the first major breakthrough, in 1954, was work by Pollock and others on the water sensitivity of barley, which showed that many samples previously classified as dormant were merely sensitive to

which 93 per cent and 89 per cent respectively were low dried or lager malt. Taylor, 'Associated British Maltsters', pp. 22–29.

[70] H. L. Philbrick, 'The Wanderhaufen System', *Brewers' Guardian*, 94 (1965), pp. 39–40.

[71] A second Wanderhaufen was built at Grantham in 1964. Hugh Baird & Sons also adopted the Wanderhaufen system because their site at Witham, Essex, was too restricted to allow Saladin boxes. New plant was installed in 1963, 1970 and 1974. H. L. Philbrick, Report on Proposed New Malting Unit (1959/60); Marsden, 'Technical Change', p. 297.

[72] Funded by the Brewers' Society with contributions from the Maltsters' Association, from 1976 the Foundation was known as the Brewery Research Foundation. The work of the Foundation is discussed in more detail in Gourvish and Wilson, *British Brewing Industry*, pp. 538–46.

[73] A. M. MacLeod, 'Twenty-Five Years of Brewing Science and Technology', *Brewing Trade Review*, October 1977, p. 17.

excessive moisture. These barleys failed to germinate under the conventional steeping system, where the grain was submerged for up to three days, but responded when exposed to limited quantities of water. Once germination had begun, they could accept the additional moisture necessary to support the full malting process. This led to the system of broken steeping, comprising a series of short steeps interspersed with longer, dry 'air-rests', which allowed oxygen to permeate the barley and facilitate respiration.[74] The result was more even germination and a reduction in process time. One problem was rapid rootlet growth which increased malting losses. This in turn prompted the use of small quantities of potassium bromate as a growth inhibitor and, subsequently, the development of various re-steeping techniques: a period of rapid germination, followed by a warm (38° C) water steep to kill root growth, then a final period of modification. This reduced malting losses by half and removed the need for turning and, although not widely adopted, made possible the development of steeping and germination in a single vessel.[75]

One of the most significant advances was the recognition of the role of the plant hormones, particularly the gibberellins, in germination. Gibberellin, derived from the fungus *Gibberella fujikuroi*, was first isolated in Japan in the 1920s. Subsequently, the Swedish chemist E. Sandegren demonstrated the ability of gibberellic acid to augment the natural gibberellins produced by the barley embryo, thus accelerating the malting process. Minute quantities added to the steep water or, more frequently, sprayed at the beginning of germination, reduced germination time, increased yield and shortened the period of dormancy.[76] First used commercially in 1959, it was estimated that by 1970 gibberellic acid was used in 73 per cent of British malting production.[77] Finally, Palmer's 'abrasion' process (mainly adopted by brewer-maltsters), where a small amount of the barley husk is removed, allowing greater and more rapid penetration of water and additives, led to a further acceleration of the malting process and a widening of the range of barleys suitable for malting.[78]

[74] R. E. Essery, B. H. Kirsop and J. R. A. Pollock, 'Studies in Barley and Malt: Effects of Water on Germination Tests', *Journal of the Institute of Brewing*, 60 (1954), pp. 471–81; Macey, 'Advances in Malting Techniques', p. 93.

[75] Hudson, 'Malting Technology', p. 117; Marsden, 'Technical Change', p. 208.

[76] By 1959 the dose was restricted to a range of 0.025 – 0.25 milligrams of gibberellic acid per kilogram of barley. Initially higher application rates were used but these could lead to unbalanced modification. Sodium or potassium bromate used in conjunction with gibberellic acid proved effective in restraining proteolysis as well as root growth. The development and use of gibberellic acid in malting is discussed more fully in Hough, *Biotechnology of Malting*, pp. 38–41; and J. S. Hough, D. E. Briggs and R. Stevens, *Malting and Brewing Science* (Cambridge, 1971), pp. 97–99.

[77] L. Nabseth and G. F. Ray, *The Diffusion of New Industrial Processes: An International Study* (Cambridge, 1971), p. 219.

[78] J. R. Hudson, 'Recent Developments in Brewing Technology', *Brewers' Guardian*, 105 (1976), p. 31.

Yet if the BIRF was instrumental in initiating malting research, attitudes within the industry were also changing. The Maltsters' Association established its own technical and research sub-committee: its annual symposium, held in conjunction with Birmingham University, played an important role in fostering a more open and cooperative environment. The larger companies, in particular, were not only receptive to new ideas but keen to exploit their commercial advantages. Several established research departments and appointed talented chemists such as Alan Macey, who joined ABM from Birmingham University in 1947, Brian Kirsop, who went to Sandars following his work on broken steeping at the BIRF, and another Birmingham graduate, Oliver Griffin, who in 1958 was appointed at Pauls. All were subsequently at the centre of scientific debate and played a leading role in future developments.

The work of Oliver Griffin and the research team at Pauls demonstrates the quality of research and development at company level. The initial breakthrough was in standardising the application of gibberellic acid, which immediately reduced the production cycle from two weeks to nine to ten days.[79] A series of trials carried out in the old floor malting at Wells-Next-The-Sea, combining gibberellic acid with broken steeping, subsequently achieved unprecedented gains in productivity. Whereas previously the malting cycle had been determined by environmental factors, a marginal adjustment to batch sizes eradicated the need for weekend loading and enabled standard process times to be introduced. The result was to improve malt quality, halve the labour force and double production. For the first time in the history of the industry, the maltster had achieved complete control over the timing of the production process.

The introduction of broken steeping and re-steeping techniques also prompted the development of several new malting systems, of which the static box, pioneered by Griffin, and the steeping-germination vessel, based on the work of Pollock and Pool, were the most important. The latter, which combined steeping and germination while maintaining separate kilning, was developed commercially by Sandars in conjunction with the engineers Robert Boby & Company. The circular, free-standing vessel was suitable for converting an existing system and, following trials at Ancaster in 1965, was installed in the Paddock Malting, built at Gainsborough before the turn of the century.[80] In contrast, the static box was a purpose-built system which enabled all three stages of production to be carried out in a single vessel. Successful trials were held at Dobson's Leeds maltings in 1962 and, three years later, the first commercial unit was completed at Mendlesham in

---

[79] The following section is based mainly on interviews with Oliver Griffin.

[80] A. A. Pool, 'Studies in Barley and Malt: Single-Vessel System for Malting without Turning', *Journal of the Institute of Brewing*, 68 (1962), pp. 476–78; *Pauls' Link*, spring 1970, pp. 10–12.

Suffolk.[81] The unit formed part of an integrated system, with the seven static boxes also doubling as grain driers during the harvest season, while a system of farm contracts (with farmers growing a specified acreage of malting barley for which they were paid on the basis of nitrogen content) ensured consistent barley quality.[82] The static box was not without its problems. Initially, the malt was not of the highest quality and it was found that the boxes required mechanical turners. Against this must be set a production cycle of six days, the low capital cost of construction and reduced malting losses. In particular, the production of large volumes of consistent quality malt ideal for distilling, coupled with the vessel's dual role of barley drier, was subsequently to ensure the system's success in Scotland.

The possibility of taking the Mendlesham 'concept' of single-vessel malting, barley store and farm contracts north of the border was initially investigated by Pauls. The decision hinged upon its potential to utilise more Scottish-grown barley but, despite promising results from initial investigations, the opinion of Hutchisons, Pauls' agents, that the climate was unsuitable, persuaded the company not to proceed. Convinced of the project's potential, Griffin, together with three of his colleagues, Klaus Nielsen (the manager of Mendlesham), Hugo Page-Croft and Michael Crowther, formed the Moray Firth Malting Company and in 1968 completed their first static-box complex at Inverness. The opportune release of *Golden Promise*, which performed well in the wet Scottish climate, was to put the final seal on their success. When three years later a second factory was opened at Arbroath, the quantity of malting barley grown locally had more than trebled, while 40 per cent of total requirements were supplied by farm contracts.[83]

A further area of research, and again one where the research team at Pauls played a leading role, was the work on enzyme syrups conducted during the 1960s. These were either barley syrups, produced from ground barley treated with industrial enzymes, or malt syrup, in effect liquid malt, derived from green malt by the action of the naturally occurring

[81] Initially the unit had a malting capacity of 47,000 quarters a year and provided storage for 120,000 quarters of barley. In 1967 five additional 300 quarter boxes increased malting capacity to 127,000 quarters, while barley storage was extended to 187,000 quarters. *East Anglian Daily Times*, 28 September 1966; 'Mendlesham Maltings', Pauls Malt Limited (typescript, n.d.); O. T. Griffin and B. C. Pinner, 'The Development of a Static Malting', *Journal of the Institute of Brewing*, 71 (1965), pp. 324–29.

[82] The contract system was based on the concept of sugar-beet contracting. Barley was delivered direct to the Mendlesham factory, eliminating the double handling, storage and drying of grain. A successful pilot scheme was run at Wells in 1964. By 1966, 115 farmers were participating in the Mendlesham project, involving almost 6000 acres producing over 40,000 quarters of barley. 'Malting Barley Made to Order', *Farmer and Stockbreeder*, 29 December 1964; Report on Mendlesham, 1966, Pauls Malt; interview with Oliver Griffin.

[83] *Golden Promise* was the only barley variety accepted for contract growing. Three further units were built in 1975 (Inverness), 1978 (Arbroath) and 1980 (Arbroath). *Financial Times*, 27 July 1971; *Farmer and Stockbreeder*, September 1969.

enzymes.[84] Unlike existing adjuncts, such as flaked maize, sugar and glucose syrups, which were widely used in conjunction with malt, these were viewed as malt substitutes and therefore caused some alarm throughout the industry.[85] Hence these developments were an important focus of research among the major malting firms. ABM combined with the sugar and flavourings firm Manbré & Garton to form ABMG (Syrups) for research and marketing. Likewise, Pauls had two subsidiaries, the Albion Sugar Company and Gillman & Spencer, with experience in similar fields, but their real interest was in the development of liquid malt. After successful trials at Ruddle's Oakham brewery, a commercial plant was built at Mendlesham. The product appeared to offer several advantages over granular malt. It was cheaper and easier to handle and store, yielded higher extracts, contained less haze-forming materials and speeded up throughput at the brewery. Nevertheless, neither liquid malt nor barley syrups were ever to achieve widespread popularity and the Mendlesham plant was closed in 1972.[86] In part this was due to technical weaknesses. But the main factors were the conservatism of some sectors of the brewing trade and, not least, resistance from their customers, reflected in the growing influence of the Campaign for Real Ale (CAMRA) and their demands for traditional beer.[87]

In the short space of thirty years, these developments transformed malting into a capital-intensive, high-technology sector. By 1970, 80 per cent of the industry's malting capacity had been replaced. Whereas in 1950 almost 90 per cent of all malt was made in floor maltings, twenty years later almost 80 per cent was produced by a variety of modern systems.[88] Process time had been reduced from fourteen to seventeen days to six to seven days and malting losses cut from 10 per cent to 4–5 per cent. Batch sizes had escalated, from 50–60 quarters to 1500–2000 quarters, while the annual output of a single malting had increased from a few thousand quarters to between 100–150,000 quarters.[89] The gains in terms of labour productivity, although difficult to calculate, were equally impressive. Whereas the 1950s floor-malting typically required one man per 1000 quarters of malt

[84] The production of liquid malt involved mixing crushed green malt with liquid to allow the enzymes to convert the starch and proteins to soluble products. The extracted material was then separated by centrifuge and evaporated to give a concentrated syrup. D. W. Ringrose, 'New Malting Procedure and the Broader Outlook in Malting', *Brewers' Guardian*, 98 (1969), pp. 50–52.

[85] Wheat and barley flours were new additives to the list of malt adjuncts. They were cost-effective and improved the 'head' on some beers. 'Brewing and Allied Trades Review', *Investors' Chronicle*, November 1970; *Sunday Times*, 17 November 1968.

[86] The Mendlesham plant produced around 60 tonnes of syrup a week which was sold both to the brewing and food trade.

[87] *Yorkshire Post*, 31 January 1969; *Sunday Times*, 17 November 1968; 'Report of the Working Party on Planning', Pauls & Whites Limited, Brewing Materials Division, 21 November 1971.

[88] 'Brewing and Allied Trades Review', *Investors' Chronicle*, November 1970; Marsden, 'Technical Change', p. 185.

[89] Macey, 'Advances in Malting Techniques', pp. 91–93.

produced per year, the modern maltings of the 1970s achieved productivity levels of 13,000 quarters per man. Even when adjusted to account for the growing numbers engaged in adminstration, maintenance, engineering and research, which offset the decline in production workers, estimates suggest average annual productivity levels ranging from 4–6000 quarters per person.[90] There is little doubt that the industry achieved its objective of increasing efficiency and maintaining costs.[91]

The mergers and rising levels of concentration which were major features of the post-war malting industry were trends common to most sectors of the British economy. In the period 1948–73 a total of 9761 manufacturing firms disappeared through merger, no fewer than 8066 in the period 1959–73, while by 1968 the hundred largest firms controlled 41 per cent of net output, compared with 22 per cent in 1949.[92] One of the foremost sectors in this process was brewing, the number of companies falling from 362 in 1950 to eighty-two twenty-five years later.[93] The main emphasis was again from the late 1950s, Gourvish identifying 172 brewing mergers in 1958–75. Seventy-five took place in 1959–61, a peak of activity significantly earlier than in most sectors. Similarly, the share of the top five companies in net output increased from 23 per cent in 1958 to 62 per cent by 1968.[94] The pattern of change in malting was similar. In 1945–46 the Maltsters' Association lists recorded eighty-nine paid-up members. By 1960 the number had fallen to seventy-two.[95] By 1970 there remained a mere twenty-four companies and by 1975 sixteen. In 1945–46 the top five companies accounted for 29.9 per cent of net output;[96] by 1970, the proportion had risen to 82 per cent, a figure which remained virtually unchanged five years later.[97]

[90] By the 1970s research and development and control of technical details accounted for 10 per cent of the ABM workforce. Interview with Alan Macey; Hudson, 'Malting Techniques', p. 116.

[91] While there are no figures which compare costs over these precise years, Hudson compared the capital costs of malting in 1885 and 1985 and estimated that in 1985 values, total outlay and charges per tonne of malt were £143 23p. in 1885 against £132 in 1985. Hudson, 'Malting Technology', p. 116.

[92] L. Hannah, *The Rise of the Corporate Economy* (London, 1976), pp. 176–77; S. J. Prais, *The Evolution of Giant Firms in Britain* (Cambridge, 1976), p. 4.

[93] Brewers' Society, *UK Statistical Handbook* (1982).

[94] Gourvish and Wilson, *British Brewing Industry*, pp. 448–49.

[95] These figures are based on subscriptions to the MAGB which are calculated on production. To 1967 they include parent and subsidiary companies, which until the 1960s, to all intents and purposes, traded in competition with one another. Three companies, ABM, Pauls and H. A. & D. Taylor, had subsidiaries, leaving a total of seventy-five firms in 1945–46 and fifty-seven in 1960–61.

[96] If subsidiaries are included with parent companies, the five largest (ABM, Pauls, Taylors, Hugh Baird & Sons and Robert Hutchison) accounted for 50.2 per cent of output.

[97] The top five companies in 1970 were ABM (37.6 per cent), Pauls (21.6 per cent), Munton & Fison (11.2 per cent), Hugh Baird (7.0 per cent) and Robert Hutchison (4.9 per cent). In 1975 the figure was 79.1 per cent: ABM (31.5 per cent), Pauls (23.6 per cent), Bairds (10.1 per

What factors underpinned the rationalisation of malting? The first phase, from 1945 to the late 1950s, reflected the demise of small companies which, either for succession or financial reasons, opted not to meet the challenges of the post-war era. Almost immediately after 1945, several ceased trading, while three firms, Woods, Sadd & Moore of Loddon, E. G. Clarke of Framlingham and Frederick May of Stisted in Essex, gave up malting but continued their grain-merchanting interests. Others sold their businesses to larger competitors or brewers: T. W. Wilson of Hadleigh joined ABM; the Shrewsbury firm of William Jones & Son, rejected by ABM, was subsequently bought by Ansells; in 1952 John Smith's Tadcaster Brewery acquired the local businesses of Frank Colley and the Selby Malt Roasting Company. Three years later, Lacons bought the Great Yarmouth firm of W. D. & A. E. Walker. By the mid 1950s, however, the pressures facing the industry were felt more widely and the experience of the Burton maltster Yeomans, Cherry & Curtis was typical of a significant number of companies. The directors' minutes chronicle a growing list of problems: labour shortages; constant expenditure on repairs and labour-saving equipment; falling profit margins and sales. This reflected both the stagnant malt market and the loss of customers – either through brewery amalgamations or because like Bass they had installed pneumatic drums and therefore became more self-sufficient. The only long-term solution was mechanised malting, but the cost (estimated at £150,000) could only be justified by greatly increased sales or by an amalgamation.[98] Similar factors underpinned several significant mergers: the acquisition in 1956 of Free Rodwell by Ind Coope and the merger in 1957 of H. A. & D. Taylor with the Ipswich Malting Company and their subsequent acquisition by ABM the following year.

From 1959 the period of intense merger activity which radically restructured the brewing industry added a new dimension to the situation. Previously, most brewing mergers involved small companies. Negotiations were amicable and frequently between personal friends or family connections. While the loss of customers had clearly posed problems for some maltsters, generally the informal code of conduct, whereby large buyers supported their established customers, persisted. From the late 1950s the scale and nature of merger changed. A number of factors, including uncertainty about the market and the search for national status, caused greater activity from within the industry. In addition, the realisation by City financiers that brewers possessed undervalued property assets attracted hostile attention from the non-brewing sector. The unsuccessful bid in 1959 by

cent), Munton & Fison (9.0 per cent) and Moray Firth (7.9 per cent). MAGB, Subscription Lists; Pauls & Whites, Board Paper, 150, 1976/7.

[98] During the period 1949–57 sales fell by 29 per cent from 34,600 quarters to 24,550 quarters. To prevent a further decline, the company purchased a smaller neighbour, W. H. Cox & Sons Limited, in 1959. Yeomans, Cherry & Curtis, Directors' Minutes, 12 November 1951, 29 December 1954, 9 December 1957, 9 September 1958, 9 September 1959.

Charles Clore, chairman of Sears Holdings, for Watney Mann, and the entry into British brewing of the Canadian brewing entrepreneur E. P. Taylor, triggered a series of defensive mergers which culminated in the formation of the 'Big Six' national brewers: Allied, Bass Charrington, Courage, Scottish & Newcastle, Watney and Whitbread. Together with Guinness, by 1967 they accounted for 73 per cent of total UK beer production and, as such, dominated the malt market.[99]

From the malting perspective the consequences were far-reaching. In scarcely more than a decade, over 200 breweries closed and were replaced by a few large, centralised concerns.[100] Production was also modernised with an emphasis on greater automation and faster throughput, which necessitated larger quantities of malt of a consistent quality. In addition, raw materials were increasingly purchased through a central office, finally ending the traditional support for the small producer. Indeed, the growing influence of accountants meant that, more than ever before, cost became the deciding factor. While many small customers disappeared, the scale of contracts rose to such an extent that they either stretched productive capacity or meant reliance on a single brewer. Pidcocks, the Nottingham maltster, suddenly faced the options of supplying to their major customer, Courage, in excess of 25,000 quarters of malt annually, the majority of their total production, or of losing their long-standing contract.[101] Smaller firms found themselves undercut by the few large competitors, particularly ABM, who could at last reap the benefits of their investment in mechanised malting. The result was a series of amalgamations from which no company, regardless of its size or position in the industry, was entirely immune.

A number of firms had neither the financial nor managerial resources to respond and, in the time-honoured way, approached one of their larger rivals with a view to merger. In 1963 Pidcocks, reluctant to accept their dependence on Courage, was bought by Sandars of Gainsborough. Yeomans, Cherry & Curtis, despite the rising demand for malt after 1958, was unable either to increase sales or maintain profit margins, and in 1965 also joined the Sandars group.[102] That same year S. Swonnell & Son, who had themselves acquired two small companies, Alfred Gough of Saffron Walden and Randells (Maltsters) of London, were acquired by Pauls.[103] In other cases, changes in

[99] These developments are discussed in detail by Gourvish and Wilson, *British Brewing Industry*, pp. 449–74; K. H. Hawkins and C. L. Pass, *The Brewing Industry: A Study in Industrial Organisation and Public Policy* (London, 1979), pp. 52–77.

[100] The number of breweries in operation fell from 399 in 1958 to 177 in 1969 and to 147 by 1975, Brewers' Society, *UK Statistical Handbook* (1982).

[101] Marsden, 'Technical Change', p. 139.

[102] Sales recovered slowly to peak at 33,371 quarters in 1962 before falling to 29,570 quarters the following year. The company was purchased for £75,000, Yeomans, Cherry & Curtis, Directors' Minutes, 23 December 1963, 18 December 1964, 15 June 1965.

[103] The business, with a trade of 45,000 quarters, including 15,000 quarters of coloured malt, was purchased for £90,000.

ownership were the direct result of the escalating cost of modernisation. Hugh Baird & Sons, one of the first companies to consider mechanised malting, had reached agreement with Canada Malting Company of Toronto in 1946 jointly to build a Saladin malting at Witham in Essex.[104] Thwarted by the refusal of a building licence, and subsequently by the dollar shortage and import restrictions on machinery, the project was dropped and for a further decade the company continued with floor malting. In 1961 the decision was taken to build a Wanderhaufen malting, with the first phase estimated at £150–200,000. Within a year, however, costs had risen so sharply that Bairds approached Canada Malting, who provided a much needed injection of capital in exchange for 50 per cent of the company's shares. The first phase was eventually completed at a cost of £374,031 and the second phase for £440,377, a total of £814,408.[105] A similar fate befell the three small Hertfordshire firms, Henry Page & Sons, J. Harrington and Henry Ward & Sons, who amalgamated in 1962–63 in order to pool their resources and build a modern malting. Halfway through they ran out of funds and were forced to approach Pauls, who bought them out and completed the plant.[106]

These last events had taken place against a strongly rising malt market, a trend which, apart from the sharp downturn of 1968, continued until 1974. Nevertheless, from the mid 1960s, the industry was under increasing pressure. The major problem was the growing situation of excess-supply. This reflected both the technological revolution, which enabled more malt to be produced from existing plant, and continued expansion, mainly to serve the Scottish distilling trade.[107] In particular, the increasing self-sufficiency of the Distillers Company, and the decision by Inver House Distillers to form a subsidiary company, Moffat Malting, and to enter the sales-malting market, caused great concern. The situation came to a head in 1967, when the completion of Moffat's initial two Wanderhaufen streets coincided with a sharp downturn in the production of grain whisky. When the following autumn maltsters made their contracts for the coming year, the consequences were all too evident. The immediate response was the closure of numerous old floor maltings across the country. Within a year Pauls had closed a total of 172,000 quarters capacity, including Ipswich Nos 2 and 4, Stonham, Barnetby, Bedford, the Oulton Broad maltings of S. Swonnell & Son

[104] Early in 1939 Bairds had visited the USA and Canada to inspect the latest developments. Negotiations with Canada Malting Company resumed immediately after the war. Hugh Baird & Sons, Directors' Minutes, 3 February 1939, 26 April, 18 October 1961, 30 September 1948.

[105] Bairds' capital was doubled to £640,000 by the issue of 240,000 £1 ordinary, and 80,000 £1 preference shares, all of which were purchased by Canada Malting Company, Ibid., 25 September, 18 December 1962, 29 March 1965.

[106] The plant, again a Wanderhaufen, with an annual capacity of 74,000 quarters, was completed in 1965. The company was purchased for £575,000.

[107] Typically, by 1966 the Albion malting, opened at Ipswich in 1962, had progressed from six- to four-day germination with a corresponding increase in annual output.

purchased three years earlier, and a string of small maltings scattered across Yorkshire. Sandars also closed 75,000 quarters of capacity.[108] Although demand recovered significantly the following year, further expansion in Scotland – six more streets at Moffat bringing capacity to almost 800,000 quarters, the formation of Moray Firth and ABM's penetration into Scotland in 1970 – perpetuated the position of excess supply. Lastly, the industry faced the problem of the likely replacement of granular malt by barley syrups. By the 1970s several of the national brewers, including Bass and Watneys, were using a high proportion of barley syrups in some commercial brews and achieving satisfactory results and significant savings.[109] Although the threat did not materialise, it was a final factor causing widespread concern about the long-term prospects of the industry.

The resulting price war, initiated by ABM, devastated profit margins already slender in comparison with those obtained in the brewing trade. By 1968–69, for example, Pauls estimated a profit margin of 15 shillings per quarter of brewing malt against 5 shillings per quarter for the non-brewing sector – distilling, exports and the less important food and vinegar trades. The importance of these figures is clear when it is appreciated that the major proportion of the increased demand for malt was accounted for by rising whisky production.[110] In 1968–69, of 640,000 quarters of malt sold by Pauls, only 280,000 quarters (43.8 per cent) went to UK brewers. In hard financial terms this represented a return on capital invested of 11 per cent for brewing sales against a mere 4 per cent elsewhere, resulting in an average return of 7.3 per cent.[111] Of course the dependence on different markets varied between companies. At the other extreme, Sandars sold almost exclusively to brewers, achieving a return on capital invested of 15.4 per cent. It is notable that, after the Second World War, the company began to develop exports and distilling sales, but virtually withdrew from both markets because of poor returns. Sandars, however, with their excellent reputation and impeccable family connections (which still carried weight among brewers), were the exception. It is clear that after years of unprecedented capital investment by the industry, involving the replacement of 80 per cent of

[108] As early as 1959, Pauls had planned their Wanderhaufen with the specific objective of replacing old floor maltings, but initially found they required all their capacity to meet rising demands. Subsequently it was expected that these maltings would be phased out gradually over the remainder of the decade, rather than in the space of a few months. File relating to the acquisition of Sandars & Company Limited, 1969.

[109] Bass, using 50 per cent barley syrup in a third of all brews at Tennents Brewery, Glasgow, achieved savings of 10–12 pence per barrel. Watneys, using cheaper enzymes at 70 per cent, reckoned on a saving of 20 pence per barrel. Average savings were estimated at £1 per quarter of raw material. *Brewer*, 57, April 1971, p. 112; Dr J. A. Collier, Report: 'Malt and the Future', September 1971 (Pauls Malt).

[110] Whisky production grew at an annual average growth rate of around 12 per cent throughout the 1960s, against 2–3 per cent for beer production. The other growth area, exports, was both variable and, because of fierce overseas competition, always subject to narrow margins.

[111] File relating to the acquisition of Sandars & Company Limited, 1969.

malting capacity, the returns achieved were, to quote the *Investors' Chronicle*, 'abysmal'.[112]

Table 7.2, which illustrates the return on capital and sales margins achieved by Pauls, provides some insight into the impact of these problems. Between 1960–63 the company achieved an annual return on capital employed of 15.65 per cent.[113] By 1969–71 this had fallen by more than half

Table 7.2

R. & W. Paul Limited,[1] *group profit, return on capital and margins on sales, 1960–75*

Year	Pre-tax group profit	Return on capital (per cent)	Group turnover (£000s)	Margins on sales (per cent) [2]	Margins on malt sales [3]
1960	469	14.13	—	—	—
1961	557	15.55	—	—	—
1962	721	18.63	—	—	—
1963	670	14.29	—	—	—
1964	796	9.73	—	—	—
1965	957	11.28	—	—	—
1966	646	7.18	—	—	—
1967	855	8.89	—	—	—
1968	997	10.09	29,999	3.32	6.68
1969	741	7.37	31,282	2.37	7.39
1970	774	6.67	34,507	2.24	4.02
1971	721	6.09	37,679	1.91	5.65
1972	1717	13.88	36,893	4.65	7.79
1973	2129	14.19	47,423	4.49	5.38
1974	2468	15.01	73,641	3.35	5.68
1975	2809	13.95	90,084	3.12	8.14

Notes:
[1] Pauls & Whites Limited from 1964
[2] Pre-tax profit as a percentage of turnover
[3] Includes other sales by the brewing materials division.

Source: R. & W. Paul Limited, Annual Accounts.

[112] 'Survey of the Brewing and Allied Trades', *Investors' Chronicle*, November 1970, p. 23.

[113] For a number of reasons, including the demise of a significant number of the 'representative' sample (see Appendix 9) and because several of the more substantial companies (such as Munton & Fison, Crisp Malting and J. P. Simpson) remained private and detailed accounts are not therefore available, it is not possible to present a comprehensive analysis of profits across the industry. A further problem is that the two large public companies, Pauls and ABM, became increasingly diversified concerns. In neither case is it possible to isolate the capital employed in malting. At Pauls it was also practice to make transfers between divisions to 'smooth' group profits. These qualifications must be remembered in the context of the following analysis.

to 6.71 per cent. In terms of margins on sales, available from 1967, these averaged a mere 2.46 per cent in 1968–71, rising to 3.90 per cent in 1972–75.

It must be emphasised that Pauls was a widely diversified enterprise (generally malting contributed between 35–50 per cent of annual profits) whose other main interest, animal feedstuffs, faced an even more competitive climate during these years. Margins on malt sales were indeed consistently higher than for total group sales, averaging 5.69 per cent at the nadir of 1969–71. Analysis of ABM's accounts reveals a similar trend: an annual average return on capital of 10.26 per cent in 1960–63, falling to 6.64 per cent in 1969–71 (with a low of 4.21 per cent in 1969), with margins on sales averaging 4.74 per cent over the latter period.[114]

It was against this background that further rationalisation occurred. In August 1969 Pauls acquired Sandars & Company for an agreed bid of £870,000.[115] Although a key reason for Colonel Sandars' approach to Pauls was the persistent problem of family succession, there is no doubt that uncertainty about the future played a major part in shaping Pauls' own expansion policy and in the decisions of other key players in the industry. In the brief space of six months, Robert Hutchison & Company and J. P. Simpson of Alnwick also approached Pauls with a view to merger. Similarly, talks were conducted with Robert Kilgour & Company regarding joint operations in Scotland. The motives were clearly defensive. While merger provided the most cost-effective route for Pauls' further expansion, it was also viewed as the means of creating a more stable environment. A further rationalisation of the industry – ideally into two large groups (ABM and Pauls) and a few smaller companies – was considered necessary to eliminate the internecine competition which had eroded profit margins.[116] As the *Investors' Chronicle* concluded, only when maltsters competed a little less with one another could they expect a more prosperous future.[117]

The acquisition of Sandars, with their valuable brewing contracts, boosted Pauls' share of the brewing market to 23 per cent and total annual production to 900–950,000 quarters (approximately 22 per cent of total output): within reach of the target of the million to a million and a half quarters considered to be the optimum economic size for a malting group.[118] This was achieved in 1972 with the acquisition of Robert Hutchison & Company, which added a further 180,000 quarters a year. The completion two years later at Kirkcaldy of three additional germinating vessels brought production to 1,417,000

[114] Throughout this period malting remained the main division, contributing 96 per cent of group profits in 1967, falling to 81 per cent by 1971 and 65 per cent by 1973, reflecting a growing interest in fine chemicals, ABM, Annual Accounts, 1960–75.

[115] This included a joint interest with Peter Walker (Warrington) Limited in the Gainsborough Malting Company. The bid involved an exchange of nine ordinary shares in Pauls & Whites for every two Sandars ordinary shares, *The Times*, 29 August 1969.

[116] File relating to the acquisition of Sandars & Company Limited, 1969.

[117] 'Survey of the Brewing and Allied Trades', *Investors' Chronicle*, November 1970, p. 24.

[118] File relating to the acquisition of Sandars & Company Limited, 1969.

quarters, representing 23 per cent of the total UK sales-malting market.[119] A further significant merger of 1972, and one which again underlined the financial limitations of smaller firms, was the purchase by Bass of the Mirfield maltster J. F. & J. Crowther. A long-standing customer, the company was forced to turn to Bass when, after installing two pneumatic plants, they faced similar problems to those encountered by Harrington Page a few years earlier.[120] The final development of the period was the attention paid by corporate raiders to the large public companies and the acquisition in October 1972 of ABM by Dalgety.

By 1975 there remained only sixteen sales-malting companies: two dominant firms, ABM and Pauls, who between them accounted for 55 per cent of sales-maltsters production; and a fringe of medium-sized companies – Bairds, Munton & Fison, Moray Firth, Crisp Malting and J. P Simpson. Between them, these seven companies produced over 94 per cent of the malt produced by the sector.[121] The few small companies which remained, such as French & Jupp's and Edwin Tucker, served a niche market. The sector closely resembled the one predicted by Pauls a few years earlier. What is also notable is the change in scale of the major sales-malting companies relative to brewer and distiller-maltsters. Whereas in earlier periods the large brewer-maltsters had dominated the malt market, only the giant Distillers Company, with an annual capacity around 1.64 million quarters, and Moffat Malting (who produced malt both for sale and for its parent company) with 1.18 million quarters, could challenge ABM's annual capacity of 1.84 million quarters and Pauls 1.4 million. In comparison, Bass the largest brewer-maltster, produced only around 550,000 quarters of malt a year.[122] These figures underline the progress made by the sector in gaining a greater share of the malt market, in particular its penetration of the distilling and world trades.

The key to this success had been the technological revolution which had transformed malting from a craft-based to a high-technology industry. Without question, much of the progress was underpinned by the work of the BIRF. Nevertheless, the review of research and development, which focused in particular on the work of Oliver Griffin and the research team at Pauls, demonstrates the contribution at company level. Research at ABM, led by

[119] Group sales accounted for 27 per cent of the UK brewing market, 18 per cent of distilling sales, 28 per cent of exports and 10 per cent of the food trade. Pauls & Sandars Group, 'Proposal for Construction of Additional Malting Capacity in Scotland', March 1977.

[120] The acquisition enabled Bass to close small floor maltings in Yorkshire, Lancashire and Lincolnshire and supply their northern breweries from one centralised plant. By the mid 1970s, the maltings supplied around half of the brewer's needs. Marsden, 'Technical Change', pp. 133, 285.

[121] Excluding malt sold by Moffatt, who acted both as sales and distiller-maltster. Pauls & Whites, Board Paper, 150, 1976–77; MAGB, Report to the Brewing Sector Working Party, 'The Malting Industry, 1977–82'.

[122] Pauls & Whites, Board Paper 150, 1976–77.

Dr Alan Macey, was similarly of an outstanding calibre. Even among the medium-sized firms such as Munton & Fison, there was both no shortage of innovation and a marked determination to remain at the forefront of progress. More importantly these developments were beyond the resources of most small companies. Those that clung to the old ways went to the wall. It is nevertheless evident that, despite a reputation for conservatism, once faced with an environment which demanded the adoption of labour and energy-saving capital equipment, the industry had been quick to respond. The rising demand for malt from the late 1950s provided the final stimulus.

8

The Family Firm, 1914–75

The years after 1914 presented a severe challenge to all malting companies. The legacy of war, recession and a falling demand for malt meant survival was by no means certain. Many companies simply ceased trading or sold up to competitors. After the Second World War, the technical revolution and the 1960s rationalisation of brewing led to a further concentration of the industry. As in earlier years, location and markets remained important. A few firms enjoyed the protection of a major brewer and were secure in a niche market. In most cases, the outcome was determined by the aims and skills of partners, directors and managers alike.

No aspect of the history of malting is more difficult to evaluate than its organisation and management. Malting records produce, as in other industries, long strings of figures and bald entries of decisions in minute books, but provide little insight into management styles: the division of responsibility between partners and directors, the functions and status of salaried staff. The few company histories, while they shed some light upon the personalities behind the well-known names, say little about any shortcomings, not least because they tell the story of *successful* firms. Betty Wharton's account of the Smiths of Ryburgh traces the rise, decline and subsequent recovery of the family firm with a refreshing frankness.[1] Generally, however, we know little about the many small firms – and in malting this was the vast majority – or those who, for whatever reason, failed. Despite these difficulties, no aspect of the industry is of greater interest to historians. Small-scale, family dominated and technologically unimpressive, by the inter-war years malting was representative of many other small business sectors. Alfred Chandler's view of them is unequivocal: conservative, resistant to change and driven by short-term objectives, they lay at the heart of Britain's relative economic decline from the late nineteenth century.[2] Peter Payne is less sweeping in his generalisations. Nevertheless, he points the finger firmly at the inter-war holding companies which remained essentially loose federations of autonomous family firms.[3] Associated British Maltsters (ABM), formed in 1928 from five old-established malting firms, seems to provide a classic example. A

[1] B. Wharton, *The Smiths of Ryburgh: 100 Years of Milling and Malting* (Crisp Malting, 1990).

[2] A. D. Chandler, Jr, *Scale and Scope: The Dynamics of Industrial Capitalism* (Cambridge, Massachusetts, 1990), pp. 235–37, 389–92.

[3] P. L. Payne, 'Family Business in Britain: A Historical and Analytical Survey', in A. Okochi and S. Yasuoka (eds), *Family Business in the Era of Industrial Growth* (Toyko, 1984), pp. 196–97.

defensive response to the problems of the 1920s, it proudly boasted of its continuity of management. Whether this was accompanied by complacency is another matter. For the sales-maltsters' business environment was closely defined by brewing – itself identified by Chandler as more personally managed than other family-dominated sectors. Terry Gourvish found it nurtured a 'cosy amateur style' and notions of 'gentlemanly conduct' even after the Second World War.[4] To what extent did the persistence of family capitalism in the British malting industry until late in the twentieth century reflect the aims and objectives of founders and their families? To what extent did the 'special relationship' with brewers inhibit structural change?

There can be few sectors of the British economy where the participation of founding families was more enduring than in malting.[5] At the end of the First World War the vast majority of firms were organised as partnerships. Of those which during the late nineteenth century had adopted limited liability status, only a handful had offered any of their shares for public subscription. Subsequently, despite the growing trend towards incorporation, the only public flotation was the formation in 1928 of Associated British Maltsters.[6] Indeed, only unprecedented capital demands after 1950 prompted even the leading companies to seek public status. Until then most remained, in every respect, private. The firm of R. & W. Paul provides a classic example. Registered in 1893, the initial capital of £250,000 was held jointly by Robert and William Paul. By 1960 the paid-up capital of £1.18 million, if more widely dispersed, was held entirely by family members, their executors and trusts.[7] The management and direction of the company was equally stable. Robert and William served as joint life managing directors, each selecting two sons who were appointed to the board in 1906: Robert, his eldest son, Robert Harold (Harry, 1872–1950) and third son, Russell (1875–1951); and William, his second and third sons, Hugh (1878–1947) and Stuart (1879–1961).[8] After

---

[4] T. R. Gourvish and R. G. Wilson, *The British Brewing Industry, 1830–1980* (Cambridge, 1994), p. 373.

[5] There are various definitions of the family firm. Alfred Chandler defined the family firm (entrepreneurial in the first generation) as one where founders and their heirs recruited salaried managers but continued to be influential shareholders, held executive managerial positions and exercised decisive influence on company policy. For Channon, in his study of the largest British companies, it was where a family member was the chief executive, where there had been at least two generations of family control and when a minimum of 5 per cent of the voting shares were held by the family or trusts associated with it. Chandler, *Scale and Scope*, p. 240; D. F. Channon, *The Strategy and Structure of British Enterprise* (London, 1971), pp. 15–16.

[6] The company was initially registered as Gilstrap Earp; see pp. 205–6.

[7] The ordinary shares were divided into eighteen holdings and the preference shares into forty holdings, R. & W. Paul, Share Registers, Companies House.

[8] William had planned to bring in his eldest son, Bernard. A lively and likeable young man, he finally kicked over the traces and was banished to a ranch in the Argentine. His place was taken by Stuart, for whom William had already purchased a corn merchants business in Dublin. His youngest son, Cyril, came into the shipping business. Robert's other sons, Hewitt, Rowland and Oscar, managed mills in Birkenhead and Coventry.

Robert's death in 1909, William continued as chairman and managing director until April 1927 when, aged seventy-seven, he resigned because of failing health. The four cousins (who controlled in equal proportions almost 90 per cent of the company's equity) assumed the role of joint managing directors, Harry serving as chairman until his death in 1950. He was succeeded by Russell and, subsequently, Stuart, who resigned at the age of eighty-one to become the company's first president. The only other changes to the board were to accommodate the next generation. In 1935 Russell's son, Russell James (Jim, 1906–85) joined, in 1940, Stuart's elder son, William Stuart (1912–84), and after the death of Hugh in 1947, his son, 'young' Hugh (1917–88) and Stuart's second son, Geoffrey (1917–85). In addition, in 1935 Joseph Causton (Jock, 1905–87), William's grandson, became the first member of the board who was not a direct male descendant of the founder. The position with many small companies was similar. The Hertfordshire firm of French & Jupp's, which traced its roots to the late seventeenth century, was converted to a private limited company in 1920. The issued capital of £50,000 has remained unchanged. Guy Horlock, appointed to the board in 1959 to ease the transition from Ronald Jupp to his son David (the eighth generation of the family), has been the only non-family shareholder.[9]

It is evident that founding families went to considerable lengths to ensure succession, usually by recruiting from the extended family, trusted managers and friends. When war broke out in 1914, the firm of Sandars & Company (founded in the late 1700s) was owned and managed by John Drysdale Sandars (1860–1922). His only son, John Eric, was eight years old. After the call-up of the other active family participant, John Drysdale's nephew Sam (1888–1967), the partnership was quickly converted to a private company. Frank Thorpe, who had joined the firm as a clerk in 1869, was appointed company secretary and director and joined on the board by Claude Leach, a family friend. Sam's return from war was marred by his severe injuries but, after John Drysdale's sudden death in 1922, he acted as joint managing director with Leach. The family solicitor, J. A. Dyson, also became a director. Four years later, John Eric joined the company. He succeeded his cousin in 1932 and remained as chairman until 1969 when the company was acquired by Pauls. Even after the addition of further outside directors – Hugh Lancaster, the well-known maltster and writer in 1940 and, a decade later, Sir Edmund Bacon (an old family friend) – 74 per cent of the ordinary stock was held by family directors.[10]

Continuity was a strongly marked feature of the industry. Among non-family managers and directors, company solicitors and financial advisers, the same tradition of long service, often encompassing several generations, was evident. At Sandars, Frank Thorpe gave sixty-four years to the company before finally retiring from the board aged seventy-nine, only months before

9 I am grateful to Guy Horlock for information relating to French & Jupp's.
10 Sandars & Company, Directors' Minutes, PM.

his death.[11] Likewise, when F. & G. Smith was incorporated in 1890, John Hill, who had worked with Frederick Smith from the 1870s, was appointed general manager and a director. His son, Edward (1864–1949), succeeded him, both as manager and, from 1917, as director, acting as chairman between 1929 and his retirement in 1933. He remained a director until his death, devoting sixty-five years of his life to the company. Similarly, three generations of the Gould family served as financial advisers: Harry Gould, who also worked with Frederick in his early days, his son, Russell, and grandson, David, who in 1953 also joined the board.[12]

On those occasions when, either for financial reasons or a lack of heirs, founders opted to sell their firms, a common response was to approach a larger competitor. By this means they frequently retained much of their autonomy and effective control. At the Beccles firm of John Crisp & Son (founded in 1734), for example, seven generations of John Crisp followed one another before in 1927 the business was sold to W. J. Robson of Leeds. However, John Francis Crisp remained as managing director and the following year became joint managing director of ABM. In other cases, the absence of heirs prompted the emergence of 'dynastic management'. A feature of other family-dominated sectors of industry, continuity in malting was often sustained by managerial, in contrast with strict hereditary, ownership.[13] At Gilstraps, succession was secured by recruiting John MacRae, the husband of Sir William's niece, and an able manager, Hubert Cherry-Downes. When in 1921 the company was incorporated, MacRae became chairman and Cherry-Downes (who held 25 per cent of the equity) managing director. Yet on the formation of ABM seven years later, MacRae almost immediately retired to his estates in Scotland, while Cherry-Downes, as joint managing director, together with his sons and grandsons, went on to play a dominant role in the new company.[14] Similarly, in 1900 William Robson converted his grandfather's business to a public company, offered 60 per cent of the ordinary shares to the public and then retired to his estates in Yorkshire. The manager, Frederick Cooke, became chairman and his son Philip a director of the company. Together with Frederick's wife, Gladys, they steadily bought small parcels of shares and by 1928 had acquired over 81 per cent of the equity.[15] Like the Cherry-Downeses, three generations of the Cookes were to be a powerful influence in the development of ABM.

Even the formation of ABM, which brought together five, old-established family firms, meant little change in terms of ownership and control. A typical

---

[11] *Gainsborough News*, 13 April 1934.

[12] F. & G. Smith, Directors' Minutes; Wharton, *Smiths of Ryburgh*, pp. 51–52.

[13] R. Church, 'The Family Firm in Industrial Capitalism: International Perspectives on Hypotheses and History', *Business History*, 35 (1993), p. 31; C. Erickson, *British Industrialists: Steel and Hosiery, 1850–1950* (Cambridge, 1959), pp. 52–53, uses the term 'bureaucratic dynasties'.

[14] Gilstrap Earp & Company, Directors' Minutes, PM.

[15] W. J. Robson & Company, Directors' Minutes, PM.

multi-firm merger of the inter-war years, it grew out of Hubert Cherry-Downes's proposals, in his role as chairman of the Maltsters' Association, for an industry-wide scheme for cooperative trading during the early 1920s. Despite the clear need to rationalise productive capacity, few firms were willing to relinquish their autonomy and there was little support. Cherry-Downes's later attempts to amalgamate Gilstrap Earp (of which he was managing director) with a number of other malting companies similarly met with little success until, in 1927, the MacRae-Gilstrap family brought in Leicester financier, Sir Arthur Wheeler, to promote the public flotation of the company.[16] Through the Charterhouse Investment Trust, of which Wheeler was a director, approaches were made to many of the more prosperous companies. Most had reservations, but ultimately Edward Sutcliffe, Samuel Thompson & Sons and W. J. Robson (and their subsidiary John Crisp) joined Gilstrap Earp. The Wakefield firm of Michael Sanderson & Son was also acquired when Charles Sutcliffe, a director, sold his holding of ordinary shares to the Charterhouse Investment Trust.[17] Thus in July 1928 Gilstrap Earp was floated as a public company with a registered capital of £1,250,000, divided into 500,000 6 per cent cumulative preference shares, 500,000 7 per cent 'A' cumulative preference shares of £1, and 1,000,000 ordinary shares of 5 shillings. The purchase price of the shares of the associated companies was £807,044, payable in a combination of cash, ordinary shares and the 6 per cent preference shares. The Charterhouse Investment Trust subscribed for the remaining 6 per cent preference shares and underwrote the 'A' preference shares and 125,000 ordinary shares which were offered for public subscription in the ratio of four to one. However, despite positive comments by the *Investors' Chronicle*, which saw the new company as well-established and soundly financed, the underwriters were left with around one-third of the shares.[18] Only 8 per cent of the equity was therefore publicly held. The Trust provided one of its directors, Walter Burt, as the first chairman of the new company and appointed Brigadier-General Lionel Milman to act as its adviser. From July 1929 he became General Managing Director. Yet with the deputy chairman, John MacRae Gilstrap, and the five joint managing directors (Hubert Cherry-Downes, Charles Sutcliffe, Frederick Cooke, John F. Crisp and S. Harold Thompson) drawn from the founding companies ownership the control of the new company rested firmly in the hands of its constituent parts, a recipe for inter-family rivalry and squabbles.[19]

[16] Gilstrap Earp, Directors' Minutes, 28 November 1925, 20 January 1926; Letter from H. Cherry-Downes to Douglas Taylor, 16 February 1928; H. St G. Gallaher, 'In the Beginning' (1970), Lincolnshire Museum of Rural Life.

[17] Michael Sanderson & Son, Directors' Minutes, 6 July, 26 July 1928, 14 November 1929.

[18] Gilstrap Earp & Company, Directors' Minutes; *Investors' Chronicle*, 14 July, 28 July 1928.

[19] Unfortunately the company's share registers disclose the preference shares, but not the equity held by the vendors. Almost certainly the several large holdings in the names of London stockbrokers belonged to the various families. Gilstrap Earp & Company, Directors' Minutes, Share Registers, Companies House.

Despite the continuity of ownership, as many maltsters had feared, brewers proved unwilling to accept a large malting merger.[20] The chairman's first annual report left little doubt about the scale of the problem: 'theirs was a business [with] a definite speed limit ... they had to carry with them the feelings and wishes of their customers'.[21] Barely a year after its formation Gilstrap Earp was therefore renamed Associated British Maltsters and restructured as a holding company for investments in associated firms: a move designed to reassure brewers that the status quo had been maintained.[22] It made expansion more acceptable, and by 1947 a total of nine companies had been acquired.[23] It also enabled the founding members to maintain their control over the group. Subsequently, acquisitions were registered as private companies, the shares issued to ABM, and the vendors given service agreements with the parent company. Each was then allocated to one of the original five founding companies of 1928 (for whom it acted as selling agent) on a regional basis.[24] Thus Sutcliffes controlled Michael Sanderson & Son, the Hull business of William Glossop & Bulay and Richard Worswick of Elland. Similarly, the Thompson group comprised James D. Taylor, the Gloucester business of G. & W. E. Downing, Thomas & Company of Abingdon and Williams Brothers of Salisbury.[25] In 1959, after the purchase of the Hertfordshire business of H. A. & D. Taylor (and its subsidiaries, the Ipswich Malting Company, J. W. & H. Branston and W. B. Walmsley), the regional structure was formally consolidated. Four zonal companies ABM (Northern) Limited, ABM (Midlands) Limited, ABM (Southern) Limited and ABM (Eastern) Limited (with the exception of the last), replaced the old groups.[26] The newly created eastern zone, with its headquarters at Bury St Edmunds, comprised the Taylor group, John Crisp & Son and T. W. Wilson of

[20] Apart from a reluctance to give up their autonomy, this was the main reason why most companies had opted not to join the merger. Letters between Douglas Taylor, Hubert Cherry-Downes and the Charterhouse Investment Trust, 14 January–16 February 1928.

[21] *Investors' Chronicle*, 1 December 1928.

[22] In particular it was thought to have been a mistake to trade under the name of Gilstrap Earp. All malting assets were transferred to a new private company named Gilstrap Earp and the whole of the share capital issued to ABM. Gallaher, 'In the Beginning'; E. F. Taylor, 'History of the Formation and Development of Associated British Maltsters Limited, 1928–78' (1978), p. 6; *Investors' Chronicle*, 31 August 1929, 3 May 1930.

[23] The assets of Smiths (Maltsters) Limited of Pontefract, Edward Mortimer of Driffield and J. N. & G. Middleborough of Selby were also purchased. ABM, Directors' Minutes, PM.

[24] Sandersons and James D. Taylor of Bath (acquired in 1929), initially wholly-owned subsidiaries, were both restructured under the new system. ABM, Directors' Minutes, 29 September 1930, 1 June 1931, PM.

[25] With the exception of the small firm of Thomas Haigh, which was merged with Sandersons, each business continued to be worked by the vendors. It is notable that the merger of Haigh and Sandersons took place only after an agreement was obtained from Haigh's main customer, Hardy's Crown Brewery, Manchester, that they would continue to buy their malt from the new company. ABM, Directors' Minutes, 29 April 1929.

[26] The zonal companies were registered as private limited companies with a capital of £100 and the shares issued to ABM.

Hadleigh.[27] Several subsidiary companies were also registered: ABM Export Company in 1939; ABM Special Products, a marketing company for coloured and roasted malts in 1959; and, finally, ABM Industrial Products, embracing malt extracts and flours and a developing interest in fine chemicals for the brewing, food and textile trades in 1963.[28]

The rapid expansion of the group was accompanied by a remarkable stability of direction. Only four months after the flotation, John MacRae Gilstrap resigned as deputy chairman and retired to Scotland, but apart from the death of Frederick Cooke in 1937 and his replacement as joint managing director by his son Philip, the only other changes during the first decade concerned the chairmanship. In September 1931 Walter Burt was killed in a railway accident and replaced by Lionel Milman (also a nominee of the Charterhouse Investment Trust). Less than sixteen months later, however, the board took the unanimous decision not to renew his service agreement and, on 31 January 1933, he resigned from the company.[29] The directors' minutes provide no explanation. According to contemporaries, neither chairman had appreciated the key relationship between brewer and maltster or had the strength of character necessary to ensure the old competitors worked in harmony.[30] Their successor, Hubert Nutcombe Hume, also managing director of the Charterhouse Investment Trust, remained in office until December 1965, when he became the first honorary president. In September 1938 the board was increased by the creation of six ordinary directors: H. Arthur Cherry-Downes, S. George and H. Leslie Thompson, Lawrence Burgess, a director of Sutcliffes, Frank Price of Robsons and, notably, Sidney Waddacor of William Glossop & Bulay, the only occasion between 1928 and 1959 that the vendor of a subsidiary company was offered a seat on the board.[31] Barely three months later, John Crisp, who for some years had suffered indifferent health, stepped down from his position as joint managing director, finally resigning from the company in March 1948.[32] In September 1941 Thomas Sutcliffe, the last of the great malting family, was asked to resign from ABM and all its associated companies. Again the

[27] In 1960 the group made its last malting acquisition, the purchase of E. Bailey & Sons of Frome, which was incorporated into the southern zone.

[28] ABM Industrial Products Limited comprised J. M. Collett and Company Limited (acquired in 1961) and Norman Evans & Rais Limited, both manufacturers of enzymes and organic chemicals, British DiaMalt Limited (acquired with H. A. & D. Taylor), and Sunvi-Torrax (ex-Sutcliffes), producers of malt extract and malt flours.

[29] ABM, Directors' Minutes, 23 January, 31 January 1933.

[30] Gallaher, 'In the Beginning'; D. L. Nicolson, Tribute to Sir Nutcombe Hume, KBE; ABM, Annual Report, 1966.

[31] The reason is unclear, but was probably to secure Waddacor's expertise with coloured malts.

[32] Because of John Crisp's poor health, Leslie Thompson was based at Beccles from 1933 onwards and supervised Crisp's production and, with Arthur Cherry-Downes, acted as barley buyer. From 1939 the business was placed more formally under the control of Thompsons, with John Crisp merely retaining responsibility for sales. Taylor, 'Associated British Maltsters', p. 21; I am grateful to George Abbott for information about the Thompson group.

reasons are unclear, although the directors' minutes suggest a long-running clash of personalities between Sutcliffe and the other founding directors.[33] Thus by the early 1940s three families, the Thompsons, Cherry-Downeses and Cookes, had secured a position of dominance in the merger. Between them, they provided six of the ten directors. When in 1947 Sidney Waddacor resigned, Hubert Cherry-Downes's younger son, Geoffrey, was also appointed to the board. The next generation – Arthur Cherry-Downes's son, Hubert Michael; Geoffrey's son, Nicholas; Philip Cooke's sons, David and Frederick; and George and Leslie Thompsons' nephew, Simon – were introduced as trainee managers. Even with the retirement in 1958 of Hubert Cherry-Downes, aged eighty-two, and Harold Thompson, at seventy-seven, the real focus of power changed little. Two years later, Philip Cooke took charge of ABM (Northern), the Thompsons ABM (Southern) and the Cherry-Downes ABM (Midlands).

Given a sector comprising almost without exception family-dominated enterprises, how did sales-maltsters *manage* their firms? First, it must be stressed that by the inter-war years most companies were small scale and therefore did not demand sophisticated management. Many, like Richard Dewing's firm, were run entirely by principals and a few working maltsters. Generally, partners and directors, each with his own network of personal contacts, concentrated on the key roles of barley buying and malt sales. Production was supervised either by a general manager or one of the principals, although commonly, especially in rural maltings, foremen were semi-autonomous and determined the precise details of the malting schedule. The Hertfordshire firm of French & Jupp's, for example, was effectively run from Surbiton in Surrey where David Jupp resided. David, and subsequently his son Claude, visited the maltings at Stanstead Abbotts once a week. The head foreman managed the workforce of around twenty-five maltsters and took responsibility for the routine decisions of malt production.[34] Even larger firms required only a modest staff. A total of nine, including the company secretary, an analyst and two salesmen, were employed at Gilstrap's head office at Newark.[35] Similarly, when Leslie Thompson joined Samuel Thompson & Sons in 1927, he brought the salaried staff to twelve. The company was by then the leading concern in the west country, with maltings as widely scattered as Devon and Wiltshire, Birmingham, Bristol, Newark and Peterborough, and with customers numbered in hundreds. Family members were responsible for barley buying and the majority of malt sales, where their

[33] Sutcliffe was offered £7000 as compensation for loss of office. He was replaced as joint managing director by Lawrence Burgess. ABM, Directors' Minutes, 15 September, 8 December 1941.
[34] Interview with Guy Horlock.
[35] Taylor, 'Associated British Maltsters', p. 3.

brewing contacts were considered essential. The routine decisions of production were again delegated to malting foremen.[36]

The demands made on partners and directors, especially in the smaller companies, were far from onerous. Like their fathers before them, most combined business with a full and active life in other circles. The Paul family again provides a good example. Of the third generation directors, Russell and Harry jointly farmed the Broxtead estate, near Ipswich. Both were also deeply involved in church work. Stuart, a noted breeder of Suffolk punches and red-poll cattle, farmed an enormous 6000 acres, extending his father's land by the purchase in 1934 of the Wherstead estate. A justice of the peace, member of East Suffolk County Council and High Sheriff of Suffolk in 1938, from 1939–46 he served as chairman of the East Suffolk War Agricultural Executive Committee.[37] Of the four, Hugh was the most divorced from the day-to-day running of the firm and the only one to adopt a lifestyle which went beyond provincial comfort to the exalted circles of London society and the yachting world. This is not to imply that the cousins were anything other than conscientious and competent directors. Hugh's government work demonstrates his real ability, while Russell, the driving force in the 1930s and 1940s, was an austere man, rigid in his interpretation of his nonconformist faith, whose capacity for work and demanding standards provided a forbidding example. The Pauls were simply typical of countless partners and directors throughout other personally managed sectors. Many, like Major Samuel Nock Thompson, who for years served as chairman of Handsworth Conservative Association, were the pillars of local politics.[38] For others, farming was an integral part of their lives. Eric Sandars, for example, lovingly and expertly managed the Gate Burton Estate. The natural accompaniment, of course, was a full range of country pursuits: hunting, shooting and fishing. Certainly the industry boasted more than its share of able horsemen: Hubert Cherry-Downes and 'Sandy' Hutchison – both won the Foxhunter Steeplechase at Liverpool – and James Simpson, who for over twenty years bred and raced his own horses. But if such interests indicate a relaxed management style, how better, in an industry straddling agriculture and brewing, to consolidate personal relationships? In the same way the paternalism which permeated most firms nurtured a loyal and enduring workforce, creating a 'high-trust' culture in every respect.

Is there also evidence of more progressive management practices, especially among the leading firms? By the inter-war years Pauls was already a diverse enterprise engaged in the corn trade, malting, manufacture of animal feedstuffs, brewers adjuncts and preservatives, and owning a range of

---

[36] Ibid., pp. 3, 16–17.

[37] *East Anglian Daily Times*, 20 November 1961; *Who's Who in Suffolk* (1959), p. 47.

[38] Adopted as Conservative candidate for Smethwick in the 'coupon' election of 1918, he gracefully if reluctantly stood down in favour of Christabel Pankhurst, who received the coalition 'ticket'.

subsidiary companies: Gillman & Spencer (1902), the Hull Malt Company (1918), the Cereals Company (1925), a 50 per cent interest in the Albion Sugar Company (1929) and the maltsters Lee & Grinling (1928) and Richard Dobson & Sons of Leeds (1941). Similarly, ABM, with over two hundred maltings strategically situated among the prime barley lands of East Anglia, the east midlands and Yorkshire, and a combined capacity of over 750,000 quarters, was advertised as the world's largest sales-malting company. Clearly, there was ample scope for economies of scale. From the early 1920s there were signs that Sutcliffes, the largest of ABM's constituent companies, was moving towards more centralised administration, based around specialised, functional departments. The seventy maltings within Sutcliffe's purview were grouped into three branches, with production controlled from the head-quarters, the Mirfield offices embracing the laboratory, barley, sales, engineering and transport departments, each in the charge of a qualified manager.[39] To what extent did ABM, building upon these foundations, realise its stated objectives: to deal effectively with the world's barley markets, form an efficient organisation, effect transport economies and apply modern business methods and technology throughout?[40]

The administration of Pauls was, in many respects, representative of other malting companies. The managing directors governed in close collaboration, each taking broad responsibility for one area of activity: Russell, the company's mills, Harry, as grain buyer, Stuart, the grain trade and personnel and Hugh, malting. The next generation followed in their footsteps only after a lengthy training both outside the company and with subsidiaries. Typically, Jock Causton joined the firm in 1926 after Harrow and Pembroke College, Cambridge, then spent time with a grain company in Antwerp and with Lee & Grinling at Grantham. On his return he worked under Hugh at Ipswich, after whose death he assumed control of the group's maltings and responsibility for the key role of barley buying.[41] 'Young' Hugh also followed his father into malting. Similarly educated at Harrow, he was apprenticed to the Leith grain merchants Herdman & McDougall, spent time with Gillman & Spencer, the Albion Sugar Company and the London consultant chemists Briant & Harman, then gained experience in barley buying at Ipswich before completing a final year with Lee & Grinling.[42] William was apprenticed to a firm of flour millers and then worked under Russell on the milling side, Jim was involved in the corn trade and Geoffrey in animal feedstuffs.[43]

[39] *Brewery Record*, 6, August 1927, pp. 10–14; September 1927, pp. 10–13.

[40] Prospectus, Gilstrap Earp & Company, *The Times*, 16 July 1928; *Brewers' Journal*, 15 July 1928.

[41] 'Background Note', Pauls & Whites Limited (1972).

[42] *Pauls' Link*, winter 1977–78.

[43] 'Background Note', Pauls & Whites Limited (1972).

All decisions of any consequence – long-term strategy, capital investment and senior appointments – were taken by the directors. Otherwise, day-to-day decisions rested very much with able managers like Jim Hendry, who took charge of the mills, and F. G. M. Burton, the head maltster, who deployed labour and organised production with minimal interference.[44] Until the Second World War, most managers worked their way up the company during a lifetime's employment. Many, like Bob Prentice (animal feeds, 1931–79), were selected from Ipswich School where the third generation directors had been educated. Alan Woodward joined the company in 1893 and retired as head buyer for the corn trade in 1946, while Jack Bedford began as office boy and rose to head buyer for the malt division. All were totally loyal to the company and the Paul family; Hubert Oxley, company secretary 1938–60, so much so that he was known to refuse a salary increase. The post-war years saw a change of policy, with the recruitment of well-qualified trainee managers who quickly assumed a senior role. There was, however, the same emphasis on able men who enjoyed a significant degree of autonomy and authority: Hugh Philbrick, who joined the company after Marlborough, five years' active service and with a diploma from the Birmingham University School of Malting and Brewing, succeeded Burton in 1951; Oliver Griffin, who first worked for Pauls in his vacations from Birmingham University, became the company's first research chemist in 1958;[45] and, in the following year, John Young (Stowe and Southampton University), who in 1960 replaced Hubert Oxley as company secretary. A chartered accountant previously employed by Plessey and the Ford Motor Company, he brought to Pauls experience of management accountancy, financial analysis and organisation and methods.

Pauls' subsidiaries, although directly controlled by the main board, enjoyed a similar degree of autonomy as those under the ABM umbrella.[46] From the beginning, Pauls provided the chairman of Lee & Grinling but took no further part in running the business. Little changed in 1928 when, after the retirement of Edward Grinling, the company became a wholly owned subsidiary. Harry Paul remained as chairman and Edward's sons, Jack and Philip, stayed as managing director and sales director respectively. Indeed, until he retired in 1958, Brigadier Jack Grinling continued to run his family firm in his own inimitable style, brooking no interference from the parent

---

[44] Jim Hendry, a technical miller, who joined in 1924 and retired in 1965, was the first graduate employed by the company.

[45] He was initially employed on a temporary basis to conduct trials with gibberellic acid, but so impressed Philbrick that he persuaded the directors to appoint him to do research. With his long hair and penchant for making his own clothes he was far removed from a traditional Pauls' employee, but was not only a brilliant industrial chemist but enjoyed excellent relations with the working maltsters. His work is discussed in Chapter 7.

[46] The evidence for the following sections is taken mainly from interviews with Oliver Griffin, Pat Hudson, Bill Nelson, George Paul and Hugh Philbrick.

company.[47] Similarly, the acquisition in 1941 of the Leeds maltster Richard Dobson & Sons made little impact on organisation and management. The business, producing 30–40,000 quarters of malt a year in a string of small, old-fashioned maltings scattered across the West Riding, continued to be run by its managing director, George Hudson, with much of the day-to-day decision making resting with rural foremen. Except for their visit to chair the annual general meeting, Pauls' directors had no involvement with the company until the death of Hudson in the mid 1950s.

In contrast to the relaxed management at Pauls, the administration of ABM clearly presented an enormous challenge to those who had instigated the merger. The early years, perhaps inevitably, were marked by many of the problems experienced by other multi-firm mergers. The group was directed and managed by men who were intensely proud of their old-established firms and reluctant to relinquish their autonomy. For years they had been keen competitors and thus found it difficult to work together. Even the Thames cruise organised by the chairman to celebrate the flotation did little to foster closer relations, with the Cherry-Downeses gathered at one end of the boat and the Thompsons at the other.[48] Not surprisingly, apart from the creation of the barley import department, there is little evidence of integration. Proposals for the collective purchase of such items as coal and sacks were repeatedly rejected. Wages and holidays were determined by individual companies that clearly undercut one another and poached each others' customers.

The board maintained responsibility for key strategic decisions throughout, including the capital expenditure of associated companies but, increasingly, day-to-day management was coordinated through a series of committees. The managing directors' committee and a number of ad hoc committees evaluated broad policy options – some with notable success. In 1946, for example, Arthur Cherry-Downes and Bedrich Lorenz, the manager of the export company, toured the major American brewer-maltsters; while Leslie Thompson, accompanied by the group's engineer, Peter Parker, visited Sweden and Central Europe. Their reports provided the basis for a bold strategy which envisaged the replacement of outdated floor maltings with ten to twelve modern factories producing a million quarters of malt a year. Subsequently, with the addition of Harold Thompson, the committee undertook the planning and design of the first mechanical malting, Louth, which became operational in 1952. Standing committees were also appointed to coordinate key operational functions: sales, raw materials, production,

---

[47] The business was profitable and had a fine reputation for quality and the brigadier never allowed malt made by Pauls to be sold under the Lee & Grinling name. Despite the fact that his production director's brother, John Clarke, as managing director of Greene King, had been responsible for installing a successful drum malting at Bury St Edmunds, he resisted the pressure to modernise and built the last unmechanised floor malting in England.

[48] Interview with Tony Chubb; Taylor, 'Associated British Maltsters', p. 5.

transport, research and administration. Most comprised three members of the main board (who each served on at least two committees) plus four or five senior managers or directors of subsidiary companies. Typically, the sales committee was responsible for developing the group's sales policy and monitoring its implementation, for organising the circulation of daily sales reports and, to improve communications, instituting annual conferences. Despite their central role, the board found difficulty in defining the precise purpose of the various committees, ultimately deciding they should 'help and guide rather than act in a functional way'.[49] Following the introduction of the regional zones, an additional management committee, consisting of all group executive directors, was formed to coordinate activities and to 'increase the efficiency of day-to-day management'.[50] Finally, in January 1963, to relieve the growing administrative burden of the company, an executive committee of the board, comprising all full-time executive directors plus the director representing the Charterhouse Investment Trust (J. G. Vaughan), was established, its purpose being to deal with all routine matters, reserving only the more significant policy decisions for the full board.[51]

In spite of all these committees, ABM remained essentially a federation of family firms. Progress towards centralised administration was painfully slow. There was, for example, no uniform system of accounting, and not until 1952 was a common policy of depreciation adopted. Barley purchases and malt sales were conducted through the zone companies which effectively competed against one another. Several of the company's subsidiaries also continued to operate maltings in similar areas.[52] The passage of time only gradually eased old rivalries. The Thompson brothers, in particular, rarely agreed with each other. Families continued to compete against one another and there were several instances when the guidelines laid down by the sales committee were transgressed and agreed margins undercut. Nothing supposedly elated George Thompson more than taking a contract from Geoffrey Cherry-Downes. Not least, the directors found it difficult to relinquish control of their family firms and to divorce themselves from day-to-day operations, resulting in the duplication evident in the many committees. As Sir Hubert

---

[49] ABM, Directors' Minutes, 17 June 1946, 4 March 1958.

[50] Subsequently, during the peak months of the season, the sales, raw materials and production committees met every Monday morning at Newark, then during the afternoon, the management committee, chaired by Philip Cooke (who served ex-officio all the operations committees), convened to consider their reports. Ibid., 22 February 1960.

[51] In 1954 the old posts of joint managing director were abolished. In many respects the executive committee (renamed the group executive committee the following year) replaced the original managing directors' committee. Ibid., 14 January 1963, 9 March 1964.

[52] In 1956, as a first step towards integrating the purchase of barley, Philip Cooke bought for the whole of Yorkshire, but the following year the northern companies were again buying under their own names with their barley buyers competing against one another on local markets. Ibid., 29 April 1952, 9 July 1956, 23 May 1957.

Nutcombe Hume told his shareholders in 1963, some thirty-five years after the merger 'the knitting together of many independent companies ... into one efficient whole takes a long time'.[53]

That there was resistance to change, particularly from some of the older directors, is evident. Equally important was the conservative attitude of brewers, especially in the key area of sales. Until the 1960s rationalisation of brewing, malt sales were governed by an informal code of conduct whereby large buyers spread their interests widely and supported small producers; head brewers held sway, and personal contacts and reputation were all important.[54] Few could exploit the personal network as effectively as the ABM directors with their connections among brewing's elite.[55] Nevertheless, the merger companies, afraid of losing trade to competitors, dare not unite under a common banner. Indeed, as late as 1948, the ABM directors considered the trade was becoming *more* personal and the employment of additional salesmen with 'good connections' worthwhile.[56] Not for another decade, thirty years after the merger, was malt supplied under the ABM label.[57] Until sales were centralised, little could be done to rationalise transport. Although after the 1947 Transport Act, the merger quickly built up a fleet of 120 vehicles, these were owned by and painted in the colours of individual firms. Not until 1960 were they finally pooled and run under ABM colours.[58] The same pressures were evident in Pauls' relationship with its malting subsidiaries, which also enjoyed a significant degree of autonomy. Undoubtedly, as at ABM, this reflected the reluctance of proprietors to relinquish control of family firms. But the influence of brewers is also clear. Pauls had first acquired a financial stake in Lee & Grinling in 1907. Remarkably, they kept this a closely guarded secret from their brewing customers until the 1960s.

For both companies, the period was also one of achievement and innovation: at ABM, the success of the Export Company, the appointment in 1947 of a talented chemist, Dr Alan Macey, to head research and development and, not least, the investment programme. By 1964 big new maltings, at Louth, Knapton and Wallingford, served three of the zones, while a

[53] Chairman's Statement, 31 July 1963.

[54] Major brewers such as Mann, Crossman & Paulin purchased malt from as many as twenty-five to thirty maltsters. Twice a year, Sir John Mann presided while the head brewer, Mr Lucas (who had already negotiated with his regular salesmen), went through the ritual of comparing samples and fixing contracts. Interview with Bill Nelson.

[55] These were both business and personal. For example, in 1901, Hubert Cherry-Downes married Adeline, daughter of Colonel Hanbury Barclay, the chairman of Barclay Perkins.

[56] ABM, Directors' Minutes, 19 July 1948.

[57] The board overruled the wishes of the sales committee who feared repercussions, especially from the northern brewers. The first consignment delivered in ABM sacks went to Flowers' Luton Brewery. Ibid., 11 August 1958.

[58] Some brewers still specified that their malt was made in a particular malting, regardless of distance. The Courage brewery at Devonport, for example, took all their malt from Bury St Edmunds. Taylor, 'Associated British Maltsters', p. 37; interview with George Abbott.

fourth, at Bury St Edmunds, was under construction.[59] Similarly, at Pauls, the appointment of a professional management team led to the steady modernisation of the company. Hugh Philbrick, in tackling the shift from imported to home-grown barley transformed the working practices of half a century.[60] Jock Causton initiated the development of malt exports and investment in the company's first mechanical malting, a Saladin box type, completed at Ipswich in 1956.[61] Lastly, the appointment of Oliver Griffin marked the beginning of a sustained programme of research and development.

Throughout most of the industry there was even less weakening of family control before the 1960s. On occasions, as at F. & G. Smith, it was accompanied by complacency and a marked resistance to change, the chairman, Vardon Smith, perceiving little need to think in terms of modern plant while the company could maintain the dividend at 10 per cent. According to Betty Wharton, the company's historian and a family member, 'the interests of shareholders and family always took precedence over those of the company'.[62] Elsewhere there were signs that most of the leading firms were adapting their organisation and management to meet the challenges of the post-war era. Long before this, Bairds had established a management committee to evaluate potential acquisitions and long-term investments, negotiations with Canada Malting Company concerning investment in a Saladin plant beginning as early as 1939. The promotion to the board in 1943 of Reginald Dennis, a chartered accountant, again suggests a growing professionalisation in executive management.[63] The same progressive attitude, resulting in the opening of the new drum malting at Stowmarket in 1950, was evident at Muntons. The employees' handbook emphasised the firm's family character. More unusually, it also included an organisation chart delineating lines of responsibility.[64] Such advances were modest. They should be set in the context of an industry where most companies were small in scale, where for many decades technology had remained unchanged, and where the attitude of brewers clearly acted as a brake on progress.

[59] Maltings at Bath, Pontefract, Louth and Abingdon were also fully mechanised, enabling the closure of many old floor maltings.

[60] This meant establishing tight control over production, implementing a rigorous system of sampling barley deliveries and ending the monopoly of large grain merchants who had been buying from smaller merchants and then adding their own margin.

[61] Between 1950–59 a total of £1.5 million was expended on modernising and building new properties. Besides the Saladin malting, war-damaged mills were all replaced or modernised and grain silos built at Ipswich, Faversham and London.

[62] Wharton, *Smiths of Ryburgh*, pp. 56, 70.

[63] Hugh Baird & Sons, Directors' Minutes, 14 October 1943, 3 February 1939, 11 May 1939; See above, p. 194.

[64] Muntona Limited, 'Notes for Employees', c. 1956, pp. 2, 14–19.

After 1960 several factors underpinned the restructuring of many of the leading malting companies. As in other sectors of the British economy, most felt the pressure of rising costs and unprecedented capital demands.[65] In addition, the industry had entered an intensely competitive era, both in domestic and export markets, providing every incentive to achieve economies in production, transport and administration. More specifically, the rapid rationalisation of the brewing industry after 1958 had sharply reduced the number of customers and had at last brought to an end the traditional methods of selling malt. As local breweries closed, the national groups began buying raw materials through a central office. Contracts escalated and the barrier to fully integrating sales was at last removed, enabling the larger firms to reap the benefits of their investment in mechanised plant.

Elsewhere decisions could no longer be delayed. Immediately after the war, Bairds had reached agreement with Canada Malting Company over joint investment in a Saladin plant – only to be refused a building licence. Sixteen years later, as the cost of their new Wanderhaufen malting soared, they again turned to the Canada company who provided the necessary capital injection in exchange for a 50 per cent interest in the business. The move also brought four directors from the much larger corporation onto a board which previously had been drawn entirely from family and long-serving managers.[66] Reorganisation at Smiths was less straightforward. After years of prevarication, the government's ultimatum over war damage compensation finally forced the hands of the board. In 1962, when the chairman, Vardon Smith, resigned, the more progressive members, determined to restore the firm's lost vitality, entered into a joint venture with John Crisp (eighth generation of the famous malting family) to construct a Saladin malting at Great Ryburgh.[67] A new company, Crisp Malting, was created, in which F. & G. Smith held a 75 per cent interest. Nevertheless, John Crisp, a man of undoubted ability and entrepreneurial drive who brought with him valuable contracts from ABM, secured 50 per cent of the voting rights. From the beginning the venture flourished: capacity at Great Ryburgh quickly doubled; Courage's Ditchingham maltings were acquired together with an agreement to supply them with malt; in 1969 the old Beccles floor maltings worked by the Crisp family in the 1920s were bought from ABM

[65] Notably higher labour costs, rates, water and effluent charges. Channon found that similar factors prompted many of the largest British manufacturing companies to restructure their organisations; *Investors' Chronicle*, Brewing Survey, 25 October 1963; Channon, *Strategy and Structure*, p. 239.

[66] Hugh Baird & Sons, Directors' Minutes, 25 September 1962–18 December 1964.

[67] The company was given the choice of £60,000 in cash or replacement maltings. The cost of the Saladin malting was £453,000, of which £195,000 was received as War Damage Compensation. F. & G. Smith, Directors' Minutes, 23 June 1958–31 March 1962; Wharton, *Smiths of Ryburgh*, p. 74.

and reopened. Two years later Crisps purchased the Mistley company, EDME, producer of malt extract and home-brew kits.[68]

Events at ABM and Pauls, perhaps inevitably given the relative scale and complexity of their organisations, were more protracted. At ABM the decision to centralise administration, further fuelled by the approaching retirement of the second-generation directors, was finally taken in July 1963. Despite the good intentions, more than a year later the executive directors were as deeply involved in their respective zones as ever. The problem was resolved, as in many other companies during this period, by management consultants, when in January 1965 the PE Consultancy Group were asked to investigate the organisation of the company. Unfortunately their report has not survived. That it was highly critical there can be little doubt. According to Stephen Aris, of the *Sunday Times*, what they found was:

> enough to turn the hair of the most ardent advocate of decentralisation grey. Although ABM was in theory a massive and coherent industrial combine, in practice it was a loose confederation of four autonomous regional units. Each had its own board and sold in competition against the other. There was no chief executive and as everything was controlled by committee there was no one man responsible for sales, for production or for research.[69]

Certainly the reorganisation which followed was, to quote the chairman, Sir Hubert Nutcombe Hume, 'drastic' and 'far-reaching'. It is to the board's credit that they were prepared to accept the recommendations of the consultants.[70] The executive management was immediately strengthened by the addition of David Nicholson, chairman of PE Consultancy, a director of the Charterhouse Group, and the man largely responsible for undertaking the investigation. In December 1965 he replaced Sir Hubert, then seventy-two years old, as chairman of the group. The role of chief executive was given to John Parry, George Thompson's deputy and sales manager of the Eastern Zone (formerly with Ipswich Malting Company), who assumed his duties in January 1966 after a crash course of three months at the Massachusetts Institute of Technology. Leslie Thompson was appointed forward planning director, a new post to which the consultants clearly attached great importance. The remaining senior executives, Geoffrey Cherry-Downes, George Thompson and Robert Brown, retained their old roles in transport, sales and finance. Hans Lorenz became the group's first technical director, with three junior executives, John West (production), Giles Cartwright (barley supplies) and Harry St. G. Gallaher (sales), completing the team.[71]

[68] From the beginning, the two companies collaborated closely, but in 1976 were brought together under the umbrella of Anglia Holdings Group. In 1971 F. & G. Smith also purchased the Dereham haulage company Walpole & Wright. Ibid., pp. 74–76.

[69] *Sunday Times*, 20 November 1966.

[70] Chairman's Statement, 31 July 1965; ABM, Directors' Minutes, 10 May 1965.

[71] Harry St G. Gallaher was initially deputy to S. George Thompson and responsible for central office sales, taking over as sales director after Thompson's retirement in 1966.

The regional structure was dissolved and the associated malting companies brought together under the umbrella of ABM (Malting) Limited.[72] Management by committee was replaced by direct line and functional management (see Fig. 8.1). The old committees were also disbanded and replaced by four advisory ones: executive, personnel, forward planning and research and development. In areas where the consultants had identified serious short-comings – cost accounting, stock and production control – they were retained to devise new systems, notably implementing for the first time a system of budgetary control. Lastly, to reduce dependence on malting, already a low-growth sector and further threatened by the introduction of malt substitutes, the corporate plan outlined the gradual shift to a multi-divisional structure embracing five divisions: malt, which was to remain the dominant product, chemicals, animal feedstuffs, human food and transport engineering (the last four initially under the auspices of ABM Industrial Products).[73] The result was a significant and rapid widening of interests: the acquisition in 1968 of R. Murfitt and the Burtonwood Mechanical Handling Company to form an engineering division specialising in bulk transport; a £1.4 million bid for Stevenson & Howell, manufacturers of flavourings and essences; a 25 per cent stake in the French chemical group Promaco; and, in malting, new plant at Cork and Carnoustie, a majority holding in the Australian maltsters, Smith Mitchell & Company, and the formation with Manbré & Garton of a joint marketing company to promote sales of barley syrups.[74]

Although in 1969 Pauls also turned to management consultants to oversee the restructuring of the firm, much of the necessary change was achieved internally. Initially, despite a public flotation in July 1960 to raise finance for an ambitious expansion programme, there was little change in terms of ownership and control.[75] A year later family holdings accounted for almost 80 per cent of the equity, with the directors holding 36.6 per cent in their

[72] ABM (Malting) Limited was registered as the main malting company on 1 August 1967 and comprised all the previous subsidiaries, ABM Export Company and ABM Special Products.

[73] The board of Industrial Products, previously dominated by maltsters, was strengthened by the appointment in place of George and Leslie Thompson of three directors with experience of the chemical industry: Philip Evans, of Norman Evans & Rais, as managing director; Keith Parker, as development and product director; and David Price MP, as deputy chairman and a member of the main board.

[74] The Bury malting, opened in 1965, cost £2¼ million and was the largest in Europe; Carnoustie, completed in 1971 was the last malting built by the group and served the Scottish distillers. The Malting Company of Ireland was a joint venture undertaken with Canadian Breweries and the Cork Distilleries, ABM holding a 50 per cent interest. ABM, Directors' Minutes and Annual Reports.

[75] The capital of the company was increased, from £1.22 million to £2.15 million, by the creation of 3,120,000 new ordinary shares of 5s. The sum of £480,000 standing to reserves was capitalised and distributed to ordinary shareholders in the ratio of eight shares for every one held; one million of the new shares (20.8 per cent of the issued equity) were offered for public subscription.

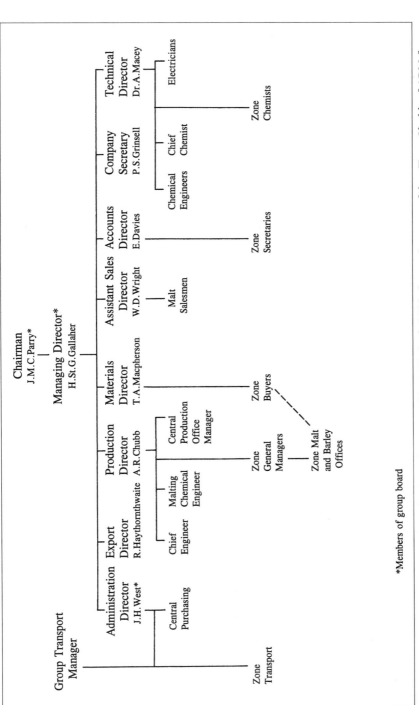

Figure 8.1 Divisional board and organisation of ABM (Malting) Limited, 1968. *Source:* I am grateful to Tony Chubb of ABM for this information.

own names.[76] Jim Paul succeeded Stuart as chairman. Otherwise there was no change in the composition of the board or in their style of management. The directors, as tradition decreed, each took a functional role in the various activities. Like the previous generation, they were also deeply involved in farming and the local community. William and Geoffrey inherited their father's estates and farmed on an extensive scale. Jim also followed closely in his father's footsteps as a justice of the peace and an active member of the Congregational Church, he was also vice-chairman of the Ipswich Dock Commission, president of the London Corn Trade Association and subsequently of the National Federation of Corn Trade Associations. Likewise, the two malting directors, Jock Causton and Hugh Paul, as members of the executive of the Maltsters' Association and the Home Grown Cereals Authority, took an active role in the wider administration of their industry. Both were rural district councillors. Jock also farmed 700 acres, was a magistrate, chairman of the St Edmundsbury and Ipswich Diocesan Board of Finance and a member of the Diocesan Synod. A man of enormous energy and determination, he emerged as the natural leader of his generation, guiding the company through its first decade of public ownership.[77]

The first significant changes in organisation came in February 1963 when Pauls merged with one of its oldest competitors, White, Tomkins & Courage of London, who also produced brewers' flakes and animal feedstuffs and with whom Pauls had already established links through their joint ownership of the Albion Sugar Company. The merger, inevitably, brought a widening of ownership and, for the first time, the appointment of 'outsiders' to the board, four of White's directors joining the five members of the Paul family: Alwyn White, grandson of the founder, Robert Wallace (who became deputy chairman of the new company), Philip Frere and Alexander Garden.[78] Nevertheless, the Pauls continued to hold large controlling blocs of shares and, relying on family holdings, accounted for over 35 per cent of the equity.[79] In all, five wholly-owned subsidiaries reported to the new holding company, Pauls & Whites: Gillman & Spencer, White, Tomkins & Courage and the Albion Sugar Company – each trading under its existing management – and two new companies formed by separating Pauls' milling and malting interests, Pauls Foods and R. & W. Paul (Maltsters). The latter, with a board drawn from all the malting subsidiaries, proved a major step in

[76] Family holdings include shares held jointly as trustees and executors. Institutions accounted for only 9.97 per cent of the equity. The largest shareholders, the Pearl Assurance and Equity and Law Life Assurance, each held 60,000 shares (£15,000). R. & W. Paul, Share Registers.

[77] From 1942–64 he was also a director, and from 1953 chairman, of the publishers Sir Joseph Causton & Sons Limited.

[78] The issued ordinary capital of the new company was £2,359,380. Shares were offered to existing shareholders of the two companies in the ratio of 61 per cent to Pauls and 39 per cent to White Tomkins & Courage.

[79] Pauls & Whites', Share Registers.

integrating the malting interests.[80] The acquisition in 1965 of S. Swonnell & Son of Oulton Broad, specialists in the production of coloured malts, and of Harrington Page of Ware, brought a further centralisation of sales and distribution. Despite opportunities to rationalise the production of animal feedstuffs, attempts to integrate Pauls Foods and White, Tomkins & Courage proved less successful, with the two companies maintaining much of their independence. The approaching retirement of Philip Frere and Jim Paul,[81] coupled with the increasingly technical nature of the group's activities, also caused concern prompting a further reorganisation of the company. In November 1966 the executive board was dissolved and Jock Causton unanimously elected chairman and managing director. Within a month, he had outlined plans for a multi-divisional structure embracing three divisions: malt, animal foodstuffs and general products. Stressing the need for functional and independent directors, he also recommended the appointment of three additional executives: Hugh Philbrick as managing director of the malt division; John Young as financial director; and John Westbrook (who had joined the group in 1965) as director of research and development. Lastly, John Harvey brought experience from a wide spectrum of industry, as a non-executive director.[82] These appointments not only marked a break with tradition but demonstrated Causton's determination to force the pace of change even at the expense of family status. Previously no senior manager had ever been appointed to the group board. In part, this reflected the continued abundance of male heirs but, of the fourth generation, only William's sons, George and Jonathan (born in 1940 and 1942) were of an age to secure family succession.[83] Some widening of the board was therefore inevitable. The appointment of Hugh Philbrick, the man largely responsible for the successful integration of the malting companies, as managing director of the malt division meant that he superseded Hugh Paul, a charming and intelligent man adept at entertaining customers but with little real appetite for business.

A further innovation the following year was a group planning committee set up to formulate long-term strategy and identify potential high-growth

[80] The board comprised Jock Causton (managing director), Hugh Paul and Hugh Philbrick, and the managing directors of Dobsons and Lee & Grinling, Peter Branston and Harry Clarke.

[81] Because of poor health, Jim Paul resigned as an executive director and chairman in November 1966 but remained as a non-executive director until 1972.

[82] Pauls & Whites, Directors' Minutes, 18 February, 8 November 1966, 24 January, 13 June 1967. John Westbrook (Cambridge and Manchester), a Fellow of the Royal Institute of Chemistry and Institute of Food Science and Technology, had previously worked for Birds Eye Foods and Beechams. John Harvey (Radley and Oxford), was managing director of Spencer Chapman & Merrel between 1946–54. Subsequently a director of Laporte Industries, Gallaher and chairman of the National Provident Institute, he was also treasurer of the Institute of Directors and served the council of the Chemical Industries Association.

[83] Both were educated at Harrow and Wye College, London University, before embarking on their internal apprenticeship, George as a trainee maltster and Jonathan in animal foods.

sectors. Despite these radical changes, two problems remained. Throughout the 1960s the group, in common with many British companies, had been unable to match growth with performance. By 1968–69 the return on assets, in excess of 15 per cent in 1959–63, had fallen to 7 per cent while the share price had more than halved.[84] There was also the need to find a managing director to succeed Causton, who was by now in his early sixties. On the advice of John Harvey, a firm of management consultants, John Tyzack, was approached and their recommendation for a detailed survey of the entire organisation by one of their directors, John Clayton, was accepted. His report emphasised not only the weaknesses but also the many strengths of the group, in particular the high proportion of loyal and able managers and the introduction of modern cost accounting. On the negative side, he stressed the need for a clear group strategy, also deprecating the overlapping and blurring of reporting lines and lack of management training.[85] The main proposal was to retain the multi-divisional structure but disband the existing general products division and reorganise the group from a production to marketing basis. This involved, for example, bringing together all products sold to the brewing and distilling trades – malt, syrups, flakes, caramels and finings – into one Brewing Materials Division (see Fig. 8.2). The remaining divisions were to be similarly focused on farming and the food trade.

Not only was Clayton's report accepted, he was invited to become the group's next managing director. First, however, Causton tackled the difficult task of restructuring the group board. As a result, Geoffrey Paul resigned and retired to devote himself to farming. Hugh Paul and Alwyn White resigned from the group board but remained as directors of R. & W. Paul (Maltsters) and White Tomkins & Courage (Reigate) respectively. In March 1970 Robert Wallace and Alex Garden, both of whom were approaching seventy and had given over forty-five years to Whites, retired, while Brigadier James Hill, deputy chairman of Powell Duffryn and previously a director of the maltsters Sandars & Company, was appointed a non-executive director. At the same time, Causton, who remained as the group's chairman, handed over the role of managing director to John Clayton – a move which marked the final transition from family ownership and control. Of the board of nine,

---

[84] Channon found that this was a common experience with many British companies failing to maintain the real value of their 1960 earnings. The main problems rested with animal foods, where for most of the decade rising costs and intense competition had, despite increased sales, depressed margins and profits. The sudden fall in the demand for distilling malt had compounded the situation. Channon, *Strategy and Structure*, p. 221.

[85] The group possessed no specialists in work study or market research while, of the thirty directors and senior managers interviewed, only nine had a degree or professional qualification. Subsequently Clayton introduced a programme of management training and a series of weekend seminars bringing together directors and middle management from the constituent companies. John Tyzack Consultants Limited, 'Report on the Management Structure of Pauls & Whites Limited', p. 5; interview with John Clayton.

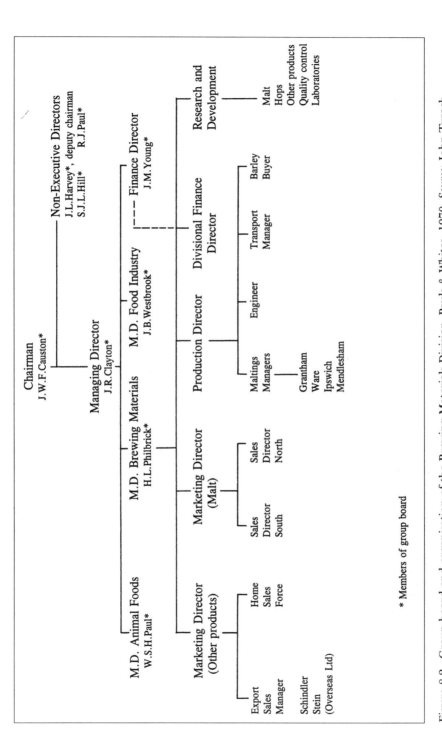

Figure 8.2. Group board and organisation of the Brewing Materials Division, Pauls & Whites, 1970. *Source*: John Tyzack Consultants Limited, 'Report on the Management Structure of Pauls & Whites'.

only three were members of the founding family. Jock Causton remained as chairman until 1973 (he was succeeded by Brigadier Hill), finally retiring in 1975 almost fifty years after joining the company, forty of them as a director. Jim Paul (a non-executive director since 1967) retired in March 1972 after forty-six years' service. Four months later, William Paul resigned his executive duties but remained as a non-executive director. He was succeeded as managing director of Pauls & Whites Foods and as group executive director by his thirty-one-year-old son George – an appointment based on the recommendation of Clayton.[86] In terms of ownership, by 1970 close family holdings accounted for almost a quarter of the company's equity; a decade later, just over 12 per cent.[87] Almost certainly this understates the full extent of family support: in 1973, for example, a third of the voting shares were held by those connected with the company. But the trend towards institutional holdings was unmistakeable. In 1973, 43 per cent of the equity was held by large institutions; by 1980, almost 70 per cent.[88]

Clayton's recommendations were quickly implemented, although unlike at ABM it was more a case of fine tuning, reflecting the steps already taken to adopt a multi-divisional structure. The planning committee was discontinued and, in its place, Clayton introduced 'board papers' (detailed reports prepared by the executive directors) as the means of formulating the group's long-term strategy. A profit-centred approach was also adopted. Expansion continued mainly by the acquisition of more companies. Hence the acquisition of Barkers & Lee Smith, who were based in Lincolnshire, Yorkshire and Norfolk, complemented the opening of the country mills at Crediton and Radstock, while the purchase of Stevenson & Howell and the Glentham Essence Company strengthened the group's interest in flavours for the food trade. The aims of the Brewing Division – to maintain domestic market share and develop interests overseas – were similarly met by acquisition. Most important was the takeover of Sandars & Company of Gainsborough. This had taken place in 1969 when Sandars had approached Pauls because

---

[86] Board Paper, 29, 1971–72; Interview with John Clayton; During the following years the board was strengthened by the addition of further outside directors. Two came from brewing backgrounds: George Duncan was previously chief executive of Truman Limited and Watney Mann and chief executive of Yule Catto; Michael Falcon had until 1968 been managing director of the brewers Lacons, was a director of Norwich Union and regional director of Lloyds Bank. Michael McCorkell was managing director of the animal food manufacturers, William McCorkell, and chairman of the International Corn Company of Antwerp.

[87] Mainly because new shares were issued to finance the group's acquisitions: 1.35 million ordinary shares in Pauls & Whites were allotted to shareholders of Robert Hutchison as part of the purchase price of the company. A further 4.8 million new shares were issued in 1977 in a 1:4 rights issue. Pauls & Whites, Share Registers; Directors' Minutes, 16 June 1972, 8 March 1977.

[88] Pauls & Whites, Share Registers; Directors' Minutes, 18 July 1973. Large institutional shareholders were those with more than 100,000 shares.

of their succession problems.[89] Subsequently a new operating company, Pauls & Sandars, was formed. Until his retirement in 1973, Colonel J. E. Sandars served as chairman, with Hugh Philbrick as managing director. Sandars brought to Pauls their high-margin contracts and good brewing connections. In contrast, the acquisition in 1972 of the Scottish maltster Robert Hutchison & Company provided the means for further penetration into the growing distilling market.[90] Finally, Britain's prospective entry into the EEC prompted a direct move into the European industry. Accordingly in 1971 the group took a quarter share in Malteries Huys NV, a Belgian company for whom Pauls had previously acted as technical consultants. Two years later Pauls acquired the French companies Usines Ethel SA and its neighbour, Grands Moulins de Strasbourg. Notably, in each case acquisition was initiated by family firms lacking the necessary management, finance or technology to maintain independence, as such underlining the progress made by Pauls during the previous decade.

Expansion was not without its difficulties. The acquisition of the European malting companies was not successful and ultimately these were sold.[91] But in comparison with ABM's investment in potentially high-growth sectors, there were relatively few problems. ABM's engineering division, in particular, had made heavy losses from the beginning and was sold in 1970. After two years the Promaco holding was also disposed of while other acquisitions, such as Stevenson & Howell, performed erratically. 'Diversification', noted the *Investors' Chronicle*, 'has proved far from an unmixed blessing.'[92] Overall, the expected returns were slow to materialise and did little to ease concern regarding the uncertainties and slow growth of malting. Yet it was in malting that changes in market share underline most clearly the contrasting fortunes of the two firms, ABM's share falling from almost 45 per cent in 1962 to 31 per cent in 1970, while that of Pauls increased from just under 10 per cent to almost 22 per cent.[93]

The real test for both companies came from outside predators. At ABM the brief period of restructuring reached its conclusion in November 1971 when the chief executive, David Nicholson, was appointed the first chairman

[89] Sandars had already acquired the Nottingham maltster, J. Pidcock & Company, and Yeomans, Cherry & Curtis of Burton-upon-Trent. The bid, valued at £870,000, offering nine Pauls & White ordinary shares of 5s. for two of Sandars £1 shares, was accepted by 99.9 per cent of shareholders. Pauls & Whites, Directors' Minutes, 15 September 1969; *The Times*, 29 August 1969.

[90] For a decade Hutchisons had acted as Pauls' agents in the distilling market and had suggested a merger between the companies as early as 1968. File covering the acquisition of Sandars & Company, 13 December 1968, 22 January 1969.

[91] This was for a variety of reasons, notably oversupply and the resultant price-war in European malt markets. The most successful was the investment in Malteries Huys, but in this case Pauls were unable to obtain a controlling interest.

[92] *Investors' Chronicle*, 31 October 1969, 28 November 1969, 4 December 1970.

[93] MAGB, Subscription Lists.

of British Airways and resigned from the board.[94] Almost simultaneously, the company became embroiled in the merger activity of the period. Barely a month after his Grand Metropolitan Hotels had acquired the brewers Trumans, Maxwell Joseph launched a surprise £10.3 million bid for the company through his industrial holding and gaming group, Giltspur Investments. Perceived by the *Investors' Chronicle* as having 'no kind of industrial logic',[95] the bid was clearly prompted by ABM's undervalued property assets, especially a potential development site at Southwark. A hasty revaluation, which raised net assets per share from 92p to 155p, record pre-tax profits and Joseph's reluctance to increase the bid beyond £11.5 million (150p. a share) ensured shareholder loyalty.[96] But the company was shaken and remained vulnerable. The following September saw a defensive agreed bid for Glovers (Chemicals), but immediately, ABM was itself approached by Dalgety, an Australian company rapidly expanding its UK interests. Dalgety's activities ranged from primary production and grain merchanting to rural properties and services, clearly complementing ABM's core business. Indeed, a major factor underpinning acceptance of the £21 million bid was the prospect of some far less desirable partner. The crucial determinant was the substantial stake in ABM acquired under nominees by Slater Walker Securities. These shares were first offered to Joseph, who was unwilling to match the asking price. Instead the 14 per cent of ABM's equity amassed by Giltspur was purchased by Slater Walker, bringing their holding to more than 25 per cent. Once promised to Dalgety, the ABM board had little choice but to accept their bid.[97] Pauls similarly became the target for speculative stake-building in 1971 when Jim Slater acquired 7½ per cent of the group's equity. Two years later, Michael Richards, the chairman of Wood Hall Trust, purchased Slater's stake and steadily amassed a total of 29.5 per cent of the ordinary shares.[98] In contrast to ABM, a bid did not materialise. The presence of predators clearly remained a threat but also provided a spur to performance. After two difficult years, the benefits of the reorganisation, in terms of integration and rationalisation, were evident in improved margins and profits.[99] The scale of Pauls' achievement as a public company

[94] His position as chairman of ABM was taken by Peter Parker, who had joined the board fourteen months earlier. He subsequently left ABM to become chairman of British Rail.

[95] The bid placed a value of approximately 130 pence per share on ABM, *Investors' Chronicle*, 24 December 1971.

[96] The revaluation excluded the uncertain value of the development site, estimated at a further 28 pence a share. *The Times*, 2 November 1971; *Investors' Chronicle*, 5, 12 November 1971, 24, 31 December 1971, The bid lapsed in January 1972.

[97] *The Times*, 21 October 1972; *Investors' Chronicle*, 27 October 1972.

[98] This was just short of the 30 per cent barrier which necessitated a bid. Pauls & Whites, Directors' Minutes.

[99] In 1969–71 average pre-tax profits were £700,000 (on a turnover of £36.1 million), well below the peak of £980,000 in 1967–68. In 1971–72 pre-tax profits more than doubled to £1.7 million (on a turnover of £36.90 million) and thereafter rose steadily to £8.9 million in 1979.

may be judged by regular inclusion after 1970 in the top quarter of *The Times* index of 1000 largest companies in the United Kingdom.

What conclusions can we draw about the management of the industry before the mid 1970s? Two points need to be made. First, it is difficult to generalise about a sector comprising small firms such as French & Jupp's, capitalised at £50,000, and, at the other end of the spectrum, Pauls & Whites, capitalised at £5½ million. Secondly, there is little to suggest that administration and organisation differed greatly from that of other family-dominated sectors of the economy:[100] a personal style of management; a predilection for partners and directors to combine business with politics and public life; an acceptance of less able family members; and a marked reluctance to retire. Yet this should not be taken as evidence of complacency. The pressures facing the industry after 1918 meant that survival was by no means certain. If advances were modest before the 1960s, in most companies there were signs of competent and progressive management. Terry Gourvish found that even the largest brewery companies tackled the structure of the board and the handling of subsidiaries with hesitancy.[101] For sales-maltsters, their relationship with brewers added a further dimension, evident in the rapid restructuring of ABM in 1929, barely a year after its formation. Until the rationalisation of the brewing industry in the 1960s, the small family firm with its prized reputation and network of personal contacts remained the most appropriate organisational form. If there were shortcomings, they were most clearly evident at ABM. Despite many positive achievements, inter-family rivalries and resistance to change meant that the company met few of its objectives. The 1960s marked the turning point. Thereafter, most of the leading companies showed a willingness to adapt organisation and structure, even at F. & G. Smith the more progressive directors finally securing managerial change which restored the firm's vitality. Of the two leading companies, Pauls' relative success in adapting to a multi-divisional structure reflected not only their experience of growth by diversification but the policy of consolidating well-established activities. At ABM the legacy of family capitalism was only too clearly evident in the group's poor performance after 1960. There is much to support Payne's hypothesis that if there was a causal link between the family firm and a loss of economic vitality, it is to be found in the multi-firm mergers of the inter-war years which failed to adopt a centralised structure and create a managerial staff necessary to overcome the diseconomies of size.[102] ABM provides a classic example.

[100] See also T. R. Gourvish, 'British Business and the Transition to a Corporate Economy: Entrepreneurship and Management Structures', *Business History*, 29 (1987), pp. 19–45.

[101] Gourvish and Wilson, *British Brewing Industry*, pp. 532–33. See in particular the example of Bass & Company, C. C. Owen, *The Greatest Brewery in the World: A History of Bass, Ratcliff & Gretton* (Chesterfield, 1992), pp. 172–190.

[102] Payne, 'Family Business', pp. 196–97.

9

The Modern Malting Industry, 1975–98

Between the end of the Second World War and the mid 1970s, the British malting industry had witnessed unprecedented change. Empirical methods had given way to modern technology and the old traditional skills were fast becoming a dim memory. So, too, was the virtual dependency upon the domestic brewing trade. Led by world-class companies, the sector was by now well placed in international markets. Yet, in the subsequent globalisation of the malt trade and in rising levels of concentration, the industry faced in the last quarter of the twentieth century some of the most far-reaching challenges of its long history.

The main force shaping British malting during these years was the changing focus of the malt market. In many respects, this marked a continuation of post-war trends, although the steady growth of the distilling trade, which had proved so critical to maltsters' fortunes since the early 1960s, came to an abrupt end in 1974. Thereafter, the market was characterised by a series of severe cyclical fluctuations (see Fig. 9.1). The first, which saw demand fall by almost a quarter in two years, reflected the sharp contraction of the crucial US market at the conclusion of the Vietnam War.[1] The upturn of 1979 was short-lived, the oil crisis and the onset of world recession prompting a lengthy period of destocking by distillers. At the nadir, four years later, the demand for malt had fallen to 296,000 tonnes, a decline of 57 per cent from the 1974 peak. Although distillers' own production was sharply curtailed, it was sales-maltsters who felt the main impact, deliveries over the same period falling by a massive 64 per cent.

To make matters worse, during the short-lived recovery of the late 1970s most of the leading companies commissioned new maltings specifically to supply the distilling trade: Moray Firth at Arbroath in 1978 and again two years later; Crisps at Portgordon and Pauls at Buckie in 1980. Bairds extended their Pencaitland plant and in 1978 ABM purchased the Airdrie Wanderhaufen plant from Moffat Malting Company. In addition, the completion in December 1981 of the Distillers Company's new plant at Roseisle forced it into export markets in direct competition with sales-maltsters. Such was the situation of excess capacity that by 1983 Pauls' Buckie plant was producing

---

[1] Underpinned in particular by the recession in the massive armaments industry which employed around 20 per cent of the workforce. K. Marsden, 'Technical Change in the British Malting Industry' (unpublished Ph.D. thesis, University of Salford, 1985), p. 146.

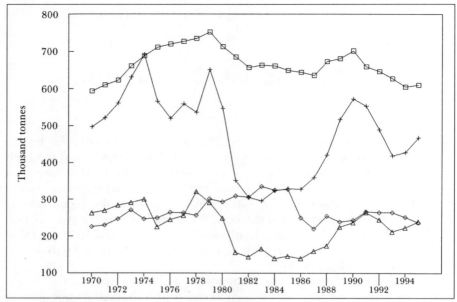

Figure 9.1 Total malt used in UK brewing and distilling, and brewers' and distillers' malt production, 1970–95 (thousand tonnes).
Key: □ Total malt used in brewing   + Total malt used in distilling
          ◇ Brewers' own production   △ Distillers' own production.
Source: MAGB, Annual Statistics.

lager malt for West Africa and Europe. Demand recovered after 1986 but four years later again gave way to world recession and a further period of destocking. By 1994 sales-maltsters' deliveries were little above those of a decade earlier and demand remained below the trough of the 1970s.

Conditions in the domestic brewing market were little better. After two decades of unchecked growth (excepting the brief downturn of 1968), beer production fell sharply in the depression of 1979–81. Although it stabilised thereafter, the relatively high price of beer, demographic and social forces (especially the growing preference for wine and issues such as health and drink driving) meant it was not to regain its previous heights. A further decline in the recession of the early 1990s, and the subsequent downward drift, indicate likely future trends. Again, the problems for sales-maltsters were exacerbated because, for much of the period, brewer-maltsters maintained their own production and reduced the quantity of malt they purchased. While the demand for malt fell 11.8 per cent in 1979–83, brewers' own production increased by almost the same amount, not least because of the decision by Bass and Allied to achieve 80 per cent self-sufficiency.[2] As sales-maltsters watched their deliveries fall by some 120,000 tonnes (27 per

[2] K. Marsden, 'Technical Change', p. 165.

cent) over the period, the completion of the Bass tower malting at Burton-upon-Trent in 1979 and Allied's tower malting five years later, could scarcely have been more ill-timed for the trade.[3] Moreover, although the statistics indicate a shift in the balance of production in favour of sales-maltsters after 1986, this is mainly accounted for by the sale of Grand Metropolitan's (formerly Watney's) four maltings (of approximately 40,000 tonnes capacity) to Simpsons. Even with the transfer of this capacity, sales-maltsters average production in 1991–95 still remained almost 20 per cent below that in 1975–79.

To a large extent, the uncertain and at times volatile domestic trade was offset by more favourable conditions in world markets. Apart from a brief setback in 1984, world beer production rose unchecked from 796 million hectolitres in 1975 to 1249 million twenty years later. Equally important from a malting viewpoint, the pattern of growth varied widely from region to region. As in Britain, beer output in Europe as a whole was sluggish, falling in the decade after 1985 from almost 45 per cent of the world total to a little over one-third. On the other hand, the Far East's share more than doubled, from almost 11 per cent to 22.5 per cent, while that of South America rose from 7 to nearly 12 per cent. Thus, while the demand for malt for brewing (which in 1995 accounted for over 94 per cent of total malt consumption) increased from 8.6 million tonnes to 13.5 million in 1975–95, the fastest growth came in regions unsuitable for barley cultivation and therefore unable to produce sufficient malt to meet their own needs.[4] Japan, for example, by far the largest malt importer by the 1990s, satisfied less than one-third of its total requirements, while overall, some two-thirds of all the countries that brewed beer produced no malt at all. Consequently, in the two decades after 1975, not only did the quantity of malt traded on the world market rise sharply, more than doubling from 1.94 million tonnes to 4.48 million (see Table 9.1), the flow was from regions with excess malting capacity, mainly Europe, North America and Australia, to the great growth markets of Asia, Africa, South and Central America.

It was this steady globalisation of the malt trade, more than any other factor, which sustained the British malting industry during the last quarter of the twentieth century (see Fig. 9.2). A few companies, especially ABM with their interests in Australia and Ireland, and Pauls, who acquired subsidiaries in Belgium, France and Germany, were already well-established overseas.[5] But the severe problems from the late 1970s prompted a sustained

[3] The first tower maltings to be built in the UK. The Bass tower, 60 metres high, houses three steeping vessels above four germinating vessels, with an adjacent single deck kiln, and can produce 84,000 tonnes of malt a year. *The Brewer*, November 1985, p. 427.

[4] The total world demand for malt in 1995 was 14.315 million tonnes. 0.54 million tonnes (3.8 per cent) were used in distilling (four-fifths in Scotland, the rest in Japan and the USA), the remaining 0.26 million tonnes (1.8 per cent) in extract and food manufacture.

[5] In 1967 ABM took a 26 per cent holding in Smith Mitchell & Company of Melbourne; this was increased to 51 per cent two years later. See p. 225 for details of Pauls' subsidiaries.

Table 9.1

*World demand for malt for brewing and proportion traded
internationally, 1975–95 (million tonnes)*

Year	(i) Total demand for brewing malt	(ii) World trade in brewing malt	(iii) Percentage of malt traded internationally
1975	8.58	1.94	22.6
1980	9.99	2.52	25.2
1985	11.18	2.70	24.2
1990	13.19	3.83	29.0
1995	13.50	4.48	33.2

Note: Column (iii) = (ii) as a percentage of (i).

Source: Pollock and Pool, 1993, table 3.3; 1997, appendix 4.3.

effort by all the leading sales-maltsters to secure a growing share of world
trade. The success of the industry in general was borne out by the surge in
UK malt exports in 1979–83, culminating in an all-time record of 446,500
tonnes and the presentation of the Queen's Award for Export Achievement
to ABM in 1981 and to Pauls and to Crisps two years later.[6] By 1984,
however, the effects of recession were widespread, reflected in a fall in world
beer production of some 4 million hectolitres. Although the downturn was
short-lived, it marked the beginning of an intensely competitive era, as
maltsters throughout Europe, Australia and Canada, experiencing similar
conditions in domestic markets as in Britain, struggled to maintain production. As a result, UK malt exports declined by over 43 per cent in two years
reflecting, in particular, the severe economic and political difficulties in
Nigeria, one of Britain's major markets, where an embargo on malt imports
followed from 1988. Much of the lost trade was recouped by rising sales to
Asia, especially Japan, where British malt was valued for its quality and
consistency. During subsequent years, a new potentially more damaging
problem emerged. In the growing situation of world overcapacity, imports
into the UK of cheap, continental malt reached unprecedented levels (see
Fig. 9.2), averaging in excess of 130,000 tonnes a year in 1989–92, against
some 40,000 in the decade after 1975. Inevitably malt margins were
squeezed. Nevertheless, faced with a shrinking home market, sales-maltsters
not only resisted further import penetration,[7] but sustained exports, to the
extent that in 1993 Pauls received their second Queen's Award. The company, which had acquired ABM six years earlier, accounted for more than

---

[6] Introduced in 1976, the award was based upon results over a three-year period. ABM also
received the award in its inaugural year.

[7] Imports of malt into the UK in 1993–95 averaged almost 83,000 tonnes, falling to 53,000
tonnes. MAGB, Annual Statistics.

half of total UK exports, with malt sold to around forty customers, including major brewers such as Heineken, Becks, Grolsch, Carlsberg and Kirin, in over thirty different countries. Whereas twenty years earlier more than two-thirds of all sales went to Africa, nearly half now was sent to Asia, and of these most were made to Japan. Indeed, it was a pattern of development closely mirrored by the other leading sales-maltsters, Bairds, Crisps and Muntons. Against an increasingly competitive background, world trade had assumed a growing importance, accounting on average for over 40 per cent of UK sales-maltsters' output in 1991–95, against a mere 16.6 per cent in 1975–79.

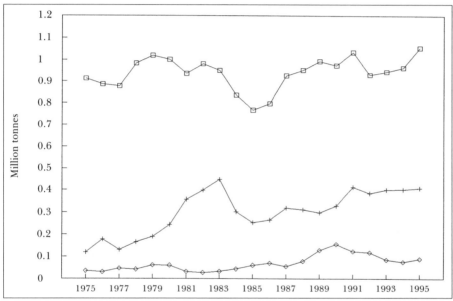

Figure 9.2 Sales-maltsters' total malt production, malt exports and imports, UK, 1975–95 (million tonnes)
Key: □ Sales-maltsters total production   + Malt exports
         ◇ Malt imports
Source: MAGB, Annual Statistics.

How did the British industry fare in relative terms? Throughout the period, seven countries dominated world trade, in 1975–85 controlling between them as much as 84 per cent of total exports (see Table 9.2). Over the next decade, this share fell to 75 per cent, mainly because of growing sales by relative newcomers, notably the United States, Uruguay, Spain, the Netherlands and Argentina.

Table 9.2

Seven leading malt exporting countries, and percentage share of world trade, 1975–95

	1975		1985		1995	
1	France	23.9	France	32.1	France	22.3
2	Belgium	18.1	Belgium	13.7	Belgium	14.3
3	Australia	10.6	UK	9.8	Germany	10.0
4	Czech Rep.	9.6	Australia	8.2	Canada	8.4
5	W. Germany	8.9	Czech Rep.	8.0	UK	8.3
6	Canada	7.8	W. Germany	6.2	Australia	7.6
7	UK	5.5	Canada	6.0	Czech Rep.	4.6
	Total	84.4	Total	84.0	Total	75.5

Source: Pollock and Pool, 1985, table 2.17; 1997, appendix 4.3, p. 2.

As in earlier years, France maintained a commanding position, her market share rising from almost 24 per cent in 1975 to peak at 32 per cent a decade later before falling again to 22 per cent. This success was based upon a number of factors: favourable investment grants and credit facilities; the production of cheaper six-row malts which proved attractive to developing countries with limited hard currency to finance imports; and aggressive marketing. Unlike the other leading exporters, France had no significant home market and therefore focused almost exclusively on world trade. Over the same period, UK market share rose from 5.5 per cent to peak at 13.7 per cent in 1983 and then fluctuated around 8–10 per cent, much on a par with Germany, Australia and Canada. Compared with their major competitors, UK maltsters enjoyed few advantages. Initially handicapped by Britain's late entry into the European Community, they faced the internal customs union and third party tariffs. In addition they were excluded from grants and subsidies. Subsequently, they were unable to offer their customers government-sponsored credit and insurance facilities, while in recent years they have lacked the support of national grain boards, such as the Canadian Wheat Board, with the power to adjust malting barley prices to give their home industry a competitive edge. When considered in the context of the world's leading malt producers, the UK industry, with an output of 1.5 million tonnes, ranked third behind the United States and Germany in 1995. More than two-thirds of this quantity was produced by sales-maltsters, an amount little short of total French output.[8] The only other country to approach this level of production was China, responding to the fastest-growing market of all. In its case, virtual self-sufficiency was achieved

[8] Total UK malt production in 1995 was 1,530,000 tonnes, of which 1,056,000 tonnes (68.9 per cent) was produced by sales-maltsters; French production in 1995 was 1,277,888 tonnes.

through the protection of heavy import tariffs. In contrast, the main assets enjoyed by British maltsters remain an environment which favours the cultivation of some of the best malting barley in the world and, not least, their reputation.

Underpinning the industry's success in world terms has been the determination to maintain costs and quality in an increasingly competitive market. This was achieved in three ways. First, there were significant improvements in the yield and quality of malting barley.[9] An important stimulus was the 1964 legislation granting plant-breeders' rights, resulting in a plethora of disease-resistant, high-yielding varieties challenging the long-established dominance of *Proctor*. Although most were short-lived, from 1980 the German-bred *Triumph* accounted for a steadily growing proportion of UK spring-sown barley.[10] However, despite these advances, Britain's entry to the European Community and the adoption of the Common Agricultural Policy, rewarding *yield* regardless of market demand, left the malting industry with two problems: a decline in the national barley acreage in favour of wheat; and a shift away from spring-sown malting barleys to higher-yielding winter varieties which, with the exception of *Maris Otter*, were not of consistent malting quality.[11] Although initially this caused great concern throughout the industry, the Institute of Brewing (IOB), working in conjunction with the National Institute of Agricultural Botany (NIAB), did much to encourage the breeding of new barley varieties attractive to both farmer and maltster. To the well-established field trials evaluating agronomic performance was added a system of micromalting and brewing trials to test malting potential. Successful varieties were included in the NIAB's 'Recommended List' and awarded the IOB's coveted (and commercially-rewarding) 'asterisk' of malting quality.[12] Consequently, from the mid 1980s, a number of elite winter varieties, combining the high-yield potential of winter barley with other

9 National average yields increased from 3.6 tonnes per hectare in the 1960s to approximately 5 tonnes by the early 1980s; more than one-third of this increase was attributable to new varieties. For details of progress in this field see R. B. Pirie, 'Review of Barley Varieties: Old and New', *The Brewer*, December 1992, pp. 534–36; and P. A. Brookes, 'Barley Breeding and Development Progress in the UK', ibid., December 1986, pp. 471–76.

10 *Triumph*, first listed in 1980, became susceptible to mildew after 1985, but was included on the NIAB Recommended List until 1994. Other significant malting varieties were *Ark Royal* (listed 1976 to 1982), *Wing* (1972–79) and *Kym* (1981–88).

11 Gutsell estimated that by 1995 farmers required a 40 per cent premium to make barley cultivation viable against high-yielding feed-quality wheat, plus a further premium to grow a lower-yielding, high-quality grain to cover the risk of low prices or rejection. M. Gutsell, 'Notes on the Supply of Barley', *The Brewer*, November 1995, p. 453.

12 Varieties are added to the Recommended List after a minimum of three years of field trials and agronomic tests. Their performance must be at least as good as that of the best variety already listed. Each variety is graded on a scale from 1–9 (in Scotland this work is undertaken by the Scottish Agricultural Colleges). The IOB then approves for malting, brewing use and distilling.

essential malting qualities – lack of dormancy and resistance to splitting and pregermination – were introduced. The best of these, *Halcyon, Pipkin, Puffin* and more recently *Fanfare*, proved readily acceptable to British brewers and distillers and, increasingly, to customers overseas. Nevertheless, spring varieties have remained popular in export markets and especially in Scotland, with its wetter climate and harsher winters. Here the dominant *Golden Promise*, which made possible the great expansion of barley cultivation during the 1970s, was superseded first by *Triumph* and then by *Prisma*. By 1995 around 80 per cent of Scottish-grown malting barley was still spring-sown. In England and Wales, despite a number of excellent spring-sown varieties, such as *Doublet, Triumph, Natasha* and more recently *Alexis, Chariot* and *Optic*, the proportion was only a quarter. Taking the UK as a whole, the balance of production has swung very firmly towards winter varieties. In 1995 they accounted for around 58 per cent of the cultivated area against 20 per cent two decades earlier.[13] Yet such has been the success of the barley breeding programmes that far from seeing a deterioration in the quality of British malt, on balance the UK has moved to being a net exporter, rather than importer, of the highest quality malting barleys.[14]

Compared with the previous period, there were few significant changes in technology. However, the progress made with energy conservation following the oil crisis of 1973 was critical in containing costs. After the Second World War maltsters had begun to move away from traditional large anthracite towards progressively cheaper fuels: anthracite grains, light oils and then the heavier gas oils.[15] The sudden explosion in fuel prices from the early 1970s brought major problems, with kiln-fuel becoming the most expensive element of production, accounting for around 40 per cent of total processing costs.[16] Subsequently, many firms switched to natural gas and focused upon more efficient kilning, investing in equipment to recover and reuse waste heat. The savings achieved were substantial. Whereas the simple, natural draught kiln of the nineteenth century used up to 80 therms of heat for each tonne of malt dried, the modern deep-bed pressure kiln, used in conjunction with a heat recovery system, uses as little as 16 therms.[17] The air-to-air heat exchangers and heat pumps installed at Louth by ABM, for

[13] K. Osman, 'The 1989 UK Barley Harvest', *The Brewer*, December 1989, p. 1107; Colin West, 'The 1995 UK Malting Barley Harvest', ibid., November 1995, p. 453.

[14] A notable trend has been the move by sales-maltsters into the grain trade. Several, including Muntons, Simpsons and Bairds, have acquired grain merchants while Moray Firth have a number spread throughout the UK.

[15] These developments were not only cost-effective but provided greater control over the kilning process. J. R. Hudson, 'Recent Developments', p. 31; A. Macey, 'Advances in Malting Techniques', *Brewers' Guardian*, Centenary Issue (1971), p. 93.

[16] K. Marsden, 'Technical Change', p. 232.

[17] O. P. Hudson, 'Malting Technology', *Journal of the Institute of Brewing*, 92 (1986), pp. 119–21.

example, despite their difficulties, cut kilning costs by as much as 45 per cent.[18]

Such dramatic savings were not achieved without problems. One negative consequence of the search for cost-efficient fuels was the nitrosamine 'crisis', a situation potentially as threatening to the industry as the arsenic scare seventy years earlier.[19] During the 1970s, it was recognised that nitrosamines were commonly found in preserved foods such as bacon and cheeses, possibly arising from the use of nitrites as preservatives. A further report in 1979 suggested that beer could also be affected and implicated malt as a likely source. The report provoked an immediate response from the MAGB and MAFF, which initiated a research programme to investigate the problem. Working in conjunction with the Brewing Research Foundation, an outline of the mechanism for nitrosamine formation was established. Levels were found to be higher when malts were kilned with gas rather than anthracite and oil in direct-fired kilns, leading to the conclusion that sulphur in the latter fuels suppressed formation of nitrosamines. Commercial solutions (employing combinations of sulphur dioxide treatment, special burners that produce low oxides of nitrogen and indirect firing during kilning) to control the formation of nitrosamines were quickly advanced. So successfully were these recommendations implemented by the industry that in September 1980, only eighteen months after the initial report, the MAGB was able to introduce a voluntary limit of 5 ppb – a level to which its membership has adhered ever since and which has precluded the need to introduce legislation on the issue.

The other major technological advance, automation, was also triggered by the search for energy savings. Driven by the need to achieve precise time-control and efficient use and reuse of heat, by the late 1970s the leading companies were installing computerised kiln controllers. Automatic steeping soon followed. Progress overall remained piecemeal but rising labour costs, which gradually superseded energy as the greatest element of processing costs, provided a further incentive. By the 1990s most modern plant had been upgraded, while new maltings, such as those built by Muntons, Bairds, Simpsons and Pauls, were fully automated. Batch sizes also increased dramatically, again influenced by the changing balance between energy and labour costs. During the 1970s and early 1980s, batches of 60 tonnes of barley, loaded every eight to twelve hours, were typical. A decade later, more labour-efficient batches of around 340 tonnes, loaded daily, were commonplace.[20] When combined with automation and modern working practices, the

[18] K. Marsden, 'Technical Change', p. 233; Muntons reuse heat for fish farming and for plant propagation by the hydroponics system.

[19] N-nitroso compounds are amongst the most powerful known carcinogens and, whilst there is no direct evidence to show that they are carcinogenic to man, they are known to have potent effects on animals. I am grateful to Dr Ian Cantrell of Pauls Malt for the information in this paragraph.

[20] Pauls' Buckie malting, commissioned in 1980, has the largest batch size in the world: 575 tonnes of barley are loaded once every four days.

savings in labour were substantial and were a major factor in maintaining the industry's competitiveness in world terms. Lastly, the shift to automation, coupled with new stainless steel plant built to food standards, has enabled the industry to achieve the levels of hygiene expected by modern-day consumers.

The third area of progress was that of transport and distribution, especially in the field of exports. In the case of the home market, the main change, the transition from 12 stone (75 Kg) sacks to bulk transport, was already complete by the 1970s. ABM led the way in the early 1950s with a specially designed dual-purpose vehicle, carrying either 50 quarters (approximately 7½ tonnes) of malt in sacks or 60 quarters (9 tonnes) in bulk.[21] Despite some resistance from small breweries, especially in the north, 'bulkers' steadily gained in popularity and by the mid 1960s, 70 per cent of UK sales-maltsters' barley supplies and 50 per cent of malt deliveries were handled in this way.[22] Subsequently, the main changes were in the speed of delivery brought about by an improved road system and in the size of loads; by 1983 gross lorry weights had increased to 38 tonnes – enabling a maximum load of approximately 25 tonnes.

Again it was ABM who pioneered the bulk shipment of malt for export. Initially, consignments for the continent were dispatched in 50 Kg bags by rail to New Holland on the Humber and then lightered to vessels offshore. Similarly, Pauls sent malt by barge to the Port of London.[23] Their first bulk shipment was sent to Becks of Bremen in 1966. For both companies, it was the more distant but increasingly important South African and South American markets which provided the main stimulus. Until the mid 1970s, this involved dispatching malt either through deep-sea ports like Tilbury or Liverpool, or via coasters for transhipment to ocean-going bulk carriers at Rotterdam. Subsequently, the development by ABM of Immingham as a deep-sea loading facility enabled ABM and Pauls jointly to charter ocean-going vessels for long-distance exports. Pauls also undertook major investment projects. First, in 1982, the company acquired a 40 per cent stake in Multimalt Limited, a Nigerian consortium which commissioned malt silos and handling facilities at Tin Can Island, Lagos. The complex was for a time highly successful, certainly in stabilising costs and maintaining quality. Unfortunately, its operation was severely curtailed, initially by restrictions imposed by the new military government and, ultimately, by a ban on malt imports. Pauls' next project was a second deep-sea loading facility at Ipswich. Completed in 1983 and complemented by the opening of the A14 (previously

---

[21] E. F. Taylor, 'History of the Formation and Development of Associated British Maltsters Ltd, 1928–1978', p. 37.

[22] ABM, Chairman's Annual Report, 1966.

[23] The company retained its own fleet of barges until 1972 but subsequently used cheaper, chartered vessels. These were loaded directly from the Albion Malting at Ipswich, as were small vessels destined for the German and Swiss breweries.

A45) trunk road and Orwell crossing, the grain terminal was capable of handling cargoes of 13,000 tonnes at the rate of 700 tonnes an hour. Again providing a facility for other malt exporters, it made possible the export at competitive prices of as much as 70,000 tonnes of malt a year, mostly to South Africa, Venezuela and Brazil.[24]

The final development of the period, the introduction from the early 1980s of containerised shipments, was similarly important for the quality-conscious Japanese market. For several years consignments were pre-packed in bags, partly to minimise damage and partly because bulk shipments required product-specific containers involving high freight charges. The development by Pauls in 1988 of specially-designed loading equipment enabled the use of general purpose containers. Subsequently an increasing proportion of exports was dispatched by this method, either from Felixstowe or Southampton. Overall, the 1990s have seen the steady shift from bulk shipments to containers: in 1993 just over half of Pauls' deliveries were shipped loose in bulk, around 40 per cent in bulk containers, and the remainder in bags – mostly to third world countries with cheap labour. Four years later, the proportions were approximately 30 per cent in bulk to 70 per cent in containers, a shift which again reflects the changing focus of the malt market and the growing importance of the Far East. Not least, these developments underline the continuing importance of the east coast ports to the British malting industry. Whereas in the eighteenth century it was the coastal trade and exports to the Dutch gin distillers, and a hundred years later the influx of cheap foreign grain, at the close of the twentieth century it is the provision of fast and cost-efficient export facilities which has been critical in maintaining a competitive edge for the industry in world markets.

These developments, inevitably, had significant consequences for the malting industry as a whole, both in terms of plant rationalisation and in rising levels of concentration. Not surprisingly, given the cyclical nature of the industry, it was a pattern which closely paralleled the booms and slumps of the period. The sharp recession after 1979, coming at a time when most firms had commissioned new plant in Scotland, prompted the closure of most of the remaining floor maltings in the country.[25] Pauls' Stoke maltings, for so many years the centrepiece of the enterprise, were closed in 1980. Part of their German subsidiary, Malzfabrik Schragmalz, was also closed in 1984 and the

---

[24] The Ipswich grain terminal was built jointly by Pauls (who held 75 per cent of the equity) and Ross T. Smythe, the UK subsidiary of the International Corn Company NV. Besides malt, the terminal handles 500,000 tonnes of cereal exports and 200,000 tonnes of imports a year.

[25] A few maltsters continue to operate floor maltings, mainly for small batches of malt for specialist beers. Those in use in the late 1990s are Ditchingham (J. P. Simpson & Company), Dereham and Ryburgh (Crisp Malting), Beeston (Moray Firth), Warminster (Warminster Maltings), Newton Abbot (Edwin Tucker & Sons), Castleford (Thomas Fawcett & Sons), and those owned by the brewers, Wolverhampton & Dudley, at Lichfield and Langley Green. A number of Scottish distillers also work small floor maltings.

remainder sold. During the same period, ABM closed Bath and Sawbridge-worth and sold their Pontefract and Abingdon drum maltings to Watneys enabling Watneys to shut their own floors. Crisps closed Halesworth, Beccles and all but one of their Dereham maltings. Bairds shut their last floor malting at Cirencester. Similarly, the two major brewer-maltsters, Bass and Allied, abandoned floor malting, including Worthington's mechanical floor malting installed as recently as 1955, when their Tower maltings were commissioned. Despite the sharp recession, only one company succumbed during this period – Cardiff Malting Company, – which ceased malting in 1981. Subsequent years, however, were to see significant changes in ownership.

The first of these was the acquisition by the brewers Scottish & Newcastle (S & N) of Moray Firth Maltings in January 1985, less than six months after Moray had become a public company. With S & N holding 29.3 per cent of the equity, the offer was readily accepted. Moray Firth retained its identity as a sales-maltster, but the arrangement enabled S & N to become partially self-sufficient in the supply of malt. Scarcely a month later, a far less welcome approach was made to Pauls by an overseas trading and plantations group, Harrisons & Crosfield (H & C). An initial bid of £100 million was firmly rejected but, with three-quarters of the equity in the hands of financial institutions, it was inevitable that the final offer of £113 million (370p. a share), made on 5 March, would be accepted.[26] Certainly, Pauls represented an attractive acquisition for H & C which had been under pressure in the Far East from policies rigorously pursued by the governments of various countries to increase the national ownership of indigenous industries. Despite a complex restructuring of the plantation companies, 1984 had seen the disposal of interests in no less than ten Malaysian companies, prompting the search for an alternative agricultural division based in the UK.[27] A second factor was Pauls' strong management 'a young and vigorous team of workers' to quote H & C's official history, which were to become 'nearly as valuable an asset ... as the Pauls business'.[28] In this respect the merger could more aptly be described as a reverse takeover, for many of Pauls' more progressive policies, especially in human resources, were adopted throughout the group. Moreover, with George Paul appointed to the H & C board (a rare accolade in their acquisitions) and, subsequently, chief executive, the company conti-nued to operate as a separate division, enjoying a large measure of autonomy.[29]

[26] *Financial Times*, 5 February, 13 February, 6 March 1985.

[27] Ibid., 5 February 1985.

[28] Peter Pugh (ed. Guy Nickalls), *Great Enterprise: A History of Harrisons & Crosfield* (1990), p. 244.

[29] After stepping down as chief executive in 1994, George Paul served as chairman until September 1997. He was succeeded as chief executive by Bill Turcan. A member of the Hutchison family, Turcan was appointed managing director of Robert Hutchison & Company in 1973, as finance director of Pauls plc in 1986 and as finance director of H & C two years later.

The financial strength of the larger group was a major factor facilitating the most important acquisition in the history of the British malting industry: Paul's purchase for £31 million of ABM from Dalgety on 1 July 1987. Dalgety's objective was to concentrate future growth on food processing and distribution. The problems facing the malting industry – the fall in whisky output and slow growth of beer consumption – leading to plant closure and head-office redundancies, also clearly played their part.[30] The final trigger was the tragic death of ABM's managing director, Tim Macpherson, who, together with his wife and daughter, were blown up by terrorists at Colombo airport, Sri Lanka, on 3 May 1986. A past chairman of the MAGB, chairman of its overseas affairs committee, and known throughout the international brewing and distilling communities, Macpherson was one of malting's most respected personalities.[31] His loss to ABM, at such a difficult time, provided the necessary signal for change of ownership. For Pauls, already the second UK sales-maltster, it created the largest European malting company and placed the new group, with an annual capacity of some 400,000 tonnes, firmly at the forefront of world malting.

The 1990s have, in many respects, witnessed a similar pattern: the closure of older maltings, the commissioning of new, food-standard plant and changes in ownership. The downturn at the outset, like that a decade earlier, came at a time when several companies had invested in new plant. Crisps increased capacity at Ditchingham and then in 1990 – their centenary year – opened a new 30,000 tonne plant at Great Ryburgh; in 1989 Simpsons completed the first phase of a 34,000 tonne installation at Tivetshall; Pauls extended and modernised Knapton and Wallingford; and in October 1991 Bairds opened a 22,000 tonne malting at Witham. In part the new plant replaced less efficient, less hygienic maltings; but, as the recession bit, there was further rationalisation, Simpsons closing their Haddington maltings in 1992, Pauls, Grimsby and Kirkcaldy and, two years later, Ware. Despite the difficulties, these have been years of growth for all the leading British malting companies. In 1994 Muntons completed the second phase of their new development at Bridlington and three years later acquired Robert Kilgour & Company from Allied Distillers. Crisps similarly completed the second phase of their Great Ryburgh development in 1996. Bairds extended their plant at Pencaitland and at Witham, bringing total capacity to approximately 180,000 tonnes. Simpsons extended capacity at Tivetshall and Berwick; while Pauls' Bury St Edmunds malting, with an annual capacity of 100,000 tonnes making the site the largest in Europe, became operational in February 1998. The previous year Pauls also purchased Glenesk Maltings, near Montrose, from United Distillers, the acquisition including an agreement to supply

---

[30] *South Notts Gazette and Newark Herald*, 21 August 1987.

[31] To mark his death, the Macpherson Memorial Trust, providing malting scholarships, was established, ABM offering £25,000 on a pound for pound basis. The trust fund has subsequently been managed by the MAGB.

distilling malt and malt to Guinness's Park Royal brewery in London. Similar agreements between Crisps and Wolverhampton & Dudley and Whitbread, and between Simpsons and Watneys (now part of Scottish Courage), not only emphasise the growing importance of 'toll', or commission, malting, but the climate of cooperation between the two sectors which has been a marked feature of the period.

There have also been casualties. In 1993, at the depths of recession, the Burton-upon-Trent firm of Peach Malt, founded in the 1880s, ceased trading. That same autumn, Guinness closed Beaven's Diss maltings, those at Warminster becoming the subject of a management buy-out the following year. The new company, Warminster Maltings Limited (part of Westcrop), continues to operate the traditional floor maltings, but whereas for many years they made malt for the world's largest brewer, they now supply around thirty small customers producing specialist beers.[32] The influence of CAMRA and the growing number of micro-breweries have been instrumental in sustaining another small west country sales-maltster, Edwin Tucker & Sons of Newton Abbot. In 1980, the firm relied upon three national brewers; fifteen years later it supplies over thirty small ones.[33] The Yorkshire firm of Thomas Fawcett & Sons, while similarly benefiting from the renewed emphasis upon small-scale brewing, has also specialised in the production of coloured malts, as have French & Jupp's. Lastly, Pure Malt Products of Haddington, originally trading under the name of Montgomerie & Company and manufacturers of *Bermaline*, have specialised in a range of concentrates for the food industry, whilst the lease of the Distillers Company's Kirkliston malting enabled them to further diversify into 'toll' malting.[34] For each of these small family firms, a successful strategy of specialisation in niche markets has enabled them to survive the rigours of the last quarter of the twentieth century.

It is, nevertheless, with the six larger companies, who between them account for over 95 per cent of sales-maltsters' total output, that the future of the British industry rests. Given the growing dependency upon exports, it is in the context of the global, rather than national, sector, that this future lies. Here the driving force has been the continuing concentration of the world brewing industry, to the extent that by the late 1990s some twenty brewers account for over half of world beer output.[35] Not surprisingly, this trend has been reflected in malting by increased company size but more significantly

[32] *Farmers Weekly*, 18 April 1997, p. 60.

[33] In 1991 Tuckers also opened their floor maltings as a working museum, complementing this three years later with an associated commercial venture, a micro-brewery. Although micro-breweries account for only around 1.5 per cent of total UK beer output, the Society of Independent Brewers Association estimates that there are approximately 350 throughout the UK, many of whom rely upon the smaller sales-maltsters for their supplies.

[34] The company produces 16–20,000 tonnes of white malt annually; initially this was for distilling purposes but, since the downturn of the early 1980s, it is mainly for brewing.

[35] D. R. Wilkes, 'The World Malt Market: Recent Developments and Future Outlook' (Pauls Malt, 1997), p. 6.

through a wave of conglomerate mergers which have transformed the structure of the industry.[36] The most important of these – and the one which involves a UK company, Hugh Baird & Sons – has been the formation of the huge ConAgra Malt group. Bairds are, of course, no strangers to international ownership or indeed changes in ownership. Thirteen years of joint-ownership with Canada Malting Company were followed by six months with the sugar and flavourings firm Manbré & Garton, and fourteen years with Tate & Lyle, before in 1989 Bairds once again came under the umbrella of Canada Malting Company. The company was by then the world's largest sales-maltster with interests in the United States, Canada and South America. Nevertheless, six years later it was acquired by the American-owned ConAgra Incorporated, a diversified food conglomerate which had entered malting only five years earlier when it purchased Barrett Burston (International), the malting assets of the Australian conglomerate, Elders. A strategic alliance with a South African food manufacturing, processing and distribution group, Tiger Oats Limited, the following year, saw the malting interests restructured into three internationally-based groups embracing nine countries with a total capacity of 1.6 million tonnes of malt.

Although unmatched in scale, the pattern of ConAgra's ascendency is repeated elsewhere. The American conglomerate Cargill Incorporated (America's third largest food company), like ConAgra, has only a brief history in malting, although it holds second place in world malting league tables with a capacity of 1.55 million tonnes. The company's first plant, at Arras in France, was acquired in 1978. In less than two decades it has acquired or built new capacity in the USA (in 1991 the 550,000 tonne Ladish Malting Company and in 1997 the 140,000 tonne Schreier Malting Company), Belgium, Spain, Germany, Holland, Argentina, Canada and China. An even more recent, if smaller, entrant, the Irish-based agriculture and sugar conglomerate Greencore Group, bought the privately owned Minch Norton maltings in 1991 and has subsequently expanded into Belgium. These mergers also highlight the global spread enjoyed by the world's leading maltsters. Again it is a trend reflected throughout the sector, with a growing number of the 'Top Twenty' (with the notable exception of the UK companies) achieving an international focus; several investing in the high-growth regions of China and South America. Lastly, there is the explosive growth of the Chinese malting industry, itself something of an enigma. Two Chinese companies, Guangdong Enterprises (formed in 1988) and COFCO, built at Dalian (1996), are already well placed in the world league.[37]

---

[36] I am grateful to John F. Alsip, president and chief executive of Rahr Malting Company, Minnesota, for access to his comprehensive research relating to the international malting industry.

[37] Guandong Enterprises was established with government money invested through Hong Kong as foreign capital. COFCO is the Chinese government grain importing agency. Two huge plants have been erected as part of a government plan to develop a local malting industry.

These developments reflect the fundamental change within the global sectors of the malting industry in the 1990s. Other aspects have altered little, not least the cyclical nature of the industry and its vulnerability to short-term fluctuations in demand. Indeed, given the growing dependence upon developing markets with their volatile economies, this is a problem which is likely to increase. To quote one commentator: 'when the Brazilian domestic brewing industry sneezes, the world malt industry catches a cold'.[38] The sluggish demand for beer in 1997, even in the high-growth regions of South-East Asia, Mexico, South America and Eastern Europe, at a time when world malt capacity is rising, has again left the industry in a situation of excess supply. Moreover, with the leading brewers struggling to maintain market share, malt margins have inevitably suffered, resulting in further pressure on the less competitive smaller firms. Other factors, particularly the interplay between political intervention and agricultural policy, play their part. In Europe, maltsters rely on the malt restitution, a payment which compensates for the artificially high barley prices maintained under the Common Agricultural Policy. Elsewhere monopolistic grain boards protect domestic markets. The world barley market is therefore far from a level playing field. The problems of individual firms are further exacerbated by fluctuations in financial markets. During 1997 and 1998, for example, UK maltsters suffered the consequences of a high pound which has made their product uncompetitive in world markets, resulting in the closure by Pauls of their Louth and Gainsborough Maltings in March 1998. Any shift in the balance between these variables clearly influences the ascendency or otherwise of the major players. Given this climate, there is little doubt that the industry will see further rationalisation. Quite what the direction will be is uncertain, for many of the 'Top Twenty' maltsters enjoy the relative security of private ownership: Cargill; the American-based Rahr Malting Company; the French companies, Groupe Lesaffre and Groupe Soufflet; and the German maltster, Weissheimer Malz, among the largest. In April 1998, as part of the restructuring of Harrisons & Crosfield into a chemical group (renamed Elementis), Pauls Malt was sold to Greencore, making the combined tonnage of the new group nearly 700,000 tonnes and placing them fourth in the world league.

How will the British industry fare in future? Lacking the global investment of many of their competitors, vulnerable to fluctuations in raw material prices and handicapped by a strong pound, the challenges facing the industry on the eve of the twenty-first century are as far-reaching as any it has experienced during the last 150 years. Nevertheless, given its resilience in the face of past crises – the Great Depression of the late nineteenth century, the 1930s and two World Wars – it will doubtless weather the storm.

---

[38] Wilkes, 'The World Malt Market', p. 5.

Appendixes

Appendix 1

Raw materials used in brewing, and total malt consumed in brewing and distilling, United Kingdom, 1831–1914

Year	(i) Malt	(ii) Malt adjuncts	(iii) Malt + adjuncts [1]	(iv) Sugar	(v) Malt for distilling	(vi) Total malt used [2]
	Thousand quarters	Thousand quarters	Thousand quarters	Thousand cwts	Thousand quarters	Thousand quarters
1831	3585	—	—	—	—	—
1832	3552	—	—	—	—	—
1833	3695	—	—	—	—	—
1834	4017	—	—	—	—	—
1835	4103	—	—	—	—	—
1836	4279	—	—	—	—	—
1837	4031	—	—	—	—	—
1838	4040	—	—	—	—	—
1839	4082	—	—	—	—	—
1840	3985	—	—	—	—	—
1841	3676	—	—	—	—	—
1842	3588	—	—	—	—	—
1843	3566	—	—	—	—	—
1844	3701	—	—	—	—	—
1845	3749	—	—	—	—	—
1846	4076	—	—	—	—	—
1847	3664	—	—	72	—	—
1848	3700	—	—	25	—	—
1849	3719	—	—	16	—	—
1850	3787	—	—	10	—	—
1851	4044	—	—	7	—	—
1852	4129	—	—	7	—	—
1853	4478	—	—	13	—	—
1854	4050	—	—	30	—	—

[1] Malt plus Malt adjuncts
[2] Malt plus Malt used in distilling

Year	(i) Malt	(ii) Malt adjuncts	(iii) Malt + adjuncts [1]	(iv) Sugar	(v) Malt for distilling	(vi) Total malt used [2]
	Thousand quarters	Thousand quarters	Thousand quarters	Thousand cwts	Thousand quarters	Thousand quarters
1855	3844	—	—	16	—	—
1856	4243	—	—	20	—	—
1857	4557	—	—	20	585	5142
1858	4549	—	—	34	683	5232
1859	4866	—	—	35	591	5457
1860	5077	—	—	92	613	5690
1861	4743	—	—	79	499	5242
1862	4046	—	—	84	448	5394
1863	5078	—	—	80	491	5569
1864	5479	—	—	38	600	6079
1865	5912	—	—	55	564	6476
1866	6380	—	—	145	629	7009
1867	5960	—	—	382	514	6474
1868	6028	—	—	352	510	6538
1869	6077	—	—	343	551	6628
1870	6209	—	—	271	602	6811
1871	6453	—	—	271	673	7126
1872	6928	—	—	336	646	7574
1873	7156	—	—	599	819	7975
1874	7258	—	—	828	801	8059
1875	7279	—	—	884	777	8056
1876	7603	—	—	860	864	8467
1877	7566	—	—	871	879	8445
1878	7424	—	—	1128	931	8355
1879	6885	—	—	1067	887	7772
1880	6981	—	—	1334	815	7796
1881	—	—	6488	1125	974	—
1882	—	—	6637	1142	859	—
1883	—	—	6416	1126	900	—
1884	—	—	6602	1152	917	—
1885	—	—	6486	1275	929	—
1886	—	—	6360	1310	819	—
1887	—	—	6540	1466	856	—
1888	—	—	6487	1524	838	—
1889	—	—	6793	1811	910	—
1890	—	—	6920	1976	946	—
1891	—	—	6962	2026	994	—

Year	(i)	(ii)	(iii)	(iv)	(v)	(vi)
	Malt	*Malt adjuncts*	*Malt + adjuncts* [1]	*Sugar*	*Malt for distilling*	*Total malt used* [2]
	Thousand quarters	*Thousand quarters*	*Thousand quarters*	*Thousand cwts*	*Thousand quarters*	*Thousand quarters*
1892	—	—	6982	2097	980	—
1893	—	—	6957	2123	1021	—
1894	—	—	6847	2194	1050	—
1895	6714	209	6924	2274	1095	7809
1896	—	—	7263	2441	1220	—
1897	7080	351	7431	2570	1394	8474
1898	7208	422	7630	2774	1566	8774
1899	7343	503	7846	2944	1411	8754
1900	7169	549	7718	2980	1197	8366
1901	7099	601	7700	2859	1196	8295
1902	6974	623	7597	2825	1178	8152
1903	6865	614	7479	2875	1164	8029
1904	6665	619	7284	2887	1211	7876
1905	6497	606	7103	2747	1158	7655
1906	6546	563	7109	2842	1151	7697
1907	6523	562	7085	2859	1144	7667
1908	6384	571	6955	2883	1020	7404
1909	6211	560	6771	2891	1121	7332
1910	6259	575	6834	2910	854	7113
1911	6470	594	7064	3011	871	7341
1912	6456	629	7085	3068	930	7386
1913	6549	712	7261	3280	1054	7603
1914	6566	697	7263	3280	1116	7682

Notes:
[1] Malt plus Malt adjuncts
[2] Malt plus Malt used in distilling

Source: See Appendix 2.

Appendix 2
Raw materials used in brewing, and total malt consumed in brewing and distilling, United Kingdom, 1915–95

Year	(i) Malt	(ii) Malt adjuncts	(iii) unmalted corn	(iv) Sugar	(v) Malt for distilling	(vi) Total malt used [1]
	Thousand quarters	Thousand cwts	Thousand cwts	Thousand cwts	Thousand quarters	Thousand quarters
1915	5554	1236	30	2679	968	6522
1916	5211	1344	29	2400	1104	6315
1917	3583	801	17	1614	997	4580
1918	2783	—	—	890	585	3368
1919	3724	351	48	1532	759	4483
1920	5253	1023	36	2136	1298	6551
1921	4917	980	26	1874	1133	6050
1922	4140	810	24	1622	1070	5210
1923	3581	804	26	1599	1081	4662
1924	3758	846	23	1700	1035	4793
1925	3818	908	24	1864	1015	4833
1926	3649	827	23	1833	661	4310
1927	3561	823	22	1817	497	4058
1928	3509	825	22	1838	617	4126
1929	3457	797	24	1817	653	4110
1930	3360	763	26	1835	581	3941
1931	3040	689	23	1698	364	3404
1932	2372	533	13	1377	182	2554
1933	2413	521	12	1380	96	2509
1934	2665	548	12	1543	381	3046
1935	2815	589	11	1632	378	3193
1936	2882	593	11	1705	456	3338
1937	3022	649	11	1836	653	3675
1938	3126	688	14	1895	761	3887
1939	3295	735	10	1986	728	4023
1940	3286	364	8	1533	413	3699
1941	3663	247	12	1398	246	3909
1942	3639	382	53	1411	93	3732
1943	3429	1238	41	1401	68	3497
1944	3540	1241	143	1459	—	3540

[1] Malt plus Malt for distilling

Year	(i)	(ii)	(iii)	(iv)	(v)	(vi)
	Malt	*Malt adjuncts*	*unmalted corn*	*Sugar*	*Malt for distilling*	*Total malt used* [1]
	Thousand quarters	*Thousand cwts*	*Thousand cwts*	*Thousand cwts*	*Thousand quarters*	*Thousand quarters*
1945	3479	1332	246	1784	284	3763
1946	3326	1133	138	1790	403	3729
1947	3151	614	93	1601	248	3399
1948	3167	607	70	1444	577	3744
1949	3029	505	61	1303	775	3804
1950	3031	455	56	1286	826	3857
1951	3094	453	58	1355	790	3884
1952	3104	467	52	1386	847	3951
1953	3029	426	58	1405	762	3791
1954	2876	462	52	1485	882	3758
1955	2879	478	47	1529	993	3872
1956	2877	487	40	1544	1032	3909
1957	2958	532	14	1565	1172	4130
1958	2881	543	11	1528	1300	4181
1959	2962	590	8	1651	1374	4693
1960	3136	573	9	1651	1557	4693
1961	3299	585	8	1746	1631	4930
1962	3322	609	11	1758	1706	5028
1963	3340	644	14	1751	1843	5183
1964	3531	712	26	1835	2174	5705
1965	3540	735	61	1814	2541	6081
1966	3563	769	133	1853	2870	6433
1967	3606	776	147	1910	3024	6630
1968	3555	748	121	1898	2742	6297
1969	3788	775	175	2133	3096	6884
1970	3823	771	234	2279	3260	7083
1971	3972	751	275	2505	3418	7390
1972	4032	452	635	2641	3680	7712
1973	4103	409	619	2602	4139	8242
1974	4438	517	624	2848	4540	8978
1975	4502	643	750	2739	3713	8215
1976	4630	680	890	2613	3411	8041
1977	4763	770	912	2749	3667	8430
1978	4813	803	810	2802	3516	8329
1979	4825	797	784	2632	4271	9096
1980	4976	875	656	2674	3588	8564

[1] Malt plus Malt for distilling

Year	(i)	(ii)	(iii)	(iv)	(v)	(vi)
	Malt	Malt adjuncts	unmalted corn	Sugar	Malt for distilling	Total malt used [1]
	Thousand quarters	Thousand cwts	Thousand cwts	Thousand cwts	Thousand quarters	Thousand quarters
1981	4614	854	663	2432	2303	6917
1982	4446	1098	435	2373	2001	6447
1983	4414	1035	437	2262	1942	6356
1984	4420	1045	447	2524	2125	6545
1985	4374	994	437	2504	2158	6532
1986	4295	1020	516	2485	2152	6447
1987	4341	1037	606	2518	2355	6696
1988	4413	1134	581	2603	2762	7175
1989	4465	1026	567	2688	3391	7856
1990	4606	996	530	2780	3752	8358
1991	4323	1020	411	2576	3628	7951
1992	4238	998	488	2235	3208	7446
1993	4116	1134	303	1948	2749	6865
1994	3870	1171	291	1752	2808	6678
1995	3924	1053	246	1878	3070	6994

Note: Year end 30 September to 1970, 31 March thereafter.

Between 1881 and 1896 no separate figures are given for malt and malt adjuncts.

To 1914 malt adjuncts (rice, rice grits, flaked rice, flaked maize) include unmalted corn (1 quarter of adjuncts = 256lbs; 1cwt = 3.5 bushels).

From 1914 adjuncts and unmalted corn are listed separately.

[1] Malt plus Malt for distilling

Source: Brewers' Almanack; UK Statistical Handbooks, Brewers' Society.

Appendix 3
Average prices of malt, per quarter, 1830–1914

Year	Truman Hanbury & Buxton		Parliamentary Papers		Year	Truman Hanbury & Buxton		Parliamentary Papers	
	s.	d.	s.	d.		s.	d.	s.	d.
1830	60	9	58	6	1873	59	6	71	5¾
1831	64	6	69	0	1874	60	7	75	8¾
1832	68	10	58	5	1875	65	5	70	3½
1833	59	9	57	10	1876	60	1	57	6
1834	60	2	—		1877	55	11	63	1
1835	58	2	—		1878	62	1	62	6
1836	57	10	—		1879	60	7	61	4
1837	60	9	—		1880	57	8	51	0
1838	58	1	59	6	1881	45	2		
1839	58	10	66	6	1882	36	3		
1840	42	6	69	6	1883	37	0		
1841	65	0	—		1884	39	2		
1842	58	0	—		1885	37	1		
1843	53	4	—		1886	36	0		
1844	56	9	—		1887	31	1		
1845	63	3	—		1888	33	0		
1846	58	3	64	4	1889	32	1		
1847	65	10	70	0	1890	34	0		
1848	62	5	60	6	1891	32	6		
1849	58	0	59	9	1892	33	6		
1850	57	8	53	9	1893	32	6		
1851	49	9	55	1	1894	31	9		
1852	53	9	55	0	1895	29	0		
1853	56	5	63	10	1896	27	6		
1854	67	0	68	0	1897	29	1		
1855	71	6	72	6	1898	30	6		
1856	69	10	73	6	1899	30	7		
1857	68	0	72	0	1900	29	7		
1858	66	10	63	10¼	1901	38	11		
1859	64	2	61	9¼	1902	30	0		
1860	62	2	63	0	1903	30	0		
1861	63	0	62	6	1904	30	0		
1862	64	0	62	9¾	1905	30	3		

Year	Truman Hanbury & Buxton		Parliamentary Papers		Year	Truman Hanbury & Buxton		Parliamentary Papers	
	s.	d.	s.	d.		s.	d.	s.	d.
1863	59	1	62	1¾	1906	31	3		
1864	61	2	58	9¾	1907	30	9		
1865	—		58	2	1908	31	10		
1866	55	0	66	4¾	1909	36	4		
1867	65	11	69	0½	1910	36	6		
1868	62	2	71	7	1911	35	0		
1869	66	10	69	7	1912	37	7		
1870	61	6	62	8	1913	39	6		
1871	59	2	64	1½	1914	38	10		
1872	58	10	67	1½					

Source: PP (1899), appendix iv, p. 383; Truman Hanbury & Buxton, Acc 73.36; Rest Books, 1831–66; Annual totals, 1867–89; Abstract Rest Book, 1889–1905, Acc 79.94, B/THB, GLRO.

Appendix 4
Malt exported from the United Kingdom, 1860–1995

Year	Thousand quarters	Year	Thousand quarters	Year	Thousand quarters
1860	36.4	1895	81.7	1930	118.8
1861	45.3	1896	98.3	1931	113.1
1862	53.1	1897	114.8	1932	100.6
1863	62.8	1898	133.9	1933	74.9
1864	57.1	1899	128.5	1934	70.1
1865	61.7	1900	129.0	1935	103.0
1866	70.8	1901	160.0	1936	86.1
1867	45.1	1902	162.6	1937	56.3
1868	54.1	1903	87.6	1938	26.0
1869	68.3	1904	97.0	1939	62.2
1870	73.1	1905	94.6	1940	19.6
1871	70.7	1906	91.3	1941	7.6
1872	58.0	1907	92.0	1942	2.1
1873	67.8	1908	87.7	1943	10.5
1874	63.3	1909	67.1	1944	11.4
1875	63.4	1910	83.5	1945	20.7
1876	65.0	1911	97.8	1946	50.8
1877	75.2	1912	96.3	1947	25.6
1878	62.9	1913	81.6	1948	93.6
1879	78.6	1914	90.9	1949	111.6
1880	52.6	1915	403.0	1950	130.8
1881	62.9	1916	176.6	1951	116.0
1882	64.8	1917	51.9	1952	141.4
1883	61.1	1918	2.3	1953	148.5
1884	85.1	1919	17.1	1954	163.2
1885	78.7	1920	35.7	1955	174.5
1886	93.8	1921	63.2	1956	190.0
1887	78.9	1922	28.3	1957	217.7
1888	90.6	1923	47.9	1958	226.1
1889	93.7	1924	97.9	1959	230.8
1890	80.5	1925	114.5	1960	264.0
1891	78.6	1926	106.7	1961	259.4
1892	75.5	1927	70.3	1962	282.9
1893	74.0	1928	80.5	1963	265.8
1894	80.8	1929	75.6	1964	313.3

The British Malting Industry

Year	Thousand quarters	Year	Thousand quarters	Year	Thousand quarters
1965	259.9	1976	1154.6	1987	2092.6
1966	268.4	1977	852.8	1988	2046.7
1967	321.7	1978	1075.8	1989	1954.9
1968	502.5	1979	1239.8	1990	2151.7
1969	453.5	1980	1600.6	1991	2702.7
1970	336.8	1981	2341.9	1992	2519.0
1971	617.6	1982	2610.9	1993	2624.0
1972	554.7	1983	2932.3	1994	2630.6
1973	818.7	1984	1981.1	1995	2669.9
1974	866.5	1985	1659.7		
1975	720.1	1986	1738.4		

Note: Includes malt flour from 1963.

Source: Annual Statement of the Overseas Trade of the United Kingdom; MAGB annual statistics.

Appendix 5
Chronology of malting company registration

Date	Company	Location	Registered capital (£)
1873	North Lincolnshire Farmers Malting and Manure	Lincoln	125,000
1873	Birmingham Malting Company	Birmingham	50,000
1878	Wolverhampton Malting	Wolverhampton	10,000
1884	S. Stanbridge & Company	Camberwell	40,000
1886	Mirfield Malting Company	Mirfield	10,000
1886	Cardiff Malting Company	Cardiff	60,000
1890	Bristol Channel Malting & Milling Company	—	20,000
1890	F. & G. Smith	Great Ryburgh and Wells-Next-The Sea	200,000
1891	L. & G. Meakin	Burton-upon-Trent	55,000
1891	Giradot & Company	Bury St Edmunds	50,000
1892	Sheppard's Corn Malting	—	45,000
1892	Thomas Sugden & Son	Brighouse, Yorkshire	23,000
1893	T. H. White & Company	Belfast and London	140,000
1893	J. Pidcock & Company	Nottingham	100,000
1893	R. & W. Paul	Ipswich	250,000
1893	Free Rodwell & Company	Mistley	130,000
1894	William Cooper & Company	Southampton	125,000
1894	Smith & Company	Newport	12,000
1894	Charles Sharpe & Company	Sleaford	100,000
1894	Hugh Baird & Sons	Glasgow	160,000
1894	Robert Hutchison & Company	Kirkcaldy	—
1895	Marriott Hall	Sheffield	20,000
1895	Thomas Bernard & Company	Leith and Haddington	150,000
1896	Pitts, Son & King	Plymouth	201,000
1896	White, Tomkins & Courage	London	360,000
1897	Liverpool Malting Company	Liverpool	20,000
1897	J. F. & J. Crowther	Mirfield	50,000
1897	J. & C. H. Evans & Company	Birmingham	100,000
1897	Michael Sanderson & Son	Wakefield	150,000
1897	F. W. Jarvis & Company	Newmarket	30,000
1898	Sleeman, Hadwen & Company	Portishead and Bristol	30,000
1898	S. Swonnell & Son	Nine Elms	50,000
1898	Parker Brothers	Mildenhall	20,000
1898	R. & G. Boby & Chapman	Bury St Edmunds and Leeds	45,000

Date	Company	Location	Registered capital (£)
1898	E. Bailey & Son	Frome	35,000
1899	Edwin Tucker & Sons	Ashburton, Devon	50,000
1899	Clowes, Walker	Needham Market	15,000
1899	James Fison & Sons	Thetford	60,000
1899	Worcester Free Licence-Holders Malting Company	Worcester	2000
1899	H. B. Walmsley & Sons	Bromley and Hammersmith	120,000
1899	Llangollen Malting	Llangollen	2000
1900	H. P. Dowson & Company	Reading	20,000
1900	W. J. Robson & Company	Leeds	120,000
1900	Yeomans, Cherry & Curtis	Burton-upon-Trent	70,000
1901	W. B. Thorpe	Nottingham	50,000
1901	T. W. Wilson & Sons	Hadleigh	32,000
1901	A. & R. Man	Wakefield	40,000
1901	William K. Pitts	Plymouth	10,000
1902	R. & S. Swires	Cleckheaton, Leeds	25,000
1902	Pneumatic Malting & Malted Foods Company	Bristol	5000
1902	Wimborne Malting Company	Wimborne Minster	16,000
1902	H. A. & D. Taylor	Sawbridgeworth	96,000
1902	A. McMullen & Company	Hertford	14,000
1902	James T. Connell & Company	Edinburgh	15,000
1903	Trent Malting Company	—	2000
1903	North Tipperary Maltings	Dublin	20,000
1903	Churton & Company	Liverpool	20,000
1903	Figgis, Son & Company	Dublin	80,000
1903	G. I. Long & Company	Nottingham	25,000
1903	Woolston & Bull	Wellingborough	50,000
1903	George Wheeldon	Bedford and Grantham	60,000
1903	William Jones & Son, Maltsters	Shrewsbury	100,000
1906	Shaws Hull Malt Company	Hull	40,000
1906	M. Minch & Son	County Kildare	55,000
1906	Smith & Eastaugh	Beccles and Lowestoft	25,000
1906	James Tyrell & Company	Dublin	14,000
1907	Austin Brothers	Castleford	55,000
1907	W. D. & A. E. Walker	Bungay	50,000
1907	Lee & Grinling	Grantham	30,000
1908	Charles Smith	Derby	1000
1908	Edward Fison	Ipswich	30,000
1909	Henry Page & Company	Ware	125,000
1909	John Crisp & Son	Beccles	40,000
1909	Ipswich Malting Company	Ipswich	100,000

Date	Company	Location	Registered capital (£)
1909	Thomas Prentice & Company	Stowmarket	20,000
1909	Randells (Maltsters)	Barking and Grays	50,000
1910	Birr Maltings	Dublin	5000
1911	Nathan Pratt & Son	Nottingham	21,000
1912	Mechanical Malting Company	Eastington, Glos.	10,000
1912	Williams Brothers Maltings	Salisbury	45,000
1913	R. Peach & Company	Burton-upon-Trent	20,000
1914	W. L. Browne & Company	Shrewsbury	45,000
1915	Sandars & Company	Gainsborough	150,000
1918	Alfred Gough	Saffron Walden	6000
1919	J. P. Simpson & Company	Alnwick	70,000
1919	Thomas Fawcett & Sons	Garforth, Leeds	55,000
1919	Richards & Company (Malt Roasters)	Burton-upon-Trent	50,000
1920	Burton Malting Company	Burton-upon-Trent	10,000
1920	French & Jupp's	Stanstead Abbotts	75,000
1920	J. R. Page & Son	Baldock	—
1920	Munton & Baker	Bedford	30,000
1920	J. W. Holmes	East Retford	30,000
1920	A. C. Hinde	Derby	40,000
1920	Plunkett Brothers	Dublin	30,000
1921	Horlick's Maltings	—	8000
1921	Wilson & Hood	Shropshire	5000
1921	David & Allester	Worcester	20,000
1921	Gilstrap Earp & Company	Newark	325,000
1921	S. E. Ridley	Bridgnorth	15,000
1922	Worcestershire Malting	Worcester	2000
1922	W. & S. Burkitt	Chesterfield	13,000
1923	W. F. Leech & Company	Liverpool	1000
1923	Shardlow Malt Extract Company	Burton-upon-Trent	10,000
1923	James Cronshay & Sons	Thetford	2500
1923	Belfast Malting Company	Belfast	2000
1924	Richard Worswick & Son	Elland, Yorkshire	15,000
1924	Frank Colley	Tadcaster	25,000
1925	James D. Taylor & Sons	Bath	40,000
1925	Smiths (Maltsters)	Sheffield	10,000
1925	Melford Malt Company	Long Melford	15,000
1925	C. E. Seed	Clayton, Bradford	25,000
1925	James Milnthorp & Sons	Goole	30,000
1926	J. A. & A. Thompson	Oldbury, West Bromwich	25,000
1926	British Malt Products	Dunbar and Accrington	46,000
1926	W. H. Cox & Sons	—	5000
1927	Edward Sutcliffe	Mirfield	250,000
1927	Brooks (Mistley)	Mistley	150,000

Date	Company	Location	Registered capital (£)
1928	Samuel Thompson & Sons	Smethwick	100,000
1928	John H. Bennett	Dublin	15,000
1929	Richard Dobson & Sons	Dewsbury, Leeds	30,000
1932	North of England Malt Roasting Company	Masham, Yorkshire	6000
1935	Henry Ward & Sons	Ware	55,000
1938	Russell Hall Maltings	Birmingham	5000

Source: Brewers' Journal, Brewing Trade Review, Brewers' Guardian, Stock Exchange Year-book and company prospectuses.

Appendix 6
R. & W. Paul Limited, malt delivered from Ipswich, 1895–1975
(thousand quarters)

Year	Malt delivered	Year	Malt delivered Home trade	Exports	Total
1895	55.8	1936	105.0	—	105.0
1896	60.4	1937	118.1	—	118.1
1897	68.9	1938	127.9	—	127.9
1898	78.7	1939	127.9	—	127.9
1899	75.4	1940	132.5	—	132.5
1900	64.6	1941	157.4	—	157.4
1901	72.2	1942	154.2	—	154.2
1902	64.6	1943	150.9	—	150.9
1903	85.3	1944	157.4	—	157.4
1904	91.8	1945	144.3	—	144.3
1905	82.0	1946	141.0	—	141.0
1906	93.2	1947	134.5	2.6	137.1
1907	91.8	1948	124.6	19.7	144.3
1908	92.5	1949	101.7	26.2	127.9
1909	91.8	1950	97.1	14.4	111.5
1910	99.1	1951	99.7	11.8	111.5
1911	118.1	1952	97.1	14.4	111.5
1912	121.4	1953	78.7	32.8	111.5
1913	144.3	1954	75.4	34.8	110.2
1914	145.0	1955	75.4	23.0	98.4
1915	150.8	1956	72.2	45.9	118.1
1916	149.6	1957	75.4	50.5	125.9
1917	75.4	1958	72.2	45.9	118.1
1918	62.3	1959	91.8	38.0	129.8
1919	98.4	1960	118.1	52.5	170.6
1920	131.9	1961	150.9	59.0	209.9
1921	131.2	1962	157.4	59.0	216.4
1922	118.1	1963	170.6	47.9	218.5
1923	101.7	1964	144.3	78.7	223.0
1924	106.3	1965	275.5	65.6	341.1
1925	111.5	1966	249.3	68.9	318.2
1926	108.2	1967	242.7	88.6	331.3
1927	112.2	1968	177.1	118.1	295.2

Year	Malt delivered	Year	Home trade	Malt delivered Exports	Total
1928	118.1	1969	164.0	131.2	295.2
1929	114.8	1970	183.7	111.5	295.2
1930	91.8	1971	170.6	177.1	347.7
1931	95.1	1972	157.4	203.4	360.8
1932	78.7	1973	147.6	265.7	413.3
1933	78.7	1974	144.3	252.6	396.9
1934	88.6	1975	249.3	154.2	403.5
1935	98.4				

Note: Year end 30 June to 1952, 31 March thereafter.

Source: Annual deliveries, Pauls Malt.

Appendix 7
R. & W. Paul Limited, group malt sales, 1951–67

Year	R. & W. Paul	Lee & Grinling [1] (Thousand quarters)	Dobsons [1]	Total
1951	117	50	30	197
1952	117	50	30	197
1953	116	50	30	196
1954	115	45	25	185
1955	104	40	25	169
1956	114	50	25	189
1957	123	45	25	193
1958	117	45	25	187
1959	129	40	25	194
1960	174	45	25	244
1961	210	46	23	279
1962	227	50	26	303
1963	209	39	25	273
1964	280	30	29	339
1965	251	77	29	450[2]
1966	299	125	29	644[2]
1967	355	186	27	666[2]

Note: Year end 31 March
[1] Figures rounded to nearest 1000 quarters, 1951—60.
[2] Includes production at Swonnells and Harrington Page

Source: Pauls Malt.

Appendix 8
R. & W. Paul Limited, profits, 1894–1959

	(i)	(ii)	(iii)	(iv)	(v)	(vi)	(vii)
Year	Capital employed	Trading profit on malt trade (£000s)	Total [1] trading profit	(ii) as per cent of (iii)	Pre-tax [2] profit (£000s)	Return [3] on capital (per cent)	Ordinary share dividends (per cent)
1894	311.0	—	24.7	—	.3	0.1	0
1895	268.2	10.7	30.6	35.0	17.9	6.7	6
1896	324.4	18.4	45.3	40.6	30.9	9.9	10.75
1897	332.0	19.0	39.5	48.1	20.9	7.3	8
1898	412.1	21.4	66.8	32.0	47.7	11.6	15.5
1899	389.8	19.2	67.7	28.4	49.2	12.1	15
1900	452.9	15.2	59.3	25.6	35.7	8.1	10.75
1901	539.4	13.9	31.8	43.7	5.7	1.5	1.25
1902	516.3	12.0	57.0	21.1	29.7	4.9	9.25
1903	478.5	10.6	53.6	19.8	33.1	7.4	10.5
1904	479.1	11.4	49.2	23.2	28.3	6.5	9
1905	552.1	13.8	67.4	20.5	57.5	10.4	16.5
1906	566.3	16.6	52.1	31.9	35.4	8.1	11
1907	647.5	19.8	54.1	36.6	45.4	7.0	13
1908	573.5	14.6	40.5	36.0	22.6	4.8	7.5
1909	692.0	15.1	39.8	37.9	26.0	4.1	8.25
1910	609.6	13.3	35.1	37.9	22.6	4.4	8.25
1911	639.1	13.9	72.2	19.3	56.6	9.2	15.75
1912	725.6	26.6	128.9	20.6	108.8	15.6	29
1913	740.7	23.9	96.5	24.8	77.8	11.2	21
1914	681.1	17.8	46.6	38.2	42.9	5.9	*10.5
1915	960.9	24.7	216.9	11.4	207.0	20.5	44
1916	1044.2	46.4	247.5	18.7	234.8	22.0	22
1917	1053.0	50.6	271.2	18.7	267.4	24.4	30
1918	758.1	27.0	207.4	13.0	211.4	24.6	36
1919	729.4	20.0	75.2	26.6	100.0	10.4	21
1920	1289.0	95.9	286.7	33.4	203.8	14.6	42
1921	1028.4	0.2	10.3	1.9	92.7	8.9	*14
1922	916.1	82.9	151.8	54.6	153.8	13.5	22.5
1923	833.5	43.7	129.2	33.8	138.2	12.3	20.25
1924	928.3	56.6	172.9	32.7	167.3	15.1	24
1925	1027.5	83.7	193.1	43.3	175.9	15.4	25.5
1926	887.5	35.1	105.2	33.4	107.6	9.2	16
1927	932.6	44.3	119.6	37.0	132.2	10.6	19.5
1928	1150.0	45.8	249.2	18.4	252.0	19.3	26

Year	(i) Capital employed	(ii) Trading profit on malt trade (£000s)	(iii) Total [1] trading profit	(iv) (ii) as per cent of (iii)	(v) Pre-tax [2] profit (£000s)	(vi) Return [3] on capital (per cent)	(vii) Ordinary share dividends (per cent)
1929	939.9	28.5	83.3	34.2	103.5	7.4	23
1930	845.9	31.7	52.1	60.8	61.5	3.4	21.5
1931	878.1	29.4	125.9	23.4	149.3	12.4	21.5
1932	1003.2	35.4	259.9	13.6	257.9	21.3	36
1933	929.8	14.9	113.5	13.1	116.7	8.7	17.5
1934	1191.0	38.6	251.1	15.4	228.7	14.6	32
1935	1212.9	41.6	173.5	24.0	186.9	10.8	20
1936	1365.8	39.1	247.0	15.8	265.8	15.0	20
1937	1726.5	63.0	427.3	14.7	329.7	15.7	20
1938	1592.1	33.1	162.5	20.4	160.0	7.5	17
1939	1357.3	39.8	113.7	35.0	139.0	6.3	17
1940	1222.8	61.3	281.4	21.8	341.9	19.3	30
1941	1396.6	53.7	224.8	23.9	254.7	12.9	16
1942	1515.7	41.4	126.5	32.7	165.3	5.7	16
1943	1304.0	173.6	281.9	61.6	334.0	19.3	30
1944	1041.1	193.5	298.0	64.9	345.2	24.8	30
1945	961.3	154.1	242.2	63.6	283.9	29.5	25
1946	886.1	139.1	268.1	51.9	318.5	25.9	28
1947	864.6	73.7	106.7	69.1	146.5	8.3	12.5
1948	1272.5	121.2	157.0	77.2	202.5	10.1	12.5
1949	1496.0	—	180.0	—	206.3	10.6	12.5
1950	2026.1	—	224.9	—	221.8	10.0	12.5
1951	3108.5	—	252.4	—	200.5	9.6	12.5
1952	3270.6	—	250.4	—	221.8	9.7	12.5
1953	3624.5	—	598.3	—	346.9	13.0	15
1954	3509.6	—	394.2	—	304.9	12.3	*7.5
1955	3800.7	—	575.7	—	470.2	16.4	11.25
1956	3155.6	—	358.4	—	257.3	11.9	10
1957	3357.2	—	290.0	—	243.4	11.6	9
1958	3055.9	—	382.2	—	313.9	14.6	11
1959	3782.5	—	499.7	—	415.7	14.8	12.5

Notes: Year end 30 June to 1910, thereafter 31 March; 1910 represents nine months profits.

[1] Trading Profit = Gross profit (sales–manufacturing cost) less rents, rates, etc. Total Trading Profit also included Flake Mills, Shipping and Shipyard.

[2] Pre-tax profit = Trading profit plus Interest on Investments (mainly subsidiary companies) less General Establishment Charges, Depreciation, Directors' Fees, but before Debenture Interest.

[3] Return on capital = Profits (Net profits plus Interest less Investment income) as a per centage of Capital (Share capital plus all creditors plus Reserves less Investments).

* Dividend paid on increased ordinary share capital

Source: R. & W. Paul, Accounts and Directors' Minute Books.

Appendix 9

Ordinary dividends of sixteen representative companies, 1895–1955
(percentage)

Co.	1895–98	1899–1903	1904–08	1909–13	1914–16	1917–20	1921–23
1	12.50	7.90	5.90	3.20	5.33	7.50	10.00
2	10.00	7.00	3.90	5.60	6.67	9.00	8.67
3	10.06	9.35	11.40	16.45	25.50	32.38	18.92
4	7.13	7.00	3.30	3.60	4.50	8.13	3.33
5	12.22 §	10.46	7.00	5.60	5.83	10.00	—
6	9.00	10.00	6.33	6.00	6.50	13.13	38.33
7	5.00	—	6.25	3.30	5.83	9.63	5.00
8	—	7.50	0	0	0	4.00	10.00
9	—	7.88	6.40	2.40	4.67	2.50	13.33
10	—	7.40	4.50	4.00	2.67	8.50	15.00
11	—	9.50	9.90	8.40	7.67	10.75	15.00 [20.00]
12	—	5.80	0.50	0.50	4.33	10.00	8.00 [9.33]
13	—	5.17	4.10	5.90	7.67	8.00	8.00
14	—	—	7.50	5.10	5.00	5.63	7.50 [9.38]
15	—	—	—	—	—	—	—
16	—	—	—	—	—	—	20.00
Av. 1	9.42	7.91	5.49	5.00	6.58	9.94	12.93
Av. 2	9.42	7.91	5.49	5.00	6.58	9.94	13.52
Av. 3	9.85	8.13	6.08	7.11	10.28	14.09	13.75
Av. 4	9.85	8.13	6.08	7.11	10.28	14.09	14.02

Averages: 1 = Unweighted average excluding bonuses
2 = Unweighted average with bonuses
3 = Weighted average excluding bonuses (by ordinary share capital)
4 = Weighted average with bonuses

Figures inside square brackets [ ] take account of the capitalisation of reserves as bonus shares, with the ordinary dividend recalculated to reflect the equivalent dividend on the ordinary capital (the effect of a 1 for 1 i.e. 100 per cent bonus would be to double the declared ordinary dividend in following years. The calculations start from scratch in 1924 and 1934).

* Calculation takes account of cash bonus of 30 per cent paid from reserves
+ 80 per cent of capital repaid to shareholders
† Capital written down by 62.5 per cent
§ Calculations from 1895–1901 based on profits paid on partners capital as proxy for ordinary dividends
‡ Subsequently included in Associated British Maltsters

1924–8	1929–33	1934–38	1939–45	1946–50	1951–55
6.00	2.00	2.60	6.79	17.50 [25.00]	12.50 [25.00]
8.20	10.30+	19.50	28.57	35.00	30.00
22.20	23.90 [27.23]	20.60	22.57	15.60	11.75 [15.50]
0	0†	0	2.86	21.00	25.00
—	8.25	10.00	10.00	15.00	14.50
30.00	22.00	28.00	31.43	—	—
15.20*	11.20	14.00	29.57	22.50	12.50 [13.35]
7.20	2.00	0.50	4.29	14.00	1.50
15.00	15.00	15.00	15.00	26.00	23.00
16.40	17.40	16.10	20.71	30.00	—
20.00	19.00	17.50	17.50	—	—
5.20	2.38 ‡	—	—	—	—
7.50 ‡	—	—	—	—	—
10.00	19.00	21.00 [23.00]	22.14 [29.52]	39.00 [52.00]	15.50 [20.67]
2.50	2.50	3.60	7.43	9.40	3.00 [7.50]
19.50	9.00	11.00	10.00	10.00	10.00
12.33	10.92	12.81	16.35	21.30	14.48
12.33	11.15	12.96	16.87	22.59	16.94
13.81	12.87	14.14	15.86	16.51	12.09
13.81	13.77	14.19	16.06	16.96	14.20

Key to companies

Companies	*Nominal capital at registration (£)*	*Issued ordinary capital (£)*
1. Hugh Baird & Sons, Glasgow	160,000	66,000
2. F. & G. Smith, Gt. Ryburgh, Norfolk	200,000	200,000
3. R. & W. Paul, Ipswich	250,000	200,000
4. Thomas Bernard & Company, Leith	150,000	75,000
5. H. A. & D. Taylor, Sawbridgeworth	96,000	78,000
6. J. Pidcock & Company, Nottingham	100,000	43,000
7. Cardiff Malting Company, Cardiff	60,000	35,000
8. J. E. & C. H. Evans, Birmingham	100,000	30,000
9. Montgomerie & Company, Glasgow [3]	10,000	60,000 [1]

Companies	Nominal capital at registration (£)	Issued ordinary capital (£)
10. S. Swonnell & Son, Oulton Broad, Suffolk	50,000	25,000
11. E. Bailey & Son, Frome, Somerset	35,000	35,000
12. M. Sanderson & Son, Wakefield	150,000	60,000
13. W. J. Robson, Leeds	120,000	55,000
14. Lee & Grinling, Grantham	30,000	23,000
15. Sandars & Company, Gainsborough	150,000	100,000 [2]
16. Gilstrap Earp/ABM, Newark	325,000	100,000

Notes:
[1] Data available from 1899 when issued ordinary capital increased to £60,000.
[2] Data available from 1925 when issued ordinary capital increased to £100,000.
[3] Montgomerie & Co. produced malt primarily for use in their range of bakery products; their inclusion in the series does not materially affect the results.
No adjustments have been made for income tax.

Source: Company financial records and Directors' Minute Books; *Manual of British Breweries*, 1914ff.; *Exchange Yearbook.*

Appendix 10
Disposal of sales-malting companies, 1915–75

Date	Company	Location	Acquired by
1915	Arthur Soames & Son	Grimsby	Sandars & Company
1918	Newson Garrett	Snape	S. Swonnell
1918	James Thorpe	Newark	Gilstrap Earp
1918	Addison Potter & Son	Newcastle-on-Tyne	Newcastle Breweries
1920	James Fison	Thetford	Edward Packard & Company; 1944, Pauls' Malt
1920	Cardiff Malting	Cardiff	Ely Brewery Company
1922	Josiah Brick	Welshpool	Ceased trading
1922	E.R. Gayford & Company	Hadleigh	Ceased trading
1922	Haworth Brothers	Wakefield	Michael Sanderson
1922	Musgrave & Sagar	Leeds	Ceased trading
1922	W. Sheard	Mirfield	Ceased trading
1922	P.A. Taylor	Wakefield	Ceased trading
1923	Wakefield & South Elmsall Malting Company	Wakefield	Edward Sutcliffe
1924	David Bassett & Company	Maidenhead	Ceased trading
1924	Harrison Gray	Chelmsford	Hugh Baird & Sons
1926	Walter Betts	Eye, Suffolk	Ceased trading
1926	D. Byass	Scarborough	Edward Sutcliffe
1926	R.W. & G. Nicholson	Doncaster	Ceased trading
1926	J. Taylor & Sons	Bishops Stortford	Ceased trading
1926	Samuel Young	Cardigan	Ceased trading
1927	John Crisp & Son	Beccles	W.J. Robson; ABM*
1927	Alfred Messenger	Cleckheaton	Edward Sutcliffe
1927	S. Passey	Breconshire	Ceased trading
1928	Lee & Grinling	Grantham	Pauls Malt
1928	Gilstrap Earp	Newark-upon-Trent	ABM*
1928	Edward Sutcliffe	Mirfield	ABM*
1928	S. Thompson & Sons	Smethwick	ABM*
1928	W.J. Robson	Leeds	ABM*
1929	A. Milnthorp	Harrowgate	Richard Dobson
1929	James D. Taylor & Sons	Bath	ABM
1930	Thomas Haigh	Wakefield	ABM

* Founder members of ABM.

Date	Company	Location	Acquired by
1930	Michael Sanderson & Son	Wakefield	ABM
1931	Tuckers & Blakes	Bristol	Hugh Baird & Sons
1931	G. & W.E. Downing	Smethwick	ABM
1932	H.B. Walmsley	London	H.A. & D. Taylor
1933	Wimborne Malting Company	Wimborne	Ceased trading
1933	J. Hole & Company	Newark-upon-Trent	Ceased trading
1934	Thomas Prentice & Company	Stowmarket	Greene King
1935	Edward Fison	Ipswich	Muntona
1935	Austin Brothers	Castleford	Thomas Fawcett
1936	W. Thomas & Company	Wolverhampton	ABM
1936	Glossop & Bulay	Hull	ABM
c. 1936	J. Gough & Sons	Bury St Edmunds	R. Peach & Company
1937	R. Bishop & Sons	Newark-upon-Trent	R. Peach & Company
1940	R. Worswick & Sons	Elland	ABM
1940	F. Hudson	Thirsk	Richard Dobson
1941	Richard Dobson & Sons	Leeds	Pauls Malt
1944	J.N. Middleborough	Selby	ABM
1945	John Garrod	Bures	Ceased trading
1945	A.H. Clarke	Wellington, Shropshire	Ceased trading
1945	Frederick Branwhite	Long Melford	Ceased trading
c. 1945	J.W. & H. Branston	Newark-upon-Trent	ABM
1946	Isaac Lord	Ipswich	Ceased malting
1946	T.W. Wilson	Hadleigh	ABM
1947	Williams Brothers	Salisbury	Ceased trading
1947	Woods, Sadd & Moore	Loddon	Ceased malting
1947	W.F. Leech	Liverpool	Ceased trading
1947	P.W. Owen	Wellington, Shropshire	Ceased trading
1947	A. Savill	Eye, Suffolk	Ceased trading
1947	E.G. Clarke	Framlingham	Ceased malting
1947	Charles Deighton	Bridgnorth	Ceased trading
1947	Frederick May	Stisted, Essex	Ceased malting
c. 1947	William Jones & Son	Shrewsbury	Ansells Brewery; Albrew
1952	Frank Colley	Tadcaster	Smith's Tadcaster Brewery
1952	Groom & Symonds	Diss	E. S. Beaven

Date	Company	Location	Acquired by
1952	P.W. Garneys	Stowmarket	Ceased trading
1952	Selby Malt Roasting Company	Selby	Smith's Tadcaster Brewery
1952	George Ikin	Leeds	Ceased trading
1952	W.& R. Williams		Ceased trading
1955	Millward Brothers	Wednesbury	Ceased trading
1955	W.D. & A.E. Walker	Great Yarmouth	Lacons; Whitbread
1955	Alexander Bonthrone	Falkland, Fifeshire	Ceased trading
1956	Free Rodwell	Mistley	Albrew Maltsters
1957	Ipswich Malting	Ipswich	H.A. & D. Taylor
1958	H.A. & D. Taylor	Sawbridgeworth	ABM
1958	Gripper Son & Wightman	Hertford	Ceased trading
1959	William Gleadall	Gainsborough	Ceased trading
1959	W.H. Cox & Sons		Yeomans, Cherry & Curtis
1960	E. Bailey	Frome	ABM
1961	A. & J. Bowker	King's Lynn	Ceased trading
1961	Vynne & Everett	Swaffham	Ceased trading
1962	Millar & Dudgeon	Bellhaven, Dunbar	Ceased trading
1962	J.R. Page	Bishops Stortford	J. Harrington
1962	F. &. G. Smith	Great Ryburgh	Reconstructed as Crisp Malting
1962	Hugh Baird & Sons	Glasgow and Witham	Canada Malt
1963	Henry Ward & Sons	Ware	Harrington Page
1963	J. Pidcock & Company	Nottingham	Sandars & Company
1964	Melford Malt	Long Melford	Ceased trading
1964	G.F. Milnthorpe	Doncaster	Ceased trading
1965	James Parry	Halesworth	Ceased trading
1965	Yeomans, Cherry & Curtis	Burton-upon-Trent	Sandars & Company
1965	Harrington Page	Hertford	Pauls Malt
1965	Alfred Gough	Saffron Walden	S. Swonnell
1965	Randells (Maltsters)	London	S. Swonnell
1965	S. Swonnell & Son	Oulton Broad	Pauls malt
1966	Battlebridge Malting Company	Chelmsford	Ceased trading
1967	Brooks (Mistley)	Mistley	ABM
1967	William Pitts	Plymouth	Ceased trading
1968	John Hare	Biggleswade	Ceased trading
1969	Sandars & Company	Gainsborough	Pauls Malt
c. 1970	Richard Dewing	Fakenham	Ceased trading

Date	Company	Location	Acquired by
1972	Robert Hutchison	Kirkcaldy	Pauls Malt
1972	J.F. & J. Crowther	Mirfield	Bass
1978	Moffat Malting Company	Airdrie	ABM; ceased trading
1981	Cardiff Malting Company	Cardiff	Ceased trading
1983	North of England Malt Roasting Company	Masham, Yorkshire	ABM; ceased trading
1985	Moray Firth Maltings	Inverness	Scottish & Newcastle
1985	Pauls Malt	Ipswich	Harrisons & Crosfield
1987	ABM	Newark-upon-Trent	Pauls/Harrisons & Crosfield
1993	Peach Malt	Burton-upon-Trent/Bury St Edmunds	Ceased trading
1993	E. S. Beaven (Guinness)	Diss	Ceased malting
1994	E. S. Beaven (Guinness)	Warminster	Warminster Maltings Limited
1997	Robert Kilgour & Company	Kirkcaldy	Muntons

Undated

—	Frederick Law	Wolverhampton	Ceased trading
—	J. R. Page	Baldock	Paine & Company, St Neots

Membership of MAGB, 1997

Full members
Hugh Baird and Sons
Crisp Malting Group
Thomas Fawcett & Sons
French and Jupp's
Moray Firth Maltings
Muntons
Pauls Malt Limited
J.P.Simpson & Company (Alnwick) Limited
Edwin Tucker & Sons
Pure Malt Products

Associate members
  Brewer-maltsters
Bass Maltings Limited
Carlsberg-Tetley Maltsters
Greene King and Sons Plc
Wolverhampton and Dudley Breweries Limited
  Distiller-maltsters
Chivas Brothers
Highland Distillers Company Plc
Robert Kilgour and Company Limited
Morrison Bowmore Distillers Limited
United Distillers Cereals Limited
United Malt and Grain Distillers Limited

Notes: * Founder members of ABM.
Source: MAGB; Brewing Trade Press; Interviews.

Bibliography

Archival Sources

Pauls Malt Archives

R. & W. Paul Limited

Directors' Minutes, 1893–1942; 1960–75
Board Papers, 1970–75
Private Ledgers
Salaries Ledger, 1899–1925
Accounts, 1893–1975
Malt Production, Annual Costings, 1895–1967
Capital Ledger (n.d.)
Report of John Tyzack Consultants, 1969
Stonham Malt and Barley Ledgers, 1900–4

Associated British Maltsters

Directors' Minutes, 1928–67
Accounts, 1928–75
Annual Reports, 1929–67

Gillman & Spencer (1902) Limited

Directors' Minutes, 1902–35
Accounts, 1902–35
Register of Directors
Agreement between the Manufacturers' of Flaked Maize, 1908

Alfred Gough Limited

Directors' Minutes, 1915–59

Edward Sutcliffe Limited

Directors' Minutes, 1927–56
Private Ledger, 1932–40
Private Journal, 1927–60

H. A. & D. Taylor Limited

J. L. & H. Taylor, Balance Book, 1871–84
Balance Books, 1886–1901
Directors' Minutes, 1938–50
Private Journals, 1885–92; 1898–1904

Henry Page & Company Limited
Ledger, 1883–94
Miscellaneous papers

Lee & Grinling Limited
Accounts, 1903–67

Michael Sanderson & Son Limited
Directors' Minutes, 1897–1929
Annual General Meeting Minutes, 1897–1957

J. Pidcock & Company Limited
Directors' Minute Books, 1893–1948

W. J. Robson & Company Limited
Directors' Minutes, 1900–57

Sandars & Company Limited
Directors' Minutes, 1915–60
Annual Meeting Book, 1915–77
Sales Ledger, 1864–69
Cash Book, Ferry Maltings
Barley Purchases Books, 1894–95, 1900–1
Inventories of Maltings, 1864

Shaws Hull Malt Company
Directors' Minutes, 1906–51
Register of Directors

S. Swonnell & Son Limited
Directors' Minutes, 1899–1935
'General Statistics', 1899–1918
Private Ledgers

Yeomans, Cherry & Curtis Limited
Directors' Minutes, 1948–75
Private Ledgers

Allied Breweries

Samuel Allsopp, Minute Books, 1a and 1b, 1865–97
Weekly Malt Returns, 1888–91, C/T/35

Bairds Malt

Hugh Baird & Sons, Directors' Minutes, 1931–80
General Meeting Minutes, 1921–80
'Annals of a Scots Family' (Anon.)

Bass Museum

Bass, Ratcliff & Gretton, Partnership Meeting Minutes, 1869–80

Companies House, London

R. & W. Paul/Pauls & Whites, Shareholders Registers
ABM, Shareholders Registers

Crisp Malting Group

F. &. G. Smith Limited, Directors' Minutes, 1890–1962
Balance Sheet, 1879

Fakenham Gasworks Museum

Richard Dewing, Stock Book, FG 190.191
Account Books, 1880–1951, FG 189.991

French & Jupp's Limited

Directors' Minutes, 1920–64
Accounts, 1922–64

Greater London Record Office

Truman, Hanbury and Buxton (B/THB)
Malt and Barley Ledgers, 1825–76, 1925–35, B/155–160
Thursday Private Memoranda, 1830–1937, A/129–137
Monthly Reports, 1884–1938, A/118–122
Stock Book, 1865–73, C/291
Rest Books, 1831–66, Abstract Rest Book, Acc 79.94

Guildhall Library, London

New Issues Prospectuses

Hertfordshire Record Office

Henry Page & Company
Malt Ledgers, 1894–1909, D/EPa B6
Malt Contract Books, 1916–55, B20–31
Sales Ledgers, 1911–42, B14–19

Henry Ward & Sons
Summaries of Annual Accounts, 1895–1940, D/EWd B1,2
Balance Sheets, 1908–11, B3
Sales Books, B5, 6
Letter Books, B18, 19, 20

Lincoln Archives

Sandars and Company (2 Sandars)
Account of Family History, Written by a Daughter of Samuel Sandars, 10/9
Executors Accounts, J. E. Sandars, 1890–91, 4/1
Account of malt produced, 1867–86, 4/6
Diaries of J. E. Sandars, 1849–88, 1/1a, 1b
Diaries of J. D. Sandars, 1880–97, 1/2–15
Letter Book of J. D. Sandars, 1887–97, 2/1–2
Malt and Trading Account, John Hyde, 1859–64, Brace 3/22
Gainsborough highways assessment, 1849, Brace 3/4
Gainsborough poor rate books, 1862, Brace 3/10

MAGB, Newark

Minutes of Executive Committee Meetings
Membership Lists
Subscription Lists
Survey, 'Beer Tax and the Malting Industry', 1932
Annual Reports, 1919–95

Norfolk Record Office

Great Yarmouth Poor Rate Books, 1846–80, Y/LI/71–3.

Public Record Office

Files of Dissolved Companies, BT31

Suffolk Record Office

Ipswich
Records of Tacket Street Chapel:
Register of Baptisms, 1721–1854, FK 3/1/5/3
Subscriptions for the Minister, FK 3/1/3/22
Sunday School Records, FK 3/1/2/10
Ipswich Poor Rate Books, 1854–80, DC2/17/5

Bury St Edmunds

Whiting Street Chapel, Subscriptions and Accounts, FK 3/502/28
Northgate Street Chapel, Rules of New Chapel, FK 3/502/95
J. Duncan, 'History of the Free Churches in Bury'

British Parliamentary Papers

Minutes of Evidence Taken before the Select Committee on Public Breweries (1819), v
Report of Select Committee on the Sale of Corn (1834), vii
Commission of Excise Inquiry, Fifteenth Report (Malt) (1835), xxxi
Select Committee on Agricultural Distress, Second Report (1836), viii
First Report of the Tidal Harbours Commission (1845), xvi
Report of Sir John Walsham on Norfolk Agriculture (1854), lxv
Select Committee on the Malt Tax:
　Report of Select Committee (1867), xi
　Minutes of Evidence (1867–68), ix
Royal Commission on Agricultural Depression (1895), xvi, xvii
Report of the Departmental Committee on Beer Materials (1899), xxx, Cmnd 9171–72
Reports of the Royal Commission on Arsenical Poisoning, First Report (1901), Cmnd
　692, x; Final Report (1904), Cmnd 1845, 1848, 1869, ix
*Committee on the Financial Aspects of Control and Purchase of the Liquor Trade by the
　State* (1917–18), Cmnd 8619, xxvi
*Report on the Proposals for the State Purchase of the Licensed Liquor Trade Reports of
　the English, Scotch and Irish Committees* (1918), Cmnd 9042, xi
Ministry of Reconstruction, Final Report of Committee on Trusts (1919), xiii

Accounts and Papers

Accounts Relating to the Public Income of Great Britain (1805), v
Return of All British Corn, Flour and Malt, Shipped at the Different Ports of
　England and Scotland (1824), xvii; (1828), xviii; (1839), xlvi
Returns Relating to Maltsters' Licences (1837), xxx; (1862), xxx; (1863), lxvii;
　(1870), lxi; (1871), lxii
Account of Number of Persons in UK Licensed as Brewers and Victuallers
　(1831–32), xxxiv; (1833), xxxiii; (1841), xxvi; (1851), liii; (1861), lviii; (1871),
　lxii; (1881), lxxxiii
Agricultural Returns for Great Britain (1866), lx; (1870), lxviii; (1874), lxix;
　(1878–79), lxxv; (1882), lxxiv; (1886), lxx; (1890–91), xci; (1895), cvi
Return Relating to the Consumption of Sugar in Brewing (1880), lxvii
Board of Trade, *Annual Statements of Trade*
Census of Production, 1924, 1935
United Nations, *Food and Agriculture Organisation: Trade Yearbook,* 25–29

Contemporary Journals and Newspapers

Brewer
Brewers' Almanack
Brewers' Gazette
Brewers' Guardian
Brewers' Journal
Brewery Record
Brewers' Society, *UK Statistical Handbook*
Brewing Trade Review
Country Brewers' Gazette
Duncan's *Manual of British and Foreign Brewery Companies*
East Anglian Daily Times
Gainsborough News
Investors' Chronicle and Stock Exchange Gazette
Ipswich Chronicle and Mercury
Ipswich Evening Star
Ipswich Journal
Journal of the Institute of Brewing
Lincolnshire Chronicle
Newark Advertiser
Pauls' Link
Stock Exchange Yearbook
Stock Exchange Official Intelligence
Suffolk Chronicle
Sunday Times
The Times
Who Was Who

Published Sources

Books

D. H. Aldcroft and M. J. Freeman (eds), *Transport in Victorian Britain* (Manchester University Press, Manchester, 1988).

W. G. Arnott, *Orwell Estuary: The Story of Ipswich River* (N. Adlard & Company, Ipswich, 1966).

N. Bacon, *Annalls of Ipswiche, the Laws, Customs and Government of the Same* (ed.) W. H. Richardson (Ipswich, 1884).

J. L. Baker, *The Brewing Industry* (Methuen, London, 1905).

A. Barnard, *The Whisky Distilleries of the United Kingdom* (Harpers Weekly Gazette, London, 1887).

—, *The Noted Breweries of Great Britain and Ireland*, i–iv (J. Causton and Sons, London, 1889–1891).

L. M. Barnett, *British Food Policy during the First World War* (George Allen & Unwin, London, 1985).

A. D. Bayne, *Royal Illustrated History of Eastern England*, i (1874).

—, *A Comprehensive History of Norwich* (Jarrold, London, 1869).

—, *A History of the Industry and Trade of Norwich and Norfolk* (2nd edn, Norwich, 1858).

E. S. Beaven, *Barley* (Duckworth, London, 1947).

W. H. Beveridge, *British Food Control* (OUP, Oxford, 1928).

W. H. Bird, *A History of the Institute of Brewing* (Institute of Brewing, London, 1955).

W. Black, *Practical Treatise on Brewing* (London, 1870).

J. S. Boswell, *The Rise and Decline of Small Firms* (George Allen and Unwin, London, 1973).

J. Boyes and R. Russell, *The Canals of Eastern England* (David and Charles, Devon, 1977).

W. Branch Johnson, *The Industrial Archaeology of Hertfordshire* (David and Charles, Devon, 1970).

J. Brown, *Steeped in Tradition: The Malting Industry in England Since the Railway Age* (University of Reading, 1983).

J. Brown and M. B. Rose (eds), *Entrepreneurship, Networks and Modern Business* (MUP, Manchester, 1993).

I. M. Burgess and C. J. Knell, *British Malting Barley: Supply and Demand* (Home-Grown Cereals Authority, London, 1978).

M. Casson, *The Entrepreneur: An Economic Theory* (Basil Blackwell, Oxford, 1982).

W. H. Chaloner and B. M. Ratcliffe (eds), *Trade and Transport: Essays in Economic History in Honour of T. S. Willan* (MUP, Manchester, 1977).

A. D. Chandler, Jr, *The Visible Hand: The Management Revolution in American Business* (Harvard University Press, Cambridge, Massachusetts, 1977).

—, *Scale and Scope: The Dynamics of Industrial Capitalism* (Harvard University Press, Cambridge, Massachusetts, 1990).

—, *Strategy and Structure: Chapters in the History of the Industrial Enterprise* (MIT Press, Cambridge, Massachusetts, 1962).

D. F. Channon, *The Strategy and Structure of British Enterprise* (MacMillan, London, 1971).

R. A. Church, *Kenricks in Hardware: A Family Business, 1791–1966* (David and Charles, Devon, 1969).

R. Clark, *Black Sailed Traders* (Pitman & Company, London, 1961).

R. Clarke and T. McGuinness (eds), *The Economics of the Firm* (Basil Blackwell, Oxford, 1987).

P. L. Cook and R. Cohen, *Effects of Mergers: Six Studies* (George Allen and Unwin, London, 1958).

H. S. Corran, *A History of Brewing* (David and Charles, Devon, 1975).

P. L. Cottrell, *Industrial Finance, 1830–1914: The Finance and Organisation of English Manufacturing Industry* (Methuen, London, 1980).

A. Crosby, *A History of Thetford* (Phillimore, Chichester, 1986).

H. R. De Salis, *Chronology of Inland Navigation* (London, 1897).

D. Defoe, *A Tour Through the Whole Island of Great Britain*, i (London, 1927).

I. Donnachie, *A History of the Brewing Industry in Scotland* (John Donald Publishers, Edinburgh, 1979).

R. Edwards, *The River Stour* (Terence Dalton, Lavenham, 1982).

B. Elbaum and W. Lazonick (eds), *The Decline of the British Economy* (OUP, Oxford, 1986).

C. Erickson, *British Industrialists: Steel and Hosiery, 1850–1950* (CUP, Cambridge, 1959).

G. E. Evans, *Where Beards Wag All: The Relevance of the Oral Tradition* (Faber & Faber, London, 1970).

R. Finch, *A Cross in the Topsail* (Boydell Press, Ipswich, 1979).

S. P. Florence, *Ownership, Control and Success of Large Companies* (Sweet & Maxwell, London, 1961).

W. Ford, *An Historical Account of the Malt Trade and Laws* (London, 1849).

A. Gall, *Manchester Breweries of Times Gone By* (Manchester, 1978–80).

J. Glyde, *Suffolk in the Nineteenth Century* (London, 1851).

T. R. Gourvish, *Norfolk Beers from English Barley: A History of Steward and Patteson, 1793–1963* (Centre of East Anglian Studies, University of East Anglia, 1987).

T. R. Gourvish and R. G. Wilson, *The British Brewing Industry, 1830–1980* (CUP, Cambridge, 1994).

R. J. Hammond, *History of the Second World War*, i, *Food* (1951), iii (HMSO, Longmans, 1962).

L. Hannah (ed.), *Management Strategy and Business Development* (MacMillan, London, 1976).

—, *The Rise of the Corporate Economy* (Methuen, London, 1976).

G. H. Hardinge, *The Development and Growth of Courage's Brewery, 1787–1932* (Jordan-Gaskell, London, 1932).

B. Harrison, *Drink and the Victorians, The Temperance Question in England, 1815–1872* (Faber & Faber, London, 1971).

K. H. Hawkins, *A History of Bass Charrington* (OUP, Oxford, 1978).

K. H. Hawkins and C. L. Pass, *The Brewing Industry: A Study in Industrial Organisation and Public Policy* (Heinemann, London, 1979).

A. G. Hollingsworth, *The History of Stowmarket* (F. Pawsey, Ipswich, 1844).

J. S. Hough, *The Biotechnology of Malting and Brewing* (CUP, Cambridge, 1985).

J. S. Hough, D. E. Briggs and R. Stevens, *Malting and Brewing Science* (CUP, Cambridge, 1971).

J. House, *Pride of Perth: The Story of Arthur Bell & Sons Ltd, Scotch Whisky Distillers* (Hutchinson, Benham, London, 1976).

E. Hughes, *Treatise on the Brewing of Beer and Porter and on the Drying and Qualities of Malt* (1798).

H. Hunter, *The Barley Crop* (Crosby Lockwood, London, 1952).

H. Janes, *The Red Barrel: A History of Watney Mann* (John Murray, London, 1963).

D. J. Jeremy, *Business and Religion in Britain* (CUP, Cambridge, 1988).

G. Jones and M. B. Rose (eds), *Family Capitalism* (Frank Cass, London, 1993).

N. Kent, *General View of the Agriculture of the County of Norfolk* (Norwich, 1796).

A. Kenwood and A. L. Lougheed, *The Growth of the International Economy, 1820–1990* (3rd edn, Routledge, London, 1992).

H. Lancaster, *Practical Floor Malting* (1906).

D. S. Landes, *The Unbound Prometheus: Technological Change and Industrial Development in Western Europe from 1750 to the Present* (CUP, Cambridge, 1969).

R. Lawrence, *Southwold River: Georgian Life in the Blyth Valley* (Suffolk Books, 1990).

A. B. Levy, *Private Corporations and their Control*, i and ii (Routledge and Kegan Paul, 1950).

H. Levy, *Monopolies, Cartels and Trusts in British Industry* (2nd edn, MacMillan, London, 1927).

E. Lisle, *Observations on Husbandry* (1757).

P. Lynch and J. Vaizey, *Guinness's Brewery in the Irish Economy, 1759–1876* (CUP, Cambridge, 1960).

C. Mackie, *Norfolk Annals*, i, *1801–50*; ii, *1851–1900* (Norwich, 1901).

H. W. Macrosty, *The Trust Movement in British Industry: A Study of Business Organisation* (Longmans, Green & Company, London, 1907).

C. A. Manning, *Suffolk Celebrities* (1893).

P. Mathias, *The Brewing Industry in England, 1700–1830* (CUP, Cambridge, 1959).

B. R. Mitchell and P. Deane, *Abstract of British Historical Statistics* (CUP, Cambridge, 1959).

M. S. Moss and J. R. Hume, *The Making of Scotch Whisky: A History of the Scotch Whisky Distilling Industry* (Edinburgh, 1981).

L. Nabseth and G. F. Ray, *The Diffusion of New Industrial Processes: An International Study* (CUP, Cambridge, 1974).

C. S. Orwin, *A History of English Farming* (Nelson, 1949).

C. C. Owen, *The Development of Industry in Burton-upon-Trent* (Shillitoe, 1978).

—, *The Greatest Brewery in the World: A History of Bass, Ratcliff & Gretton* (Derbyshire Record Society, Chesterfield, 1992).

P. L. Payne, *The Early Scottish Limited Companies, 1856–1895: An Historical and Analytical Survey* (Scottish Academic Press, 1980).

—, *British Entrepreneurship in the Nineteenth Century* (MacMillan, London, 1974).

I. A. Peaty, *Brewery Railways* (David and Charles, Devon, 1985).

—, *Essex Brewers and the Malting and Hop Industries of the County* (Brewing History Society, 1992).

E. T. Penrose, *The Theory of the Growth of the Firm* (Basil Blackwell, Oxford, 1959).

M. E. Porter, *Competitive Strategy: Techniques for Analysing Industries and Competitors* (MacMillan, London, 1980).

S. J. Prais, *The Evolution of Giant Firms in Britain* (CUP, Cambridge, 1976).

P. Pugh, *Great Enterprise: A History of Harrisons & Crosfield* (Harrisons & Crosfield, 1990).

L. Richmond and A. Turton (eds), *The Brewing Industry: A Guide to Historical Records* (Manchester, 1990).

J. Ross-Mackenzie, *Brewing and Malting* (Sir Isaac Pitman & Son, London, 1921).

M. Silver, *Enterprise and the Scope of the Firm* (Robertson, Oxford, 1984).

J. N. Slater, *A Brewer's Tale* (Greenall Whitley, 1980).

J. L. Smith-Dampier, *East Anglian Worthies* (1949).

B. Spiller, *The Chameleon's Eye: James Buchanan & Company Limited, 1884–1984* (James Buchanan, London, 1984).

J. Steel, *Malting and Brewing* (London, 1881).

P. Stephens (ed.), *Newark: The Magic of Malt* (Nottinghamshire County Council, 1993).

H. Stopes, *Malt and Malting* (F. W. Lyon, London, 1885).

D. Stuart, *History of Burton-upon-Trent*, ii, *1914–74* (Wood Mitchell, 1977).

F. Thatcher, *A Treatise of Practical Brewing and Malting* (The Country Brewers' Gazette Limited, London, 1905).

J. Vaizey, *The Brewing Industry, 1886–1951, An Economic Study* (Sir Isaac Pitman and Sons, London, 1960).

R. B. Weir, *The History of the Malt Distillers' Association of Scotland, 1874–1974* (Elgin, 1974).

—, *The History of the Distillers' Company, 1877–1939: Diversification and Growth in Whisky and Chemicals* (OUP, Oxford, 1995).

B. Wharton, *The Smiths of Ryburgh: 100 Years of Milling and Malting* (Crisp Malting, 1990).

M. J. Wiener, *English Culture and the Decline of the Industrial Spirit, 1850–1980* (Cambridge, Penguin edition, 1981).

G. B. Wilson, *Alcohol and the Nation* (Nicholson and Watson, London, 1940).

R. G. Wilson, *Gentlemen Merchants: The Merchant Community in Leeds, 1700–1830* (MUP, Manchester, 1971).

—, *Greene King: A Business and Family History* (The Bodley Head & Jonathan Cape, London, 1983).

N. R. Wright, *Lincolnshire Towns and Industry, 1700–1914* (History of Lincolnshire Committee, 1982).

A. Young, *General View of the Agriculture of the County of Norfolk* (David and Charles Reprint, 1969).

Directories

W. White, *Directory* for Norfolk, 1836–83.

W. White, *Directory* for Lincolnshire, 1826–82.

W. White, *Directory* for Suffolk, 1844–85.

W. White, *Directory* for Staffordshire, 1872–90.

Kelly's, *Directory* for Norfolk, 1846–83.

Kelly's, *Directory* for Lincolnshire, 1849–92.

Kelly's, *Directory* for Suffolk, 1846–86.

Kelly's, *Directory of the Wine and Spirit Trade*, 1902.

London Trades and Court Directory, 1883.
Universal British Directory, 1790.

Articles and Essays

H. G. Aldous, 'The Free Mash-Tun', *Journal of the Institute of Brewing*, 4 (1898), pp. 570–81.

E. S. Beaven, 'Barley for Brewing Since 1886', *Journal of the Institute of Brewing*, 42 (1936), pp. 487–95.

D. W. Bemment, 'Speciality Malts', *The Brewer*, 71 (1985), pp. 457–60.

K. J. Blois, 'Vertical Quasi-Integration', *Journal of Industrial Economics*, 20 (1972), pp. 253–72.

L. Briant, 'Drum Malting', *Brewing Trade Review*, 16 (1902), pp. 41–44.

M. Casson, 'Entrepreneurship and Business Culture', in J. Brown and M. B. Rose (eds), *Entrepreneurship, Networks and Modern Business* (MUP, 1993), pp. 30–54.

J. F. W. Causton, 'One Hundred Years of Malting: Some Notes on its Growth and Development', *Brewers' Journal*, Centenary Issue (1965), pp. 128–34.

A. C. Chapman, 'Unmalted Grain and its Use as a Partial Malt Substitute', *Journal of the Institute of Brewing*, 1 (1895), pp. 149–59.

—, 'The Production of Light Bottled Beer', *Journal of the Institute of Brewing*, 2 (1896), pp. 274–86.

H. A. D. Cherry-Downes, 'Mechanisation of Maltings', *Journal of the Institute of Brewing*, 54 (1948), pp. 208–13.

R. Church, 'The Family Firm in Industrial Capitalism: International Perspectives on Hypotheses and History', *Business History*, 35 (1993), pp. 17–43.

—, 'The Limitations of the Personal Capitalism Paradigm', in R. Church et al., 'Scale and Scope: A Review Colloquium', *Business History Review*, 64 (1990), pp. 703–10.

R. Church, B. Baldwin and B. Berry, 'Accounting for Profitability at the Consett Iron Company before 1914: Measurement, Sources and Uses', *Economic History Review*, 47 (November 1994), pp. 703–24.

C. Dagleish, 'Twenty-Five Years of Brewing Research', *Brewing Review* (March 1976), pp. 109–13.

T. Davies, 'Development of New Varieties of Barley', *Brewers' Guardian*, Centenary Issue (1971), pp. 77–82.

R. E. Essery, B. H. Kirsop and J. R. A. Pollock, 'Studies in Barley and Malt: Effects of Water on Germination Tests', *Journal of the Institute of Brewing*, 60 (1954), pp. 473–81.

R. Free, 'Barley from a Maltster's Point of View', *Brewers' Journal* (1888), pp. 603–8.

T. R. Gourvish, 'British Business and the Transition to a Corporate Economy: Entrepreneurship and Management Structures', *Business History*, 29 (1987), pp. 19–45.

T. R. Gourvish and R. G. Wilson, 'Profitability in the Brewing Industry, 1885–1914', *Business History*, 27 (1985), pp. 146–65.

O. T. Griffin and B. C. Pinner, 'The Development of a Static Malting', *Journal of the Institute of Brewing*, 71 (1965), pp. 324–29.

L. Hannah, 'Mergers in British Manufacturing Industry, 1880–1918,' *Oxford Economic Papers*, 26 (1974), pp. 1–20.

G. T. Harrop, 'Notes on the Construction and Design of Breweries and Maltings', *Journal of the Institute of Brewing*, 1 (1895), pp. 48–49.

W. L. Hiepe, 'The Establishment of Maltings on the Manchester Ship Canal', *Journal of the Institute of Brewing*, 4 (1898), pp. 237–47.

J. R. Hudson, 'Recent Development in Brewing Technology', *Brewers' Guardian*, 105 (1976), pp. 31–35.

O. P. Hudson, 'The Malting Industry', *The Brewer* (1987), pp. 554–56.

—, 'Malting Technology', *Journal of the Institute of Brewing*, 92 (1986), pp. 115–22.

D. Hutchinson and N. Stephen, 'Modelling the Growth Strategies of British Firms', *Business History*, 29–30, Special Edition (1987), pp. 79–96.

H. M. Lancaster, 'Advances Made during the Last Fifty Years in Malting', *Journal of the Institute of Brewing*, 42 (1936), pp. 496–500.

D. Landes, 'Technological Change and Development in Western Europe, 1750–1914', in *The Cambridge Economic History of Europe*, vi, *The Industrial Revolution and After*, ed. H. J. Habakkuk and M. M. Postan (Cambridge, 1965).

R. Lawrence, 'An Early Nineteenth-Century Malting Business in East Suffolk', *Proceedings of the Suffolk Institute of Archaeology*, 36 (1986), pp. 115–29.

H. Leak and A. Maizels, 'The Structure of British Industry', *Journal of the Royal Statistical Society*, 108 (1945), pp. 46–59.

R. Lloyd-Jones and A. A. LeRoux, 'Marshall and the Birth and Death of Firms: The Growth and Size Distribution of Firms in the Early Nineteenth-Century Cotton Industry', *Business History*, 24 (1982), pp. 141–55.

A. M. MacLeod, 'Twenty-Five Years of Brewing Science and Technology', *Brewing Review* (October 1977), pp. 16–19.

A. Macey, 'Advances in Malting Techniques', *Brewers' Guardian*, Centenary Issue (1971), pp. 89–93.

R. Maltster, 'Maltings in Suffolk', *Suffolk Industrial Archaeological Society Journal* (1984), pp. 2–6.

M. Manning, 'Great Ryburgh Maltings', *Norfolk Industrial Archaeology Society Journal*, 2 (1976–80), pp. 14–19.

S. Marriner, 'Company Financial Statements as Source Material for Business Historians', *Business History*, 22 (1980), pp. 201–35.

J. Mason, 'Accounting for Beer: An Investigation into the Accounting Practice of Three Northamptonshire Breweries', *Accounting History*, 5 (1981), pp. 63–77.

K. Monteverde and D. J. Teece, 'Appropriable Rents and Quasi-Vertical Integration', *Journal of Law and Economics*, 25 (1982), pp. 321–28.

E. R. Moritz, 'The Alleged Deterioration of English Malting Barley', *Brewers' Journal* (1895), pp. 329–39.

E. R. Moritz and H. Lancaster, 'The Economics of Brewery Malting', *Journal of the Institute of Brewing*, 11 (1905), pp. 491–507.

S. Nenadic, 'The Small Firm in Victorian Britain', in G. Jones and M. B. Rose (eds), *Family Capitalism* (Frank Cass, London, 1993), pp. 86–114.

S. Nyman and A. Silberston, 'The Ownership and Control of Industry', *Oxford Economic Papers*, new series (1978), pp. 84–102.

P. L. Payne, 'The Emergence of the Large-Scale Company in Great Britain, 1870–1914', *Economic History Review* 20 (1967), pp. 519–42.

—, 'Family Business in Britain: A Historical and Analytical Survey', in A. Okochi and S. Yasuoka (eds), *Family Business in the Era of Industrial Growth* (Tokyo, 1984), pp. 171–206.

H. L. Philbrick, 'The Wanderhaufen System', *Brewers' Guardian*, 94 (1965), pp. 39–40.

A. A. Pool, 'Studies in Barley and Malt: Single-Vessel System for Malting without Turning', *Journal of the Institute of Brewing*, 68 (1962), pp. 476–78.

G. B. Richardson, 'The Organisation of Industry', *Economic Journal*, 82 (1972), pp. 883–96.

D. W. Ringrose, 'New Malting Procedure and the Broader Outlook in Malting', *Brewers' Guardian*, 98 (1969), pp. 43–53.

J. C. Ritchie, 'The Use of Flaked Malts', *Journal of the Institute of Brewing*, 13 (1907), pp. 502–11.

M. B. Rose, 'Beyond Buddenbrooks: The Family Firm and the Management of Succession in Nineteenth-Century Britain', in J. Brown and M. B. Rose (eds), *Entrepreneurship, Networks and Modern Business* (MUP, 1993), pp. 127–43.

—, 'Diversification of Investment by the Greg Family, 1800–1914', *Business History*, 21 (1979), pp. 79–96.

J. Saunders, 'Modern Malting from an Engineering Point of View', *Brewers' Journal* (1905), p. 445–48.

H. A. Shannon, 'The Coming of General Limited Liability', *Economic History*, 2 (1931), pp. 358–79.

—, 'The First Five Thousand Limited Companies and Their Duration', *Economic History*, 2 (1931), pp. 396–419.

—, 'The Limited Companies of 1866–1883', *Economic History Review*, 4 (1933), pp. 380–405.

E. M. Sigsworth, 'Science and the Brewing Industry, 1850–1900', *Economic History Review*, 17 (1965), pp. 536–50.

R. Simper, 'The Maltings of Suffolk', *Suffolk Fair*, 1, no. 9 (January 1972), pp. 2–6.

—, 'Over Snape Bridge: The Story of Snape Maltings', *East Anglian Magazine* (1967), pp. 6–14.

J. Turner, 'State Purchase of the Liquor Trade in the First World War', *Historical Journal*, 23 (1980), pp. 589–615.

M. A. Utton, 'Some Features of the Early Merger Movements in British Manufacturing Industry', *Business History*, 14 (1972), pp. 51–60.

G. Valentine, 'Roasting of Barley and Malt', *Journal of the Institute of Brewing*, 26 (1920), pp. 573–79.

O. E. Williamson, 'The Vertical Integration of Production: Market Failure Considerations', *American Economic Review*, 61 (1971), pp. 112–23.

Privately Printed

Crisp Malt, *One Hundred Years of Malting, 1890–1990, Anglia Maltings Group Review* (1990).

Munton & Fison, *A Brief History of Munton & Fison Limited to Mark Their Fiftieth Anniversary, 1921–1971* (1971).

Munton & Fison, *Muntona Limited and Edward Fison Limited: Notes for Employees* (1956).

Munton & Fison, *Muntona Limited: The Drying and Storage of Combine Harvested Grain* (n.d.).

Muntona, *This is Fisons* (n.d.).

Pauls & Whites, *Pauls and Whites: Background Note* (1972).

R. & W. Paul, *Handbook* (1957).

M. Ripley, *'Beer is Best': The Collective Advertising of Beer, 1933–1970* (Brewers and Licensed Retailers Association, 1994).

Sandars & Company, *Of Malt and Men: Sandars & Company Limited, Gainsborough and Grimsby* (1965).

Edward Sandars, *The Sandars Years* (1972).

Typescripts

Anon., 'History of the Guinness Barley Research Station' (1987).

Anon., 'The History of the Family and Firm of J. P. Simpson and Company (Alnwick) Limited.

Anon., 'The Hutchisons of Kirkcaldy: A History of the Family and the Firm'.

S. R. Dennison and O. MacDonagh, 'History of Guinness, 1886–1939'.

G. Hemingway, 'The Branston Family of Newark' (1980).

G. Hemingway, 'The Gilstraps of Newark' (1982).

B. A. Holderness, 'Pauls of Ipswich' (*c.* 1980)

I. R. Murrell, 'Malting History' (n.d.).

E. F. Taylor, 'History of the Formation and Development of Associated British Maltsters Limited, 1928–78' (1978).

J. P. Tucker, 'An Autobiography of John Parnell Tucker in Commerce, Public Life and Sport' (*c.* 1934).

Theses

E. Doble, 'History of the Eastern Counties Railways in Relation to Economic Development' (unpublished Ph.D. thesis, University of London,1939).

A. Douet, 'Norfolk Agriculture 1914–1972' (unpublished Ph.D. thesis, University of East Anglia 1989).

C. G. Finch, 'The Hertfordshire Malt Factors, 1780–1835: A Study of Commercial Strength' (unpublished MA dissertation, 1976, unknown).

K. Hawkins, 'The Conduct and Development of the Brewing Industry in England and Wales, 1888–1938: A Study of the Role of Entrepreneurship in Determining Business Strategy with Particular Reference to Samuel Allsopp and Sons Limited' (unpublished Ph.D. thesis, University of Bradford, 1981).

D. M. Knox, 'The London Brewing Industry, 1830–1914: With Special Reference to Messrs Whitbread and Company (unpublished B.Litt., University of Oxford, 1956).

S. A. Levy, 'The Brewing Industry, Politics and Taxation, 1852–1880' (unpublished Ph.D. thesis, University of Cambridge, 1992).

J. C. Lincoln, 'Sleaford Maltings: History of Architecture and Design, 1890–1939' (unpublished BA dissertation, Open University, n.d.).

K. Marsden, 'Technical Change in the British Malting Industry' (unpublished Ph.D. thesis, University of Salford, 1985).

J. D. Murphy, 'The Town and Trade of Great Yarmouth, 1740–1850' (unpublished Ph.D. thesis, University of East Anglia, 1979).

K. Watson, 'Industrial Finance in the UK: The Brewing Experience, 1880–1913' (unpublished D.Phil., University of Oxford, 1990).

F. Wood, 'The Development of Inland Transport in the Hinterland of King's Lynn, 1760–1840' (unpublished Ph.D. thesis, University of Cambridge, 1992).

Index

Index of Companies

Companies including Christian names or initials are indexed by these